BRITISH POEMS

FROM "CANTERBURY TALES" TO "RECESSIONAL"

EDITED BY

PERCY ADAMS HUTCHISON, Ph.D.

FORMERLY INSTRUCTOR IN ENGLISH, HARVARD UNIVERSITY

NEW YORK

CHARLES SCRIBNER'S SONS

1912

BRITISH POEMS

FROM "CANTERBURY TALES" TO "RECESSIONAL"

TO THE MEMORY

OF

MY MOTHER

1041

1901

PREFACE

Iᴛ has been my endeavor in preparing this anthology to present, as adequately as might be possible within the limits of a handy volume, the best in Great Britain's non-dramatic poetry from Chaucer to Kipling, and this without exaggerating or minimizing the importance of any poet or period.

The unusual resources of the Harvard library, in point of first editions, reprints, and definitive editings, have made it possible for me to obtain always an authoritative text, and in not a few instances to correct errors. As I have chosen to keep the pages free from foot-notes (except for glosses on words not found in modern English dictionaries) I have not, as a rule, indicated the source of a text.

The too common practice of printing isolated stanzas as if they were complete poems is one from which I have refrained. Nor have I sought to improve a poet's work by excising weak lines or stanzas. If a poem is not printed in its entirety, the fact is noted. The only poem from which any integral part has been omitted without apprising the reader of the fact is Tʜᴇ Pʀɪᴏ-ʀᴇssᴇs Tᴀʟᴇ of Chaucer, which has been shorn of a final stanza expressive of a race-hatred fortunately now abated and better forgotten. For excerpts, a title descriptive of the subject-matter of the extract has been provided, and at the close is given the title of the poem from which the extract is drawn, and also the location of the part within the whole. In a few cases only, when a poem would require more space than could be afforded it, I have allowed myself to make an abridgment. To distinguish abridgments from excerpts, I have preserved to them the title of the original, and printed at the end, "From the poem of the same title." An exception is the excerpt-abridgment from A Mɪʀʀᴏʀ ғᴏʀ Mᴀɢɪsᴛʀᴀᴛᴇs.

It has made for uniformity to designate sonnets from sequences by the word "Sonnets" merely, and when the sequence possessed a title to indicate it after the last sonnet. Unless for adequate cause, modern spellings have been adopted; and, except for reasons that will be obvious, poets follow chronological order of birth rather than of production. The selections under each poet have been arranged chronologically with occasional exceptions (when such exceptions would not be of moment) if a slight change of sequence would produce a more pleasing arrangement of the pages.

I wish to acknowledge my indebtedness to Professors George Lyman Kittredge, William Allan Neilson, and Barrett Wendell, of Harvard University, for the interest they have taken in the book, and for valuable suggestions:

To Professor George Herbert Palmer, also of Harvard, not only for the interest he has shown, but also for the generous way in which at all times he has given me access to his wide collection of rare editions:

To Professor Henry MacCracken, of Yale University, for the text of a recently discovered poem by John Lydgate:

To Miss Lydia Adams Richardson, of the Rock Ridge School, for assistance in preparing the manuscript for the press:

To Mr. Rudyard Kipling and to Messrs. Doubleday, Page and Company for permission to reprint THE LAST CHANTEY:

And to Mr. Rudyard Kipling for permission to reprint RECESSIONAL.

P. A. HUTCHISON.

Cambridge, Mass.,
June, 1912.

CONTENTS

ix

PAGE

CONTENTS

CONTENTS

CONTENTS

CONTENTS xxiii

BRITISH POEMS

FROM "CANTERBURY TALES" TO "RECESSIONAL"

GEOFFREY CHAUCER [1340?–1400]

THE PILGRIMS

WHAN that Aprille with his shoures soote[1]
The droghte of Marche hath percèd[2] to the roote,
And bathèd every veyne in swich[3] licour,
Of which vertu engendrèd is the flour;
Whan Zephirus eek with his swete breeth
Inspirèd hath in every holt[4] and heeth
The tendre croppes,[5] and the yonge sonne
Hath in the Ram his halfe cours y-ronne,
And smale fowles maken melodye,
That slepen al the night with open ye,
(So priketh hem nature in hir corages[6]):
Than longen folk to goon on pilgrimages,
(And palmers for to seken straunge strondes,)
To ferne halwes, couthe[7] in sondry londes;
And specially, from every shires ende
Of Engelond, to Caunterbury they wende,
The holy blisful martir for to seke,
That hem hath holpen, whan that they were seke.

Bifel that, in that sesoun on a day,
In Southwerk at the Tabard as I lay
Redy to wenden on my pilgrimage
To Caunterbury with ful devout corage,
At night was come in-to that hostelrye
Wel[8] nyne and twenty in a compaignye,
Of sondry folk, by aventure y-falle
In felawshipe, and pilgrims were they alle,

---

[1] sweet.   [2] pierced.   [3] such.   [4] wood.   [5] young shoots.   [6] hearts.
[7] known.   [8] full.

1

That toward Caunterbury wolden ryde;
The chambres and the stables weren wyde,
And wel we weren esèd atte beste.
And shortly, whan the sonne was to reste,
So hadde I spoken with hem everichon,
That I was of hir felawshipe anon,
And made forward erly for to ryse,
To take our wey, ther as I yow devyse.

But natheles, whyl I have tyme and space,
Er that I ferther in this tale pace,
Me thinketh it acordaunt to resoun,
To telle yow al the condicioun
Of ech of hem, so as it semèd me,
And whiche they weren, and of what degree;
And eek in what array that they were inne:
And at a knight than wol I first biginne.

A KNIGHT ther was, and that a worthy man,
That fro the tyme that he first bigan
To ryden out, he lovèd chivalrye,
Trouthe and honour, fredom[9] and curteisye.
Ful worthy was he in his lordes werre,[10]
And thereto[11] hadde he riden (no man ferre[12])
As wel in Cristendom as hethenesse,
And evere honourèd for his worthinesse.
At Alisaundre he was, whan it was wonne;
Ful ofte tyme he hadde the bord bigonne[13]
Aboven alle naciouns in Pruce.
In Lettow hadde he reysèd and in Ruce,
No Cristen man so ofte of his degree.
In Gernade at the sege eek hadde he be
Of Algezir, and riden in Belmarye.
At Lyeys was he, and at Satalye,
Whan they were wonne; and in the Grete See
At many a noble aryve hadde he be.
At mortal batailles hadde he been fiftene,
And foughten for our feith at Tramissene

---

[9] liberality.   [10] war.   [11] besides.   [12] farther.
[13] sat at the head of the table.

In listes thryes, and ay slayn his foo.
This ilke worthy knight hadde been also
Somtyme with the lord of Palatye,
Ageyn another hethen in Turkye:
And everemore he hadde a sovereyn prys.[14]
And though that he were worthy, he was wys,
And of his port as meek as is a mayde.
He nevere yet no vileinye[15] ne sayde
In al his lyf, un-to no maner wight.
He was a verray parfit gentil knight.

But for to tellen yow of his array,
His hors were gode, but he was nat gay;
Of fustian he werèd a gipoun
Al bismotered with his habergeoun,
For he was late y-come from his viage
And wente for to doon his pilgrymage.

Ther was also a Nonne, a PRIORESSE,
That of hir smyling was ful simple and coy;
Hir gretteste ooth was but by seynt Loy;[16]
And she was clepèd madame Eglentyne.
Ful wel she song the service divyne,
Entunèd in hir nose ful semely;
And Frensh she spak ful faire and fetisly,
After the scole of Stratford atte Bowe,
For Frensh of Paris was to hir unknowe.
At mete wel y-taught was she with-alle;
She leet no morsel from hir lippes falle,
Ne wette hir fingres in hir sauce depe.
Wel coude she carie a morsel, and wel kepe,
That no drope ne fille up-on hir brest.
In curteisye was set ful moche hir lest.[17]
Hir over lippe wypèd she so clene,
That in hir coppe was no ferthing[18] sene
Of grece, whan she dronken hadde hir draughte.
Ful semely after hir mete she raughte,[19]

---

[14] reputation.   [15] discourtesy.   [16] *i. e.*, she did not swear at all.
[17] delight.   [18] particle.   [19] reached.

And sikerly[20] she was of greet disport,[21]
And ful plesaunt, and amiable of port,
And peynèd hir to countrefete chere[22]
Of court, and been estatlich of manere,
And to ben holden digne[23] of reverence.
But, for to speken of hir conscience,
She was so charitable and so pitous,
She wolde wepe, if that she sawe a mous
Caught in a trappe, if it were deed or bledde.
Of smale houndes had she, that she fedde
With rostèd flesh, or milk and wastel breed.
But sore weep she if oon of hem were deed,
Or if men smoot it with a yerde smerte:
And al was conscience and tendre herte.
Ful semely hir wimpel pinchèd[24] was;
Hir nose tretys;[25] hir eyen greye as glas;
Hir mouth ful smal, and ther-to softe and reed;
But sikerly she hadde a fair forheed.
It was almost a spanne brood, I trowe;
For, hardily, she was nat undergrowe.
Ful fetis was hir cloke, as I was war.
Of smal coral aboute hir arm she bar
A peire of bedes, gauded al with grene;[26]
And ther-on heng a broche of gold ful shene,
On which ther was first write a crownèd A,
And after, *Amor vincit omnia.*

A Clerk ther was of Oxenford also,
That un-to logik hadde longe y-go.[27]
As lene was his hors as is a rake,
And he was nat right fat, I undertake;
But lokèd holwe, and there-to soberly.
Ful thredbar was his overest courtepy;[28]
For he had geten him yet no benefyce,
Ne was so worldly for to have offyce.
For him was levere have at his beddes heed
Twenty bookes, clad in blak or reed

---

[20] certainly.   [21] high spirits.   [22] took pains to imitate courtly manners.
[23] worthy.   [24] plaited kerchief.   [25] well formed.
[26] a string of beads every eleventh one of which was green.
[27] devoted himself.   [28] short coat.

Of Aristotle and his philosophye,
Then robes riche, or fithele,[29] or gay sautrye,[30]
But al be that he was a philosophre,
Yet hadde he but litel gold in cofre;
But al that he mighte of his frendes hente,
On bookes and on lerninge he it spente,
And bisily gan for the soules preye
Of hem that yaf him where-with to scoleye.
Of studie took he most cure and most hede.
Noght o word spak he more than was nede,
And that was seyd in forme and reverence,
And short and quik, and ful of hy sentence.
Sowninge in[31] moral vertu was his speche;
And gladly wolde he lerne, and gladly teche.

A good WYF was ther of bisyde BATHE,
But she was som-del deef, and that was scathe.
Of cloth-making she hadde swiche an haunt,[32]
She passèd hem of Ypres and of Gaunt.
In al the parisshe wyf ne was ther noon
That to the offring bifore hir sholde goon;
And if ther dide, certeyn, so wrooth was she,
That she was out of alle charitee.
Hir coverchiefs ful fyne were of ground;[33]
I dorste swere they weyeden ten pound
That on a Sonday were upon hir heed.
Hir hosen weren of fyn scarlet reed,
Ful streite y-teyd, and shoos ful moiste and newe.
Bold was hir face, and fair, and reed of hewe.
She was a worthy womman al hir lyve,
Housbondes at chirche-dore she hadde fyve,
Withouten other compaignye in youthe;
But thereof nedeth nat to speke as nouthe.[34]
And thryes hadde she been at Ierusalem;
She hadde passèd many a straunge streem;
At Rome she hadde been, and at Boloigne,
In Galice at seint Iame, and at Coloigne.

---

[29] fiddle. [30] psaltery. [31] tending to. [32] skill
[33] texture. [34] at present.

She coude muche of wandring by the weye.
Gat-tothèd[35] was she, soothly for to seye.
Up-on an amblere esily she sat,
Y-wimplèd wel, and on hir heed an hat
As brood as is a bokeler or a targe;
A foot-mantel aboute hir hipes large,
And on hir feet a paire of spores sharpe.
In felaweschip wel coude she laughe and carpe.[36]
Of remedies of love she knew per-chaunce,
For she coude of that art the olde daunce.[37]

A good man was ther of religioun,
And was a povre PERSOUN[38] of a toun;
But riche he was of holy thoght and werk.
He was also a lernèd man, a clerk,
That Cristes gospel trewely wolde preche;
His parisshens devoutly wolde he teche.
Benigne he was, and wonder diligent,
And in adversitee ful pacient;
And swich he was y-prevèd ofte sythes.[39]
Ful looth were him to cursen[40] for his tythes,
But rather wolde he yeven, out of doute,
Un-to his povre parisshens aboute
Of his offring, and eek of his substaunce.
He coude in litel thing han suffisaunce.
Wyd was his parisshe, and houses fer a-sonder,
But he ne lafte nat, for reyn ne thonder,
In siknes nor in meschief to visyte
The ferreste in his parisshe, muche and lyte,[41]
Up-on his feet, and in his hand a staf.
This noble ensample to his sheep he yaf,
That first he wroghte, and afterward he taughte;
Out of the gospel he tho[42] wordes caughte;
And this figure he added eek ther-to,
That if gold ruste, what shal yren do?
For if a preest be foul, on whom we truste,
No wonder is a lewèd[43] man to ruste;

---

[35] gap-toothed. [36] talked. [37] the whole game. [38] parson. [39] often proved.
[40] excommunicate. [41] great and small. [42] those. [43] ignorant.

And shame it is, if a preest take keep,[44]
A [dirty] shepherde and a clene sheep.
Wel oghte a preest ensample for to yive,
By his clennesse, how that his sheep shold live.
He sette nat his benefice to hyre,
And leet his sheep encombrèd in the myre,
And ran to London, un-to seynt Poules,
To seken him a chaunterie for soules,
Or with a bretherhed to been withholde;
But dwelte at hoom, and kepte wel his folde,
So that the wolf ne made it nat miscarie;
He was a shepherde and no mercenarie.
And though he holy were, and vertuous,
He was to sinful man nat despitous,[45]
Ne of his speche daungerous[46] ne digne,[47]
But in teching discreet and benigne.
To drawen folk to heven by fairnesse
By good ensample, this was his bisynesse:
But it were any persone obstinat,
What so he were, of heigh or lowe estat,
Him wolde he snibben sharply for the nones.
A bettre preest, I trowe that nowher non is.
He wayted after no pompe and reverence,
Ne makèd him a spycèd[48] conscience,
But Cristes lore, and his apostles twelve,
He taughte, but first he folwèd it him-selve.

[From THE PROLOGUE to the CANTERBURY TALES.]

THE PRIORESSES TALE

THER was in Asie, in a gret citee,
Amonges Cristen folk a Iewerye,
Sustened by a lord of that contree,
For foule usure, and lucre of vilanye,
Hateful to Crist, and to his compagnye:
And thurgh the strete men mighten ride or wende
For it was free, and open at eyther ende.

[44] heed   [45] contemptuous.   [46] overbearing.   [47] haughty.   [48] over fine.

A litel scole of Cristen folk ther stood
Doun at the ferther ende, in which ther were
Children an heep, y-comen of Cristen blood,
That lernèd in that scole yeer by yere,
Swiche manere doctrine as men usèd there:
This is to seyn, to singen and to rede,
As smale children doon in hir childhede.

Among thise children was a widwes sone,
A litel clergeon, seven yeer of age,
That day by day to scole was his wone,
And eek also, wheras he saugh th'image
Of Cristes moder, had he in usage,
As him was taught, to knele adoun, and seye,
His *Ave Marie*, as he goth by the weye.

Thus hath this widwe hir litel sone y-taught
Our blisful Lady, Cristes moder dere,
To worship ay, and he forgat it naught:
For sely childe wol alday sone lere.
But ay, whan I remembre on this matere,
Seint Nicholas stant ever in my presence,
For he so yong to Crist did reverence.

This litel child his litel book lerninge,
As he sate in the scole at his primer,
He *"Alma redemptoris"* herde singe,
As children lernèd hir antiphoner:
And, as he dorste, he drough him ner and ner,
And herkned ay the wordes and the note,
Til he the firste vers coude al by rote.

Noght wiste he what this latin was to saye,
For he so yong and tendre was of age;
But on a day his felaw gan he preye
Texpounden him this song in his langage,
Or telle him why this song was in usage:
This preyde he him to construe and declare,
Ful ofte tyme upon his knees bare.

His felaw, which that elder was than he,
Answerde him thus: "This song, I have herd seye,
Was makèd of our blisful Lady fre,
Hir to salue, and eek hir for to preye
To ben our help, and socour whan we deye.
I can no more expound in this matere:
I lerne song, I can but smal grammere."

"And is this song makèd in reverence
Of Cristes moder?" said this Innocent.
"Now certes I wol do my diligence
To conne it all or Cristemasse be went,
Though that I for my primer shal be shent,[1]
And shall be beten thryes in an houre,
I wol it conne, our Ladie for to honoure."

His felaw taughte him homward prively
Fro day to day, til he coude it by rote,
And than he song it wel and boldely
Fro word to word according with the note:
Twyes a day it passèd thurgh his throte,
To scoleward and homeward whan he wente
On Cristes moder set was his entente.

As I have seyd, thurghout the Iewerye
This litel child, as he cam to and fro,
Ful merily than wold he singe, and crye
"O Alma redemptoris" ever-mo:
The swetnes hath his herte percèd so
Of Cristes moder, that to hire to preye
He cannot stint of singing by the weye.

Our firste foo, the serpent Sathanas,
That hath in Iewes herte his waspes nest,
Up swal and seid, "O Ebraik peple, alas!
Is this to yow a thing that is honest,
That swich a boy shal walken as him lest
In your despyt, and singe of swich sentence,
Which is agayn your lawes reverence?"

[1] scolded.

Fro thennes forth the Iewes han conspyrèd
This Innocent out of this world to chace:
An homicyde there-to han they hyrèd,
That in an aley had a privee place,
And as the child gan forthby for to pace,
This cursèd Iew him hent,[2] and heeld him faste
And kitte his throte, and in a pit him caste.

I say that in a wardrobe they him threwe,
Wher as thise Iewes purgen hir entraille.
O cursèd folk, of Herodes alle newe,
What may your yvil entente you availle?
Mordre wol out, certein it wol not faille.
And namely ther th' honour of God shal sprede:
The blood out cryeth on your cursèd dede.

"O martyr, souded in virginitee!
Now mayst thou singen, and folwen ever in on
The White Lamb celestial," quod she,
"Of which the gret Evangelist, Seint John
In Pathmos wrote, which sayth that they that goon
Beforn this Lamb, and singe a song al newe,
That never fleshly woman they ne knewe."

This poure widwe awaiteth al that night
After hir litel childe, and he cam noght:
For which, as sone as it was dayes light,
With face pale of drede and bisy thoght,
She hath at scole and elleswher him soght,
Til finally she gan so fer espye
That he last seyn was in the Iewerye.

With modres pitee in hir brest enclosèd
She gooth, as she were half out of hir mynde,
To every place wher she hath supposèd
By lyklihede hir litel child to fynde:
And ever on Cristes moder meke and kynde
She cryde, and at the laste thus she wroughte,
Among the cursèd Iewes she him soughte.

[2] seized.

She freyneth and she preyeth pitously
To every Iew that dwelte in thilke place,
To telle hir, if hir child wente ought for-by.
They seyde, "Nay"; but Iesu, of his grace,
Yaf in hir thought, inwith a litel space,
That in that place after hir sone she cryde,
Wher he was casten in a pit besyde.

O grete God, that parformest thy laude
By mouth of Innocentz, lo heer thy myght!
This gemme of chastitee, this Emeraude,
And eek of martirdom the Rubie bright,
Ther he with throte y-korven lay upryght,
He "*Alma redemptoris*" gan to singe
So loude, that all the place gan to ringe.

The Cristen folk that thurgh the strete wente,
In coomen, for to wondre upon this thing:
And hastily they for the Provost sente.
He cam anon withouten tarying,
And herieth[3] Crist, that is of heven king,
And eek his moder, honour of mankynd,
And after that the Iewes let he bynde.

This child with pitous lamentacioun
Up-taken was, singing his song alway:
And with honour and gret processioun,
They carien him unto the next abbay.
His moder swowning by the bere lay;
Unnethe might the peple that was there
This newe Rachel bringe fro his bere.

With torment and with shamful deth eche on
This Provost doth thise Iewes for to sterve,
That of this morder wiste, and that anon;
He nolde no swiche cursednesse observe:
Yvil shal he have, that yvil wol deserve.
Therfor with wilde hors he dide hem drawe,
And after that he heng hem by the lawe.

[3] praise.

Upon his bere ay lyth this Innocent
Biforn the chief auter whyl masse laste,
And after that, the abbot with his covent
Han sped hem for to burien him ful faste;
And whan they holy water on him caste,
Yet spak this child, whan spreynd was holy water,
And sang—"*O Alma redemptoris mater!*"

This abbot, which that was an holy man,
As monkes been, or elles oughten to be,
This yonge child to conjure he bigan,
And seyd; "O dere child, I halse thee
In vertue of the holy Trinitee,
Tel me what is thy cause for to singe,
Sith that thy throte is cut, to my seminge?"

"My throte is cut unto my nekke-boon,"
Seyd this child, "and, as by wey of kynde,
I sholde have deyèd, ye, longe tyme agoon:
But Iesu Crist, as ye in bookes fynde,
Wil that his glorie laste, and be in mynde,
And, for the worship of his moder dere,
Yet may I singe '*O Alma*' loude and clere.

"This welle of mercy, Cristes moder swete,
I lovèd alwey, as after my conninge;
And whan that I my lyf sholde forlete,
To me she cam, and bad me for to singe
This antem veraily in my deyinge,
As ye han herd, and, whan that I had songe,
Me thoughte she leyde a grain upon my tonge.

"Wherfor I singe, and singe I mote certeyn
In honour of that blisful mayden free,
Til fro my tonge of-taken is the greyn;
And after that thus seyde she to me,
'My litel child, than wol I fetchen thee
Whan that the greyn is fro thy tonge y-take:
Be nat agaste, I wol thee nat forsake.'"

This holy monk, this abbot, him mene I,
His tonge out-caughte, and toke away the greyn,
And he yaf up the gost ful softely.
And whan this abbot had this wonder seyn,
His salte teres trikled doun as reyn.
And gruf he fell al plat upon the grounde,
And stille he lay, as he had ben y-bounde.

The covent eek lay on the pavement
Weping, and herying Cristes moder dere.
And after that they rise, and forth ben went,
And toke awey this martir fro his bere,
And in a tombe of marble-stones clere
Enclosen they his litel body swete;
Ther he is now, God leve us for to mete.

BALADE DE BON CONSEYL

FLEE fro the prees, and dwelle with sothfastnesse,
Suffyce unto thy good, though hit be smal;
For hord hath hate, and clymbing tikelnesse,[1]
Prees[2] hath envye, and wele blent overal;[3]
Savour no more than thee bihove shal;
Werk wel thy-self, that other folk canst rede;[4]
And trouthe shal delivere, hit is no drede.[5]

Tempest[6] thee noght al croked to redresse,
In trust of hir that turneth as a bal;[7]
Gret reste stant[8] in litel besinesse.
And eek be war[9] to sporne[10] ageyn an al;[11]
Strive noght, as doth the crokke[12] with the wal.
Daunte thy-self, that dauntest otheres dede;
And trouthe shal delivere, hit is no drede.

---

[1] insecurity.
[2] the crowd.
[3] prosperity blinds everywhere.
[4] advise.
[5] doubt.
[6] disturb.
[7] i. e., fortune.
[8] stands, resides.
[9] cautious.
[10] kick.
[11] awl.
[12] crock, earthen pot.

That thee is sent, receyve in buxumnesse,[13]
The wrastling for this worlde axeth a fal.
Her nis non hom, her nis but wildernesse:
Forth, pilgrim, forth! Forth, beste, out of thy stal!
Know thy contree; lok up, thank God of al;
Hold the hye-wey, and lat thy gost[14] thee lede!
And trouthe shal delivere, hit is no drede.

ENVOY

Therfore, thou vache,[15] leve thyn old wrecchednesse;
Unto the worlde leve[16] now to be thral;
Crye Him mercy that of His hy goodnesse
Made thee of noght, and in especial
Draw unto Him, and pray in general
For thee, and eek for other, hevenlich mede;
And trouthe shal delivere, hit is no drede.
        Explicit Le bon counseill de G. Chaucer

JOHN LYDGATE [1370?–1451?]

THE CHILD JESUS TO MARY THE ROSE

My Fader above, beholdyng thy mekenesse,
  As dewe on rosis doth his bawme sprede,
Sendith his Gost, most soverayne of clennesse,
  Into thy breste, A! Rose of Wommanhede!
  Whan I for man was borne in my manhede—
For which, with rosis of hevenly influence
I me rejoyse to pley in thy presence.

Benygne Moder, who first dide inclose
  The blessèd budde that sprang out of Jesse,
Thow of Juda the verray perfit Rose,
  Chose of my Fader for thyn humylite
  Without fadyng, most clennest to bere me—
For which with roses of chast innocence
I me rejoyse to pley in thy presence.

---

[13] willing obedience.   [14] spirit.   [15] cow.   [16] cease

O Moder! Moder! of mercy most habounde,
  Fayrest moder that ever was alyve,
Though I for man have many a bloody wounde,
  Among theym alle there be rosis fyve,
  Agayne whos mercy fiendis may nat stryve;—
Mankynde to save, best rosis of defence,
Whan they me pray for helpe in thy presence.

ROBERT HENRYSON [1425?—?]

THE BLUDY SERK

This hindir yeir I hard be tald,
  Thair was a worthy King;
Dukis, Erlis, and Barronis bald,
  He had at his bidding.
The Lord was anceane, and ald,
  And sexty yeiris cowth ring;
He had a Dochter, fair to fald,[1]
  A lusty lady ying.[2]

Off all fairheid scho[3] bur[4] the flour;
  And eik hir faderis air;[5]
Off lusty laitis,[6] and he[7] honour;
  Meik, bot and[8] debonair.
Scho wynnit[9] in a bigly bour,
  On fold wes non so fair;
Princis luvit hir *par amour*,
  In cuntreis our all quhair.[10]

Thair dwelt a lyt besyde the King
  A fowll Gyane[11] of ane;
Stollin he hes the Lady ying,
  Away with hir is gane;

---

[1] "to fald": on earth.   [2] young.   [3] she.   [4] bore.   [5] heir.
[6] "lusty laitis": pleasant demeanour.   [7] high.   [8] "bot and": but also, yet.
[9] dwelt.   [10] *i. e.*, everywhere.   [11] giant.

And kest hir in his dungering,
    Quhair licht scho micht se nane:
Hungir and cauld, and grit thristing,
    Scho fand in to hir waine.[12]

He wes the laithliest on to luk
    That on the grund mycht gang:
His nailis wes lyk ane hellis cruk,
    Thairwith fyve quarteris lang.
Thair wes nane that he our-tuk,
    In rycht or yit in wrang,
Bot all in schondir[13] he thame schuke;
    The Gyane wes so strang.

He held the Lady day and nycht,
    Within his deip dungeoun;
He wald nocht gif of hir a sicht
    For gold nor yit ransoun,
Bot gife[14] the King mycht get a Knycht,
    To fecht with his persoun,
To fecht with him, bot day and nycht,
    Quhill ane were dungin doun.

The King gart seik baith fer and neir,
    Beth be se and land,
Off ony Knycht gife he micht heir,
    Wald fecht with that Gyand.
A worthy Prince, that had no peir,
    Hes tane the deid on hand,
For the luve of the Lady cleir;
    And held full trew cunnand.[15]

That Prince come prowdly to the toun,
    Of that Gyane to heir;
And fawcht with him, his awin persoun,
    And tuke him presoneir;

---

[12] dwelling.   [13] sunder.   [14] " Bot gife ": unless.   [15] covenant.

And kest him in his awin dungeoun,
　　Allane withouttin feir,
With hungir, cauld, and confusioun,
　　As full weill worthy weir.

Syne brak the bour, had hame the Bricht,[16]
　　Unto hir Fadir deir.
Saw evill wondit was the Knycht,
　　That he behuvit[17] to de.
Unlufum was his likame[18] dicht,
　　His sark was all bludy;
In all the warld was thair a wicht
　　So peteouss for to se!

The Lady murnyt, and maid grit mone,
　　With all hir mekle micht:
"I luvit nevir lufe, bot one,
　　That dulfully now is dicht!
God sen my lyfe wer fra me tone,
　　Or I had sene yone ficht;
Or ellis in begging evir to gone
　　Furth with yone curtass Knycht."

He said, "Fair Lady now mone I
　　De,[19] trestly[20] ye me trow:
Tak ye my sark that is bludy,
　　And hing it forrow yow.
First think on it, and syne on me,
　　Quhen men cumis yow to wow."[21]
The lady said, "Be[22] Mary fre,
　　Thairto I make a vow."

Quhen that scho lukit to the serk,
　　Scho thocht on the persoun:
And prayit for him with all hir harte,
　　That lowsd hir of bandoun:[23]

---

[16] bright. fair: *i. e.*, the Lady.　　[17] must.　　[18] body.　　[19] die.
[20] truly.　　[21] woo.　　[22] by.　　[23] bondage.

Quhair scho was wont to sit full merk[24]
 In that deip dungeoun:
And evir quhill scho wes in quert,[25]
 That wass hir a lessoun.

So weill the Lady luvit the Knycht,
 That no man wald scho tak.
So suld we do our God of micht
 That did all for us mak;
Quhilk fullely to deid wes dicht,
 For sinfull manis saik.
Sa suld we do, both day and nycht,
 With prayaris to him mak.

MORALITAS

This King is lyk the Trinitie
 Baith in hevin and heir.
The[26] Manis saule to the Lady:
 The Gyane to Lucefeir.
The Knycht to Chryst, that deit on tre,
 And coft[27] our synnis deir:
The pit to hell, with panis fell;
 The[26] syn to the woweir.[28]

The Lady was wowd, but scho said "Nay"
 With men that wald hir wed;
Sa suld we wryth[29] all syn away,
 That in our breist is bred.
I pray to Jesu Chryst verrey
 For us his blud that bled,
To be our help on Domysday,
 Quhair lawis ar straitly led.

The saule[30] is Godis dochtir deir,
 And eik his handewerk,
That was betrasit with Lucifeir,
 Quha sittis in hell, full merk.

[24] dark. [25] joyful. [26] "The" is superfluous. [27] bought.
[28] wooer.   [29] remove.   [30] soul.

Borrowit[31] with Chrystis angell cleir,
Hend[32] men! will ye nocht herk?
For his lufe that bocht us deir,
Think on the Bludy Serk!

WILLIAM DUNBAR [1460?–1520?]

TO A LADYE

SWET rois of vertew and of gentilness,
Delytsum lily of everie lustyness,
Richest in bontie and in bewtie clear,
And everie vertew that is [esteemèd] deer,
Except onlie that ye ar mercyless.

Into your garth this day I did persew;
There saw I flowris that fresche wer of hew;
Baith quhyte and reid most lusty wer to seyne,
And halesome herbis upon stalkis grene;
Yet leaf nor flowr fynd could I nane of rew.

I dout that Merche, with his cauld blastis keyne,
Has slain this gentil herbe, that I of mene,
Quhois piteous death dois to my heart sic paine
That I wald mak to plant his root againe—
So confortand his levis unto me bene.

[31] redeemed.   [32] courteous.

JOHN SKELTON [1460?-1529]

TO MISTRESS MARGARET HUSSEY

MIRRY MARGARET,
As mydsomer flowre;
Jentill as fawcoun
Or hawke of the towere:
With solace and gladnes,
Moche mirthe and no madness,
All good and no badness,
   So joyously,
   So maydenly,
   So womanly,
   Her demenyng
   In every thynge,
   Far, far passynge
   That I can endyght,
   Or suffyce to wryghte,
   Of mirry Margarete,
As mydsomer flowre,
Jentyll as fawcoun
Or hawke of the towre:
As pacient and as styll,
And as full of good wyll
As faire Isaphill;
   Colyaunder,
   Swete pomaunder,
   Goode cassaunder;
   Stedfast of thought,
   Wele made, wele wrought;
   Far may be sought,
   Erst that ye can fynde
   So corteise, so kynde,
   As mirry Margaret,
This mydsomer floure,
Jentyll as fawcoun
Or hawke of the towre.

[From A GARLANDE OF LAURELL.]

ENGLISH AND SCOTTISH POPULAR BALLADS

SIR PATRICK SPENS

THE king sits in Dumferling toune,
    Drinking the blude-reid wine:
"O whar will I get guid sailor,
    To sail this schip of mine?"

Up and spak an eldern knicht,
    Sat at the kings richt kne:
"Sir Patrick Spence is the best sailor,
    That sails upon the se."

The king has written a braid letter,
    And signd it wi his hand,
And sent it to Sir Patrick Spence,
    Was walking on the sand.

The first line that Sir Patrick red,
    A loud lauch lauchèd he;
The next line that Sir Patrick red,
    The teir blinded his ee.

"O wha is this has don this deid,
    This ill deid don to me,
To send me out this time o' the yeir,
    To sail upon the se!

"Mak hast, mak haste, my mirry men all,
    Our guid schip sails the morne:"
"O say na sae, my master deir,
    For I feir a deadlie storme.

"Late, late yestreen I saw the new moone,
    Wi the auld moone in hir arme,
And I feir, I feir, my deir master,
    That we will cum to harme."

O our Scots nobles wer richt laith
   To weet their cork-heild schoone;
Bot lang owre a' the play wer playd,
   Thair hats they swam aboone.

O lang, lang may the ladies sit,
   Wi thair fans into their hand,
Or eir they se Sir Patrick Spence
   Cum sailing to the land.

O lang, lang may the ladies stand,
   Wi thair gold kems in their hair,
Waiting for thair ain deir lords,
   For they'll se thame na mair.

Haf owre, haf owre to Aberdour,
   It's fiftie fadom deip,
And thair lies guid Sir Patrick Spence,
   Wi the Scots lords at his feit.

THE DOUGLAS TRAGEDY

"RISE up, rise up, now, Lord Douglas," she says,
   "And put on your armour so bright;
Let it never be said, that a daughter of thine
   Was married to a lord under night.

"Rise up, rise up, my seven bold sons,
   And put on your armour so bright,
And take better care of your youngest sister,
   For your eldest's awa the last night."

He's mounted her on a milk-white steed,
   And himself on a dapple grey,
With a bugelet horn hung down by his side,
   And lightly they rode away.

Lord William lookit o'er his left shoulder,
   To see what he could see,
And there he spy'd her seven brethren bold,
   Come riding over the lea.

"Light down, light down, Lady Margret," he said,
   And hold my steed in your hand,
Until that against your seven brethren bold,
   And your father, I mak a stand."

She held his steed in her milk-white hand,
   And never shed one tear,
Until that she saw her seven brethren fa,
   And her father hard fighting, who loved her so dear.

"O hold your hand, Lord William!" she said,
   "For your strokes they are wondrous sair;
True lovers I can get many a ane,
   But a father I can never get mair."

O she's ta'en out her handkerchief,
   It was o' the holland sae fine,
And aye she dighted[1] her father's bloody wounds,
   That were redder than the wine.

"O chuse, O chuse, Lady Margret," he said,
   "O whether will ye gang or bide?"
"I'll gang, I'll gang, Lord William," she said,
   "For ye have left me no other guide."

He's lifted her on a milk-white steed,
   And himself on a dapple grey,
With a bugelet horn hung down by his side,
   And slowly they baith rade away.

O they rade on, and on they rade,
   And a' by the light of the moon,
Until they came to yon wan water,
   And there they lighted down.

---

[1] wiped.

They lighted down to tak a drink
  Of the spring that ran sae clear;
And down the stream ran his gude heart's blood,
  And sair she gan to fear.

"Hold up, hold up, Lord William," she says
  "For I fear that you are slain!"
"'Tis naething but the shadow of my scarlet cloak,
  That shines in the water sae plain."

O they rade on, and on they rade,
  And a' by the light of the moon,
Until they cam' to his mother's ha' door,
  And there they lighted down.

"Get up, get up, lady mother," he says,
  "Get up, and let me in!—
Get up, get up, lady mother," he says
  "For this night my fair ladye I've win.

"O mak my bed, lady mother," he says,
  "O mak it braid and deep!
And lay Lady Margret close at my back,
  And the sounder I will sleep."

Lord William was dead lang ere midnight,
  Lady Margret lang ere day—
And all true lovers that go thegither,
  May they have mair luck than they!

Lord William was buried in St. Mary's kirk,
  Lady Margaret in Mary's quire;
Out o' the lady's grave grew a bonny red rose,
  And out o' the knight's a brier.

And they twa met, and they twa plat,[2]
  And fain they wad be near;
And a' the warld might ken right weel,
  They were twa lovers dear.

             [2] twined.

But bye and rade the Black Douglas,
  And wow but he was rough!
For he pull'd up the bonny brier,
  And flang't in St. Mary's loch.

THE DEATH AND BURIAL OF ROBIN HOOD

WHEN Robin Hood and Little John
  Down, a down, a down, a down,
Went oer yon bank of broom,
  Said Robin Hood bold to Little John,
"We have shot for many a pound."
  Hey down, a down, a down.

"But I am not able to shoot one shot more,
  My broad arrows will not flee;
But I have a cousin lives down below,
  Please God, she will bleed me."

Now Robin he is to fair Kirkly gone,
  As fast as he can win;
But before he came there, as we do hear,
  He was taken very ill.

And when he came to fair Kirkly-hall,
  He knockd all at the ring,
But none was so ready as his cousin herself
  For to let bold Robin in.

"Will you please to sit down, cousin Robin," she said,
  "And drink some beer with me?"
"No, I will neither eat nor drink,
  Till I am bleeded by thee."

"Well, I have a room, cousin Robin," she said,
  "Which you did never see,
And if you please to walk therein,
  You blooded by me shall be."

She took him by the lily-white hand,
  And led him to a private room,
And there she blooded bold Robin Hood,
  While one drop of blood would run down.

She blooded him in a vein of the arm,
  And locked him up in the room;
Then did he bleed all the live-long day,
  Until the next day at noon.

He then bethought him of a casement there,
  Thinking for to get down;
But was so weak he could not leap,
  He could not get him down.

He then bethought him of his bugle-horn,
  Which hung low down to his knee;
He set his horn unto his mouth,
  And blew out weak blasts three.

Then Little John, when hearing him,
  As he sat under a tree,
"I fear my master is now near dead,
  He blows so wearily."

Then Little John to fair Kirkly is gone,
  As fast as he can dree;
But when he came to Kirkly-hall,
  He broke locks two or three:

Until he came bold Robin to see,
  Then he fell on his knee;
"A boon, a boon," cries Little John,
  "Master, I beg of thee."

"What is that boon," said Robin Hood,
  "Little John, thou begs of me?"
"It is to burn fair Kirkly-hall,
  And all their nunnery."

"Now nay, now nay," quoth Robin Hood,
　"That boon I'll not grant thee;
I never hurt woman in all my life,
　Nor men in woman's company.

"I never hurt fair maid in all my time,
　Nor at mine end shall it be;
But give me my bent bow in my hand,
　And a broad arrow I'll let flee,
And where this arrow is taken up,
　There shall my grave digg'd be.

"Lay me a green sod under my head,
　And another at my feet;
And lay my bent bow by my side,
　Which was my music sweet;
And make my grave of gravel and green,
　Which is most right and meet.

" Let me have length and breadth enough,
　With a green sod under my head;
That they may say, when I am dead,
　Here lies bold Robin Hood."

These words they readily granted him,
　Which did bold Robin please:
And there they buried bold Robin Hood,
　Within the fair Kirkleys.

THE HUNTING OF THE CHEVIOT

The Persë owt off Northombarlonde,
　and avowe to God mayd he
That he wold hunte in the mowntayns
　off Chyviat within days thre,
In the magger[1] of doughte Dogles,
　and all that ever with him be.

[1] spite.

The fattiste hartes in all Cheviat
    he sayd he wold kyll, and cary them away:
"Be my feth," sayd the dougheti Doglas agayn,
    "I wyll let[2] that hontyng yf that I may."

Then the Persë owt off Banborowe cam,
    with him a myghtee meany,[3]
With fifteen hondrith archares bold off blood and bone;
    the[4] wear chosen owt of shyars thre.

This begane on a Monday at morn,
    in Cheviat the hillys so he;[5]
The chylde may rue that ys unborn,
    it wos the more pitte.

The dryvars thorowe the woodes went,
    for to reas the dear;
Bomen byckarte[6] uppone the bent[7]
    with ther browd aros cleare.

Then the wyld[8] thorowe the woodes went,
    on every syde shear;[9]
Greahondes thorowe the grevis[10] glent,[11]
    for to kyll thear dear.

This begane in Chyviat the hyls abone,
    yerly on a Monnyn-day;
Be that it drewe to the oware off none,
    a hondrith fat hartes ded ther lay.

The[12] blewe a mort uppone the bent,
    the[12] semblyde on sydis shear;
To the quyrry then the Persë went,
    to se the bryttlynge[13] off the deare.

He sayd, "It was the Duglas promys,
    this day to met me hear;
But I wyste he wolde faylle, verament;"
    a great oth the Persë swear.

---

[2] prevent.	[3] company.	[4] they.	[5] high.	[6] attacked.	[7] field.
[8] deer.	[9] several.	[10] groves.	[11] glided.	[12] they.	[13] cutting up.

At the laste a squyar off Northomberlonde
    lokyde at his hand full ny;
He was war a the doughetie Doglas commynge,
    with him a myghtte meany.

Both with spear, bylle, and brande,
    yt was a myghtti sight to se;
Hardyar men, both off hart nor hande,
    wear not in Cristiante.

The wear twenti hondrith spear-men good,
    withoute any feale;
The wear borne along be the watter a Twyde,
    yth[14] bowndes of Tividale.

"Leave of the brytlyng of the dear," he sayd,
    "and to your boys[15] lock ye tayk good hede;
For never sithe ye wear on your mothars borne
    had ye never so mickle nede."

The dougheti Dogglas on a stede,
    he rode alle his men beforne;
His armor glytteryde as dyd a glede;[16]
    a boldar barne was never born.

"Tell me whos men ye ar," he says,
    "or whos men that ye be:
Who gave youe leave to hunte in this Chyviat chays,
    in the spyt of myn and of me."

The first mane that ever him an answear mayd,
    yt was the good lord Persë:
"We wyll not tell the whoys men we ar," he says,
    "nor whos men that we be;
But we wyll hounte hear in this chays,
    in the spyt of thyne and of the.

"The fattiste hartes in all Chyviat,
    we have kyld, and cast to carry them away.
"Be my troth," sayd the doughete Dogglas agayn,
    "therfor the ton[17] of us shall de this day."

[14] with.   [15] bows.   [16] glowing coal.   [17] one.

Then sayd the doughte Doglas
  unto the lord Persë:
"To kyll alle these giltles men,
  alas, it wear great pittie!

"But, Persë, thowe art a lord of lande,
  I am a yerle callyd within my contre;
Let all our men uppone a parti stande,
  and do the battell off the and of me."

"Nowe Cristes cors on his crowne," sayd the lord
    Persë,
  "who-so-ever ther-to says nay;
Be my troth, doughtte Doglas," he says,
  "thow shalt never se that day,

"Nethar in Ynglonde, Skottlonde, nar France,
  nor for no man of a woman born,
But, and fortune be my chance,
  I dar met him on[18] man for on."

Then bespayke a squyar off Northombarlonde,
  Richard Wytharyngton was his nam:
"It shall never be told in Sothe-Ynglonde," he says,
  "to Kyng Herry the Fourth for sham.

"I wat youe byn great lordes twaw,
  I am a poor squyar of lande:
I wylle never se my captayne fyght on a fylde,
  and stande my selffe and loocke on,
But whylle I may my weppone welde,
  I wylle not fayle both hart and hande."

That day, that day, that dredfull day!
  the first fit here I fynde;
And youe wyll here any mor a the hountyng a the
    Chyviat,
  yet ys ther mor behynde.

[18] one.

The Yngglyshe men hade ther bowys yebent,
 ther hartes wer good yenoughe;
The first off arros that the shote off,
 seven skore spear-men the sloughe.[19]

Yet byddys the yerle Doglas uppon the bent,
 a captayne good yenoughe,
And that was sene verament,
 for he wrought hom both woo and wouche.[20]

The Dogglas partyd his ost in thre,
 lyk a cheffe cheften off pryde;
With suar[21] spears off myghtte tre,
 the cum in on every syde:

Thrughe our Yngglyshe archery
 gave many a wounde fulle wyde;
Many a doughete the garde[22] to dy,
 which ganyde them no pryde.

The Ynglyshe men let ther boys be,
 and pulde owt brandes that wer brighte;
It was a hevy syght to se
 bryght swordes on basnites lyght.

Thorowe ryche male and myneyeple,[23]
 many sterne the strocke done streght;
Many a freyke[24] that was fulle fre,
 ther undar foot dyd lyght.

At last the Duglas and the Persë met,
 lyk to captayns of myght and of mayne;
The swapte togethar tylle the both swat,
 with swordes that wear of fyn myllan.

Thes worthe freckys for to fyght,
 ther-to the wear fulle fayne,
Tylle the bloode owte off thear basnetes sprente
 as ever dyd heal or rayn.

[19] slew.   [20] harm.   [21] trusty.   [22] made.   [23] gauntlets.   [24] man.

"Yelde the, Persë," sayde the Doglas,
    "and i feth I shalle the brynge
Wher thowe shalte have a yerls wagis
    of Jamy our Skottish kynge.

"Thou shalte have thy ransom fre,
    I hight[25] the hear this thinge;
For the manfullyste man yet art thowe
    that ever I conqueryd in filde fighttynge."

"Nay," sayd the lord Persë,
    "I tolde it the beforne,
That I wolde never yeldyde be
    to no man of a woman born."

With that ther cam an arrowe hastely,
    forthe off a myghtte wane:[26]
Hit hathe strekene the yerle Duglas
    in at the brest-bane.

Thorowe lyvar and longes bathe
    the sharpe arrowe ys gane,
That never after in all his lyffe-days
    he spayke mo wordes but ane:
That was, "Fyghte ye, my myrry men, whyllys ye
        may,
    for my lyff-days ben gan."

The Persë leanyde on his brande,
    and sawe the Duglas de;
He tooke the dede mane by the hande,
    and sayd, "Wo ys me for the!

"To have savyde thy lyffe, I wolde have partyde
        with
    my landes for years thre,
For a better man, of hart nare of hande,
    was nat in all the north contre."

----

[25] promise.   [26] flight.

Off all that se a Skottishe knyght,
   was callyd Ser Hewe the Monggombyrry;
He sawe the Duglas to the deth was dyght,
   he spendyd[27] a spear, a trusti tre.

He rod uppone a corsiare
   throughe a hondrith archery:
He never stynttyde, nar never blane,[28]
   tylle he cam to the good lord Persë.

He set uppone the lorde Persë
   a dynte that was full soare;
With a suar spear of a myghtte tre
   clean thorow the body he the Persë ber,

A the tothar syde that a man myght se
   a large cloth-yard and mare:
Towe bettar captayns wear nat in Cristiante
   then that day slan wear ther.

An archar off Northomberlonde
   say[29] slean was the lord Persë;
He bar a bende bowe in his hand,
   was made off trusti tre.

An arow, that a cloth-yarde was lang,
   to the harde stele halyde[30] he;
A dynt that was both sad and soar
   he sat[31] on Ser Hewe the Monggombyrry.

The dynt yt was both sad and sar,
   that he of Monggomberry sete;
The swane-fethars that his arrowe bar
   with his hart-blood the wear wete.

Ther was never a freake wone foot wolde fle,
   but still in stour dyd stand,
Heawyng on yche othar, whylle the myghte dre,[32]
   with many a balfull brande.

[27] grasped.   [28] stopped.   [29] saw.   [30] drew.   [31] set upon.   [32] endure.

This battell begane in Chyviat
    an owar before the none,
And when even-songe bell was rang,
    the battell was nat half done.

The tocke . . . [33] on ethar hande
    be the lyght off the mone;
Many hade no strenght for to stande,
    in Chyviat the hillys abon.

Of fifteen hondrith archars of Ynglonde
    went away but seventi and thre;
Of twenti hondrith spear-men of Skotlonde,
    but even five and fifti.

But all wear slayne Cheviat within;
    the hade no strengthe to stand on hy;
The chylde may rue that ys unborne,
    it was the mor pitte.

Thear was slayne, withe the lord Persë,
    Sir Johan of Agerstone,
Ser Rogar, the hinde[34] Hartly,
    Ser Wyllyam, the bolde Hearone.

Ser Jorg, the worthe Loumle,
    a knyghte of great renowen,
Ser Raff, the ryche Rugbe,
    with dyntes wear beaten dowene.

For Wetharryngton my harte was wo,
    that ever he slayne should be;
For when both his leggis wear hewyne in to,
    yet he knyled and fought on hys kny.

Ther was slayne, with the dougheti Duglas,
    Ser Hewe the Monggombyrry,
Ser Dany Lwdale, that worthe was,
    his sistars son was he.

[33] break in the text.   [34] courteous.

Ser Charls a Murre in that place,
  that never a foot wolde fle;
Ser Hewe Maxwelle, a lorde he was,
  with the Doglas dyd he dey.

So on the morrowe the mayde them by ears
  off birch and hasell so grey;
Many wedous, with wepying tears,
  cam to fache ther makys[35] away.

Tivydale may carpe off care,
  Northombarlond may mayk great mon,
For towe such captayns as slayne wear thear,
  on the March-parti shall never be non.

Word ys commen to Eddenburrowe,
  to Jamy the Skottische kynge,
That dougheti Duglas, lyff-tenant of the Marches,
  he lay slean Chyviot within.

His handdes dyd he weal and wryng,
  he sayd, "Alas, and woe ys me!
Such an othar captayn Skotland within,"
  he sayd, "ye-feth shuld never be."

Worde ys commyn to lovly Londone,
  till the fourth Harry our kynge,
That lord Persë, leyff-tenante of the Marchis,
  he lay slayne Chyviat within.

"God have merci on his solle," sayde Kyng Harry,
  "good Lord, yf thy will it be!
I have a hondrith captayns in Ynglonde," he sayd,
  "as good as ever was he:
But, Persë, and I brook my lyffe,
  thy deth well quyte shall be."

[35] mates.

As our noble kynge mayd his avowe,
　　lyke a noble prince of renowen,
For the deth of the lord Persë
　　he dyde the battell of Hombyll-down;

Wher syx and thritte Skottishe knyghtes
　　on a day wear beaten down:
Glendale glytteryde on ther armor bryght,
　　over castille, towar, and town.

This was the hontynge off the Cheviat,
　　that tear[36] began this spurn;[37]
Old men that knowen the grownde well yenoughe
　　call it the battell of Otterburn.

At Otterburn begane this spurne
　　uppone a Monnynday;
Ther was the doughte Doglas slean,
　　the Persë never went away.

Ther was never a tym on the Marche-partes
　　sen the Doglas and the Persë met,
But yt ys mervele and the rede blude ronne not,
　　as the reane[38] doys in the stret.

Ihesue Crist our balys bete,[39]
　　and to the blys us brynge!
Thus was the hountynge of the Chivyat:
　　God sent us alle good endyng!

THE DÆMON LOVER

"O where have you been, my long, long love,
　　This long seven years and mair?"
"O I'm come to seek my former vows
　　Ye granted me before."

[36] e'er.　　　[37] fight.　　　[38] rain.　　　[39] abate.

"O hold your tongue of your former vows,
    For they will breed sad strife;
O hold your tongue of your former vows,
    For I am become a wife."

He turnd him right and round about,
    And the tear blinded his ee:
"I wad never hae trodden on Irish ground,
    If it had not been for thee.

"I might hae had a king's daughter,
    Far, far beyond the sea;
I might have had a king's daughter,
    Had it not been for love o thee."

"If ye might have had a king's daughter,
    Yersel ye had to blame;
Ye might have taken the king's daughter,
    For ye kend that I was nane.

"If I was to leave my husband dear,
    And my two babes also,
O what have you to take me to,
    If with you I should go?"

"I hae seven ships upon the sea—
    The eighth brought me to land—
With four-and-twenty bold mariners,
    And music on every hand."

She has taken up her two little babes,
    Kissd them baith cheek and chin:
"O fair ye weel, my ain two babes,
    For I'll never see you again."

She set her foot upon the ship,
    No mariners could she behold;
But the sails were o the taffetie,
    And the masts o the beaten gold.

She had not sayld a league, a league,
   A league but barely three,
When dismal grew his countenance,
   And drumlie grew his ee.

They had not sayld a league, a league,
   A league but barely three,
Until she espied his cloven foot,
   And she wept right bitterlie.

"O hold your tongue of your weeping," says he,
   "Of your weeping now let me be;
I will shew you how the lilies grow
   On the banks of Italy."

"O what hills are yon, yon pleasant hills,
   That the sun shines sweetly on?"
"O yon are the hills of heaven," he said,
   "Where you will never win."

"O whaten a mountain is yon," she said,
   "All so dreary wi frost and snow?"
"O yon is the mountain of hell," he cried,
   "Where you and I will go."

He strack the tap-mast wi his hand,
   The fore-mast wi his knee,
And he brake that gallant ship in twain,
   And sank her in the sea.

SIR THOMAS WYATT [1503–1542]

THE LOVER TO HIS MISTRESS

FORGET not yet the tried intent
Of such a truth as I have meant;
My great travail so gladly spent,
Forget not yet!

Forget not yet when first began
The weary life ye know, since whan
The suit, the service, none tell can;
Forget not yet!

Forget not yet the great assays,
The cruel wrong, the scornful ways,
The painful patience in delays,
Forget not yet!

Forget not! O, forget not this,
How long ago hath been, and is,
The mind that never meant amiss—
Forget not yet!

Forget not then thine own approved,
The which so long hath thee so loved,
Whose steadfast faith yet never moved:
Forget not this!

TO HIS UNKIND MISTRESS

AND wilt thou leave me thus?
Say nay, say nay, for shame!
To save thee from the blame
Of all my grief and grame.
And wilt thou leave me thus?
Say nay! say nay!

And wilt thou leave me thus,
That hath loved thee so long
In wealth and woe among:
And is thy heart so strong ·
As for to leave me thus?
Say nay! say nay!

And wilt thou leave me thus,
That hath given thee my heart
Never for to depart
Neither for pain nor smart:
And wilt thou leave me thus?
Say nay! say nay!

And wilt thou leave me thus,
And have no more pity
Of him that loveth thee?
Alas, thy cruelty!
And wilt thou leave me thus?
Say nay! say nay!

THE LOVER COMPLAINETH

My lute, awake! perform the last
Labour that thou and I shall waste;
And end that I have now begun:
And when this song is sung and past,
My lute, be still, for I have done.

As to be heard where ear is none;
As lead to grave in marble stone;
My song may pierce her heart as soon.
Should we then sigh, or sing, or moan?
No, no, my lute, for I have done.

The rocks do not so cruelly
Repulse the waves continually

As she my suit and affection:
So that I am past remedy;
Whereby my lute and I have done.

Proud of the spoil that thou hast got
Of simple hearts thorough Love's shot,
By whom unkind thou hast them won:
Think not he hath his bow forgot,
Although my lute and I have done.

Vengeance shall fall on thy disdain,
That makst but game on earnest pain;
Think not alone under the sun
Unquit to cause thy lovers plain;
Although my lute and I have done.

May chance, thee lie wither'd and old
In winter nights, that are so cold,
Plaining in vain unto the moon;
Thy wishes then dare not be told:
Care then who list, for I have done.

And then may chance thee to repent
The time that thou hast lost and spent,
To cause thy lovers sigh and swoon:
Then shalt thou know beauty but lent,
And wish and want as I have done.

Now cease, my lute, this is the last
Labour that thou and I shall waste;
And ended is that we begun:
Now is this song both sung and past:
My lute, be still, for I have done.

THE LOVER LIKE TO A SHIP TOSSED ON THE SEA

My galley chargèd with forgetfulness
Thorough sharp seas, in winter nights doth pass,
'Tween rock and rock; and eke my foe, alas,
That is my lord, steereth with cruelness;
And every hour, a thought in readiness,
As though that death were light in such a case.
An endless wind doth tear the sail apace
Of forcèd sighs, and trusty fearfulness.
A rain of tears, a cloud of dark disdain
Hath done the wearied cords great hinderance,
Wreathèd with error, and with ignorance.
The stars be hid that led me to this pain;
    Drownèd is reason that should be my comfort,
    And I remain, despairing of the port.

HENRY HOWARD, EARL OF SURREY
[1517?–1547]

SPRING

THE LOVER ONLY IS SORROWFUL

The soote[1] season, that bud and bloom forth brings,
With green hath clad the hill, and eke the vale.
The nightingale with feathers new she sings;
The turtle to her make[2] hath told her tale.
Summer is come, for every spray now springs:
The hart hath hung his old head on the pale;
The buck in brake his winter coat he slings;
The fishes flete[3] with new repaired scale;
The adder all her slough away she slings;
The swift swallow pursueth the flies smale;
The busy bee her honey now she mings;[4]
Winter is worn, that was the flowers' bale.

    And thus I see among these pleasant things
    Each care decays, and yet my sorrow springs!

[1] sweet.   [2] mate.   [3] float.   [4] mixes.

THE MEANS TO ATTAIN HAPPY LIFE

MARTIAL, the things that do attain
  The happy life be these, I find:
The riches left, not got with pain;
  The fruitful ground, the quiet mind;
The equal friend, no grudge, no strife;
  No charge of rule nor governance;
Without disease, the healthful life;
  The household of continuance.
The mean[1] diet, no delicate fare;
  True wisdom joined with simpleness;
The night dischargèd of all care,
  Where wine the wit may not oppress;
The faithful wife, without debate;
  Such sleeps as may beguile the night:
Contented with thine own estate,
  Ne wish for death, ne fear his might.

GEORGE GASCOIGNE [1525?–1577]

THE ARRAIGNMENT OF A LOVER

AT Beauty's bar as I did stand,
When false Suspect accused me,
"George," quoth the Judge, "hold up thy hand,
Thou art arraigned of flattery:
Tell therefore how thou wilt be tried:
Whose judgment here wilt thou abide?"

"My Lord," quoth I, "this Lady here,
Whom I esteem above the rest,
Doth know my guilt if any were:
Wherefore her doom shall please me best.
Let her be Judge and Juror both,
To try me, guiltless, by mine oath!"

[1] moderate.

Quoth Beauty, "No, it fitteth not
A prince herself to judge the cause:
Will is our Justice, well you wot,
Appointed to discuss our laws:
If you will guiltless seem to go,
God and your country quit you so."

Then Craft the crier called a quest,
Of whom was Falsehood foremost fere,
A pack of pickthanks were the rest,
Which came false witness for to bear;
The jury such, the judge unjust:
Sentence was said I should be trussed.

Jealous the jailer bound me fast,
To hear the verdict of the bill,
"George," quoth the Judge, "now thou art cast,
Thou must go hence to Heavy Hill,
And there be hanged all but the head,
God rest thy soul when thou art dead."

Down fell I then upon my knee,
All flat before Dame Beauty's face,
And cried, "Good Lady, pardon me,
Which here appeal unto your grace,
You know if I have been untrue,
It was in too much praising you.

"And though this Judge do make such haste
To shed with shame my guiltless blood,
Yet let your pity first be placed
To save the man that meant you good,
So shall you show yourself a Queen,
And I may be your servant seen."

Quoth Beauty, "Well: because I guess,
What thou dost mean henceforth to be,
Although thy faults deserve no less
Than Justice here hath judged thee,

Wilt thou be bound to stint all strife
And be true prisoner all thy life ?"

"Yea madam," quoth I, "that I shall,
Lo, Faith and Truth my sureties."
"Why then," quoth she, "come when I call,
I ask no better warrantise."
Thus am I Beauty's bounden thrall,
At her command when she doth call.

THOMAS SACKVILLE, LORD BUCKHURST
[1536–1608]

THE GODDESS OF SORROW SHOWETH
THE POET HELL

An hideous hole all vast, withouten shape,
Of endless depth, o'erwhelmed with ragged stone,
With ugly mouth, and grisly jaws doth gape,
And to our sight confounds itself in one:
Here entered we, and yeding[1] forth, anon
An horrible loathly lake we might discern,
As black as pitch, that clepèd is Avern:

A deadly gulf, where naught but rubbish grows,
With foul black swelth in thickened lumps that lies,
Which up in th' air such stinking vapors throws,
That over there may fly no fowl but dies
Choked with the pestilent savours that arise:
Hither we come; whence forth we still did pace,
In dreadful fear amid the dreadful place:

And first, within the porch and jaws of Hell,
Sat deep Remorse of Conscience, all besprent
With tears; and to herself oft would she tell
Her wretchedness, and cursing never stent
To sob and sigh; but ever thus lament,

[1] going.

With thoughtful care, as she that, all in vain,
Would wear, and waste continually in pain.

Her eyes unsteadfast, rolling here and there,
Whirled on each place, as place that vengeance brought,
So was her mind continually in fear,
Tossed and tormented with the tedious thought
Of those detested crimes which she had wrought;
With dreadful cheer, and looks thrown to the sky,
Wishing for death, and yet she could not die.

And next, within the entry of this lake,
Sat fell Revenge, gnashing her teeth for ire,
Devising means how she may vengeance take,
Never in rest, till she have her desire:
But frets within so far forth with the fire
Of wreaking flames, that now determines she
To die by death, or venged by death to be.

When fell Revenge, with bloody foul pretence
Had showed herself, as next in order set,
With trembling limbs we softly parted thence,
Till in our eyes another sight we met:
When from my heart a sigh forthwith I fet,
Ruing, alas! upon the woeful plight
Of Misery, that next appeared in sight.

His face was lean, and somedeal pined away,
And eke his hands consumèd to the bone,
But what his body was, I cannot say,
For on his carcass raiment had he none,
Save clouts and patches, piecèd one by one;
With staff in hand, and scrip on shoulders cast,
His chief defence against the winter's blast.

His food, for most, was wild fruits of the tree,
Unless sometimes some crumbs fell to his share,
Which in his wallet long, God wot, kept he,

As on the which full daint'ly would he fare:
His drink, the running stream; his cup, the bare
Of his palm closed; his bed, the hard cold ground:
To this poor life was Misery ybound.

Whose wretched state when we had well beheld,
With tender ruth on him, and on his fears,
In thoughtful cares forth then our pace we held;
And, by and by, another shape appears,
Of greedy Care, still brushing up the breres,[2]
His knuckles knobbed,[3] his flesh deep dented in,
With tawèd[4] hands, and hard ytannèd skin.

The morrow gray no sooner hath begun
To spread his light, even peeping in our eyes,
When he is up, and to his work yrun:
But let the night's black misty mantles rise,
And with foul dark never so much disguise
The fair, bright day, yet ceaseth he no while,
But has his candles to prolong his toil.

Lastly, stood War, in glittering arms yclad,
With visage grim, stern looks, and blackly hued;
In his right hand a naked sword he had,
That to the hilts was all with blood imbrued;
And in his left (that kings and kingdoms rued)
Famine and fire he held, and therewithal
He razèd towns, and threw down towers and all:

Cities he sacked; and realms that whilom flowered
In honor, glory, and rule, above the best,
He overwhelmed, and all their fame devoured,
Consumed, destroyed, wasted, and never ceased,
Till he their wealth, their name, and all, oppressed:
His face fore-hewed with wounds, and by his side
There hung his targe, with gashes deep and wide.

[From the INDUCTION TO A MIRROR FOR MAGISTRATES.

[2] briars.   [3] hardened.   [4] roughened.

NICHOLAS BRETON [1545?–1626?]

PHYLLIDA AND CORYDON

In the merry month of May,
In a morn by break of day,
Forth I walked by the wood-side,
When as May was in her pride:
There I spièd all alone
Phyllida and Corydon.
Much ado there was, God wot!
He would love and she would not.
She said, never man was true;
He said, none was false to you.
He said, he had loved her long;
She said, love should have no wrong.
Corydon would kiss her then;
She said, maids must kiss no men,
Till they did for good and all;
Then she made the shepherd call
All the heavens to witness truth:
Never loved a truer youth.
Thus with many a pretty oath,
Yea and nay, and faith and troth,
Such as silly shepherds use
When they will not love abuse,
Love which had been long deluded,
Was with kisses sweet concluded;
And Phyllida, with garlands gay,
Was made the Lady of the May.

SIR WALTER RALEIGH [1552?–1618]

HIS PILGRIMAGE

GIVE me my scallop-shell of quiet,
  My staff of faith to walk upon,
My scrip of joy, immortal diet,
  My bottle of salvation,
My gown of glory, hope's true gage;
And thus I'll take my pilgrimage.

Blood must be my body's balmer;
  No other balm will there be given;
Whilst my soul, like quiet palmer,
  Travelleth towards the land of heaven,
Over the silver mountains,
Where spring the nectar fountains:
    There will I kiss
    The bowl of bliss;
And drink mine everlasting fill
Upon every milken hill.
My soul will be a-dry before;
But after, it will thirst no more.

Then, by that happy blissful day,
  More peaceful pilgrims I shall see,
That have cast off their rags of clay,
  And walk apparelled fresh like me.
    I'll take them first
    To quench their thirst
And taste of nectar suckets,
    At those clear wells
    Where sweetness dwells,
Drawn up by saints in crystal buckets.

And when our bottles and all we
Are filled with immortality,

Then the blessèd paths we'll travel,
Strowed with rubies thick as gravel;
Ceilings of diamonds, sapphire floors,
High walls of coral, and pearly bowers.
From thence to heaven's bribeless hall,
Where no corrupted voices brawl;
No conscience molten into gold,
No forged accuser bought or sold,
No cause deferred, no vain-spent journey,
For there Christ is the king's Attorney,
Who pleads for all without degrees,
And He hath angels, but no fees.
And when the grand twelve-million jury
Of our sins, with direful fury,
Against our souls black verdicts give,
Christ pleads His death, and then we live—
Be Thou my speaker, taintless pleader,
Unblotted lawyer, true proceeder!
Thou givest salvation even for alms;
Not with a bribed lawyer's palms.

And this is mine eternal plea
To Him that made heaven, earth, and sea.
That, since my flesh must die so soon,
And want a head to dine next noon,
Just at the stroke, when my veins start and spread,
Set on my soul an everlasting head!
Then am I ready, like a palmer fit,
To tread those blest paths which before I writ.
    Of death and judgment, heaven and hell,
    Who oft doth think, must needs die well.

VERSES

FOUND IN HIS BIBLE IN THE GATE-HOUSE AT WESTMINSTER

EVEN such is time, that takes in trust
   Our youth, our joys, our all we have,
And pays us but with earth and dust;
   Who, in the dark and silent grave,
When we have wandered all our ways,
Shuts up the story of our days;
But from this earth, this grave, this dust,
My God shall raise me up, I trust!

SIR PHILIP SIDNEY [1554–1586]

SONNETS

WITH how sad steps, O Moon, thou climb'st the skies!
How silently, and with how wan a face!
What, may it be that even in heavenly place
That busy archer his sharp arrows tries!
Sure, if that long-with-love-acquainted eyes
Can judge of love, thou feel'st a lover's case,
I read it in thy looks; thy languisht grace,
To me, that feel the like, thy state descries.
Then, even of fellowship, O Moon, tell me,
Is constant love deemed there but want of wit?
Are beauties there as proud as here they be?
Do they above love to be loved, and yet
   Those lovers scorn whom that love doth possess?
   Do they call virtue there ungratefulness?

COME, Sleep! O Sleep, the certain knot of peace,
The baiting-place of wit, the balm of woe,
The poor man's wealth, the prisoner's release,
Th' indifferent judge between the high and low;

With shield of proof shield me from out the prease[1]
Of those fierce darts Despair at me doth throw:
O make in me those civil wars to cease;
I will good tribute pay, if thou do so.
Take thou of me smooth pillows, sweetest bed,
A chamber deaf to noise and blind to light,
A rosy garland and a weary head:
And if these things, as being thine in right,
  Move not thy heavy grace, thou shalt in me,
  Livelier than elsewhere, Stella's image see.

HIGHWAY, since you my chief Parnassus be,
And that my Muse, to some ears not unsweet,
Tempers her words to trampling horses' feet
More oft than to a chamber-melody.
Now, blessèd you bear onward blessèd me
To her, where I my heart, safe-left, shall meet;
My Muse and I must you of duty greet
With thanks and wishes, wishing thankfully.
Be you still fair, honoured by public heed;
By no encroachment wronged, nor time forgot;
Nor blam'd for blood, nor sham'd for sinful deed;
And that you know I envy you no lot
  Of highest wish, I wish you so much bliss,—
  Hundreds of years you Stella's feet may kiss.

No more, my Dear, no more these counsels try;
O give my passions leave to run their race!
Let Fortune lay on me her worst disgrace;
Let folk o'ercharg'd with brain against me cry;
Let clouds bedim my face, break in mine eye;
Let me no steps but of lost labour trace;
Let all the earth with scorn account my case,—
But do not will me from my Love to fly.
I do not envy Aristotle's wit,
Nor do aspire to Cæsar's bleeding fame;

[1] press.

Nor aught do care though some above me sit;
Nor hope nor wish another course to fame,
    But that which once may win thy cruel heart:
    Thou art my wit, and thou my virtue art.

[From ASTROPHEL AND STELLA.]

PHILOMELA

THE nightingale, as soon as April bringeth
    Unto her rested sense a perfect waking,
(While late-bare earth, proud of new clothing, springeth)
    Sings out her woes, a thorn her song-book making;
        And mournfully bewailing,
        Her throat in tunes expresseth
        What grief her breast oppresseth
For Tereus' force on her chaste will prevailing.

O Philomela fair, O take some gladness,
That here is juster cause of plaintful sadness:
        Thine earth now springs, mine fadeth;
Thy thorn without, my thorn my heart invadeth.

Alas, she hath no other cause of anguish
    But Tereus' love, on her by strong hand wroken,
Wherein she suffering, all her spirits languish,
    Full womanlike complains her will was broken.
        But I, who, daily craving,
        Cannot have to content me,
        Have more cause to lament me,
Since wanting is more woe than too much having.

O Philomela fair, etc.

DORUS TO PAMELA

My sheep are thoughts, which I both guide and serve;
Their pasture is fair hills of fruitless love;
On barren sweets they feed, and feeding starve.
I wail their lot, but will not other prove.
My sheephook is wan Hope, which all upholds;
My weeds Desire, cut out in endless folds;
　　What wool my sheep shall bear, whilst thus they live,
　　In you it is, you must the judgment give.

　　　　　　　　　　　　　　　　　　[From ARCADIA]

SONNET

Leave me, O Love, which reachest but to dust;
And thou, my mind, aspire to higher things;
Grow rich in that which never taketh rust;
Whatever fades, but fading pleasure brings.
Draw in thy beams, and humble all thy might
To that sweet yoke where lasting freedoms be;
Which breaks the clouds, and opens forth the light,
That doth both shine, and give us sight to see.
O take fast hold; let that light be thy guide
In this small course which birth draws out to death,
And think how ill becometh him to slide,
Who seeketh heaven, and comes of heavenly breath.
　　Then farewell, world; thy uttermost I see:
　　Eternal Love, maintain thy life in me!

EDMUND SPENSER [1552-1599]

PROTHALAMION

CALME was the day, and through the trembling ayre
Sweete breathing Zephyrus did softly play,
A gentle spirit, that lightly did delay
Hot Titans beames, which then did glyster fayre:
When I, whom sullein care,
Through discontent of my long fruitlesse stay
In princes court, and expectation vayne
Of idle hopes, which still doe fly away,
Like empty shaddowes, did aflict my brayne,
Walkt forth to ease my payne
Along the shoare of silver streaming Themmes;
Whose rutty bancke, the which his river hemmes,
Was paynted all with variable flowers,
And all the meades adornd with daintie gemmes,
Fit to decke maydens bowres,
And crowne their paramours,
Against the brydale day, which is not long:
  Sweete Themmes, runne softly, till I end my song.

There, in a meadow, by the rivers side,
A flocke of nymphes I chauncèd to espy,
All lovely daughters of the flood thereby,
With goodly greenish locks all loose untyde,
As each had bene a bryde:
And each one had a little wicker basket,
Made of fine twigs entraylèd curiously,
In which they gathered flowers to fill their flasket;
And with fine fingers cropt full feateously
The tender stalkes on hye.
Of every sort, which in that meadow grew,
They gathered some; the violet pallid blew,
The little dazie, that at evening closes,
The virgin lillie, and the primrose trew,

With store of vermeil roses,
To decke their bridegromes posies
Against the brydale day, which was not long:
   Sweete Themmes, runne softly, till I end my song.

With that I saw two swannes of goodly hewe
Come softly swimming downe along the lee;
Two fairer birds I yet did never see:
The snow which doth the top of Pindus strew
Did never whiter shew,
Nor Jove himselfe, when he a swan would be
For love of Leda, whiter did appear:
Yet Leda was, they say, as white as he,
Yet not so white as these, nor nothing neare:
So purely white they were,
That even the gentle streame, the which them bare,
Seemd foule to them, and bad his billowes spare
To wet their silken feathers, least they might
Soyle their fayre plumes with water not so fayre,
And marre their beauties bright,
That shone as heavens light,
Against their brydale day, which was not long:
   Sweete Themmes, runne softly, till I end my song.

Eftsoones the nymphes, which now had flowers their fill,
Ran all in haste to see that silver brood,
As they came floating on the christal flood;
Whom when they sawe, they stood amazèd still,
Their wondring eyes to fill.
Them seemd they never saw a sight so fayre,
Of fowles so lovely, that they sure did deeme
Them heavenly borne, or to be that same payre
Which through the skie draw Venus silver teeme;
For sure they did not seeme
To be begot of any earthly seede,
But rather angels or of angels breede:
Yet were they bred of Somers-heat, they say,
In sweetest season, when each flower and weede

The earth did fresh aray;
So fresh they seemd as day,
Even as their brydale day, which was not long:
  Sweete Themmes, runne softly, till I end my song.

Then forth they all out of their baskets drew
Great store of flowers, the honour of the field,
That to the sense did fragrant odours yield,
All which upon those goodly birds they threw,
And all the waves did strew,
That like old Peneus waters they did seeme,
When downe along by pleasant Tempes shore,
Scattred with flowres, through Thessaly they streeme,
That they appeare, through lillies plenteous store,
Like a brydes chamber flore.
Two of those nymphes, meane while, two garlands bound
Of freshest flowres which in that mead they found,
The which presenting all in trim array,
Their snowie foreheads therewithall they crownd,
Whil'st one did sing this lay,
Prepar'd against that day,
Against their brydale day, which was not long:
  Sweete Themmes, runne softly, till I end my song.

"Ye gentle birdes, the worlds faire ornament,
And heavens glorie, whom this happie hower
Doth leade unto your lovers blissfull bower,
Joy may you have and gentle hearts content
Of your loves couplement:
And let faire Venus, that is Queene of Love,
With her heart-quelling sonne upon you smile,
Whose smile, they say, hath vertue to remove
All loves dislike, and friendships faultie guile
For ever to assoile.
Let endlesse peace your steadfast hearts accord,
And blessèd plentie wait upon your bord;
And let your bed with pleasures chast abound,
That fruitfull issue may to you afford,
Which may your foes confound,
And make your joyes redound,

Upon your brydale day, which is not long;
  Sweete Themmes, runne softlie, till I end my song."

So ended she; and all the rest around
To her redoubled that, her undersong,
Which said, their bridale daye should not be long.
And gentle Eccho from the neighbour ground
Their accents did resound.
So forth those joyous birdes did passe along,
Adowne the lee, that to them murmurde low,
As he would speake, but that he lackt a tong,
Yeat did by signes his glad affection show,
Making his streame run slow.
And all the foule which in his flood did dwell
Gan flock about these twaine, that did excell
The rest so far as Cynthia doth shend
The lesser starres.   So they, enrangèd well,
Did on those two attend,
And their best service lend,
Against their wedding day, which was not long:
  Sweete Themmes, runne softly, till I end my song.

At length they all to mery London came,
To mery London, my most kyndly nurse,
That to me gave this lifes first native sourse:
Though from another place I take my name,
An house of auncient fame.
There when they came whereas those bricky towers
The which on Themmes brode agèd backe doe ryde,
Where now the studious lawyers have their bowers,
There whylome wont the Templar Knights to byde,
Till they decayd through pride:
Next whereunto there standes a stately place,
Where oft I gainèd giftes and goodly grace
Of that great lord, which therein wont to dwell,
Whose want too well now feeles my freendles case:
But ah! here fits now well
Olde woes, but joyes to tell,
Against the brydale daye, which is not long:
  Sweete Themmes, runne softly, till I end my song.

Yet therein, now doth lodge a noble peer,
Great Englands glory and the worlds wide wonder,
Whose dreadful name late through all Spaine did thunder,
And Hercules two pillars standing neere
Did make to quake and feare.
Faire branch of honour, flower of chevalrie,
That fillest England with thy triumphs fame,
Joy have thou of thy noble victorie,
And endlesse happinesse of thine owne name
That promiseth the same:
That through thy prowesse and victorious arms
Thy country may be freed from forraigne harms;
And great Elisaes glorious name may ring
Through al the world, filled with thy wide alarmes,
Which some brave Muse may sing
To ages following:
Upon the brydale daye, which is not long:
   Sweete Themmes, runne softly, till I end my song.

From those high towers this noble lord issuing,
Like radiant Hesper when his golden hayre
In th' ocean billows he hath bathèd fayre,
Descended to the rivers open viewing,
With a great traine ensuing.
Above the rest were goodly to bee seene
Two gentle knights of lovely face and feature,
Beseeming well the bower of anie queene,
With gifts of wit and ornaments of nature,
Fit for so goodly stature:
That like the twins of Jove they seem'd in sight,
Which decke the bauldricke of the heavens bright.
They two, forth pacing to the rivers side,
Received those two fair brydes, their loves delight.
Which, at th' appointed tyde,
Each one did make his bryde,
Against their brydale day, which is not long:
   Sweete Themmes, runne softly, till I end my song.

SONNETS

MORE then most faire, full of the living fire
Kindled above unto the Maker neere:
No eies, but joyes, in which al powers conspire,
That to the world naught else be counted deare:
Thrugh your bright beams doth not the blinded guest
Shoot out his darts to base affections wound;
But angels come, to lead fraile mindes to rest
In chast desires, on heavenly beauty bound.
You frame my thoughts, and fashion me within,
You stop my toung, and teach my hart to speake,
You calme the storme that passion did begin,
Strong thrugh your cause, but by your vertue weak.
    Dark is the world where your light shinèd never;
    Well is he borne that may behold you ever.

LYKE as a ship, that through the ocean wyde,
By conduct of some star, doth make her way;
Whenas a storme hath dimd her trusty guyde,
Out of her course doth wander far astray;
So I, whose star, that wont with her bright ray
Me to direct, with cloudes is overcast,
Doe wander now, in darknesse and dismay,
Through hidden perils round about me plast.
Yet hope I well, that when this storme is past,
My Helice, the lodestar of my lyfe,
Will shine again, and looke on me at last,
With lovely light to cleare my cloudy grief,
    Till then I wander carefull, comfortlesse,
    In secret sorow, and sad pensivenesse.

MEN call you fayre, and you doe credit it,
For that your selfe ye dayly such doe see:
But the trew fayre, that is the gentle wit
And vertuous Mind, is much more praysd of me.
For all the rest, how ever fayre it be,
Shall turne to nought and loose that glorious hew:

But onely that is permanent, and free
From frayle corruption, that doth flesh ensew.
That is true Beautie: that doth argue you
To be divine, and borne of heavenly seed,
Derived from that fayre spirit from whom al true
And perfect beauty did at first proceed.
    He onely fayre, and what he fayre hath made;
    All other fayre, lyke flowers, untymely fade.

[From AMORETTI.]

LUCIFERA RIDETH FORTH FROM THE HOUSE OF PRIDE

A STATELY pallace built of squarèd bricke,
    Which cunningly was without morter laid,
    Whose wals were high, but nothing strong, nor thick,
    And golden foile all over them displaid,
    That purest skye with brightnesse they dismaid:
    High lifted up were many loftie towres,
    And goodly galleries farre over laid,
    Full of faire windowes and delightful bowres;
And on the top a diall told the timely howres.

It was a goodly heape for to behould,
    And spake the praises of the workmans witt;
    But full great pittie, that so faire a mould
    Did on so weake foundation ever sitt:
    For on a sandie hill, that still did flitt
    And fall away, it mounted was full hie,
    That every breath of heaven shakèd itt:
    And all the hinder parts, that few could spie,
Were ruinous and old, but painted cunningly.

Arrivèd there, they passèd in forth right;
    For still to all the gates stood open wide:
    Yet charge of them was to a porter hight
    Cald Malvenù; who entrance none denide:
    Thence to the hall, which was on every side

With rich array and costly arras dight:
Infinite sorts of people did abide,
There waiting long to win the wishèd sight
Of her that was the Lady of that pallace bright.

By them they passe, all gazing on them round,
And to the Presence mount; whose glorious vew
Their frayle amazèd senses did confound:
In living princes court none ever knew
Such endlesse richesse, and so sumptuous shew;
Ne Persia selfe, the nourse of pompous pride,
Like ever saw.   And there a noble crew
Of lordes and ladies stood on every side,
Which with their presence faire the place much beautifide.

High above all a cloth of state was spred,
And a rich throne, as bright as sunny day,
On which there sate most brave embellished
With royall robes and gorgeous array,
A mayden Queene, that shone as Titans ray,
In glistring gold, and peerelesse pretious stone;
Yet her bright blazing beautie did assay
To dim the brightnesse of her glorious throne,
As envying her selfe, that too exceeding shone:

Exceeding shone, like Phœbus fayrest childe,
That did presume his fathers firie wayne,
And flaming mouthes of steedes unwonted wilde
Through highest heaven with weaker hand to rayne;
Proud of such glory and advancement vayne,
While flashing beames do daze his feeble eyen,
He leaves the welkin way most beaten playne,
And, rapt with whirling wheeles, inflames the skyen,
With fire not made to burne, but fayrely for to shyne.

So proud she shyned in her princely state,
Looking to heaven; (for earth she did disdayne)
And sitting high; (for lowly she did hate)
Lo, underneath her scornefull feete was layne

A dreadfull Dragon with an hideous trayne,
And in her hand she held a mirrhour bright,
Wherein her face she often vewed fayne,
And in her selfe-lov'd semblance tooke delight;
For she was wondrous faire, as any living wight.

Of griesly Pluto she the daughter was,
And sad Proserpina, the queene of hell;
Yet did she thinke her pearelesse worth to pas
That parentage, with pride so did she swell;
And thundring Jove, that high in heaven doth dwell,
And wield the world, she claymed for her syre,
Or if that any else did Jove excell:
For to the highest she did still aspyre,
Or if ought higher were than that, did it desyre.

And proud Lucifera men did her call,
That made her selfe a queene, and crownd to be;
Yet rightfull kingdome she had none at all,
Ne heritage of native soveraintie,
But did usurpe with wrong and tyrannie
Upon the sceptre, which she now did hold:
Ne ruld her realmes with lawes, but pollicie,
And strong advizement of six wisards old,
That with their counsels bad her kingdome did uphold.

Soone as the Elfin Knight in presence came,
And false Duessa, seeming lady fayre,
A gentle husher, Vanitie by name,
Made rowme, and passage for them did prepaire:
So goodly brought them to the lowest stayre
Of her high throne, where they on humble knee
Making obeyssaunce, did the cause declare,
Why they were come, her royall state to see,
To prove the wide report of her great majestee.

With loftie eyes, halfe loth to looke so lowe,
She thankèd them in her disdainefull wise;
Ne other grace vouchsafèd them to showe

Of princesse worthy, scarse them bad arise.
Her lordes and ladies all this while devise
Themselves to setten forth to straungers sight:
Some frounce their curled haire in courtly guise,
Some prancke their ruffes, and others trimly dight
Their gay attire: each others greater pride does spight.

Goodly they all that knight do entertayne,
  Right glad with him to have increast their crew:
  But to Duess each one himselfe did payne
  All kindnesse and faire courtesie to shew;
  For in that court whylome her well they knew:
  Yet the stout Faerie mongst the middest crowd
  Thought all their glorie vayne in knightly vew,
  And that great Princesse too exceeding prowd,
That to strange knight no better countenance allowd.

Suddein upriseth from her stately place
  The royall Dame, and for her coche doth call:
  All hurtlen forth, and she with princely pace,
  As faire Aurora in her purple pall
  Out of the east the dawning day doth call:
  So forth she comes: her brightnesse brode doth blaze;
  The heapes of people thronging in the hall
  Do ride each other, upon her to gaze:
Her glorious glitter and light doth all mens eyes amaze.

So forth she comes, and to her coche does clyme,
  Adornèd all with gold, and girlonds gay,
  That seemed as fresh as Flora in her prime,
  And strove to match, in royall rich array,
  Great Junoes golden chaire, the which they say
  The gods stand gazing on, when she does ride
  To Joves high house through heavens bras-pavèd way
  Drawne of faire pecocks, that excell in pride,
And full of Argus eyes their tayles dispredden wide.

But this was drawne of six unequall beasts,
  On which her six sage Counsellours did ryde,

Taught to obay their bestiall beheasts,
With like conditions to their kinds applyde:
Of which the first, that all the rest did guyde,
Was sluggish Idlenesse, the nourse of sin;
Upon a slouthfull asse he chose to ryde,
Arayd in habit blacke, and amis thin,[1]
Like to an holy monck, the service to begin.

And in his hand his portesse[2] still he bare,
That much was worne, but therein little redd,
For of devotion he had little care,
Still drownd in sleepe, and most of his dayes dedd;
Scarse could he once uphold his heavie hed,
To looken whether it were night or day:
May seeme the wayne was very evill led,
When such an one had guiding of the way,
That knew not whether right he went, or else astray.

From worldly cares himselfe he did esloyne,[3]
And greatly shunned manly exercise;
From every worke he chalenged essoyne,[4]
For contemplation sake: yet otherwise,
His life he led in lawlesse riotise;
By which he grew to grievous malady;
For in his lustlesse limbs, through evill guise,
A shaking fever raignd continually:
Such one was Idlenesse, first of this company.

And by his side rode loathsome Gluttony,
Deformèd creature, on a filthie swyne;
His belly was up-blowne with luxury,
And eke with fatnesse swollen were his eyne;
And like a crane his necke was long and fyne,
With which he swallowed up excessive feast,
For want whereof poore people oft did pyne;
And all the way, most like a brutish beast,
He spuèd up his gorge, that all did him deteast.

---

[1] very thin.   [2] breviary.   [3] keep aloof.   [4] excuse.

In greene vine leaves he was right fitly clad;
　　For other clothes he could not weare for heat;
　　And on his head an yvie girland had,
　　From under which fast trickled downe the sweat:
　　Still as he rode, he somewhat still did eat,
　　And in his hand did beare a bouzing can,
　　Of which he supt so oft, that on his seat
　　His dronken corse he scarse upholden can:
In shape and life more like a monster, than a man.

Unfit he was for any worldly thing,
　　And eke unhable once to stirre or go,
　　Not meet to be of counsell to a king,
　　Whose mind in meat and drinke was drowned so,
　　That from his frend he seldome knew his fo:
　　Full of diseases was his carcas blew,
　　And a dry dropsie through his flesh did flow
　　Which by misdiet daily greater grew:
Such one was Gluttony, the second of that crew.

And next to him rode lustfull Lechery,
　　Upon a bearded goat, whose rugged haire,
　　And whally eyes (the signe of gelosy)
　　Was like the person selfe whom he did beare,
　　Who rough, and blacke, and filthy did appeare:
　　Unseemely man to please faire ladies eye;
　　Yet he of ladies oft was loved deare,
　　When fairer faces were bid standen by:
O who does know the bent of womens fantasy?

In a greene gowne he clothèd was full faire,
　　Which underneath did hide his filthinesse,
　　And in his hand a burning hart he bare,
　　Full of vaine follies, and new fanglenesse,
　　For he was false, and fraught with ficklenesse;
　　And learned had to love with secret lookes;
　　And well could daunce, and sing with ruefulnesse,
　　And fortunes tell, and read in loving bookes,
And thousand other wayes, to bait his fleshly hookes.

Inconstant man, that loved all he saw,
  And lustèd after all that he did love;
  Ne would his looser life be tide to law,
  But joyd weak wemens hearts to tempt, and prove,
  If from their loyall loves he might them move;
  Which lewdnesse fild him with reprochfull paine
  Of that foule evill, which all men reprove,
  That rotts the marrow and consumes the braine:
Such one was Lechery, the third of all this traine.

And greedy Avarice by him did ride,
  Uppon a camell loaden all with gold;
  Two iron coffers hong on either side,
  With precious metall full as they might hold;
  And in his lap an heape of coine he told;
  For of his wicked pelfe his God he made,
  And unto hell him selfe for money sold;
  Accursèd usurie was all his trade,
And right and wrong ylike in equall ballaunce waide.

His life was nigh unto deaths doore yplaste,
  And thred-bare cote, and cobled shoes, he ware,
  Ne scarse good morsell all his life did taste,
  But both from backe and belly still did spare,
  To fill his bags, and richesse to compare;
  Yet chylde ne kinsman living had he none
  To leave them to; but thorough daily care
  To get, and nightly feare to lose his owne,
He led a wretched life, unto him selfe unknowne.

Most wretched wight, whom nothing might suffise,
  Whose greedy lust did lacke in greatest store,
  Whose need had end, but no end covetise,
  Whose wealth was want, whose plenty made him pore,
  Who had enough, yett wishèd ever more;
  A vile disease, and eke in foote and hand
  A grievous gout tormented him full sore,
  That well he could not touch, nor go, nor stand:
Such one was Avarice, the fourth of this faire band.

And next to him malicious Envie rode,
　　Upon a ravenous wolfe, and still did chaw
　　Betweene his cankred teeth a venemous tode,
　　That all the poison ran about his chaw;
　　But inwardly he chawed his owne maw
　　At neighbours wealth, that made him ever sad;
　　(For death it was when any good he saw,
　　And wept, that cause of weeping none he had);
But when he heard of harme, he wexèd wondrous **glad.**

All in a kirtle of discolourd say[5]
　　He clothèd was, ypainted full of eyes;
　　And in his bosome secretly there lay
　　An hatefull snake, the which he taile uptyes
　　In many folds, and mortall sting implyes.
　　Still as he rode, he gnasht his teeth, to see
　　Those heapes of gold with griple[6] Covetyse;
　　And grudged at the great felicitie
Of proud Lucifera, and his owne companie.

He hated all good workes and vertuous deeds,
　　And him no lesse that any like did use,
　　And who with gracious bread the hungry feeds
　　His almes for want of faith he doth accuse;
　　So every good to bad he doth abuse:
　　And eke the verse of famous poets witt.
　　He does backebite, and spightfull poison spues
　　From leprous mouth on all that ever writt:
Such one vile Envie was, that fifte in row did sitt.

And him beside rides fierce revenging Wrath,
　　Upon a lion, loth for to be led;
　　And in his hand a burning brond he hath,
　　The which he brandisheth about his hed;
　　His eyes did hurle forth sparkles fiery red,
　　And stared sterne on all that him beheld;
　　As ashes, pale of hew and seeming ded;

---

[5] quality.　　　　　　　　　　　　　[6] grasping.

And on his dagger still his hand he held,
Trembling through hasty rage, when choler in him sweld.

His ruffin raiment all was staind with blood,
  Which he had spilt, and all to rags yrent,
  Through unadvizèd rashnesse woxen wood;[7]
  For of his hands he had no governement,
  Ne cared for bloud in his avengement:
  But when the furious fitt was overpast,
  His cruell facts he often would repent;
  Yet, wilfull man, he never would forecast
How many mischieves should ensue his heedlesse hast.

Full many mischiefes follow cruell Wrath;
  Abhorrèd bloodshed and tumultuous strife,
  Unmanly murder, and unthrifty scath,
  Bitter despight, with rancours rusty knife,
  And fretting griefe the enemy of life;
  All these, and many evils moe haunt ire,
  The swelling splene, and frenzy raging rife,
  The shaking palsey, and Saint Fraunces fire:
Such one was Wrath, the last of this ungodly tire.

And, after all, upon the wagon beame
  Rode Sathan, with a smarting whip in hand,
  With which he forward lasht the laesie teme,
  So oft as Slowth still in the mire did stand.
  Huge routs of people did about them band,
  Showting for joy; and still before their way
  A foggy mist had covered all the land;
  And underneath their feet, all scattered lay
Dead sculs and bones of men, whose life had gone astray.

[From Book I, Canto IV, THE FAERIE QUEENE.]

[7] mad.

THE PAGEANT OF MUTABILITIE WHO MAIN-
TAINETH SHE RULETH ALL THINGS

So forth issew'd the seasons of the yeare:
    First, lusty Spring, all dight in leaves of flowres
    That freshly budded and new bloomes did beare
    (In which a thousand birds had built their bowres,
    That sweetly sung, to call forth paramours):
    And in his hand a javelin he did beare,
    And on his head (as fit for warlike stoures)
    A gilt engraven morion he did weare;
That, as some did him love, so others did him feare.

Then came the jolly Sommer, being dight
    In a thin silken cassock coloured greene,
    That was unlynèd all, to be more light:
    And on his head a girlond well beseene
    He wore, from which, as he had chauffed been,
    The sweat did drop; and in his hand he bore
    A bowe and shaftes, as he in forrest greene
    Had hunted late the libbard or the bore,
And now would bathe his limbes, with labor heated sore.

Then came Autumne, all in yellow clad,
    As though he joyèd in his plentious store,
    Laden with fruits that made him laugh, full glad
    That he had banisht hunger, which to-fore
    Had by the belly oft him pinchèd sore.
    Upon his head a wreath, that was enrold
    With eares of corne of every sort, he bore:
    And in his hand a sickle he did holde,
To reape the ripened fruits the which the earth had yold.

Lastly came Winter, clothèd all in frize,
    Chattering his teeth for cold that did him chill,
    Whil'st on his hoary beard his breath did freese,
    And the dull drops, that from his purpled bill,
    As from a limbeck, did adown distill.

In his right hand a tippèd staffe he held,
With which his feeble steps he stayèd still:
For he was faint with cold, and weak with eld;
That scarse his loosed limbes he hable was to weld.

These, marching softly, thus in order went,
    And after them the monthes all riding came:
First, sturdy March, with brows full sternly bent,
    And armed strongly, rode upon a ram,
    The same which over Hellespontus swam:
Yet in his hand a spade he also hent,
    And in a bag all sorts of seeds ysame,
    Which on the earth he strowèd as he went,
And fild her womb with fruitfull hope of nourishment.

Next came fresh Aprill, full of lustyhed,
    And wanton as a kid whose horne new buds:
Upon a bull he rode, the same which led
    Europa floting through th' Argolick fluds:
    His hornes were gilden all with golden studs,
And garnishèd with garlonds goodly dight
    Of all the fairest flowres and freshest buds
    Which th' earth brings forth, and wet he seem'd in sight
With waves, through which he waded for his loves delight.

Then came faire May, the fayrest mayd on ground,
    Deckt all with dainties of her seasons pryde,
    And throwing flowres out of her lap around:
Upon two brethrens shoulders she did ride,
    The twinnes of Leda; which on eyther side
Supported her like to their soveraine queene.
    Lord! how all creatures laught, when her they spide,
    And leapt and daunc't as they had ravisht beene!
And Cupid selfe about her fluttred all in greene.

And after her came jolly June, arrayd
    All in greene leaves, as he a player were;
    Yet in his time he wrought as well as playd,
    That by his plough-yrons mote right well appeare:

Upon a crab he rode, that him did beare
With crooked, crawling steps an uncouth pase,
And backward yode, as bargemen wont to fare
Bending their force contrary to their face,
Like that ungracious crew which faines demurest grace.

Then came hot July boyling like to fire,
  That all his garments he had cast away:
  Upon a lyon raging yet with ire
  He boldly rode, and made him to obay:
  It was the beast that whylome did forray
  The Nemæan forrest, till th' Amphytrionide
  Him slew, and with his hide did him array:
  Behinde his back a sithe, and by his side
Under his belt he bore a sickle circling wide.

The sixt was August, being rich arrayd
  In garment all of gold downe to the ground:
  Yet rode he not, but led a lovely mayd
  Forth by the lilly hand, the which was cround
  With eares of corne, and full her hand was found:
  That was the righteous virgin[1] which of old
  Lived here on earth, and plenty made abound;
  But, after wrong was loved and justice solde,
She left th' unrighteous world and was to heaven extold.

Next him September marchèd eeke on foote;
  Yet was he heavy laden with the spoyle
  Of harvests riches, which he made his boot,
  And him enricht with bounty of the soyle:
  In his one hand, as fit for harvests toyle,
  He held a knife-hook; and in th' other hand
  A paire of waights, with which he did assoyle
  Both more and lesse, where it in doubt did stand,
And equall gave to each as justice duly scannd.

Then came October full of merry glee;
  For yet his noule[2] was totty[3] of the must,

---

[1] Astræa   [2] noddle, head, brain.   [3] tottering, unsteady.

Which he was treading in the wine-fats see,
And of the joyous oyle, whose gently gust
Made him so frollick and so full of lust;
Upon a dreadfull scorpion he did ride,
The same which by Dianæs doom unjust
Slew great Orion: and eeke by his side
He had his ploughing-share and coulter ready tyde.

Next was November; he full grosse and fat,
As fed with lard, and that right well might seeme;
For he had been a fatting hogs of late,
That yet his browes with sweat did reek and steem,
And yet the season was full sharp and breem;[4]
In planting eeke he took no small delight.
Whereon he rode, not easie was to deeme;
For it a dreadfull centaure was in sight,
The seed of Saturne and faire Nais, Chiron hight.

And after him came next the chill December:
Yet he through merry feasting which he made,
And great bonfires, did not the cold remember;
His Saviours birth his mind so much did glad:
Upon a shaggy-bearded goat he rade,
The same wherewith Dan Jove in tender yeares,
They say, was nourisht by th' Idæan mayd;
And in his hand a broad deepe boawle he beares,
Of which he freely drinks an health to all his peeres.

Then came old January, wrappèd well
In many weeds to keep the cold away;
Yet did he quake and quiver like to quell,
And blowe his nayles to warme them if he may:
For they were numbd with holding all the day
An hatchet keene, with which he fellèd wood,
And from the trees did lop the needlesse spray:
Upon an huge great earth-pot steane[5] he stood,
From whose wide mouth there flowed forth the Romane floud.

4 fierce, bitter.   5 large jar.

And lastly came cold February, sitting
 In an old wagon, for he could not ride;
 Drawne of two fishes for the season fitting,
 Which through the flood before did softly slyde
 And swim away: yet had he by his side
 His plough and harnesse fit to till the ground,
 And tooles to prune the trees, before the pride
 Of hasting Prime did make them burgein round.
So past the twelve months forth, and their dew places found.

And after these there came the Day and Night,
 Riding together both with equall pase,
 Th' one on a palfrey blacke, the other white:
 But Night had cover'd her uncomely face
 With a blacke veile, and held in hand a mace,
 On top whereof the moon and stars were pight,
 And Sleep and Darknesse round about did trace:
 But Day did beare, upon his scepters hight,
The goodly sun, encompast all with beamës bright.

Then came the Howres, faire daughters of high Jove
 ⸓ And timely Night, the which were all endewd
 With wondrous beauty fit to kindly love;
 But they were virgins all, and love eschewd,
 That might forslack the charge to them fore-shewd
 By mighty Jove, who did them porters make
 Of heaven's gate (whence all the gods issued)
 Which they did dayly watch, and nightly wake
By even turnes, ne ever did their charge forsake.

And after all came Life, and lastly Death:
 Death with most grim and griesly visage seene,
 Yet is he nought but parting of the breath;
 Ne ought to see, but like a shade to weene,
 Unbodièd, unsoul'd, unheard, unseene:
 But Life was like a faire young lusty boy,
 Such as they faine Dan Cupid to have beene,
 Full of delightfull health and lively joy,
Deckt all with flowres, and wings of gold fit to employ.

When these were past, thus gan the Titanesse:
　"Lo! mighty mother, now be judge, and say
　Whether in all thy creatures more or lesse
　Change doth not raign and beare the greatest sway:
　For who sees not that Time on all doth pray?
　But times do change and move continually:
　So nothing here long standeth in one stay:
　Wherefore, this lowere world who can deny
But to be subject still to Mutabilitie?"

[From Book VII, Canto VII, THE FAERIE QUEENE.]

MUTABILITY SUBJECT TO ETERNITY

WHEN I bethinke me on that speech whyl-eare
　Of Mutability, and well it way,
　Me seemes, that though she all unworthy were
　Of the heav'ns rule, yet, very sooth to say,
　In all things else she beares the greatest sway;
　Which makes me loath this state of life so tickle,
　And love of things so vaine, to cast away,
　Whose flowring pride, so fading and so fickle,
Short Time shall soon cut down with his consuming sickle.

Then gin I thinke on that which Nature sayd,
　Of that same time when no more change shall be,
　But stedfast rest of all things, firmely stayd
　Upon the pillours of Eternity,
　That is contrayr to Mutabilitie:
　For all that moveth doth in change delight:
　But thence-forth all shall rest eternally
　With him that is the God of Sabbaoth hight:
O that great Sabbaoth-God graunt me that Sabaoths
　　sight! [1]

[Book VIII, THE FAERIE QUEENE.]

[1] Either the death of Spenser halted THE FAERIE QUEENE at this point, or the poet relinquished his design. But as Book VIII—of which these two stanzas alone seem to be all that was written—is called "Unperfite," the first is the more probable.

JOHN LYLY [1554?–1606]

APELLES' SONG

Cupid and my Campaspe play'd
At cards for kisses; Cupid paid.
He stakes his quiver, bows and arrows,
His mother's doves and team of sparrows;
Loses them too; then down he throws
The coral of his lip, the rose
Growing on's cheek (but none knows how);
With these, the crystal of his brow,
And then the dimple of his chin;
All these did my Campaspe win.
At last he set her both his eyes;
She won, and Cupid blind did rise.
O Love, has she done this to thee?
What shall, alas! become of me?

[From Alexander and Campaspe.]

THOMAS LODGE [1558?–1625]

ROSALYND'S MADRIGAL

Love in my bosom, like a bee,
    Doth suck his sweet;
Now with his wings he plays with me,
    Now with his feet.
    Within mine eyes he makes his nest,
    His bed amidst my tender breast;
    My kisses are his daily feast,
    And yet he robs me of my rest:
        Ah! wanton, will ye?

And if I sleep, then percheth he
    With pretty flight,

And makes his pillow of my knee
    The livelong night.
   Strike I my lute, he tunes the string;
   He music plays if so I sing;
   He lends me every lovely thing,
   Yet cruel he my heart doth sting:
    Whist, wanton, will ye?

Else I with roses every day
    Will whip you hence,
And bind you, when you long to play,
    For your offence;
   I'll shut my eyes to keep you in;
   I'll make you fast it, for your sin;
   I'll count your power not worth a pin:
   Alas! what hereby shall I win,
    If he gainsay me?

What if I beat the wanton boy
    With many a rod?
He will repay me with annoy,
    Because a god.
   Then sit thou safely on my knee,
   And let thy bower my bosom be;
   Lurk in mine eyes; I like of thee.
   O Cupid! so thou pity me,
    Spare not, but play thee.

GEORGE PEELE [1558?–1597?]

DUET

ŒNONE. Fair and fair, and twice so fair,
    As fair as any may be;
   The fairest shepherd on our green,
    A love for any lady.

PARIS.   Fair and fair, and twice so fair,
              As fair as any may be;
          Thy love is fair for thee alone,
              And for no other lady.

ŒN.   My love is fair, my love is gay,
              As fresh as bin the flowers in May:
          And of my love my roundelay,
              My merry, merry roundelay,
          Concludes with Cupid's curse—
              "They that do change old love for new,
          Pray gods they change for worse!"

AMBO.   Fair and fair, etc.

[From THE ARRAIGNMENT OF PARIS.]

GEORGE CHAPMAN [1559?–1634]

OF MAN

MAN is so sovereign and divine a state,
That not, contracted and elaborate,
The world he bears about with him alone;
But even the Maker makes his breast His throne.

ROBERT GREENE [1560?–1592]

SEPHESTIA'S SONG

WEEP not, my wanton, smile upon my knee,
When thou art old there's grief enough for thee.
          Mother's wag, pretty boy,
          Father's sorrow, father's joy;
          When thy father first did see
          Such a boy by him and me,
          He was glad, I was woe,
          Fortune changèd made him so

When he left his pretty boy,
Last his sorrow, first his joy.

Weep not, my wanton, smile upon my knee,
When thou art old there's grief enough for thee.
    Streaming tears that never stint,
    Like pearl drops from a flint,
    Fell by course from his eyes,
    That one another's place supplies;
    Thus he grieved in every part,
    Tears of blood fell from his heart,
    When he left his pretty boy,
    Father's sorrow, father's joy.

Weep not, my wanton, smile upon my knee,
When thou art old there's grief enough for thee.
    The wanton smiled, father wept,
    Mother cried, baby leapt;
    More he crow'd, more we cried,
    Nature could not sorrow hide:
    He must go, he must kiss
    Child and mother, baby bless,
    For he left his pretty boy,
    Father's sorrow, father's joy.
Weep not, my wanton, smile upon my knee,
When thou art old there's grief enough for thee.

ROBERT SOUTHWELL [1561?–1595]

THE BURNING BABE

As I in hoary winter's night stood shivering in the snow,
Surprised I was with sudden heat which made my heart to glow;
And lifting up a fearful eye to view what fire was near,
A pretty babe all burning bright did in the air appear,
Who, scorchèd with exceeding heat, such floods of tears did shed
As though His floods should quench His flames with what His
    tears were fed;

"Alas!" quoth He, "but newly born, in fiery heats of fry,
Yet none approach to warm their hearts or feel my fire but I!
My faultless breast the furnace is, the fuel wounding thorns;
Love is the fire and sighs the smoke, the ashes shame and scorns;
The fuel Justice layeth on, and Mercy blows the coals;
The metal in this furnace wrought are men's defilèd souls;
For which, as now on fire I am, to work them to the good,
So will I melt into a bath, to wash them in my blood."
With this He vanish'd out of sight, and swiftly shrunk away,
And straight I called unto mind that it was Christmas-day.

SAMUEL DANIEL [1562–1619]

SLEEP

CARE-CHARMER Sleep, son of the sable Night,
Brother to Death, in silent darkness born:
Relieve my anguish, and restore the light;
With dark-forgetting of my care, return!
And let the day be time enough to mourn
The shipwreck of my ill-adventured youth:
Let waking eyes suffice to wail their scorn,
Without the torment of the night's untruth.
Cease, dreams, the images of day-desires,
To model forth the passions of the morrow;
Never let rising sun approve you liars,
To add more grief to aggravate my sorrow.
    Still let me sleep, embracing clouds in vain;
    And never wake to feel the day's disdain.

[FROM SONNETS TO DELIA.]

MICHAEL DRAYTON [1563–1631]

LOVE'S FAREWELL

SINCE there's no help, come let us kiss and part.
Nay, I have done, you get no more of me!
And I am glad, yea, glad with all my heart,
That thus so cleanly I myself can free.
Shake hands for ever! Cancel all our vows!
And when we meet at any time again,
Be it not seen in either of our brows
That we one jot of former love retain.
Now at the last gasp of Love's latest breath,
When, his pulse failing, Passion speechless lies,
When Faith is kneeling by his bed of death,
And Innocence is closing up his eyes—
　　Now, if thou would'st, when all have given him over,
　　From death to life thou might'st him yet recover!

[From the sonnet-sequence IDEA.]

BALLAD OF AGINCOURT

FAIR stood the wind for France,
When we our sails advance,
Nor now to prove our chance,
　　Longer will tarry;
But putting to the main,
At Caux, the mouth of Seine,
With all his martial train,
　　Landed King Harry.

And taking many a fort,
Furnished in warlike sort,
Marcheth tow'rds Agincourt
　　In happy hour;
Skirmishing day by day,

With those that stopp'd his way,
Where the French general lay
    With all his power.

Which in his height of pride,
King Henry to deride,
His ransom to provide
    To the King sending.
Which he neglects the while,
As from a nation vile,
Yet with an angry smile
    Their fall portending.

And turning to his men,
Quoth our brave Henry then,
" Though they to one be ten,
    Be not amazed.
Yet have we well begun;
Battles so bravely won,
Have ever to the sun
    By fame been raised.

"And for myself," quoth he,
" This my full rest shall be,
England ne'er mourn for me,
    Nor more esteem me.
Victor I will remain,
Or on this earth lie slain,
Never shall she sustain
    Loss to redeem me.

" Poitiers and Cressy tell,
When most their pride did swell,
Under our swords they fell:
    No less our skill is
Than when our Grandsire great,
Claiming the regal seat,
By many a warlike feat
    Lopp'd the French lilies."

The Duke of York so dread
The eager vanward led:
With the main, Henry sped,
    Amongst his henchmen.
Exeter had the rear,
A braver man not there:
O Lord, how hot they were,
    On the false Frenchmen!

They now to fight are gone,
Armour on armour shone,
Drum now to drum did groan,
    To hear was wonder;
That with the cries they make,
The very earth did shake,
Trumpet to trumpet spake,
    Thunder to thunder.

Well it thine age became,
O noble Erpingham,
Which didst the signal aim
    To our hid forces;
When from a meadow by,
Like a storm suddenly,
The English archery
    Stuck the French horses.

With Spanish yew so strong,
Arrows a cloth-yard long,
That like to serpents stung,
    Piercing the weather;
None from his fellow starts,
But playing manly parts,
And like true English hearts,
    Stuck close together.

When down their bows they threw,
And forth their bilboes drew,
And on the French they flew,
    Not one was tardy;

Arms were from shoulders sent,
Scalps to the teeth were rent,
Down the French peasants went,
 Our men were hardy.

This while our noble King,
His broad sword brandishing,
Down the French host did ding,
 As to o'erwhelm it,
And many a deep wound lent,
His arms with blood besprent,
And many a cruel dent
 Bruised his helmet.

Gloucester, that duke so good,
Next of the royal blood,
For famous England stood,
 With his brave brother;
Clarence, in steel so bright,
Though but a maiden knight,
Yet in that furious fight
 Scarce such another.

Warwick in blood did wade,
Oxford the foe invade,
And cruel slaughter made,
 Still as they ran up;
Suffolk his axe did ply,
Beaumont and Willoughby,
Bare them right doughtily
 Ferrers and Fanhope.

Upon Saint Crispin's day
Fought was this noble fray,
Which fame did not delay
 To England to carry;
O when shall English men
With such acts fill a pen,
Or England breed again
 Such a King Harry?

CHRISTOPHER MARLOWE [1564–1593]

THE PASSIONATE SHEPHERD TO HIS LOVE

Come live with me and be my Love,
And we will all the pleasures prove
That valleys, groves, hills and fields,
Woods or steepy mountain yields.

And we will sit upon the rocks
Seeing the shepherds feed their flocks,
By shallow rivers, to whose falls
Melodious birds sing madrigals.

And I will make thee beds of roses
And a thousand fragrant posies,
A cap of flowers, and a kirtle
Embroidered all with leaves of myrtle.

A gown made of the finest wool,
Which from our pretty lambs we pull,
Fair linèd slippers for the cold,
With buckles of the purest gold.

A belt of straw and ivy buds,
With coral clasps and amber studs:
And if these pleasures may thee move,
Come live with me and be my Love.

The shepherd swains shall dance and sing
For thy delight each May-morning:
If these delights thy mind may move,
Then live with me and by my Love.

DESCRIPTION OF HERO

On Hellespont, guilty of true love's blood,
In view and opposite two cities stood,
Sea-borderers, disjoined by Neptune's might;
The one Abydos, the other Sestos hight.
At Sestos Hero dwelt; Hero the fair,
Whom young Apollo courted for her hair,
And offered as a dower his burning throne,
Where she should sit, for men to gaze upon.
The outside of her garments were of lawn,
The lining purple silk, with gilt stars drawn;
Her wide sleeves green, and bordered with a grove,
Where Venus in her naked glory strove
To please the careless and disdainful eyes
Of proud Adonis, that before her lies;
Her kirtle blue, whereon was many a stain,
Made with the blood of wretched lovers slain.
Upon her head she ware a myrtle wreath,
From whence her veil reached to the ground beneath;
Her veil was artificial flowers and leaves,
Whose workmanship both man and beast deceives.
Many would praise the sweet smell as she past,
When 'twas the odor which her breath forth cast;
And there, for honey, bees have sought in vain,
And, beat from thence, have lighted there again.
About her neck hung chains of pebblestone,
Which, lightened by her neck, like diamonds shone.
She ware no gloves; for neither sun nor wind
Would burn or parch her hands, but, to her mind,
Or warm or cool them, for they took delight
To play upon those hands, they were so white.
Buskins of shells, all silvered, usèd she,
And branched with blushing coral to the knee;
Where sparrows perched of hollow pearl and gold,
Such as the world would wonder to behold:
Those with sweet water oft her handmaid fills,
Which, as she went, would chirrup through the bills.
Some say, for her the fairest Cupid pined,
And, looking in her face, was strooken blind.

But this is true; so like was one the other,
As he imagined Hero was his mother;
And oftentimes into her bosom flew,
About her naked neck his bare arms threw,
And laid his childish head upon her breast,
And, with still panting rockt, there took his rest.
So lovely-fair was Hero, Venus' nun,
As Nature wept, thinking she was undone,
Because she took more from her than she left,
And of such wondrous beauty her bereft;
Therefore, in sign her treasure suffered wrack,
Since Hero's time hath half the world been black.

[From HERO AND LEANDER.]

RICHARD BARNFIELD [1574–1627]

AN ODE

As it fell upon a day
In the merry month of May,
Sitting in a pleasant shade
Which a grove of myrtles made,
Beasts did leap, and birds did sing,
Trees did grow, and plants did spring;
Everything did banish moan,
Save the nightingale alone:
She, poor bird, as all forlorn,
Leaned her breast up-till a thorn,
And there sung the dolefull'st ditty,
That to hear it was great pity:
"Fie, fie, fie," now would she cry;
"Teru, teru!" by and by;
That to hear her so complain,
Scarce I could from tears refrain;
For her griefs, so lively shown,
Made me think upon mine own.
Ah, thought I, thou mourn'st in vain!
None takes pity on thy pain:

Senseless trees they cannot hear thee;
Ruthless beasts they will not cheer thee:
King Pandion he is dead;
All thy friends are lapped in lead;
All thy fellow birds do sing,
Careless of thy sorrowing.
    Even so, poor bird, like thee,
None alive will pity me.
Whilst as fickle Fortune smiled,
Thou and I were both beguiled.
Every one that flatters thee
Is no friend in misery.
Words are easy, like the wind;
Faithful friends are hard to find:
Every man will be thy friend
Whilst thou hast wherewith to spend;
But if store of crowns be scant,
No man will supply thy want.
If that one be prodigal,
Bountiful they will him call,
And with such-like flattering,
"Pity but he were a king;"
If he be addict to vice,
Quickly him they will entice;
If to women he be bent,
They have at commandement:
But if Fortune once do frown,
Then farewell his great renown;
They that fawned on him before
Use his company no more.
    He that is thy friend indeed,
He will help thee in thy need:
If thou sorrow, he will weep;
If thou wake, he cannot sleep;
Thus of every grief in heart
He with thee doth bear a part.
These are certain signs to know
Faithful friend from flattering foe.

WILLIAM SHAKSPERE [1564–1616]

VENUS BEWAILETH THE DEATH OF ADONIS

"My tongue cannot express my grief for one,
And yet," quoth she, "behold two Adons dead!
My sighs are blown away, my salt tears gone,
Mine eyes are turned to fire, my heart to lead:
　　Heavy heart's lead, melt at mine eyes' red fire!
　　So shall I die by drops of hot desire.

"Alas, poor world, what treasure hast thou lost!
What face remains alive that's worth the viewing?
Whose tongue is music now? what canst thou boast
Of things long since, or anything ensuing?
　　The flowers are sweet, their colors fresh and trim;
　　But true-sweet beauty lived and died with him.

"Bonnet nor veil henceforth no creature wear!
Nor sun nor wind will ever strive to kiss you:
Having no fair to lose, you need not fear;
The sun doth scorn you and the wind doth hiss you:
　　But when Adonis lived, sun and sharp air
　　Lurked like two thieves, to rob him of his fair.

"And therefore would he put his bonnet on,
Under whose brim the gaudy sun would peep;
The wind would blow it off, and, being gone,
Play with his locks: then would Adonis weep;
　　And straight, in pity of his tender years,
　　They both would strive who first should dry his tears.

"To see his face the lion walked along
Behind some hedge, because he would not fear him;
To recreate himself when he hath sung,
The tiger would be tame and gently hear him;
　　If he had spoke, the wolf would leave his prey
　　And never fright the silly lamb that day.

"When he beheld his shadow in the brook,
The fishes spread on it their golden gills;
When he was by, the birds such pleasure took,
That some would sing, some other in their bills
 Would bring him mulberries and ripe-red cherries;
 He fed them with his sight, they him with berries.

"But this foul, grim, and urchin-snouted boar,
Whose downward eye still looketh for a grave,
Ne'er saw the beauteous livery that he wore;
Witness the entertainment that he gave:
 If he did see his face, why then I know
 He thought to kiss him, and hath killed him so.

"'Tis true, 'tis true; thus was Adonis slain:
He ran upon the boar with his sharp spear,
Who did not whet his teeth at him again,
But by a kiss thought to persuade him there;
 And nuzzling in his flank, the loving swine
 Sheathed unaware the tusk in his soft groin.

"Had I been toothed like him, I must confess,
With kissing him I should have killed him first;
But he is dead, and never did he bless
My youth with his; the more am I accurst."
 With this, she falleth in the place she stood,
 And stains her face with his congealèd blood.

She looks upon his lips, and they are pale;
She takes him by the hand, and that is cold;
She whispers in his ears a heavy tale,
As if they heard the woeful words she told;
 She lifts the coffer-lids that close his eyes,
 Where, lo, two lamps, burnt out, in darkness lies;

Two glasses, where herself herself beheld
A thousand times, and now no more reflect;
Their virtue lost, wherein they late excelled,

And every beauty robbed of his effect:
 "Wonder of time," quoth she, "this is my spite,
 That, thou being dead, the day should yet be light.

"Since thou art dead, lo, here I prophesy:
Sorrow on love hereafter shall attend:
It shall be waited on with jealousy,
Find sweet beginning, but unsavoury end,
 Ne'er settled equally, but high or low,
 That all love's pleasure shall not match his woe.

"It shall be fickle, false, and full of fraud;
Bud, and be blasted, in a breathing-while;
The bottom poison, and the top o'erstrawed
With sweets that shall the truest sight beguile:
 The strongest body shall it make most weak,
 Strike the wise dumb and teach the fool to speak.

"It shall be sparing, and too full of riot,
Teaching decrepit age to tread the measures;
The staring ruffian shall it keep in quiet,
Pluck down the rich, enrich the poor with treasures;
 It shall be raging-mad and silly-mild,
 Make the young old, the old become a child.

"It shall suspect where is no cause of fear;
It shall not fear where it should most mistrust;
It shall be merciful and too severe,
And most deceiving when it seems most just;
 Perverse it shall be where it shows most toward;
 Put fear to valour, courage to the coward.

"It shall be cause of war and dire events,
And set dissension 'twixt the son and sire;
Subject and servile to all discontents,
As dry combustious matter is to fire:
 Sith in his prime Death doth my love destroy,
 They that love best their loves shall not enjoy."

By this, the boy that by her side lay killed
Was melted like a vapor from her sight,
And in his blood that on the ground lay spilled,
A purple flower sprung up, chequered with white,
  Resembling well his pale cheeks and the blood
  Which in round drops upon their whiteness stood.

She bows her head, the new-sprung flower to smell,
Comparing it to her Adonis' breath,
And says, within her bosom it shall dwell,
Since he himself is reft from her by death:
  She crops the stalk, and in the breach appears
  Green dropping sap, which she compares to tears.

"Poor flower," quoth she, "this was thy father's guise—
Sweet issue of a more sweet-smelling sire—
For every little grief to wet his eyes:
To grow unto himself was his desire,
  And so 'tis thine; but know, it is as good
  To wither in my breast as in his blood.

"Here was thy father's bed, here in my breast;
Thou art the next of blood, and 'tis thy right:
Lo, in this hollow cradle take thy rest,
My throbbing heart shall rock thee day and night;
  There shall not be one minute in an hour
  Wherein I will not kiss my sweet love's flower."

[From VENUS AND ADONIS.]

LYRICS FROM THE PLAYS

SILVIA

WHO is Silvia? what is she,
  That all our swains commend her?
Holy, fair, and wise is she;
  The heaven such grace did lend her,
That she might admired be.

Is she kind as she is fair?
  For beauty lives with kindness.
Love doth to her eyes repair,
  To help him of his blindness,
And, being helped, inhabits there.

Then to Silvia let us sing,
  That Silvia is excelling;
She excels each mortal thing
  Upon the dull earth dwelling:
To her let us garlands bring.

[FROM TWO GENTLEMEN OF VERONA.]

UNDER THE GREENWOOD TREE

UNDER the greenwood tree
Who loves to lie with me
And turn his merry note
Unto the sweet bird's throat
Come hither! come hither! come hither!
  Here shall he see
  No enemy
But winter and rough weather.

Who doth ambition shun
And loves to live i' the sun,

Seeking the food he eats
And pleased with what he gets,
Come hither! come hither! come hither!
Here shall he see
No enemy
But winter and rough weather.

[From As You Like It.]

BLOW, BLOW, THOU WINTER WIND

Blow, blow, thou winter wind!
Thou art not so unkind
As man's ingratitude;
Thy tooth is not so keen,
Because thou art not seen,
Although thy breath be rude.

Heigh ho! sing, heigh ho! unto the green holly:
Most friendship is feigning, most loving mere folly:
Then, heigh ho, the holly!
This life is most jolly.

Freeze, freeze, thou bitter sky!
That dost not bite so nigh
As benefits forgot;
Though thou the waters warp,
Thy sting is not so sharp
As friend remembered not.

Heigh ho! sing, heigh ho! etc.

[From As You Like It.]

O MISTRESS MINE

O MISTRESS mine, where are you roaming?
O stay and hear! your true-love's coming
    That can sing both high and low;
Trip no further, pretty sweeting:
Journeys end in lovers meeting
    Every wise man's son doth know.

What is love? 'tis not hereafter;
Present mirth hath present laughter;
    What's to come is still unsure:
In delay there lies no plenty:
Then come kiss me, Sweet-and-twenty,
    Youth's a stuff will not endure.

                          [From TWELFTH NIGHT.]

LAMENT

COME away, come away, Death,
    And in sad cypress let me be laid;
Fly away, fly away, breath;
    I am slain by a fair cruel maid.
My shroud of white, stuck all with yew,
    O prepare it!
My part of death, no one so true
    Did share it.

Not a flower, not a flower sweet
    On my black coffin let there be strown;
Not a friend, not a friend greet
    My poor corpse, where my bones shall be thrown:
A thousand thousand sighs to save,
    Lay me, O, where
Sad true lover never find my grave
    To weep there.

                          [From TWELFTH NIGHT.]

TAKE, O, TAKE THOSE LIPS AWAY

TAKE, O, take those lips away,
    That so sweetly were forsworn;
And those eyes, the break of day,
    Lights that do mislead the morn:
But my kisses bring again,
                    Bring again;
Seals of love, but sealed in vain,
                    Sealed in vain!

[From MEASURE FOR MEASURE.]

HARK! HARK! THE LARK!

HARK! hark! the lark at heaven's gate sings,
    And Phœbus 'gins arise,
His steeds to water at those springs
    On chaliced flowers that lies;
And winking Mary-buds begin
    To ope their golden eyes:
With every thing that pretty is,
    My lady sweet, arise:
        Arise, arise!

[From CYMBELINE.]

DIRGE

FEAR no more the heat o' th' sun,
    Nor the furious winter's rages;
Thou thy worldly task hast done,
    Home art gone, and ta'en thy wages:
Golden lads and girls all must,
As chimney-sweepers, come to dust.

Fear no more the frown o' th' great;
  Thou art past the tyrant's stroke;
Care no more to clothe and eat;
  To thee the reed is as the oak:
The Sceptre, Learning, Physic, must
All follow this, and come to dust.

Fear no more the lightning-flash,
  Nor th' all-dreaded thunder-stone;
Fear not slander, censure rash;
  Thou hast finished joy and moan:
All lovers young, all lovers must
Consign to thee, and come to dust.

No exorciser harm thee!
  Nor no witchcraft charm thee!
Ghost unlaid forbear thee!
  Nothing ill come near thee!
Quiet consummation have;
And renowned be thy grave!

[From CYMBELINE.]

WHERE THE BEE SUCKS

WHERE the bee sucks, there suck I:
In a cowslip's bell I lie;
There I couch, when owls do cry:
On the bat's back I do fly
After summer merrily.
  Merrily, merrily, shall I live now,
  Under the blossom that hangs on the bough!

[From THE TEMPEST.]

A SEA DIRGE

FULL fathom five thy father lies;
    Of his bones are coral made;
Those are pearls that were his eyes:
    Nothing of him that doth fade
But doth suffer a sea-change
Into something rich and strange.
Sea-nymphs hourly ring his knell:
                Ding-dong.
Hark! now I hear them,—Ding-dong, bell.

                      [From THE TEMPEST]

SONNETS

SHALL I compare thee to a summer's day?
Thou art more lovely and more temperate:
Rough winds do shake the darling buds of May,
And summer's lease hath all too short a date:
Sometime too hot the eye of heaven shines,
And often is his gold complexion dimmed;
And every fair from fair sometime declines,
By chance or nature's changing course untrimmed;
But thy eternal summer shall not fade
Nor lose possession of that fair thou owest;
Nor shall Death brag thou wander'st in his shade,
When in eternal lines to time thou growest:
    So long as men can breathe or eyes can see,
    So long lives this, and this gives life to thee.

WHEN, in disgrace with fortune and men's eyes,
I all alone beweep my outcast state,
And trouble deaf heaven with my bootless cries
And look upon myself and curse my fate—
Wishing me like to one more rich in hope,
Featured like him, like him with friends possest,

Desiring this man's art, and that man's scope,
With what I most enjoy contented least—
(Yet in these thoughts myself almost despising),
Haply I think on thee, and then my state,
Like to the lark at break of day arising
From sullen earth, sings hymns at heaven's gate!
  For thy sweet love remembered such wealth brings
   That then I scorn to change my state with kings.

WHEN to the sessions of sweet silent thought
I summon up remembrance of things past,
I sigh the lack of many a thing I sought,
And with old woes new wail my dear time's waste:
Then can I drown an eye, unused to flow,
For precious friends hid in death's dateless night,
And weep afresh love's long since cancelled woe,
And moan th' expense of many a vanished sight:
Then can I grieve at grievances forgone,
And heavily from woe to woe tell o'er
The sad account of fore-bemoanèd moan,
Which I new pay as if not paid before.
  But if the while I think on thee, dear friend,
   All losses are restored and sorrows end.

WHEN I have seen by Time's fell hand defaced
The rich proud cost of outworn buried age;
When sometime lofty towers I see down-razed,
And brass eternal slave to mortal rage;
When I have seen the hungry ocean gain
Advantage on the kingdom of the shore,
And the firm soil win of the watery main,
Increasing store with loss and loss with store;
When I have seen such interchange of state,
Or state itself confounded to decay,
Ruin hath taught me thus to ruminate—
That Time will come and take my love away.
  This thought is as a death, which cannot choose
   But weep to have that which it fears to lose.

SINCE brass, nor stone, nor earth, nor boundless sea,
But sad mortality o'er-sways their power,
How with this rage shall beauty hold a plea,
Whose action is no stronger than a flower?
O, how shall summer's honey breath hold out
Against the wreckful siege of battering days,
When rocks impregnable are not so stout,
Nor gates of steel so strong, but Time decays?
O fearful meditation! where, alack,
Shall Time's best jewel from Time's chest lie hid?
Or what strong hand can hold his swift foot back?
Or who his spoil of beauty can forbid?
   O, none, unless this miracle have might,
   That in black ink my love may still shine bright.

THAT time of year thou mayst in me behold
When yellow leaves, or none, or few, do hang
Upon those boughs which shake against the cold,
Bare ruined choirs, where late the sweet birds sang.
In me thou see'st the twilight of such day
As after sunset fadeth in the west,
Which by and by black night doth take away,
Death's second self, that seals up all in rest.
In me thou see'st the glowing of such fire
That on the ashes of his youth doth lie,
As the death-bed whereon it must expire,
Consumed with that which it was nourished by.
   This thou perceiv'st, which makes thy love more strong,
   To love that well which thou must leave ere long.

How like a winter hath my absence been
From thee, the pleasure of the fleeting year!
What freezings have I felt, what dark days seen!
What old December's bareness every where!
And yet this time removed was summer's time,
The teeming autumn, big with rich increase,
Bearing the wanton burden of the prime,
Like widowed wombs after their lords' decease:
Yet this abundant issue seemed to me

But hope of orphans and unfathered fruit;
For summer and his pleasures wait on thee,
And, thou away, the very birds are mute;
   Or, if they sing, 'tis with so dull a cheer
   That leaves look pale, dreading the winter's near.

LET me not to the marriage of true minds
Admit impediments. Love is not love
Which alters when it alteration finds,
Or bends with the remover to remove:
O, no! it is an ever-fixed mark
That looks on tempests and is never shaken;
It is the star to every wandering bark,
Whose worth's unknown, although his height be taken.
Love's not Time's fool, though rosy lips and cheeks
Within his bending sickle's compass come;
Love alters not with his brief hours and weeks,
But bears it out even to the edge of doom.
   If this be error and upon me proved,
   I never writ, nor no man ever loved.

POOR soul, the centre of my sinful earth,
Thrall to these rebel powers that thee array,
Why dost thou pine within and suffer dearth,
Painting thy outward walls so costly gay?
Why so large cost, having so short a lease,
Dost thou upon thy fading mansion spend?
Shall worms, inheritors of this excess,
Eat up thy charge? is this thy body's end?
Then, soul, live thou upon thy servant's loss,
And let that pine to aggravate thy store;
Buy terms divine in selling hours of dross;
Within be fed, without be rich no more:
   So shalt thou feed on Death, that feeds on men,
   And Death once dead, there's no more dying then.

THOMAS NASHE [1567–1601]

SPRING

Spring, the sweet Spring, is the year's pleasant king;
Then blooms each thing, then maids dance in a ring,
Cold doth not sting, the pretty birds do sing,
    Cuckoo, jug-jug, pu-we, to-witta-woo!

The palm and may[1] make country houses gay,
Lambs frisk and play, the shepherds pipe all day,
And we hear aye birds tune this merry lay,
    Cuckoo, jug-jug, pu-we, to-witta-woo.

The fields breathe sweet, the daisies kiss our feet,
Young lovers meet, old wives a-sunning sit,
In every street these tunes our ears do greet,
    Cuckoo, jug-jug, pu-we, to-witta-woo!
        Spring! the sweet Spring!

[From Summer's Last Will.]

THOMAS CAMPION [1567?–1619]

CHERRY–RIPE

There is a garden in her face
    Where roses and white lilies blow;
A heavenly paradise is that place,
    Wherein all pleasant fruits do flow[2]:
      There cherries grow which none may buy
      Till "Cherry-ripe" themselves do cry.

Those cherries fairly do enclose
    Of orient pearl a double row,

---

[1] flowers of the hawthorn.   [2] flower (verb).

Which when her lovely laughter shows,
  They look like rosebuds filled with snow;
    Yet them nor peer nor prince can buy
    Till "Cherry-ripe" themselves do cry.

Her eyes like angels watch them still;
  Her brows like bended bows do stand,
Threat'ning with piercing frowns to kill
  All that attempt with eye or hand
    Those sacred cherries to come nigh
    Till "Cherry-ripe" themselves do cry.

WHEN TO HER LUTE CORINNA SINGS

When to her lute Corinna sings,
Her voice revives the leaden strings,
And doth in highest notes appear,
As any challenged echo clear:
But when she doth of mourning speak,
E'en with her sighs, the strings do break,
And as her lute doth live or die,
Led by her passion, so must I:
For when of pleasure she doth sing,
My thoughts enjoy a sudden spring,
But if she doth of sorrow speak,
E'en from my heart the strings do break.

A RENUNCIATION

Thou art not fair, for all thy red and white,
  For all those rosy ornaments in thee,—
Thou art not sweet, though made of mere delight,
  Nor fair, nor sweet—unless thou pity me!
I will not soothe thy fancies; thou shalt prove
That beauty is no beauty without love.

Yet love not me, nor seek not to allure
   My thoughts with beauty, were it more divine:
Thy smiles and kisses I cannot endure,
   I'll not be wrapped up in those arms of thine.
Now show it, if thou be a woman right—
Embrace and kiss and love me in despite!

THE MAN OF LIFE UPRIGHT

THE man of life upright,
   Whose guiltless heart is free
From all dishonest deeds,
   Or thought of vanity;

The man whose silent days
   In harmless joys are spent,
Whom hopes cannot delude
   Nor sorrow discontent:

That man needs neither towers
   Nor armour for defence,
Nor secret vaults to fly
   From thunder's violence.

He only can behold
   With unaffrighted eyes
The horrors of the deep
   And terrors of the skies.

Thus scorning all the cares
   That fate or fortune brings,
He makes the heaven his book,
   His wisdom heavenly things;

Good thoughts his only friends,
   His wealth a well-spent age,
The earth his sober inn
   And quiet pilgrimage.

SIC TRANSIT GLORIA MUNDI

COME, cheerful day, part of my life to me;
　For while thou view'st me with thy fading light
Part of my life doth still depart with thee,
　And I still onward haste to my last night:
Time's fatal wings do ever forward fly—
So every day we live, a day we die.

But O ye nights, ordained for barren rest,
　How are my days deprived of life in you
When heavy sleep my soul hath dispossest,
　By feignèd death life sweetly to renew!
Part of my life in that, you life deny:
So every day we live, a day we die.

SIR HENRY WOTTON [1568-1639]

THE CHARACTER OF A HAPPY LIFE

How happy is he born and taught
　That serveth not another's will;
Whose armour is his honest thought;
　And simple truth his utmost skill;

Whose passions not his masters are;
　Whose soul is still prepared for death,
Untied unto the world by care
　Of public fame or private breath;

Who envies none that chance doth raise,
　Nor vice; who never understood
How deepest wounds are given by praise,
　Nor rules of state, but rules of good;

Who hath his life from rumours freed;
　Whose conscience is his strong retreat;

Whose state can neither flatterers feed,
    Nor ruin make oppressors great;

Who God doth late and early pray
    More of his grace than gifts to lend;
And entertains the harmless day
    With a religious book or friend—

This man is freed from servile bands
    Of hope to rise or fear to fall:
Lord of himself, though not of lands,
    And, having nothing, yet hath all.

SIR JOHN DAVIES [1569-1626]

TRUE KNOWLEDGE OF THE SOUL

Thou! that hast fashioned twice this soul of ours,
    So that she is by double title Thine!
Thou only knowst her nature and her powers;
    Her subtle form Thou only canst define!

To judge herself, she must herself transcend;
    As greater circles comprehend the less;
But she wants power her own powers to extend;
    As fettered men cannot their strength express.

But Thou, bright morning Star![1] Thou, rising Sun!
    Which, in these later times, hast brought to light
Those mysteries that, since the world begun,
    Lay hid in darkness and eternal night—

Thou, like the sun, dost with indifferent ray
    Into the palace and the cottage shine,
And showst the soul, both to the clerk and lay,
    By the clear lamp of thy oracle Divine?

[1] See Revelation xxii, 16.

This Lamp, through all the regions of my brain,
 Where my soul sits, doth spread such beams of grace,
 As now, methinks, I do distinguish plain
 Each subtle line of her immortal face.

[From NOSCE TEIPSUM.]

THOMAS DEKKER [1570?-1641]

SONG

COLD's the wind, and wet's the rain,
 Saint Hugh be our good speed!
Ill is the weather that bringeth no gain,
 Nor helps good hearts in need.

Trowl the bowl, the jolly nut-brown bowl,
 And here, kind mate, to thee:
Let's sing a dirge for Saint Hugh's soul,
 And down it merrily.

Down a down! hey down a down!
 Hey derry derry, down a down!
Ho well done; to me let come!
 Ring, compass, gentle joy.

Trowl the bowl, etc.

[From THE SHOEMAKER's HOLIDAY.]

RUSTIC SONG

HAYMAKERS, rakers, reapers, and mowers,
 Wait on your Summer-Queen!
Dress up with musk-rose her eglantine bowers,
 Daffodils strew the green!
 Sing, dance, and play,
 'Tis holiday!

The sun does bravely shine
On our ears of corn.
    Rich as a pearl
    Comes every girl—
This is mine, this is mine, this is mine!
Let us die ere away they be borne.

Bow to the sun, to our Queen, and that fair one
    Come to behold our sports:
Each bonny lass here is counted a rare one,
    As those in princes' courts.
        These and we
        With country glee
Will teach the woods to resound,
And the hills with echoes hollow:
        Skipping lambs
        Their bleating dams
'Mongst kids shall trip it round—
For joy thus our wenches we follow.

Wind, jolly huntsmen, your neat bugles shrilly!
    Hounds, make a lusty cry!
Spring up, you falconers, partridges freely,
    Then let your brave hawks fly!
        Horses amain,
        Over ridge, over plain,
The dogs have the stag in chase:
'Tis a sport to content a king.
        So ho! ho! through the skies
        How the proud bird flies,
And sousing, kills with a grace!
Now the deer falls—hark! how they ring!

[From THE SUN'S DARLING, by Dekker and Ford.]

BEN JONSON [1573?-1637]*

SONG TO CELIA

DRINK to me only with thine eyes,
  And I will pledge with mine;
Or leave a kiss but in the cup,
  And I'll not look for wine.
The thirst that from the soul doth rise
  Doth ask a drink divine;
But might I of Jove's nectar sup,
  I would not change for thine.

I sent thee late a rosy wreath,
  Not so much honouring thee,
As giving it a hope that there
  It could not withered be.
But thou thereon didst only breathe,
  And sent'st it back to me;
Since when it grows, and smells, I swear,
  Not of itself, but thee.

HYMN TO DIANA

QUEEN and Huntress, chaste and fair,
  Now the sun is laid to sleep,
Seated in thy silver chair,
    State in wonted manner keep:
      Hesperus entreats thy light,
      Goddess excellently bright.

Earth, let not thy envious shade
  Dare itself to interpose;
Cynthia's shining orb was made
    Heaven to clear when day did close:
      Bless us then with wishèd sight,
      Goddess excellently bright.

* See note on page 130.

Lay thy bow of pearl apart
　　And thy crystal-shining quiver;
Give unto the flying hart
　　Space to breathe, how short soever:
　　　　Thou that mak'st a day of night,
　　　　Goddess excellently bright!

[From CYNTHIA'S REVELS.]

THE TRIUMPH OF CHARIS

SEE the chariot at hand here of Love,
　　Wherein my Lady rideth!
Each that draws is a swan or a dove,
　　And well the car Love guideth.
As she goes, all hearts do duty
　　　　　　Unto her beauty;
And enamour'd, do wish, so they might
　　　　　　But enjoy such a sight,
That they still were to run by her side,
Through swords, through seas, whither she would ride.

Do but look on her eyes, they do light
　　All that Love's world compriseth!
Do but look on her hair, it is bright
　　As Love's star when it riseth!
Do but mark, her forehead's smoother
　　　　　　Than words that soothe her;
And from her arched brows, such a grace
　　　　　　Sheds itself through the face
As alone there triumphs to the life
All the gain, all the good, of the elements' strife.

Have you seen but a bright lily grow,
　　Before rude hands have touched it?
Have you marked but the fall of the snow
　　Before the soil hath smutched it?
Have you felt the wool of the beaver?

Or swan's down ever?
Or have smelt o' the bud of the briar?
Or the nard in the fire?
Or have tasted the bag of the bee?
O so white! O so soft! O so sweet is she!

ECHO'S LAMENT OF NARCISSUS

SLOW, slow, fresh fount, keep time with my salt tears:
Yet slower, yet; O faintly, gentle springs:
List to the heavy part the music bears,
Woe weeps out her division, when she sings.
Droop herbs and flowers,
Fall grief in showers,
Our beauties are not ours;
O, I could still,
Like melting snow upon some craggy hill,
Drop, drop, drop, drop,
Since nature's pride is now a withered daffodil.

[From CYNTHIA'S REVELS.]

SONG

STILL to be neat, still to be drest,
As you were going to a feast;
Still to be powdered, still perfumed:
Lady, it is to be presumed,
Though art's hid causes are not found,
All is not sweet, all is not sound.

Give me a look, give me a face,
That makes simplicity a grace;
Robes loosely flowing, hair as free:
Such sweet neglect more taketh me
Than all the adulteries of art:
They strike mine eyes, but not my heart.

[From EPICÆNE; OR, THE SILENT WOMAN.]

AN HYMN TO GOD THE FATHER

HEAR me, O God!
  A broken heart
  Is my best part:
Use still thy rod,
That I may prove,
  Therein, Thy love.

If thou hadst not
  Been stern to me,
  But left me free,
I had forgot
  Myself and Thee.

For, sin's so sweet,
  As minds ill-bent
  Rarely repent,
Unless they meet
  Their punishment.

Who more can crave
  Than Thou hast done?
  Thou gav'st a Son
To free a slave,
  First made of nought,
  With all since bought.

Sin, death, and hell
  His glorious Name
  Quite overcame;
Yet I rebel,
  And slight the same.

But, I'll come in
  Before my loss
  Me farther toss;
As sure to win
  Under his cross.

JOHN DONNE [1573–1631]

SONG

Go and catch a falling star,
Get with child a mandrake root,
Tell me where all times past are,
Or who cleft the devil's foot;
Teach me to hear mermaids singing,
Or to keep off envy's stinging,
      And find
      What wind
Serves to advance an honest mind.

If thou be'st born to strange sights,
Things invisible go see,
Ride ten thousand days and nights
Till age snow white hairs on thee;
Thou, when thou return'st, wilt tell me
All strange wonders that befell thee,
      And swear
      No where
Lives a woman true and fair.

If thou find'st one let me know,
Such a pilgrimage were sweet;
Yet do not; I would not go,
Though at next door we might meet.
Though she were true when you met her,
And last till you write your letter,
      Yet she
      Will be
False, ere I come, to two or three.

THE DREAM

DEAR love, for nothing less than thee
Would I have broke this happy dream;
    It was a theme
For reason, much too strong for fantasy.
Therefore thou waked'st me wisely; yet
My dream thou brok'st not, but continued'st it.
Thou art so true that thoughts of thee suffice
To make dreams truths, and fables histories;
Enter these arms, for since thou thought'st it best
Not to dream all my dream, let's act the rest.

As lightning, or a taper's light,
Thine eyes, and not thy noise, waked me;
    Yet I thought thee—
For thou lov'st truth—an angel, at first sight;
But when I saw thou saw'st my heart,
And knew'st my thoughts beyond an angel's art,
When thou knew'st what I dreamt, when thou knew'st when
Excess of joy would wake me, and cam'st then,
I must confess it could not choose but be
Profane to think thee anything but thee.

Coming and staying show'd thee, thee;
But rising makes me doubt that now
    Thou art not thou;
That love is weak where fear's as strong as he:
'Tis not all spirit, pure and brave,
If mixture it of fear, shame, honour have.
Perchance as torches, which must ready be,
Men light and put out, so thou deal'st with me.
Thou cam'st to kindle, go'st to come: then I
Will dream that hope again, but else would die.

LOVE'S DEITY

I LONG to talk with some old lover's ghost
  Who died before the God of Love was born.
I cannot think that he who then loved most
  Sunk so low as to love one which did scorn.
But since this God produced a destiny;
And that vice-nature, custom, lets it be;
  I must love her that loves not me.

Sure, they which made him god, meant not so much,
  Nor he in his young godhead practiced it.
But when an even flame two hearts did touch,
  His office was indulgently to fit
Actives to passives. Correspondency
Only his subject was; it cannot be
  Love till I love her who loves me.

But every modern god will not extend
  His vast prerogative as far as Jove.
To rage, to lust, to write to, to commend,
  All is the purlieu of the God of Love.
O! were we waken'd by this tyranny
To ungod this child again, it could not be
  I should love her who loves not me.

Rebel and atheist too, why murmur I,
  As though I felt the worst that Love could do?
Love may make me leave loving, or might try
  A deeper plague, to make her love me too;
Which, since she loves before, I'm loth to see.
Falsehood is worse than hate; and that must be,
  If she whom I love, should love me.

THE FUNERAL

WHOEVER comes to shroud me, do not harm
          Nor question much
That subtle wreath of hair about mine arm;
The mystery, the sign, you must not touch,
          For 'tis my outward soul,
Viceroy to that which, unto heav'n being gone,
          Will leave this to control
And keep these limbs, her provinces, from dissolution.

For if the sinewy thread my brain lets fall
          Through every part
Can tie those parts, and make me one of all;
Those hairs, which upward grew, and strength and art
          Have from a better brain,
Can better do't: except she meant that I
          By this should know my pain,
As prisoners then are manacled, when they're condemn'd
          to die.

Whate'er she meant by't, bury it with me,
          For since I am
Love's martyr, it might breed idolatry
If into other hands these reliques came.
          As 'twas humility
T'afford to it all that a soul can do,
          So 'tis some bravery
That, since you would have none of me, I bury some of you.

THE WILL

BEFORE I sigh my last gasp, let me breathe,
Great Love, some legacies. Here I bequeath
Mine eyes to Argus, if mine eyes can see;
If they be blind, then Love, I give them thee:
My tongue to Fame: to ambassadors mine ears:
     To women, or the sea, my tears.

Thou, Love, hast taught me heretofore
By making me serve her who had twenty more,
That I should give to none but such as had too much before.

My constancy I to the planets give;
My truth to them who at the court do live:
Mine ingenuity and openness
To Jesuits: to buffoons my pensiveness:
My silence to any who abroad hath been:
   My money to a Capuchin.
Thou, Love, taught'st me, by appointing me
To love there, where no love receiv'd can be,
Only to give to such as have an incapacity.

My faith I give to Roman Catholics:
All my good works unto the schismatics
Of Amsterdam: my best civility
And courtship, to an university:
My modesty I give to shoulders bare:
   My patience let gamesters share.
Thou, Love, taught'st me, by making me
Love her that holds my love disparity,
Only to give to those that count my gifts indignity.

I give my reputation to those
Which were my friends; my industry to foes:
To schoolmen I bequeath my doubtfulness:
My sickness to physicians, or excess:
To Nature, all that I in rhyme have writ:
   And to my company my wit.
Thou, Love, by making me adore
Her, who begot this love in me before,
Taught'st me to make as though I gave, when I did but restore.

To him for whom the passing bell next tolls
I give my physic books: my written rolls
Of moral counsels I to bedlam give:
My brazen medals, unto them which live

In want of bread: to them which pass among
    All foreigners, my English tongue.
Thou, Love, by making me love one
Who thinks her friendship a fit portion
For younger lovers, dost my gifts thus disproportion.

Therefore I'll give no more; but I'll undo
The world by dying, because love dies too.
Then all your beauties will be no more worth
Than gold in mines where none doth draw it forth:
And all your graces no more use shall have
    Than a sun-dial on a grave.
Thou Love, taughtest me, by making me
Love her, who doth neglect both me and thee,
To invent and practise this one way to annihilate all three.

A HYMN TO GOD THE FATHER

WILT Thou forgive that sin where I begun,
    Which was my sin, though it were done before?
Wilt Thou forgive that sin through which I run,
    And do run still, though still I do deplore?
When Thou hast done, Thou hast not done;
      For I have more.

Wilt Thou forgive that sin which I have won
    Others to sin, and made my sins their door?
Wilt Thou forgive that sin which I did shun
    A year or two, but wallowed in a score?
When Thou hast done, Thou hast not done;
      For I have more.

I have a sin of fear, that when I've spun
    My last thread, I shall perish on the shore;
But swear by Thyself that at my death Thy Son
    Shall shine as He shines now, and heretofore;
And, having done that, Thou hast done;
      I fear no more.

FORGET

IF poisonous minerals, and if that tree
Whose fruit threw death on else-immortal us,
If lecherous goats, if serpents envious
Cannot be damned, alas! why should I be?
Why should intent or reason, born in me,
Make sins, else equal, in me more heinous?
And, mercy being easy and glorious
To God, in his stern wrath why threatens He?
—But who am I, that dare dispute with Thee?
O God, O! of Thine only worthy blood,
And my tears, make a heavenly Lethean flood,
And drown in it my sin's black memory.
  That Thou remember them, some claim as debt;
  I think it mercy if Thou wilt forget.

DEATH

DEATH, be not proud, though some have callèd thee
Mighty and dreadful, for thou art not so;
For those whom thou think'st thou dost overthrow
Die not, poor Death: nor yet canst thou kill me.
From rest and sleep, which but thy picture be,
Much pleasure; then from thee much more must flow;
And soonest our best men with thee do go—
Rest of their bones and souls' delivery!
Thou'rt slave to Fate, chance, kings, and desperate men,
And dost with poison, war, and sickness dwell;
And poppy or charms can make us sleep as well,
And better than thy stroke. Why swell'st thou then?
  One short sleep past, we wake eternally,
  And Death shall be no more. Death, thou shalt die!

JOHN FLETCHER [1579–1625]

SONG TO BACCHUS

God Lyæus, ever young,
Ever honoured, ever sung;
Stained with blood of lusty grapes.
In a thousand lusty shapes,
Dance upon the mazer's brim,
In the crimson liquor swim;
From thy plenteous hand divine
Let a river run with wine;
God of youth, let this day here
Enter neither care nor fear!

[From Valentian.]

WEEP NO MORE

Weep no more, nor sigh, nor groan;
Sorrow calls no time that's gone;
Violets plucked the sweetest rain
Makes not fresh nor grow again;
Trim thy locks, look cheerfully;
Fate's hid ends eyes cannot see;
Joys as winged dreams fly fast,
Why should sadness longer last?
Grief is but a wound to woe;
Gentlest fair, mourn, mourn no mo.

[From The Queen of Corinth.]

ASPATIA'S SONG

Lay a garland on my hearse
    Of the dismal yew;
Maidens, willow branches bear;
    Say, I dièd true.

My love was false, but I was firm
    From my hour of birth.
Upon my buried body lie
    Lightly, gentle earth!

[From The Maid's Tragedy.]

FRANCIS BEAUMONT [1584–1616]

LINES ON THE TOMBS IN WESTMINSTER

Mortality, behold and fear!
What a change of flesh is here!
Think how many royal bones
Sleep within this heap of stones;
Here they lie had realms and lands,
Who now want strength to stir their hands;
Where from their pulpits sealed with dust
They preach, "In greatness is no trust."
Here's an acre sown indeed
With the richest royal'st seed
That the earth did e'er suck in,
Since the first man died for sin;
Here the bones of birth have cried,
"Though gods they were, as men they died."
Here are sands, ignoble things,
Dropt from the ruined sides of kings:
Here's a world of pomp and state,
Buried in dust, once dead by fate.

GILES FLETCHER [1585?-1623]

NATURE AWAITETH THE TRIUMPH OF CHRIST

Say, Earth, why hast thou got thee new attire,
And stick'st thy habit full of dasies red?
Seems that thou doest to some high thought aspire,
And some new-found-out Bridegroom mean'st to wed:
Tell me, ye trees, so fresh apparellèd—
 So never let the spiteful canker waste you!
 So never let the heav'ns with light'ning blast you!
Why go you now so trimly drest, or whither haste you?

Answer me, Jordan, why thy crooked tide
So often wanders from his nearest way,
As though some other way thy stream would slide,
And fain salute the place where something lay?
And you, sweet Birds, that, shaded from the ray,
 Sit carolling, and piping grief away,
 The while the lambs do hear you dance and play—
Tell me, sweet Birds, what is it you so fain would say?

And thou, fair Spouse of Earth, that every year
Gett'st such a numerous issue of thy bride,
How chance thou hotter shin'st, and draw'st more near?
Sure thou somewhere some worthy sight hast spy'd,
That in one place, for joy, thou canst not bide!
 And you dead swallows, that so lively now
 Through the flit air you wingèd passage row,
How could new life into your frozen ashes flow?

Ye Primroses and purple Violets—
Tell me, why blaze ye from your leafy bed,
And woo men's hands to rend you from your seats,
As though you would somewhere be carrièd,
With fresh perfumes, and velvets garnishèd?

But, ah! I need not ask—'tis surely so!
You all would to your Saviour's triumph go,
There would ye all await, and humble homage do.

There should the Earth herself (with garlands new,
And lovely flow'rs embellishèd) adore:
Such roses never in her garland grew;
Such lilies never in her breast she wore;
Like beauty never yet did shine before:
    There should the sun another Sun behold,
    From whence himself borrows his locks of gold
That kindle heav'n and Earth with beauties manifold.

There might the Violet and Primrose sweet [1]
Beams of more lively and more lovely grace,
Arising from their beds of incense meet;
There should the Swallow see new life embrace
Dead ashes, and the grave unheal his face
    To let the living from his bowels creep,
    Unable longer his own dead to keep:
There heav'n and Earth should see their Lord awake from sleep:

Their Lord! before, by other judg'd to die;
Now judge of all himself: before, forsaken
Of all the world, that from his aid did fly;
Now, by the Saints into their armies taken:
Before, for an unworthy man mistaken;
    Now, worthy to be God confest; before,
    With blasphemies by all the basest lore;
Now, worshippèd by Angels that him low adore.

[From CHRIST'S TRIUMPH AFTER DEATH.]

[1] exhale.

JOHN WEBSTER [1580?–1625?]

DIRGE

CALL for the robin-redbreast and the wren,
Since o'er shady groves they hover
And with leaves and flowers do cover
The friendless bodies of unburied men.
Call unto his funeral dole
The ant, the field-mouse, and the mole
To rear him hillocks that shall keep him warm
And (when gay tombs are robb'd) sustain no harm;
But keep the wolf far thence that's foe to men,
For with his nails he'll dig them up again.

[From THE WHITE DEVIL.]

THREE ANONYMOUS LYRICS

I

O WALY, waly up the bank,
  And waly waly down the brae,
And waly waly yon burn-side
  Where I and my Love wont to gae!
I leant my back unto an aik,
  I thought it was a trusty tree;
But first it bow'd, and syne it brak,
  Sae my true Love did lichtly [1] me.

O waly waly, but love be bonny
  A little time while it is new;
But when 'tis auld, it waxeth cauld
  And fades awa' like morning dew.
O wherefore should I busk my head?
  Or wherefore should I kame my hair?
For my true Love has me forsook,
  And says he'll never loe me mair.

[1] slight.

Now Arthur-seat[2] sall be my bed;
   The sheets shall ne'er be prest by me:
Saint Anton's well sall be my drink,
   Since my true Love has forsaken me.
Marti'mas wind, when wilt thou blaw
   And shake the green leaves aff the tree?
O gentle Death, when wilt thou come?
   For of my life I am wearíe.

'Tis not the frost, that freezes fell,
   Nor blawing snaw's inclemencie;
'Tis not sic cauld that makes me cry,
   But my Love's heart grown cauld to me.
When we came in by Glasgow town
   We were a comely sight to see;
My Love was clad in the black velvét,
   And I mysell in cramasie.[3]

But had I wist, before I kist,
   That love had been sae ill to win;
I had lockt my heart in a case of gowd
   And pinn'd it with a siller pin.
And, O! if my young babe were born,
   And set upon the nurse's knee,
And I mysell were dead and gane,
   And the green grass growing over me!

II

MY Love in her attire doth shew her wit,
It doth so well become her:
For every season she hath dressings fit,
For winter, spring, and summer.
   No beauty she doth miss
   When all her robes are on:
   But Beauty's self she is
   When all her robes are gone.

[2] Arthur's Seat is a hill near Edinburgh: on one of its slopes is Saint Anton's well.
[3] crimson.

III

LADY, when I behold the roses sprouting
    Which clad in damask mantles deck the arbours,
    And then behold your lips where sweet love harbours,
  My eyes present me with a double doubting:
For viewing both alike, hardly my mind supposes
Whether the roses be your lips, or your lips the roses.

WILLIAM DRUMMOND [1585–1649]

SUMMONS TO LOVE

PHŒBUS, arise!
And paint the sable skies
With azure, white, and red:
Rouse Memnon's mother from her Tithon's bed
That she may thy career with roses spread:
The nightingales thy coming each-where sing:
Make an eternal Spring!
Give life to this dark world which lieth dead;
Spread forth thy golden hair
In larger locks than thou wast wont before,
And emperor-like decore
With diadem of pearl thy temples fair:
Chase hence the ugly night
Which serves but to make dear thy glorious light.

—This is that happy morn,
That day, long-wishèd day
Of all my life so dark,
(If cruel stars have not my ruin sworn
And fates my hopes betray),
Which, purely white, deserves
An everlasting diamond should it mark.
This is the morn should bring unto this grove
My Love, to hear and recompense my love.

Fair King, who all preserves,
But show thy blushing beams,
And thou two sweeter eyes
Shalt see than those which by Penèus' streams
Did once thy heart surprise.
Now, Flora, deck thyself in fairest guise:
If that ye winds would hear
A voice surpassing far Amphion's lyre,
Your furious chiding stay;
Let Zephyr only breathe,
And with her tresses play.
—The winds all silent are,
And Phoebus in his chair
Ensaffroning sea and air
Makes vanish every star:
Night like a drunkard reels
Beyond the hills, to shun his flaming wheels:
The fields with flowers are deck'd in every hue,
The clouds with orient gold spangle their blue;
Here is the pleasant place—
And nothing wanting is, save She, alas!

HUMAN FOLLY

OF this fair volume which we World do name
If we the sheets and leaves could turn with care,
Of Him who it corrects, and did it frame,
We clear might read the art and wisdom rare:
Find out His power which wildest powers doth tame,
His providence extending everywhere,
His justice which proud rebels doth not spare,
In every page, no period of the same.
But silly we, like foolish children, rest
Well pleased with colour'd vellum, leaves of gold,
Fair dangling ribbands, leaving what is best,
On the great Writer's sense ne'er taking hold;
  Or if by chance we stay our minds on aught,
  It is some picture on the margin wrought.

SAINT JOHN BAPTIST

THE last and greatest herald of Heaven's King
Girt with rough skins, hies to the deserts wild,
Among that savage brood the woods forth bring,
Which he more harmless found than man, and mild.
His food was locusts, and what there doth spring,
With honey that from virgin hives distill'd;
Parch'd body, hollow eyes, some uncouth thing
Made him appear, long since from earth exiled.
There burst he forth: "All ye whose hopes rely
On God, with me amidst these deserts mourn,
Repent, repent, and from old errors turn!"
Who listen'd to his voice, obey'd his cry?
   Only the echoes, which he made relent,
   Rung from their flinty caves, "Repent! Repent!"

GEORGE WITHER [1588–1667]

THE LOVER'S RESOLUTION

SHALL I, wasting in despair,
Die, because a woman's fair?
Or make pale my cheeks with care,
'Cause another's rosy are?
Be she fairer than the day,
Or the flowery meads in May,
   If she be not so to me,
   What care I how fair she be?

Should my seely heart be pined,
'Cause I see a woman kind?
Or a well-disposèd nature
Joinèd with a lovely feature?
Be she meeker, kinder than
Turtle dove, or pelican,
   If she be not so to me,
   What care I how kind she be?

Shall a woman's virtues move
Me to perish for her love?
Or her well-deservings known
Make me quite forget mine own?
Be she with that goodness blest
Which may gain her name of best,
    If she be not such to me,
    What care I how good she be?

'Cause her fortune seems too high,
Shall I play the fool, and die?
He that bears a noble mind,
If not outward helps he find,
Thinks what, with them, he would do,
That, without them, dares her woo.
    And unless that mind I see,
    What care I though great she be?

Great, or good, or kind, or fair,
I will ne'er the more despair!
If she love me (this believe!)
I will die, ere she shall grieve!
If she slight me when I woo,
I can scorn, and let her go!
    For if she be not for me,
    What care I for whom she be?

WILLIAM BROWNE [1591–1643]

MAN

LIKE to a silkworm of one year,
Or like a wrongèd lover's tear,
Or on the waves a rudder's dint,
Or like the sparkles of a flint,
Or like to little cakes perfumed,
Or fireworks made to be consumed—

Even such is man, and all that trust
In weak and animated dust.
The silkworm droops; the tear's soon shed;
The ship's way lost; the sparkle dead;
The cake is burnt; the firework done;
And man as these as quickly gone.

ON A ROPE–MAKER HANGED

HERE lies a man much wronged in his hopes,
Who got his wealth backwards by making of ropes:
It was his hard chance in his fortunes to falter
For he lived by the ropes, and died by the halter.

ON THE COUNTESS DOWAGER OF PEMBROKE*

UNDERNEATH this sable hearse
Lies the subject of all verse:
SIDNEY'S sister, PEMBROKE'S mother:
Death, ere thou hast slain another
Fair and learned and good as she,
Time shall throw a dart at thee.

Marble piles let no man raise
To her name: for after days
Some kind woman, born as she,
Reading this, like Niobe
Shall turn marble, and become
Both her mourner and her tomb.

---

*For upward of a century this epitaph has been ascribed to Ben Jonson. Its authorship was eventually established when it was found in a MS. in Trinity College, Dublin, signed with Browne's name. The second, and vastly inferior sextain, is possibly by another hand, that of the (then) Earl of Pembroke.

ROBERT HERRICK [1591–1674]

CHERRY–RIPE

CHERRY-RIPE, ripe, ripe, I cry,
Full and fair ones, come and buy!
If so be you ask me where
They do grow, I answer, "There,
Where my Julia's lips do smile;
There's the land, or cherry-isle,
Whose plantations fully show
All the year where cherries grow."

HOW ROSES CAME RED

ROSES at first were white,
  Till they could not agree
Whether my Sapho's breast
  Or they more white should be.

But being vanquished quite,
  A blush their cheeks bespread;
Since which, believe the rest,
  The roses first came red.

SWEET DISORDER

A SWEET disorder in the dress
Kindles in clothes a wantonness:
A lawn about the shoulders thrown
Into a fine distraction—
An erring lace, which here and there
Enthrals the crimson stomacher—
A cuff neglectful, and thereby
Ribbands to flow confusedly—
A winning wave, deserving note,
In the tempestuous petticoat—

A careless shoe-string, in whose tie
I see a wild civility—
Do more bewitch me than when art
Is too precise in every part.

UPON JULIA'S CLOTHES

WHENAS in silks my Julia goes
Then, then (methinks) how sweetly flows
The liquefaction of her clothes.

Next, when I cast mine eyes and see
That brave vibration each way free;
O how that glittering taketh me!

TO THE VIRGINS TO MAKE MUCH OF TIME

GATHER ye rosebuds while ye may,
   Old Time is still a-flying:
And this same flower that smiles to-day
   To-morrow will be dying.

The glorious lamp of heaven, the sun,
   The higher he's a-getting
The sooner will his race be run,
   And nearer he's to setting.

That age is best which is the first,
   When youth and blood are warmer;
But being spent, the worse, and worst
   Times, still succeed the former.

Then be not coy, but use your time;
   And while ye may, go marry:
For having lost but once your prime,
   You may for ever tarry.

TO DAFFODILS

FAIR Daffodils! we weep to see
  You haste away so soon;
As yet the early-rising sun
  Has not attained his noon.
   Stay, stay,
  Until the hasting day
   Has run
  But to the even-song;
And, having prayed together, we
  Will go with you along.

We have short time to stay, as you;
  We have as short a spring;
As quick a growth to meet decay
  As you, or any thing.
   We die,
  As your hours do, and dry
   Away
  Like to the summer's rain;
Or as the pearls of morning's dew
  Ne'er to be found again.

A NIGHT PIECE

HER eyes the glowworm lend thee,
The shooting stars attend thee;
  And the elves also,
  Whose little eyes glow
Like the sparks of fire, befriend thee.

No Will-o'-th'-Wisp mislight thee,
Nor snake or slowworm bite thee;
  But on, on thy way,
  Not making a stay,
Since ghost there's none to affright thee.

Let not the dark thee cumber;
What though the moon does slumber?
   The stars of the night
   Will lend thee their light,
Like tapers clear, without number.

Then, Julia, let me woo thee,
Thus, thus to come unto me;
   And when I shall meet
   Thy silvery feet,
My soul I'll pour into thee.

A THANKSGIVING TO GOD FOR HIS HOUSE

LORD, Thou hast given me a cell
   Wherein to dwell,
A little house, whose humble roof
   Is weather-proof,
Under the spars of which I lie
   Both soft and dry;
Where Thou, my chamber for to ward,
   Hast set a guard
Of harmless thoughts, to watch and keep
   Me while I sleep.
Low is my porch, as is my fate,
   Both void of state;
And yet the threshold of my door
   Is worn by th' poor,
Who thither come, and freely get
   Good words or meat.
Like as my parlour so my hall
   And kitchen's small;
A little buttery, and therein
   A little bin,
Which keeps my little loaf of bread
   Unchipp'd, unflead;
Some little sticks of thorn or briar
   Make me a fire,

Close by whose living coal I sit,
  And glow like it.
Lord, I confess too, when I dine,
  The pulse is Thine,
And all those other bits that be
  There placed by Thee;
The worts, the purslain, and the mess
  Of water-cress,
Which of Thy kindness Thou hast sent;
  And my content
Makes those, and my beloved beet,
  To be more sweet.
'Tis Thou that crown'st my glittering hearth
  With guiltless mirth,
And giv'st me wassail bowls to drink,
  Spiced to the brink.
Lord, 'tis Thy plenty-dropping hand
  That soils my land,
And giv'st me, for my bushel sown,
  Twice ten for one;
Thou mak'st my teeming hen to lay
  Her egg each day;
Besides my healthful ewes to bear
  Me twins each year;
The while the conduits of my kine
  Run cream, for wine.
All these, and better, Thou dost send
  Me, to this end,
That I should render, for my part,
  A thankful heart;
Which, fired with incense, I resign,
  As wholly thine.
But the acceptance, that must be,
  My Christ, by Thee.

CORINNA'S GOING A–MAYING

GET up, get up for shame! The blooming morn
Upon her wings presents the god unshorn.
    See how Aurora throws her fair
    Fresh-quilted colours through the air:
    Get up, sweet slug-a-bed, and see
    The dew bespangling herb and tree.
Each flower has wept and bowèd toward the east
Above an hour since: yet you not dressed;
    Nay! not so much as out of bed?
    When all the birds have matins said
    And sung their thankful hymns, 'tis sin,
    Nay, profanation, to keep in,
Whenas a thousand virgins on this day
Spring, sooner than the lark, to fetch in May.

Rise, and put on your foliage, and be seen
To come forth, like the spring-time, fresh and green,
    And sweet as Flora. Take no care
    For jewels for your gown or hair:
    Fear not; the leaves will strew
    Gems in abundance upon you:
Besides, the childhood of the day has kept,
Against you come, some orient pearls unwept;
    Come and receive them while the light
    Hangs on the dew-locks of the night:
    And Titan on the eastern hill
    Retires himself, or else stands still
Till you come forth. Wash, dress, be brief in praying:
Few beads are best when once we go a-Maying.

Come, my Corinna, come; and, coming mark
How each field turns a street, each street a park
    Made green and trimm'd with trees; see how
    Devotion gives each house a bough
    Or branch: each porch, each door, ere this
    An ark, a tabernacle is,

Made up of white-thorn, neatly interwove;
As if here were those cooler shades of love.
    Can such delights be in the street
    And open fields and we not see 't?
    Come, we'll abroad; and let's obey
    The proclamation made for May:
And sin no more, as we have done, by staying;
But, my Corinna, come, let's go a-Maying.

There's not a budding boy or girl this day
But is got up, and gone to bring in May.
    A deal of youth, ere this, is come
    Back, and with white-thorn laden, home.
    Some have despatch'd their cakes and cream
    Before that we have left to dream:
And some have wept, and wooed, and plighted troth,
And chose their priest, ere we can cast off sloth:
    Many a green-gown has been given;
    Many a kiss, both odd and even:
    Many a glance too has been sent
    From out the eye, love's firmament;
Many a jest told of the keys betraying
This night, and locks pick'd, yet we're not a-Maying.

Come, let us go while we are in our prime;
And take the harmless folly of the time.
    We shall grow old apace, and die
    Before we know our liberty.
    Our life is short, and our days run
    As fast away as does the sun;
And, as a vapour or a drop of rain,
Once lost, can ne'er be found again,
    So when or you or I are made
    A fable, song, or fleeting shade,
    All love, all liking, all delight
    Lies drown'd with us in endless night.
Then while time serves, and we are but decaying,
Come, my Corinna, come let's go a-Maying.

UPON PREW HIS MAID

IN this little urn is laid
Prewdence Baldwin, once my maid,
From whose happy spark here let
Spring the purple violet.

FRANCIS QUARLES [1592–1644]

AN ECSTASY

E'EN like two little bank-dividing brooks,
    That wash the pebbles with their wanton streams,
And having ranged and search'd a thousand nooks,
    Meet both at length in silver-breasted Thames,
      Where in a greater current they conjoin:
So I my Best-belovèd's am; so He is mine.

E'en so we met; and after long pursuit,
    E'en so we joined; we both became entire;
No need for either to renew a suit,
    For I was flax, and He was flames of fire:
      Our firm-united souls did more than twine;
So I my Best-belovèd's am; so He is mine.

If all those glittering monarchs, that command
    The servile quarters of this earthly ball,
Should tender in exchange their shares of land,
    I would not change my fortunes for them all:
      Their wealth is but a counter to my coin:
The world's but theirs; but my Belovèd's mine.

GEORGE HERBERT [1593–1633]

VIRTUE

SWEET day, so cool, so calm, so bright,
    The bridal of the earth and sky!
The dew shall weep thy fall to-night;
    For thou must die.

Sweet rose, whose hue, angry and brave,
    Bids the rash gazer wipe his eye,
Thy root is ever in its grave,
    And thou must die.

Sweet spring, full of sweet days and roses,
    A box where sweets compacted lie,
My music shows ye have your closes,
    And all must die.

Only a sweet and virtuous soul,
    Like seasoned timber, never gives;
But though the whole world turn to coal,
    Then chiefly lives.

THE COLLAR

I STRUCK the board, and cry'd "No more!
        I will abroad.
What? shall I ever sigh and pine?
My lines and life are free; free as the road,
  Loose as the wind, as large as store.[1]
        Shall I be still in suit?
  Have I no harvest but a thorn
  To let me blood, and not restore,
What I have lost, with cordial fruit?
        Sure there was wine

[1] abundance.

Before my sighs did dry it: there was corn
Before my tears did drown it.
Is the year only lost to me?
Have I no bays to crown it?
No flowers, no garlands gay? All blasted?
All wasted?
Not so, my heart! but there is fruit,
And thou hast hands.
Recover all thy sigh-blown age
On double pleasures. Leave thy cold dispute
Of what is fit and not. Forsake thy cage;
Thy rope of sands
Which petty thoughts have made, and made to thee
Good cable, to enforce and draw,
And be thy law,
While thou didst wink and wouldst not see.
Away! Take heed!
I will abroad.
Call in thy death's-head there. Tie up thy fears.
He that forbears
To suit and serve his need
Deserves his load."
But as I raved, and grew more fierce and wild
At every word,
Methought I heard one calling, "Child."
And I reply'd, "My Lord."

THE QUIP

THE merry World did on a day
With his train-bands and mates agree
To meet together where I lay,
And all in sport to jeer at me.

First, Beauty crept into a rose;
Which when I pluckt not, "Sir," said she,
"Tell me, I pray, whose hands are those?"
But Thou shalt answer, Lord, for me.

Then Money came, and chinking still,
"What tune is this, poor man?" said he:
"I heard in Music you had skill."
But Thou shalt answer, Lord, for me.

Then came brave Glory puffing by
In silks that whistled, who but he!
He scarce allow'd me half an eye.
But Thou shalt answer, Lord, for me.

Then came quick Wit and Conversation,
And he would needs a comfort be,
And, to be short, make an oration.
But Thou shalt answer, Lord, for me.

Yet when the hour of Thy design
To answer these fine things shall come,
Speak not at large: say, " I am Thine; "
And then they have their answer home.

THE PULLEY

WHEN God at first made man,
Having a glass of Blessings standing by;
"Let us," said he, "pour on him all we can:
Let the world's riches, which dispersèd lie,
    Contract into a span."

So Strength first made a way;
Then Beauty flow'd; then Wisdom, Honour, Pleasure.
    When almost all was out, God made a stay,
Perceiving that alone, of all his treasure,
    Rest in the bottom lay.

"For if I should," said he,
"Bestow this jewel also on my creature,
    He would adore my gifts instead of me,
And rest in Nature, not the God of Nature;
    So both should losers be.

"Yet let him keep the rest,
But keep them with repining restlessness;
    Let him be rich and weary, that at least,
If goodness lead him not, yet weariness
    May toss him to my breast."

DIVINE LOVE

THOU art too hard for me in Love.
There is no dealing with Thee in that art.
    That is Thy masterpiece, I see.
    When I contrive and plot to prove
Something that may be conquest on my part,
    Thou still, O Lord, outstrippest me.

Sometimes, whenas I wash, I say,—
And shrodely[1] as I think,—Lord, wash my soul,
    More spotted than my flesh can be!
    But then there comes into my way
Thy ancient baptism, which when I was foul
    And knew it not, yet cleansèd me.

I took a time when Thou didst sleep,
Great waves of trouble combating my breast:
    I thought it brave to praise Thee then.
    Yet then I found that Thou didst creep
Into my heart with joy, giving more rest
    Than flesh did lend Thee back again.

Let me but once the conquest have
Upon the matter, 'twill Thy conquest prove.
    If Thou subdue mortality,
    Thou dost no more than doth the grave;
Whereas if I o'ercome Thee and Thy love,
    Hell, death, and devil come short of me.

---

[1] shrewdly.

LOVE'S ANSWER

LOVE bade me welcome; yet my soul drew back,
     Guilty of dust and sin.
But quick-eyed Love, observing me grow slack
     From my first entrance in,
Drew nearer to me, sweetly questioning,
     If I lack'd anything.

"A guest," I answer'd, "worthy to be here:"
     Love said, "You shall be he."
"I, the unkind, ungrateful? Ah, my dear,
     I cannot look on Thee!"
Love took my hand and smiling did reply,
     "Who made the eyes but I?"

"Truth, Lord; but I have marr'd them: let my shame
     Go where it doth deserve."
"And know you not," says Love, "who bore the blame?"
     "My dear, then I will serve."
"You must sit down," says Love, "and taste my meat."
     So I did sit and eat.

JAMES SHIRLEY [1596–1666]

THE GLORIES OF OUR BLOOD AND STATE

THE glories of our blood and state
     Are shadows, not substantial things;
There is no armour against fate;
     Death lays his icy hand on kings:
       Sceptre and crown
       Must tumble down,
And in the dust be equal made
With the poor crooked scythe and spade.

Some men with swords may reap the field,
　　And plant fresh laurels where they kill:
But their strong nerves at last must yield;
　　They tame but one another still:
　　　　Early or late
　　　　They stoop to fate,
And must give up their murmuring breath
When they, pale captives, creep to death.

The garlands wither on your brow;
　　Then boast no more your mighty deeds;
Upon Death's purple altar now
　　See where the victor-victim bleeds:
　　　　Your heads must come
　　　　To the cold tomb;
Only the actions of the just
Smell sweet, and blossom in their dust.

[From THE CONTENTION OF AJAX AND ULYSSES.]

THOMAS CAREW [1598?–1639?]

SONG

Ask me no more where Jove bestows,
When June is past, the fading rose,
For in your beauty's orient deep
These flowers, as in their causes, sleep.

Ask me no more whither do stray
The golden atoms of the day,
For, in pure love, heaven did prepare
Those powders to enrich your hair.

Ask me no more whither doth haste
The nightingale when May is past,
For in your sweet dividing throat
She winters and keeps warm her note.

Ask me no more where those stars light
That downwards fall in dead of night,
For in your eyes they sit, and there
Fixed become as in their sphere.

Ask me no more if east or west
The Phœnix builds her spicy nest,
For unto you at last she flies,
And in your fragrant bosom dies.

INGRATEFUL BEAUTY THREATENED

KNOW, Celia, since thou art so proud,
　'Twas I that gave thee thy renown.
Thou hadst in the forgotten crowd
　Of common beauties lived unknown,
Had not my verse exhaled thy name,
And with it imp'd the wings of Fame.

That killing power is none of thine;
　I gave it to thy voice and eyes;
Thy sweets, thy graces, all are mine;
　Thou art my star, shin'st in my skies;
Then dart not from thy borrow'd sphere
Lightning on him that fixt thee there.

Tempt me with such affrights no more,
　Lest what I made I uncreate;
Let fools thy mystic form adore,
　I know thee in thy mortal state.
Wise poets, that wrapt Truth in tales,
Knew her themselves through all her veils.

AN EPITAPH

THIS little vault, this narrow room,
Of love and beauty is the tomb;
The dawning beam, that 'gan to clear
Our clouded sky, lies darken'd here;
For ever set to us: by death
Sent to enflame the world beneath.
'Twas but a bud, yet did contain
More sweetness than shall spring again;
A budding star, that might have grown
Into a sun when it had blown.
This hopeful beauty did create
New life in love's declining state;
But now his empire ends, and we
From fire and wounding darts are free;
His brand, his bow, let no man fear:
The flames, the arrows, all lie here.

WILLIAM HABINGTON [1605–1654]

TO ROSES IN THE BOSOM OF CASTARA

YE blushing virgins happy are
In the chaste nunn'ry of her breasts,
For he'd profane so chaste a fair,
Who e'er should call them Cupid's nests.

Transplanted thus how bright ye grow,
How rich a perfume do ye yield!
In some close garden cowslips so
Are sweeter than i' th' open field.

In those white cloisters live secure
From the rude blasts of wanton breath,
Each hour more innocent and pure,
Till you shall wither into death.

Then that which living gave you room
Your glorious sepulchre shall be:
There wants no marble for a tomb,
Whose breast has marble been to me.

SIR WILLIAM DAVENANT [1606–1668]

SONG

THE lark now leaves his wat'ry nest,
  And climbing, shakes his dewy wings,
He takes this window for the east,
  And to implore your light, he sings.
Awake! Awake! the morn will never rise,
Till she can dress her beauty at your eyes.

The merchant bows unto the seaman's star,
  The ploughman from the sun his season takes;
But still the lover wonders what they are
  Who look for day before his mistress wakes.
Awake! Awake! break through your veils of lawn!
Then draw your curtains and begin the dawn!

ABRAHAM COWLEY [1618–1667]

DRINKING

THE thirsty earth soaks up the rain,
And drinks, and gapes for drink again,
The plants suck in the earth, and are
With constant drinking fresh and fair:
The sea itself (which one would think
Should have but little need of drink)
Drinks twice ten thousand rivers up,
So fill'd that they o'erflow the cup:
The busy sun (and one would guess
By 's drunken fiery face no less)

Drinks up the sea, and when he's done,
The moon and stars drink up the sun:
They drink and dance by their own light,
They drink and revel all the night:
Nothing in Nature 's sober found,
But an eternal health goes round.
—Fill up the bowl then! fill it high!
Fill all the glasses there! for why
Should every creature drink but I?
Why, man of morals, tell me why?

[From ANACREONTIQUES.]

THE WISH

WELL then! I now do plainly see
This busy world and I shall ne'er agree.
The very honey of all earthly joy
Does of all meats the soonest cloy;
    And they, methinks, deserve my pity
Who for it can endure the stings,
The crowd and buzz and murmurings,
    Of this great hive, the city.

Ah, yet, ere I descend to th' grave
May I a small house and large garden have;
And a few friends, and many books; both true,
Both wise, and both delightful too!
    And since love ne'er will from me flee,
A Mistress moderately fair,
And good as guardian-angels are,
    Only beloved and loving me.

O founts! O when in you shall I
Myself, eased of unpeaceful thoughts, espy?
O fields! O woods! when, when shall I be made
The happy tenant of your shade?
    Here's the spring-head of pleasure's flood:

[Here's wealthy Nature's treasury,] *
Where all the riches lie that she
          Has coin'd and stamp'd for good.

Pride and ambition here
Only in far-fetch'd metaphors appear;
Here nought but winds can hurtful murmurs scatter,
And nought but echo flatter.
          The Gods, when they descend, hither
From heaven did always choose their way:
And therefore we may boldly say
          That 'tis the way too thither.

How happy here should I
And one dear She live, and embracing die!
She who is all the world, and can exclude,
In deserts, solitude.
          I should have then this only fear:
Lest men, when they my pleasures see,
Should hither throng to live like me,
          And so make a city here.

ON THE DEATH OF MR. WILLIAM HERVEY

It was a dismal and a fearful night,—
Scarce could the morn drive on th' unwilling light,
When sleep, death's image, left my troubled breast,
          By something liker death possest.
My eyes with tears did uncommanded flow,
          And on my soul hung the dull weight
          Of some intolerable fate.
What bell was that? Ah me! Too much I know!

My sweet companion, and my gentle peer,
Why hast thou left me thus unkindly here,

---

* This line, which modern editors print, does not appear in any of the earlier
editions of Cowley.

Thy end for ever, and my life, to moan?
　　O thou hast left me all alone!
Thy soul and body, when death's agony
　　　Besieged around thy noble heart,
　　　Did not with more reluctance part
Than I, my dearest friend, do part from thee.

Ye fields of Cambridge, our dear Cambridge, say,
Have ye not seen us walking every day?
Was there a tree about which did not know
　　　The love betwixt us two?
Henceforth, ye gentle trees, for ever fade,
　　　Or your sad branches thicker join,
　　　And into darksome shades combine,
Dark as the grave wherein my friend is laid.

Large was his soul; as large a soul as e'er
Submitted to inform a body here;
High as the place 'twas shortly in heaven to have,
　　　But low and humble as his grave;
So high that all the virtues there did come
　　　As to their chiefest seat
　　　Conspicuous, and great;
So low that for me too it made a room.

Knowledge he only sought, and so soon caught,
As if for him knowledge had rather sought;
Nor did more learning ever crowded lie
　　　In such a short mortality.
Whene'er the skilful youth discoursed or writ,
　　　Still did the notions throng
　　　About his eloquent tongue;
Nor could his ink flow faster than his wit.

His mirth was the pure spirits of various wit,
Yet never did his God or friends forget.
And when deep talk and wisdom came in view,
　　　Retired, and gave to them their due.

For the rich help of books he always took,
  Though his own searching mind before
  Was so with notions written o'er,
As if wise Nature had made that her book.

With as much zeal, devotion, piety,
He always lived, as other saints do die.
Still with his soul severe account he kept,
  Weeping all debts out ere he slept.
Then down in peace and innocence he lay,
  Like the sun's labourious light,
  Which still in water sets at night.
Unsullied with his journey of the day.

     [From the poem of the same title.]

SIR JOHN DENHAM [1615–1669]

THE RIVER THAMES

MY eye, descending from the hill, surveys
Where Thames amongst the wanton valleys strays;
Thames, the most loved of all the Ocean's sons,
By his old sire, to his embraces runs,
Hasting to pay his tribute to the sea,
Like mortal life to meet Eternity;
Though with those streams he no resemblance hold,
Whose foam is amber, and their gravel gold,
His genuine and less guilty wealth t' explore,
Search not his bottom, but survey his shore,
O'er which he kindly spreads his spacious wing,
And hatches plenty for th' ensuing spring;
Nor then destroys it with too fond a stay,
Like mothers which their infants overlay,
Nor, with a sudden and impetuous wave,
Like profuse kings, resumes the wealth he gave;
No unexpected inundations spoil
The mower's hopes, nor mock the ploughman's toil,
But godlike his unwearied bounty flows,
First loves to do, then loves the good he does;

Nor are his blessings to his banks confined,
But free and common as the sea or wind;
When he to boast or to disperse his stores,
Full of the tributes of his grateful shores,
Visits the world, and in his flying towers,
Brings home to us, and makes both Indies ours,
Finds wealth where 'tis, bestows it where it wants,
Cities in deserts, woods in cities plants;
So that to us no thing, no place is strange,
While his fair bosom is the world's exchange.
O could I flow like thee, and make thy stream
My great example, as it is my theme!
Though deep, yet clear, though gentle, yet not dull,
Strong without rage, without o'erflowing full.

[From COOPER'S HILL.]

EDMUND WALLER [1606–1687]

TO PHYLLIS

PHYLLIS! why should we delay
Pleasures shorter than the day?
Could we (which we never can)
Stretch our lives beyond their span,
Beauty like a shadow flies,
And our youth before us dies.
Or would youth and beauty stay,
Love hath wings, and will away.
Love hath swifter wings than Time;
Change in love to heaven does climb.
Gods, that never change their state,
Vary oft their love and hate.
Phyllis! to this truth we owe
All the love betwixt us two.
Let not you and I inquire
What has been our past desire;
On what shepherds you have smiled,
Or what nymphs I have beguiled;

Leave it to the planets too,
What we shall hereafter do;
For the joys we now may prove,
Take advice of present love.

ON A GIRDLE

THAT which her slender waist confined,
Shall now my joyful temples bind;
No monarch but would give his crown
His arms might do what this has done.

It was my Heaven's extremest sphere,
The pale which held that lovely deer;
My joy, my grief, my hope, my love,
Did all within this circle move.

A narrow compass! and yet there
Dwelt all that's good, and all that's fair;
Give me but what this ribband bound,
Take all the rest the sun goes round.

GO, LOVELY ROSE

Go, lovely Rose!
Tell her that wastes her time and me,
That now she knows,
When I resemble her to thee
How sweet and fair she seems to be.

Tell her that's young,
And shuns to have her graces spied,
That had'st thou sprung
In deserts where no men abide,
Thou must have uncommended died.

Small is the worth
Of beauty from the light retired;

Bid her come forth!
Suffer herself to be desired,
And not blush so to be admired.

Then die: that she
The common fate of all things rare
May read in thee;
How small a part of time they share,
They are so wondrous sweet and fair.

SIR JOHN SUCKLING [1609–1642]

A REFUSAL OF MARTYRDOM

O FOR some honest lover's ghost,
  Some kind unbodied post
      Sent from the shades below!
      I strangely long to know
Whether the nobler chaplets wear,
Those that their mistress' scorn did bear
      Or those that were used kindly.

For whatsoe'er they tell us here
  To make those sufferings dear,
      'Twill there, I fear, be found
      That to the being crown'd
T' have loved alone will not suffice,
Unless we also have been wise
      And have our loves enjoy'd.

What posture can we think him in
  That, here unloved, again
      Departs, and 's thither gone
      Where each sits by his own?
Or how can that Elysium be
Where I my mistress still must see
      Circled in other's arms?

For there the judges all are just,
  And Sophronisba must
    Be his whom she held dear,
    Not his who loved her here.
The sweet Philoclea, since she died,
Lies by her Pirocles his side,
    Not by Amphialus.

Some bays, perchance, or myrtle bough
  For difference crowns the brow
    Of those kind souls that were
    The noble martyrs here:
And if that be the only odds
(As who can tell?), ye kinder gods,
    Give me the woman here!

THE CONSTANT LOVER

OUT upon it! I have loved
  Three whole days together!
And am like to love three more,
  If it prove fair weather.

Time shall moult away his wings
  Ere he shall discover
In the whole wide world again
  Such a constant lover.

But the spite on't is, no praise
  Is due at all to me:
Love with me had made no stays,
  Had it any been but she.

Had it any been but she,
  And that very face,
There had been at least ere this
  A dozen dozen in her place.

WHY SO PALE AND WAN

WHY so pale and wan, fond lover?
    Prythee, why so pale?
Will, if looking well can't move her,
    Looking ill prevail?
    Prythee, why so pale?

Why so dull and mute, young sinner?
    Prythee, why so mute?
Will, when speaking well can't win her,
    Saying nothing do't?
    Prythee, why so mute?

Quit, quit, for shame! This will not move;
    This cannot take her.
If of herself she will not love,
    Nothing can make her:
    The D—l take her!

                        [From AGLAURA.]

WILLIAM CARTWRIGHT [1611–1643]

ON A VIRTUOUS YOUNG GENTLEWOMAN THAT DIED SUDDENLY

WHEN the old flaming Prophet climb'd the sky,
Who, at one glimpse, did vanish, and not die,
He made more preface to a death than this:
So far from sick, she did not breathe amiss.
She, who to Heaven more heaven doth annex,
Whose lowest thought was above all our sex,
Accounted nothing death but t' be repriev'd,
And died as free from sickness as she lived.
Others are dragg'd away, or must be driven,
She only saw her time and stept to Heaven,
Where Seraphim view all her glories o'er
As one return'd, that had been there before.

For while she did this lower world adorn,
Her body seem'd rather assumed than born:
So rarefied, advanced, so pure and whole,
That body might have been another's soul;
And equally a miracle it were,
That she could die, or that she could live here.

RICHARD CRASHAW [1613?–1649]

THE FLAMING HEART

UPON THE BOOK AND PICTURE OF THE SERAPHICAL SAINT TERESA

LIVE in these conquering leaves: live all the same;
And walk through all tongues one triumphant flame;
Live here, great Heart; and love, and die, and kill:
And bleed, and wound, and yield, and conquer still.
Let this immortal life where'er it comes
Walk in a crowd of loves and martyrdoms.
Let mystic deaths wait on't; and wise souls be
The love-slain witnesses of this life of thee.
O sweet Incendiary! show here thy art
Upon this carcase of a hard cold heart;
Let all thy scatter'd shafts of light, that play
Among the leaves of thy large books of day,
Combined against this breast at once break in,
And take away from me myself and sin;
This gracious robbery shall thy bounty be
And my best fortunes such fair spoils of me.
O thou undaunted Daughter of Desires!
By all thy dower of lights and fires;
By all the eagle in thee, all the dove;
By all thy lives and deaths of love;
By thy large draughts of intellectual day,
And by thy thirsts of love more large than they;
By all thy brim-filled bowls of fierce desire,
By thy last morning's draught of liquid fire;

By the full kingdom of that final kiss
That seized thy parting soul, and sealed thee His;
By all the Heav'n thou hast in Him
(Fair sister of the Seraphim!);
By all of Him we have in thee;
Leave nothing of myself in me.
Let me so read thy life, that I
Unto all life of mine may die!

[From THE FLAMING HEART, etc.]

RICHARD LOVELACE [1618–1658]

TO LUCASTA ON GOING TO THE WARS

TELL me not, Sweet, I am unkind,
  That from the nunnery
Of thy chaste breast and quiet mind
  To war and arms I fly.

True, a new mistress now I chase,
  The first foe in the field;
And with a stronger faith embrace
  A sword, a horse, a shield.

Yet this inconstancy is such
  As you too shall adore—
I could not love thee, Dear, so much,
  Loved I not honour more.

TO LUCASTA ON GOING BEYOND SEAS

IF to be absent were to be
    Away from thee;
  Or that when I am gone
  You or I were alone;
Then, my Lucasta, might I crave
Pity from blustering wind, or swallowing wave.

But I'll not sigh one blast or gale
    To swell my sail,
  Or pay a tear to 'suage
  The foaming blue-god's rage;
For whether he will let me pass
Or no, I'm still as happy as I was.

  Though seas and land betwixt us both,
    Our faith and troth,
  Like separated souls,
  All time and space controls:
Above the highest sphere we meet
Unseen, unknown, and greet as Angels greet.

  So then we do anticipate
    Our after-fate,
  And are alive i' the skies,
  If thus our lips and eyes
Can speak like spirits unconfined
In Heaven, their earthy bodies left behind.

TO ALTHEA FROM PRISON

  WHEN love with unconfinèd wings
    Hovers within my gates,
  And my divine Althea brings
    To whisper at the grates;
  When I lie tangled in her hair,
    And fetter'd to her eye,
  The birds that wanton in the air
    Know no such liberty.

  When flowing cups run swiftly round
    With no allaying Thames,
  Our careless heads with roses crown'd,
    Our hearts with loyal flames;
  When thirsty grief in wine we steep,
    When healths and draughts go free—

Fishes that tipple in the deep
   Know no such liberty.

When, like committed linnets, I
   With shriller throat shall sing
The sweetness, mercy, majesty,
   And glories of my King;
When I shall voice aloud, how good
   He is, how great should be,
Enlargèd winds that curl the flood
   Know no such liberty.

Stone walls do not a prison make,
   Nor iron bars a cage;
Minds innocent and quiet take
   That for an hermitage;
If I have freedom in my love—
   And in my soul am free,
Angels alone, that soar above,
   Enjoy such liberty.

HENRY VAUGHAN [1622–1695]

THE RETREAT

HAPPY those early days, when I
Shined in my Angel-infancy!
Before I understood this place
Appointed for my second race,
Or taught my soul to fancy ought
But a white, celestial thought;
When yet I had not walk'd above
A mile or two, from my first love,
And looking back—at that short space—
Could see a glimpse of His bright face:
When on some gilded cloud or flower
My gazing soul would dwell an hour,

And in those weaker glories spy
Some shadows of eternity;
Before I taught my tongue to wound
My conscience with a sinful sound,
Or had the black art to dispense,
A sev'ral sin to ev'ry sense,
But felt through all this fleshly dress
Bright shoots of everlastingness.
    O how I long to travel back,
And tread again that ancient track!
That I might once more reach that plain,
Where first I left my glorious train;
From whence th' enlightened spirit sees
That shady City of Palm Trees.
But ah! my soul with too much stay
Is drunk, and staggers in the way!
Some men a forward motion love,
But I by backward steps will move;
And when this dust falls to the urn,
In that state I came, return.

DEPARTED FRIENDS

THEY are all gone into the world of Light,
    And I alone sit ling'ring here;
Their very memory is fair and bright,
    And my sad thoughts doth clear.

It glows and glitters in my cloudy breast,
    Like stars upon some gloomy grove,
Or those faint beams in which this hill is drest,
    After the sun's remove.

I see them walking in an air of glory,
    Whose light doth trample on my days:
My days, which are at best but dull and hoary,
    Mere glimmerings and decays.

O holy Hope, and high Humility,
    High as the heavens above!
These are your walks, and you have show'd them me,
    To kindle my cold love.

Dear, beauteous Death, the jewel of the just,
    Shining nowhere but in the dark;
What mysteries do lie beyond thy dust,
    Could man outlook that mark!

He that hath found some fledged bird's nest, may know
    At first sight if the bird be flown;
But what fair well or grove he sings in now,
    That is to him unknown.

And yet, as angels in some brighter dreams
    Call to the soul when man doth sleep,
So some strange thoughts transcend our wonted themes,
    And into glory peep.

If a star were confined into a tomb,
    The captive flames must needs burn there;
But when the hand that lock'd her up, gives room,
    She'll shine through all the sphere.

O Father of eternal life, and all
    Created glories under Thee!
Resume Thy spirit from this world of thrall
    Into true liberty.

Either disperse these mists, which blot and fill
    My perspective still as they pass;
Or else remove me hence unto that hill,
    Where I shall need no glass.

THE WORLD

I SAW Eternity the other night,
Like a great ring of pure and endless light,
  All calm, as it was bright;
And round beneath it, Time, in hours, days, years,
  Driv'n by the spheres
Like a vast shadow moved; in which the world
  And all her train were hurled.

The doting Lover in his quaintest strain
  Did there complain;
Near him, his lute, his fancy, and his flights,
  Wit's sour delights,
With gloves, and knots, the silly snares of pleasure,
  Yet his dear treasure,
All scatter'd lay, while he his eyes did pour
  Upon a flower.

The darksome Statesman, hung with weights and woe,
Like a thick midnight-fog, moved there so slow,
  He did not stay, nor go;
Condemning thoughts—like sad eclipses—scowl
  Upon his soul,
And clouds of crying witnesses without
  Pursued him with one shout.
Yet digg'd the mole, and lest his ways be found,
  Work'd under ground,
Where he did clutch his prey; but one did see
  That policy;
Churches and altars fed him; perjuries
  Were gnats and flies;
It rain'd about him blood and tears, but he
  Drank them as free.

The fearful Miser on a heap of rust
Sate pining all his life there, did scarce trust
  His own hands with the dust,

Yet would not place one piece alone, but lives
    In fear of thieves.
Thousands there were as frantic as himself,
    And hugg'd each one his pelf;
The downright Epicure placed heav'n in sense
    And scorn'd pretence;
While others, slipt into a wide excess,
    Said little less;
The weaker sort, slight trivial wares enslave,
    Who think them brave;
And poor despised Truth sate counting by
    Their victory.

Yet some, who all this while did weep and sing,
And sing, and weep, soar'd up into the ring;
    But most would use no wing.
O fools—said I—thus to prefer dark night
    Before true light!
To live in grots, and caves, and hate the day
    Because it shews the way,
The way, which from this dead and dark abode
    Leads up to God;
A way where you might tread the sun, and be
    More bright than he!
But as I did their madness so discuss
    One whisper'd thus,
"This ring the Bridegroom did for none provide,
    But for His bride."

JOHN MILTON [1608–1674]

L'ALLEGRO

HENCE, loathèd Melancholy,
  Of Cerberus and blackest Midnight born,
In Stygian cave forlorn
  'Mongst horrid shapes, and shrieks, and sights unholy!
Find out some uncouth cell
  Where brooding Darkness spreads his jealous wings
And the night-raven sings;
  There under ebon shades, and low-browed rocks
As ragged as thy locks,
  In dark Cimmerian desert ever dwell.

  But come, thou Goddess fair and free,
  In heaven ycleped Euphrosyne,
  And by men, heart-easing Mirth,
  Whom lovely Venus at a birth
  With two sister Graces more
  To ivy-crownèd Bacchus bore;
  Or whether (as some sager sing)
  The frolic wind that breathes the spring,
  Zephyr, with Aurora playing,
  As he met her once a-Maying,
  There on beds of violets blue
  And fresh-blown roses washt in dew
  Filled her with thee, a daughter fair,
  So buxom, blithe, and debonair.
  Haste thee, Nymph, and bring with thee
  Jest, and youthful jollity,
  Quips, and cranks, and wanton wiles,
  Nods, and becks, and wreathèd smiles
  Such as hang on Hebe's cheek,
  And love to live in dimple sleek;
  Sport that wrinkled Care derides,
  And Laughter holding both his sides.
  Come, and trip it as ye go
  On the light fantastic toe;

And in thy right hand lead with thee
The mountain Nymph, sweet Liberty;
And if I give thee honour due
Mirth, admit me of thy crew,
To live with her, and live with thee
In unreprovèd pleasures free;
To hear the lark begin his flight
And singing startle the dull night
From his watch-tower in the skies,
Till the dappled Dawn doth rise;
Then to come, in spite of sorrow,
And at my window bid good-morrow
Through the sweetbriar, or the vine,
Or the twisted eglantine:
While the cock with lively din
Scatters the rear of Darkness thin,
And to the stack, or the barn-door,
Stoutly struts his dames before:
Oft list'ning how the hounds and horn
Cheerly rouse the slumbring Morn,
From the side of some hoar hill,
Through the high wood echoing shrill:
Sometime walking, not unseen,
By hedge-row elms, on hillocks green,
Right against the eastern gate
Where the great Sun begins his state
Robed in flames and amber light,
The clouds in thousand liveries dight;
While the ploughman, near at hand,
Whistles o'er the furrowed land,
And the milkmaid singeth blithe,
And the mower whets his scythe,
And every shepherd tells his tale
Under the hawthorn in the dale.
  Straight mine eye hath caught new pleasures
Whilst the lantskip [1] round it measures:
Russet lawns,[2] and fallows gray,
Where the nibbling flocks do stray;

[1] landscape.   [2] pastures

Mountains, on whose barren breast
The labouring clouds do often rest;
Meadows trim with daisies pied,
Shallow brooks, and rivers wide;
Towers and battlements it sees
Bosomed high in tufted trees,
Where perhaps some Beauty lies,
The Cynosure of neighbouring eyes.
Hard by, a cottage chimney smokes
From betwixt two aged oaks,
Where Corydon and Thyrsis met
Are at their savoury dinner set
Of herbs and other country messes,
Which the neat-handed Phillis dresses;
And then in haste her bower she leaves
With Thestylis to bind the sheaves;
Or, if the earlier season lead,
To the tanned haycock in the mead.
  Sometimes with secure delight
The upland hamlets will invite,
When the merry bells ring round,
And the jocund rebecks [3] sound
To many a youth and many a maid,
Dancing in the chequered shade;
And young and old come forth to play
On a sun-shine holyday,
Till the live-long day-light fail:
Then to the spicy nut-brown ale,
With stories told of many a feat,
How fairy Mab the junkets eat:—
She was pincht and pulled, she said;
And he, by Friar's lantern led,
Tells how the drudging goblin sweat
To earn his cream-bowl duly set,
When in one night, ere glimpse of morn,
His shadowy flail hath threshed the corn
That ten day-labourers could not end;
Then lies him down, the lubbar fend,

[3] fiddles.

And stretcht out all the chimney's length,
Basks at the fire his hairy strength,
And crop-full out of doors he flings,
Ere the first cock his matin rings.

Thus done the tales, to bed they creep,
By whispering winds soon lulled asleep.

Towered cities please us then,
And the busy hum of men,
Where throngs of knights and barons bold,
In weeds of peace, high triumphs hold,
With store of ladies, whose bright eyes
Rain influence, and judge the prize
Of wit or arms, while both contend
To win her grace, whom all commend.
There let Hymen oft appear
In saffron robe, with taper clear,
And pomp, and feast, and revelry,
With mask and antique pageantry;
Such sights as youthful poets dream
On summer eves by haunted stream.
Then to the well-trod stage anon,
If Jonson's learnèd sock be on,
Or sweetest Shakspere, Fancy's child,
Warble his native wood-notes wild.

And ever against eating cares,
Lap me in soft Lydian airs,
Married to immortal verse,
Such as the meeting soul may pierce,
In notes with many a winding bout
Of linkèd sweetness long drawn out,
With wanton heed and giddy cunning,
The melting voice through mazes running,
Untwisting all the chains that tie
The hidden soul of harmony;
That Orpheus' self may heave his head
From golden slumber on a bed
Of heapt Elysian flowers, and hear
Such strains as would have won the ear

Of Pluto to have quite set free
His half-regained Eurydice.
   These delights if thou canst give,
Mirth, with thee I mean to live.

IL PENSEROSO

HENCE, vain deluding Joys,
   The brood of Folly without father bred!
How little you bestead,
   Or fill the fixèd mind with all your toys!
Dwell in some idle brain,
   And fancies fond with gaudy shapes possess,
As thick and numberless
   As the gay motes that people the sunbeams,
Or likest hovering dreams,
   The fickle pensioners of Morpheus' train.

   But hail, thou Goddess sage and holy!
Hail, divinest Melancholy!
Whose saintly visage is too bright
To hit the sense of human sight,
And therefore to our weaker view
O'erlaid with black, staid Wisdom's hue;
Black, but such as in esteem
Prince Memnon's sister might beseem,
Or that starred Ethiop Queen that strove
To set her beauty's praise above
The Sea-Nymphs, and their powers offended.
Yet thou art higher far descended:
Thee bright-haired Vesta, long of yore
To solitary Saturn bore;
His daughter she; in Saturn's reign
Such mixture was not held a stain.
Oft in glimmering bowers and glades
He met her, and in secret shades
Of woody Ida's inmost grove,
While yet there was no fear of Jove.

Come, pensive Nun, devout and pure,
Sober, steadfast, and demure,
All in a robe of darkest grain,
Flowing with majestic train,
And sable stole of cypress lawn
Over thy decent shoulders drawn.
Come; but keep thy wonted state,
With even step, and musing gait,
And looks commercing with the skies,
Thy rapt soul sitting in thine eyes:
There, held in holy passion still,
Forget thyself to marble, till
With a sad leaden downward cast
Thou fix them on the earth as fast.
And join with thee calm Peace, and Quiet,
Spare Fast, that oft with gods doth diet,
And hears the Muses in a ring
Aye round about Jove's altar sing;
And add to these retired Leisure,
That in trim gardens takes his pleasure;
But, first and chiefest, with thee bring
Him that yon soars on golden wing,
Guiding the fiery-wheelèd throne,
The Cherub Contemplation;
And the mute Silence hist along,
'Less Philomel will deign a song,
In her sweetest saddest plight,
Smoothing the rugged brow of Night,
While Cynthia checks her dragon yoke
Gently o'er th' accustomed oak.
—Sweet bird, that shunn'st the noise of folly,
Most musical, most melancholy!
Thee, Chauntress, oft the woods among
I woo, to hear thy even-song;
And, missing thee, I walk unseen
On the dry smooth-shaven green,
To behold the wandering Moon,
Riding near her highest noon,
Like one that had been led astray
Through the heaven's wide pathless way,

And oft, as if her head she bowed,
Stooping through a fleecy cloud.

  Oft, on a plat of rising ground,
I hear the far-off curfew sound
Over some wide-watered shore,
Swinging slow with sullen roar;
Or, if the air will not permit,
Some still removèd place will fit,
Where glowing embers through the room
Teach light to counterfeit a gloom,
Far from all resort of mirth,
Save the cricket on the hearth,
Or the Bellman's drowsy charm
To bless the doors from nightly harm.

  Or let my lamp, at midnight hour,
Be seen in some high lonely tower,
Where I may oft out-watch the Bear,
With thrice-great Hermes, or unsphere
The spirit of Plato, to unfold
What words or what vast regions hold
Th' immortal mind that hath forsook
Her mansion in this fleshly nook;
And of those Dæmons that are found
In fire, air, flood, or under ground,
Whose power hath a true consent
With planet or with element.
Sometime let gorgeous Tragedy
In sceptred pall come sweeping by,
Presenting Thebes, or Pelops' line,
Or the tale of Troy divine,
Or what (though rare) of later age
Ennobled hath the buskined stage.

  But, O sad Virgin! that thy power
Might raise Musæus from his bower;
Or bid the soul of Orpheus sing
Such notes as, warbled to the string,
Drew iron tears down Pluto's cheek,
And made hell grant what Love did seek;
Or call up him that left half-told
The story of Cambuscan bold,

Of Camball, and of Algarsife,
And who had Canace to wife
That owned the virtuous ring and glass,
And of the wondrous horse of brass
On which the Tartar King did ride;
And if aught else great Bards beside
In sage and solemn tunes have sung
Of turneys, and of trophies hung,
Of forests, and enchantments drear,
Where more is meant than meets the ear.
    Thus, Night, oft see me in thy pale career,
Till civil-suited Morn appear,
Not trickèd and frounced, as she was wont
With the Attic Boy to hunt,
But kerchieft in a comely cloud,
While rocking winds are piping loud,
Or ushered with a shower still,
When the gust hath blown his fill,
Ending on the rustling leaves,
With minute drops from off the eaves.
And, when the sun begins to fling
His flaring beams, me, Goddess, bring
To archèd walks of twilight groves,
And shadows brown, that Sylvan loves,
Of pine, or monumental oak,
Where the rude axe with heavèd stroke
Was never heard the Nymphs to daunt,
Or fright them from their hallowed haunt.
There, in close covert, by some brook,
Where no profaner eye may look,
Hide me from Day's garish eye,
While the bee with honeyed thigh,
That at her flowery work doth sing,
And the waters murmuring,
With such consort as they keep,
Entice the dewy-feathered Sleep.
And let some strange mysterious dream,
Wave at his wings in airy stream,

Of lively portraiture displayed,
Softly on my eyelids laid.
And as I wake, sweet music breathe
Above, about, or underneath,
Sent by some Spirit to mortals good,
Or th' unseen Genius of the wood.

But let my due feet never fail
To walk the studious cloister's pale,
And love the high-embowèd roof,
With antic pillars massy proof,
And storied windows richly dight,
Casting a dim religious light.
There let the pealing organ blow,
To the full-voiced Quire below,
In service high and anthems clear,
As may with sweetness, through mine ear,
Dissolve me into ecstasies,
And bring all Heaven before mine eyes.

And may at last my weary age
Find out the peaceful hermitage,
The hairy gown and mossy cell,
Where I may sit and rightly spell,
Of every star that Heaven doth shew,
And every herb that sips the dew;
Till old experience do attain
To something like prophetic strain.

These pleasures, Melancholy, give,
And I with thee will choose to live.

LYCIDAS

ELEGY ON A FRIEND DROWNED IN THE
IRISH CHANNEL 1637

YET once more, O ye Laurels, and once more
Ye Myrtles brown, with ivy never sere,
I come to pluck your berries harsh and crude,
And with forced fingers rude

Shatter your leaves before the mellowing year.
Bitter constraint and sad occasion dear
Compels me to disturb your season due;
For Lycidas is dead, dead ere his prime,
Young Lycidas, and hath not left his peer.
Who would not sing for Lycidas? he knew
Himself to sing, and build the lofty rhyme.
He must not float upon his watery bier
Unwept, and welter to the parching wind,
Without the meed of some melodious tear.

   Begin then, Sisters of the sacred well
That from beneath the seat of Jove doth spring;
Begin, and somewhat loudly sweep the string.
Hence with denial vain and coy excuse:
So may some gentle Muse
With lucky words favour *my* destined urn,
And as he passes, turn
And bid fair peace be to my sable shroud!
For we were nursed upon the self-same hill,
Fed the same flock, by fountain, shade, and rill:

   Together both, ere the high lawns appeared
Under the opening eyelids of the Morn,
We drove a-field, and both together heard
What time the grey-fly winds her sultry horn,
Battening our flocks with the fresh dews of night,
Oft till the star that rose at evening bright
Toward heaven's descent had sloped his westering wheel.
Meanwhile the rural ditties were not mute;
Tempered to the oaten flute
Rough Satyrs danced, and Fauns with cloven heel
From the glad sound would not be absent long;
And old Damœtas loved to hear our song.

   But, oh! the heavy change, now thou art gone,
Now thou art gone and never must return!
Thee, Shepherd, thee the woods and desert caves
With wild thyme and the gadding vine o'er-grown,
And all their echoes, mourn.
The willows, and the hazel copses green,
Shall now no more be seen

Fanning their joyous leaves to thy soft lays.
As killing as the canker to the rose,
Or taint-worm to the weanling herds that graze,
Or frost to flowers that their gay wardrobe wear
When first the white-thorn blows;
Such, Lycidas, thy loss to shepherd's ear.

Where were ye, Nymphs, when the remorseless deep
Closed o'er the head of your loved Lycidas?
For neither were ye playing on the steep
Where your old bards, the famous Druids, lie,
Nor on the shaggy top of Mona high,
Nor yet where Deva spreads her wizard stream.
Ay me! I fondly dream
"Had ye been there" . . . For what could that have done?
What could the Muse herself that Orpheus bore,
The Muse herself, for her enchanting son,
Whom universal nature did lament,
When, by the rout that made the hideous roar,
His gory visage down the stream was sent,
Down the swift Hebrus to the Lesbian shore?

Alas! what boots it with uncessant care
To tend the homely, slighted, Shepherd's trade
And strictly meditate the thankless Muse?
Were it not better done, as others use,
To sport with Amaryllis in the shade,
Or with the tangles of Neæra's hair?
Fame is the spur that the clear spirit doth raise
(That last infirmity of noble mind)
To scorn delights, and live labourious days;
But the fair guerdon when we hope to find,
And think to burst out into sudden blaze,
Comes the blind Fury with the abhorrèd shears
And slits the thin-spun life.   "But not the praise,"
Phœbus replied, and touched my trembling ears:
"Fame is no plant that grows on mortal soil,
Nor in the glistering foil
Set off to the world, nor in broad rumour lies,
But lives and spreads aloft by those pure eyes
And perfect witness of all-judging Jove;

As he pronounces lastly on each deed,
Of so much fame in heaven expect thy meed."
   O fountain Arethuse, and thou honoured flood,
Smooth-sliding Mincius, crowned with vocal reeds,
That strain I heard was of a higher mood.
But now my oat proceeds,
And listens to the Herald of the Sea
That came in Neptune's plea.
He asked the waves, and asked the felon winds,
What hard mishap hath doomed this gentle swain?
And questioned every gust of rugged wings
That blows from off each beaked promontory.
They knew not of his story;
And sage Hippotades their answer brings,
That not a blast was from his dungeon strayed:
The air was calm, and on the level brine
Sleek Panope with all her sisters played.
It was that fatal and perfidious bark,
Built in th' eclipse, and rigged with curses dark,
That sunk so low that sacred head of thine.
   Next Camus, reverend Sire, went footing slow,
His mantle hairy, and his bonnet sedge,
Inwrought with figures dim, and on the edge
Like to that sanguine flower inscribed with woe.
"Ah! who hath reft," quoth he, "my dearest pledge!"
Last came, and last did go,
The Pilot of the Galilean lake;
Two massy keys he bore of metals twain
(The golden opes, the iron shuts amain)
He shook his mitred locks, and stern bespake:—
"How well could I have spared for thee, young swain,
Enow of such, as for their bellies' sake
Creep, and intrude, and climb into the fold!
Of other care they little reck'ning make
Than how to scramble at the shearers' feast,
And shove away the worthy bidden guest.
Blind mouths! that scarce themselves know how to hold
A sheep-hook, or have learnèd aught else the least
That to the faithful herdman's art belongs!

What recks it them? What need they? They are sped;
And, when they list, their lean and flashy songs
Grate on their scrannel pipes of wretched straw;
The hungry sheep look up, and are not fed,
But swoln with wind and the rank mist they draw
Rot inwardly, and foul contagion spread;
Besides what the grim wolf with privy paw
Daily devours apace, and nothing said.
—But that two-handed engine at the door
Stands ready to smite once, and smite no more."
     Return, Alpheus; the dread voice is past
That shrunk thy streams; return, Sicilian Muse,
And call the vales, and bid them hither cast
Their bells and flowerets of a thousand hues.
Ye valleys low, where the mild whispers use
Of shades, and wanton winds, and gushing brooks,
On whose fresh lap the swart star sparely looks,
Throw hither all your quaint enamelled eyes,
That on the green turf suck the honeyed showers,
And purple all the ground with vernal flowers.
Bring the rathe primrose that forsaken dies,
The tufted crow-toe, and pale jessamine,
The white pink, and the pansy freaked with jet,
The glowing violet,
The musk-rose, and the well-attired woodbine,
With cowslips wan that hang the pensive head,
And every flower that sad embroidery wears.
Bid amaranthus all his beauty shed,
And daffodillies fill their cups with tears,
To strew the laureat hearse where Lycid lies.
For so, to interpose a little ease,
Let our frail thoughts dally with false surmise.
Ay me! whilst thee the shores and sounding seas
Wash far away, where'er thy bones are hurled;
Whether beyond the stormy Hebrides,
Where thou perhaps under the whelming tide
Visit'st the bottom of the monstrous world;
Or whether thou, to our moist vows denied,
Sleep'st by the fable of Bellerus old,

Where the great Vision of the guarded mount
Looks toward Namancos and Bayona's hold.
Look homeward, Angel, now, and melt with ruth:
And, O ye dolphins, waft the hapless youth!

    Weep no more, woeful shepherds, weep no more,
For Lycidas, your sorrow, is not dead,
Sunk though he be beneath the watery floor.
So sinks the day-star in the ocean-bed,
And yet anon repairs his drooping head
And tricks his beams, and with new-spangled ore
Flames in the forehead of the morning sky:
So Lycidas sunk low, but mounted high
Through the dear might of Him that walked the waves;
Where, other groves and other streams along,
With nectar pure his oozy locks he laves,
And hears the unexpressive nuptial song,
In the blest kingdoms meek of joy and love.
There entertain him all the Saints above
In solemn troops, and sweet societies,
That sing, and singing in their glory move,
And wipe the tears for ever from his eyes.
Now, Lycidas, the shepherds weep no more;
Henceforth thou art the Genius of the shore
In thy large recompense, and shalt be good
To all that wander in that perilous flood.

    Thus sang the uncouth swain to the oaks and rills,
While the still morn went out with sandals grey:
He touched the tender stops of various quills,
With eager thought warbling his Doric lay:
And now the sun had stretched out all the hills,
And now was dropt into the western bay.
At last he rose, and twitched his mantle blue:
To-morrow to fresh woods, and pastures new.

ON THE LATE MASSACRE IN PIEDMONT

Avenge, O Lord! Thy slaughtered Saints, whose bones
Lie scattered on the Alpine mountains cold;
Even them who kept Thy truth so pure of old
When all our fathers worshiped stocks and stones,
Forget not: in Thy book record their groans
Who were Thy sheep, and in their ancient fold
Slain by the bloody Piemontese, that rolled
Mother with infant down the rocks. Their moans
The vales redoubled to the hills, and they
To Heaven. Their martyred blood and ashes sow
O'er all the Italian fields, where still doth sway
The triple Tyrant: that from these may grow
A hundred-fold, who, having learnt Thy way,
Early may fly the Babylonian woe.

ON HIS BLINDNESS

When I consider how my light is spent,
Ere half my days in this dark world and wide,
And that one Talent which is death to hide
Lodged with me useless, though my soul more bent
To serve therewith my Maker, and present
My true account, lest He returning chide,
"Doth God exact day-labour, light denied?"
I fondly ask. But patience, to prevent
That murmur, soon replies: "God doth not need
Either man's work, or His own gifts. Who best
Bear His mild yoke, they serve Him best. His state
Is kingly: thousands at His bidding speed
And post o'er land and ocean without rest.
They also serve who only stand and wait."

ON HIS DECEASED WIFE

METHOUGHT I saw my late espousèd saint
Brought to me like Alcestis from the grave,
Whom Jove's great son to her glad husband gave,
Rescued from Death by force, though pale and faint.
Mine, as whom washed from spot of childbed taint
Purification in the Old Law did save,
And such as yet once more I trust to have
Full sight of her in Heaven without restraint,
Came vested all in white, pure as her mind.
Her face was veiled; yet to my fancied sight
Love, sweetness, goodness, in her person shined
So clear as in no face with more delight.
But, oh! as to embrace me she inclined,
I waked, she fled, and day brought back my night.

THE FALLEN HOSTS IN HELL

ALL in a moment through the gloom were seen
Ten thousand banners rise into the air.
With orient colours waving: with them rose
A forest huge of spears; and thronging helms
Appeared, and serried shields in thick array
Of depth immeasurable. Anon they move
In perfect phalanx to the Dorian mood
Of flutes and soft recorders—such as raised
To height of noblest temper heroes old
Arming to battle—and instead of rage
Deliberate valour breathed, firm, and unmoved
With dread of death to flight or foul retreat;
Nor wanting power to mitigate and 'suage
With solemn touches troubled thoughts, and chase
Anguish and doubt and fear and sorrow and pain
From mortal or immortal minds. Thus they,
Breathing united force, with fixèd thought,
Moved on in silence to soft pipes that charmed

Their painful steps o'er the burnt soil; and now
Advanced in view they stand—a horrid front
Of dreadful length and dazzling arms, in guise
Of warriors old with ordered spear and shield,
Awaiting what command their mighty Chief
Had to impose. He through the armèd files
Darts his experienced eye, and soon traverse
The whole battalion views—their order due,
Their visages and stature as of gods:
Their number last he sums. And now his heart
Distends with pride, and, hardening in his strength,
Glories: for never since created man
Met such embodied force as, named with these,
Could merit more than that small infantry
Warred on by cranes—though all the giant brood
Of Phlegra with the heroic race were joined
That fought at Thebes and Ilium, on each side
Mixed with auxiliar gods; and what resounds
In fable or romance of Uther's son
Begirt with British and Armoric knights;
And all who since, baptized or infidel,
Jousted in Aspramont, or Montalban,
Damasco, or Marocco, or Trebizond,
Or whom Biserta sent from Afric shore,
When Charlemain with all his peerage fell
By Fontarabbia. Thus far these beyond
Compare of mortal prowess, yet observed
Their dread Commander. He, above the rest
In shape and gesture proudly eminent,
Stood like a tower. His form had yet not lost
All its original brightness, nor appeared
Less than Archangel ruined, and th' excess
Of glory obscured: as when the sun new-risen
Looks through the horizontal misty air
Shorn of his beams, or, from behind the moon,
In dim eclipse, disastrous twilight sheds
On half the nations, and with fear of change
Perplexes monarchs. Darkened so, yet shon
Above them all th' Archangel: but his face

Deep scars of thunder had entrenched, and care
Sat on his faded cheek; but under brows
Of dauntless courage, and considerate pride
Waiting revenge. Cruel his eye, but cast
Signs of remorse and passion, to behold
The fellows of his crime, the followers rather
(Far other once beheld in bliss), condemned
For ever now to have their lot in pain—
Millions of Spirits for his fault amerced
Of Heaven, and from eternal splendours flung
For his revolt—yet faithful how they stood,
Their glory withered; as when heaven's fire
Hath scathed the forest oaks, or mountain pines,
With singèd top their stately growth, though bare,
Stands on the blasted heath. He now prepared
To speak; whereat their doubled ranks they bend
From wing to wing, and half enclose him round
With all his peers. Attention held them mute.
Thrice he essayed, and thrice, in spite of scorn,
Tears such as angels weep, burst forth; at last
Words, interwove with sighs, found out their way.
"O myriads of immortal Spirits! O Powers
Matchless, but with the Almighty!—and that strife
Was not inglorious, though th' event was dire,
As this place testifies, and this dire change,
Hateful to utter. But what power of mind,
Foreseeing or presaging, from the depth
Of knowledge, past or present, could have feared
How such united force of gods, how such
As stood like these, could ever know repulse?
For who can yet believe, though after loss,
That all these puissant legions, whose exile
Hath emptied Heaven, shall fail to reascend
Self-raised, and re-possess their native seat?
For me, be witness all the host of Heaven,
If counsels different, or dangers shunned
By me, have lost our hopes. But he who reigns
Monarch in Heaven till then as one secure
Sat on his throne, upheld by old repute,

Consent or custom, and his regal state
Put forth at full: but still his strength concealed
Which tempted our attempt, and wrought our fall.
Henceforth his might we know, and know our own,
So as not either to provoke, or dread
New war provoked: our better part remains
To work in close design, by fraud or guile,
What force effected not; that he no less
At length from us may find, who overcomes
By force, hath overcome but half his foe.
Space may produce new Worlds; whereof so rife
There went a fame in Heaven that He ere long
Intended to create, and therein plant
A generation, whom his choice regard
Should favour equal to the Sons of Heaven.
Thither, if but to pry, shall be perhaps
Our first eruption—thither, or elsewhere;
For this infernal pit shall never hold
Celestial Spirits in bondage, nor th' Abyss
Long under darkness cover. But these thoughts
Full counsel must mature. Peace is despaired;
For who can think submission? War, then, war
Open or understood, must be resolved."

He spake; and, to confirm his words, outflew
Millions of flaming swords, drawn from the thighs
Of mighty Cherubim; the sudden blaze
Far round illumined Hell. Highly they raged
Against the Highest, and fierce with graspèd arms
Clashed on their sounding shields the din of war,
Hurling defiance toward the vault of Heaven.

There stood a hill not far, whose grisly top
Belched fire and rolling smoke; the rest entire
Shon with a glossy scurf, undoubted sign
That in his womb was hid metallic ore,
The work of sulphur. Thither, winged with speed,
A numerous brigade hastened: as when bands
Of pioneers, with spade and pickaxe armed,
Forerun the royal camp, to trench a field,
Or cast a rampart. Mammon led them on—

Mammon, the least erected Spirit that fell
From Heaven; for even in Heaven his looks and thoughts
Were always downward bent, admiring more
The riches of Heaven's pavement, trodden gold,
Than aught, divine or holy, else enjoyed
In vision beatific. (By him first
Men also, and by his suggestion taught,
Ransacked the Centre, and with impious hands
Rifled the bowels of their mother Earth
For treasures, better hid.) Soon had his crew
Opened into the hill a spacious wound,
And digged out ribs of gold. Let none admire
That riches grow in Hell; that soil may best
Deserve the precious bane. And here let those
Who boast in mortal things, and wondering tell
Of Babel, and the works of Memphian kings,
Learn how their greatest monuments of fame,
And strength and art, are easily outdone
By Spirits reprobate, and in an hour
What in an age, they, with incessant toil
And hands innumerable, scarce perform.
Nigh on the plain, in many cells prepared,
That underneath had veins of liquid fire
Sluiced from the lake, a second multitude
With wondrous art founded the massy ore,
Severing each kind, and scummed the bullion-dross.
A third as soon had formed within the ground
A various mold, and from the boiling cells,
By strange conveyance, filled each hollow nook,
As in an organ, from one blast of wind,
To many a row of pipes the sound-board breathes.
Anon, out of the earth a fabric huge
Rose like an exhalation, with the sound
Of dulcet symphonies and voices sweet—
Built like a temple, where pilasters round
Were set, and Doric pillars overlaid
With golden architrave; nor did there want
Cornice or frieze, with bossy scupltures graven
The roof was fretted gold. Not Babilon,

Nor great Alcairo, such magnificence
Equaled in all their glories, to enshrine
Belus or Serapis their gods, or seat
Their kings, when Egypt with Assyria strove
In wealth and luxury. Th' ascending pile
Stood fixed her stately highth: and straight the doors,
Opening their brazen folds, discover, wide
Within, her ample spaces, o'er the smooth
And level pavement; from the archèd roof,
Pendent by subtle magic, many a row
Of starry lamps and blazing cressets, fed
With naphtha and asphaltus, yielded light
As from a sky. The hasty multitude
Admiring entered; and the work some praise,
And some the Architect. His hand was known
In Heaven by many a towered structure high
Where sceptred Angels held their residence,
And sat as Princes, whom the supreme King
Exalted to such power, and gave to rule,
Each in his hierarchy, the Orders bright.
Nor was his name unheard or unadored
In ancient Greece; and in Ausonian land
Men called him Mulciber; and how he fell
From Heaven they fabled, thrown by angry Jove
Sheer o'er the crystal battlements: from morn
To noon he fell, from noon to dewy eve,
A summer's day; and with the setting sun
Dropped from the zenith, like a falling star,
On Lemnos, th' Ægean isle. Thus they relate,
Erring; for he with this rebellious rout
Fell long before; nor aught availed him now
To have built in Heaven high towers; nor did he 'scape
By all his engines, but was headlong sent
With his industrious crew to build in Hell.

[From Book I, Paradise Lost.]

ANDREW MARVELL [1621–1678]

SONG OF THE EMIGRANTS IN BERMUDA

WHERE the remote Bermudas ride
In th' ocean's bosom unespy'd,
From a small boat that row'd along
The list'ning winds received this song.
"What should we do but sing His praise
That led us through the wat'ry maze
Unto an isle so long unknown,
And yet far kinder than our own?
Where He the huge sea-monsters wracks,
That lift the deep upon their backs;
He lands us on a grassy stage,
Safe from the storms, and prelate's rage:
He gave us this eternal Spring
Which here enamels everything,
And sends the fowls to us in care
On daily visits through the air.
He hangs in shades the orange bright
Like golden lamps in a green night,
And does in the pomegranates close
Jewels more rich than Ormus shows:
He makes the figs our mouths to meet
And throws the melons at our feet;
But apples, plants of such a price,
No tree could ever bear them twice.
With cedars chosen by His hand
From Lebanon He stores the land;
And makes the hollow seas that roar
Proclaim the ambergris on shore.
He cast (of which we rather boast)
The Gospel's pearl upon our coast;
And in these rocks for us did frame
A temple where to sound His name.
Oh! let our voice His praise exalt
Till it arrive at Heaven's vault,

Which thence (perhaps) rebounding may
Echo beyond the Mexique bay!"
—Thus sung they in the English boat
A holy and a cheerful note:
And all the way, to guide their chime,
With falling oars they kept the time.

THE GARDEN

How vainly men themselves amaze
To win the palm, the oak, or bays,
And their uncessant labours see
Crown'd from some single herb or tree,
Whose short and narrow-vergéd shade
Does prudently their toils upbraid;
While all the flowers and trees do close
To weave the garlands of repose.

Fair Quiet, have I found thee here,
And Innocence thy sister dear!
Mistaken long, I sought you then
In busy companies of men:
Your sacred plants, if here below,
Only among the plants will grow:
Society is all but rude
To this delicious solitude.

No white nor red was ever seen
So am'rous as this lovely green.
Fond lovers, cruel as their flame,
Cut in these trees their mistress' name;
Little, alas, they know or heed
How far these beauties hers exceed!
Fair trees! wheres'e'er your barks I wound,
No name shall but your own be found.

When we have run our passions' heat
Love hither makes his best retreat:

The gods, who mortal beauty chase,
Still in a tree did end their race;
Apollo hunted Daphne so
Only that she might laurel grow;
And Pan did after Syrinx speed
Not as a nymph, but for a reed.

What wondrous life is this I lead!
Ripe apples drop about my head;
The luscious clusters of the vine
Upon my mouth do crush their wine;
The nectarine and curious peach
Into my hands themselves do reach;
Stumbling on melons, as I pass,
Ensnared with flowers, I fall on grass.

Meanwhile the mind, from pleasure less,
Withdraws into its happiness;
The mind, that ocean where each kind
Does straight its own resemblance find;
Yet it creates, transcending these,
Far other worlds, and other seas;
Annihilating all that's made
To a green thought in a green shade.

Here at the fountain's sliding foot
Or at some fruit-tree's mossy root,
Casting the body's vest aside
My soul into the boughs does glide;
There, like a bird, it sits and sings,
Then whets· and claps its silver wings,
And, till prepared for longer flight,
Waves in its plumes the various light.

Such was that happy Garden-state
While man there walk'd without a mate:
After a place so pure and sweet,
What other help could yet be meet!

But 'twas beyond a mortal's share
To wander solitary there:
Two paradises 'twere in one
To live in Paradise alone.

How well the skilful gardner drew
Of flowers and herbs this dial new!
Where, from above, the milder sun
Does through a fragrant zodiac run:
And, as it works, th' industrious bee
Computes its time as well as we.
How could such sweet and wholesome hours
Be reckon'd, but with herbs and flowers!

SIR CHARLES SEDLEY [1639?–1701]

TO CELIA

Not, Celia, that I juster am
    Or better than the rest;
For I would change each hour, like them,
    Were not my heart at rest.

But I am tied to very thee
    By every thought I have;
Thy face I only care to see,
    Thy heart I only crave.

All that in woman is adored
    In thy dear self I find—
For the whole sex can but afford
    The handsome and the kind.

Why then should I seek further store,
    And still make love anew?
When change itself can give no more,
    'Tis easy to be true.

JOHN WILMOT, EARL OF ROCHESTER
[1647–1680.]

CONSTANCY

I CANNOT change, as others do,
    Though you unjustly scorn,
Since that poor swain that sighs for you,
    For you alone was born;
No, Phillis, no, your heart to move
    A surer way I'll try,
And to revenge my slighted love,
    Will still love on, and die.

When killed with grief Amintas lies,
    And you to mind shall call
The sighs that now unpitied rise,
    The tears that vainly fall,
That welcome hour that ends his smart,
    Will then begin your pain,
For such a faithful tender heart
    Can never break in vain.

ON CHARLES II

HERE lies our Sovereign Lord the King,
    Whose word no man relies on,
Who never said a foolish thing,
    Nor ever did a wise one.

JOHN DRYDEN [1631–1700]

A SONG FOR ST. CECILIA'S DAY, 1687

FROM harmony, from heavenly harmony
 This universal frame began:
 When Nature underneath a heap
  Of jarring atoms lay
 And could not heave her head,
The tuneful voice was heard from high,
 "Arise, ye more than dead!"
Then cold, and hot, and moist, and dry,
In order to their stations leap,
 And Music's power obey.
From harmony, from heavenly harmony
 This universal frame began:
 From harmony to harmony
Thro' all the compass of the notes it ran,
The diapason closing full in Man.

What passion cannot Music raise and quell!
 When Jubal struck the chorded shell
 His listening brethren stood around,
 And, wondering, on their faces fell
 To worship that celestial sound.
Less than a god they thought there could not dwell
 Within the hollow of that shell
 That spoke so sweetly and so well.
What passion cannot Music raise and quell!

The trumpet's loud clangor
 Excites us to arms,
With shrill notes of anger
 And mortal alarms.
The double double double beat
 Of the thundering drum
 Cries: "Hark! the foes come;
Charge, charge, 'tis too late to retreat!"

The soft complaining flute
In dying notes discovers
The woes of hopeless lovers,
Whose dirge is whisper'd by the warbling lute.

Sharp violins proclaim
Their jealous pangs and desperation,
Fury, frantic indignation,
Depth of pains, and height of passion
For the fair disdainful dame.

But oh! what art can teach,
What human voice can reach
The sacred organ's praise?
Notes inspiring holy love,
Notes that wing their heavenly ways
To mend the choirs above.

Orpheus could lead the savage race,
And trees unrooted left their place
Sequacious of the lyre:
But bright Cecilia raised the wonder higher:
When to her Organ vocal breath was given
An Angel heard, and straight appear'd—
Mistaking earth for heaven.

GRAND CHORUS

As from the power of sacred lays
The spheres began to move,
And sung the great Creator's praise
To all the blest above;
So when the last and dreadful hour
This crumbling pageant shall devour,
The trumpet shall be heard on high,
The dead shall live, the living die,
And Music shall untune the sky.

ALEXANDER'S FEAST; OR, THE POWER OF MUSIC

AN ODE IN HONOUR OF ST. CECILIA'S DAY, 1697

I

'Twas at the royal feast for Persia won
 By Philip's warlike son:
 Aloft in awful state
 The godlike hero sate
 On his imperial throne;
 His valiant peers were placed around;
Their brows with roses and with myrtles bound:
 (So should desert in arms be crown'd.)
The lovely Thais, by his side,
Sate like a blooming Eastern bride,
In flower of youth and beauty's pride.
  Happy, happy, happy pair!
   None but the brave,
   None but the brave,
  None but the brave deserves the fair.

CHORUS

  Happy, happy, happy pair!
   None but the brave,
   None but the brave,
  None but the brave deserves the fair.

II

 Timotheus, placed on high
  Amid the tuneful choir,
With flying fingers touch'd the lyre:
 The trembling notes ascend the sky,
  And heavenly joys inspire.
The song began from Jove,
Who left his blissful seats above,
(Such is the power of mighty love)
A dragon's fiery form belied the god:
Sublime on radiant spires he rode,

When he to fair Olympia press'd;
    And while he sought her snowy breast:
Then, round her slender waist he curl'd,
And stamp'd an image of himself, a sovereign of the world.
    The listening crowd admire the lofty sound,
    "A present deity," they shout around;
    "A present deity," the vaulted roofs rebound:
        With ravished ears
        The monarch hears,
        Assumes the god,
        Affects to nod,
    And seems to shake the spheres.

CHORUS: With ravished ears, etc.

III

The praise of Bacchus then the sweet musician sung,
    Of Bacchus, ever fair and ever young.
    The jolly god in triumph comes;
    Sound the trumpets, beat the drums;
        Flush'd with a purple grace
        He shows his honest face:
Now give the hautboys breath; he comes, he comes.
    Bacchus, ever fair and young,
        Drinking joys did first ordain;
    Bacchus' blessings are a treasure,
    Drinking is the soldier's pleasure;
        Rich the treasure,
        Sweet the pleasure,
    Sweet is pleasure after pain.

CHORUS: Bacchus' blessings are a treasure, etc.

IV

Sooth'd with the sound, the king grew vain;
    Fought all his battles o'er again;
And thrice he routed all his foes, and thrice he slew the slain.

The master saw the madness rise,
His glowing cheeks, his ardent eyes;
And while he heaven and earth defied,
Changed his hand, and check'd his pride.
 He chose a mournful Muse,
 Soft pity to infuse;
He sung Darius great and good,
 By too severe a fate,
Fallen, fallen, fallen, fallen,
 Fallen from his high estate,
And weltering in his blood;
Deserted at his utmost need
By those his former bounty fed;
On the bare earth exposed he lies,
With not a friend to close his eyes.

With downcast looks the joyless victor sate,
 Revolving in his alter'd soul
  The various turns of chance below:
 And, now and then, a sigh he stole,
 And tears began to flow.

CHORUS: Revolving in his alter'd soul, etc.

V

The mighty master smiled to see
That love was in the next degree;
'Twas but a kindred sound to move,
For pity melts the mind to love.
 Softly sweet, in Lydian measures,
 Soon he soothed his soul to pleasures.
" War," he sung, " is toil and trouble;
Honour but an empty bubble;
 Never ending, still beginning,
Fighting still, and still destroying:
 If the world be worth thy winning,
Think, O think it worth enjoying:

Lovely Thais sits beside thee,
Take the good the gods provide thee."

The many rend the skies with loud applause:
So Love was crown'd, but Music won the cause.
 The prince, unable to conceal his pain,
   Gazed on the fair
   Who caused his care,
 And sigh'd and look'd, sigh'd and look'd,
 Sigh'd and look'd, and sigh'd again;
At length, with love and wine at once oppress'd,
The vanquish'd victor sunk upon her breast.

CHORUS: The prince, unable to conceal his pain, etc.

VI

Now strike the golden lyre again;
A louder yet, and yet a louder strain.
Break his bands of sleep asunder,
And rouse him, like a rattling peal of thunder.
 Hark, hark, the horrid sound
  Has raised up his head;
  As awaked from the dead,
 And, amazed, he stares around.
"Revenge, revenge!" Timotheus cries;
 "See the Furies arise;
 See the snakes that they rear,
 How they hiss in their hair,
And the sparkles that flash from their eyes?
 Behold a ghastly band,
 Each a torch in his hand!
Those are Grecian ghosts, that in battle were slain,
  And unburied remain
  Inglorious on the plain:
  Give the vengeance due
  To the valiant crew.
Behold how they toss their torches on high,
 How they point to the Persian abodes,
And glittering temples of their hostile gods."

The princes applaud with a furious joy;
And the king seized a flambeau with zeal to destroy;
  Thais led the way,
  To light him to his prey,
And, like another Helen, fired another Troy.

CHORUS: And the king seized a flambeau with zeal to destroy, etc.

VII

  Thus, long ago,
 Ere heaving bellows learned to blow,
  While organs yet were mute,
  Timotheus, to his breathing flute
  And sounding lyre,
Could swell the soul to rage, or kindle soft desire.
 At last divine Cecilia came,
 Inventress of the vocal frame;
The sweet enthusiast, from her sacred store,
 Enlarged the former narrow bounds,
 And added length to solemn sounds,
With nature's mother wit, and arts unknown before.
 Let old Timotheus yield the prize,
  Or both divide the crown:
 He raised a mortal to the skies;
  She drew an angel down.

GRAND CHORUS

 At last divine Cecilia came,
 Inventress of the vocal frame;
The sweet enthusiast, from her sacred store,
 Enlarged the former narrow bounds,
 And added length to solemn sounds,
With nature's mother wit, and arts unknown before.
 Let old Timotheus yield the prize,
  Or both divide the crown:
 He raised a mortal to the skies;
  She drew an angel down.

MILTON

THREE poets, in three distant ages born,
Greece, Italy, and England did adorn.
The first in loftiness of thought surpass'd,
The next in majesty, in both the last.
The force of Nature could no farther go;
To make a third she join'd the former two.

WILLIAM CONGREVE [1670–1729]

AMORET

FAIR Amoret is gone astray;
    Pursue and seek her every lover;
I'll tell the signs by which you may
    The wandering shepherdess discover.

Coquet and coy at once her air,
    Both studied, though both seem neglected;
Careless she is with artful care,
    Affecting to seem unaffected.

With skill her eyes dart every glance,
    Yet change so soon you'd ne'er suspect 'em;
For she'd persuade they wound by chance,
    Though certain aim and art direct 'em.

She likes herself, yet others hates
    For that which in herself she prizes;
And, while she laughs at them, forgets
    She is the thing that she despises.

LADY WINCHILSEA [1661–1720]

TO THE NIGHTINGALE

Exert thy voice, sweet harbinger of Spring!
This moment is thy time to sing,
This moment I attend to praise,
And set my numbers to thy lays;
Free as thine shall be my song,
As thy music, short or long;
Poets, wild as thou, were born,
Pleasing best when unconfined,
When to please is least designed,
Soothing but their cares to rest;
Cares do still their thoughts molest,
And still th' unhappy poet's breast
Like thine, when best he sings, is placed against a thorn.
She begins! Let all be still!
Muse, thy promise now fulfil!
Sweet, oh! sweet, still sweeter yet!
Can thy words such accents fit?
Canst thou syllables refine,
Melt a sense that shall retain
Still some spirit of the brain,
Till with sounds like these it join?
'Twill not be! then change thy note,
Let division shake thy throat!
Hark! division now she tries,
Yet as far the Muse outflies!
Cease then, prithee, cease thy tune,
Trifler, wilt thou sing till June?
Till thy business all lies waste
And the time of building's past?
Thus we poets that have speech
Unlike what thy forests teach,
If a fluent vein be shown
That's transcendent to our own,
Criticise, reform or preach,
Censuring what we cannot reach.

MATTHEW PRIOR [1664–1721]

TO A CHILD OF QUALITY FIVE YEARS OLD

Lords, knights, and 'squires, the numerous band,
　That wear the fair Miss Mary's fetters,
Were summoned by her high command,
　To show their passions by their letters.

My pen among the rest I took,
　Lest those bright eyes that cannot read
Should dart their kindling fires, and look
　The power they have to be obeyed.

Nor quality, nor reputation,
　Forbid me yet my flame to tell;
Dear Five-years-old befriends my passion,
　And I may write till she can spell.

For, while she makes her silk-worms beds
　With all the tender things I swear;
Whilst all the house my passion reads
　In papers round her baby's hair;

She may receive and own my flame;
　For, though the strictest prudes should know it,
She'll pass for a most virtuous dame,
　And I for an unhappy poet.

Then, too, alas! when she shall tear
　The lines some younger rival sends;
She'll give me leave to write, I fear,
　And we shall still continue friends.

For, as our different ages move,
　'Tis so ordained, (would Fate but mend it!)
That I shall be past making love,
　When she begins to comprehend it.

CUPID MISTAKEN

As, after noon, one summer's day,
  Venus stood bathing in a river,
Cupid a-shooting went that way,
  New-strung his bow, new-filled his quiver.

With skill he chose his sharpest dart:
  With all his might his bow he drew:
Swift to his beauteous parent's heart
  The too-well-guided arrow flew.

I faint! I die! the goddess cried;
  O cruel, could'st thou find none other
To wreck thy spleen on? Parricide!
  Like Nero, thou hast slain thy mother.

Poor Cupid sobbing scarce could speak;
  Indeed, mamma, I did not know ye:
Alas! how easy my mistake!
  I took you for your likeness, Chloe.

THE DYING ADRIAN TO HIS SOUL

Poor, little, pretty, fluttering thing,
  Must we no longer live together?
And dost thou prune thy trembling wing
  To take thy flight, thou know'st not whither?
Thy humourous vein, thy pleasing folly,
  Lies all neglected, all forgot:
And pensive, wavering, melancholy,
  Thou dread'st and hop'st, thou know'st not what.

EPIGRAMS

I

I SENT FOR RATCLIFFE

I SENT for Ratcliffe; was so ill,
 That other doctors gave me over:
He felt my pulse, prescribed his pill,
 And I was likely to recover.

But when the wit began to wheeze,
 And wine had warm'd the politician,
Cured yesterday of my disease,
 I died last night of my physician.

II

FOR HIS OWN TOMB-STONE

To me 'twas given to die: to thee 'tis given
To live: alas! one moment sets us even.
Mark! how impartial is the will of Heaven!

JONATHAN SWIFT [1667–1745]

THE BEASTS' CONFESSION

WHEN beasts could speak, (the learned say
They still can do so every day,)
It seems they had religion then,
As much as now we find in men.
It happen'd, when a plague broke out,
(Which therefore made them more devout,)
The king of brutes (to make it plain,
Of quadrupeds I only mean)
By proclamation gave command,
That every subject in the land

Should to the priest confess their sins;
And thus the pious Wolf begins:—
" Good father, I must own with shame,
That often I have been to blame:
I must confess, on Friday last,
Wretch that I was! I broke my fast:
But I defy the basest tongue
To prove I did my neighbour wrong;
Or ever went to seek my food,
By rapine, theft, or thirst of blood."

The Ass approaching next, confess'd,
That in his heart he loved a jest:
A wag he was, he needs must own,
And could not let a dunce alone:
Sometimes his friend he would not spare,
And might perhaps be too severe:
But yet the worst that could be said,
He was a wit both born and bred;
And, if it be a sin and shame,
Nature alone must bear the blame:
One fault he has, is sorry for't,
His ears are half a foot too short;
Which could he to the standard bring,
He'd show his face before the king:
Then for his voice, there's none disputes
That he's the nightingale of brutes.

The Swine with contrite heart allow'd.
His shape and beauty made him proud:
In diet was perhaps too nice,
But gluttony was ne'er his vice:
In every turn of life content,
And meekly took what fortune sent:
Inquire through all the parish round,
A better neighbour ne'er was found;
His vigilance might some displease;
'Tis true, he hated sloth like pease.

The mimic Ape began his chatter,
How evil tongues his life bespatter;
Much of the censuring world complain'd,
Who said, his gravity was feign'd:

Indeed, the strictness of his morals
Engaged him in a hundred quarrels:
He saw, and he was grieved to see't,
His zeal was sometimes indiscreet:
He found his virtues too severe
For our corrupted times to bear;
Yet such a lewd licentious age
Might well excuse a stoic's rage.

The Goat advanced with decent pace,
And first excused his youthful face;
Forgiveness begg'd that he appear'd
('Twas Nature's fault) without a beard.
'Tis true, he was not much inclined
To fondness for the female kind:
Not, as his enemies object,
From chance, or natural defect;
Not by his frigid constitution;
But through a pious resolution:
For he had made a holy vow
Of Chastity, as monks do now:
Which he resolved to keep for ever hence
And strictly too, as doth his reverence.

Apply the tale, and you shall find,
How just it suits with human kind.
Some faults we own; but can you guess?
—Why, virtue's carried to excess,
Wherewith our vanity endows us,
Though neither foe nor friend allows us.

The Lawyer swears (you may rely on't)
He never squeezed a needy client;
And this he makes his constant rule,
For which his brethren call him fool;
His conscience always was so nice,
He freely gave the poor advice;
By which he lost, he may affirm,
A hundred fees last Easter term;
While others of the learned robe,
Would break the patience of a Job.
No pleader at the bar could match
His diligence and quick dispatch;

Ne'er kept a cause, he well may boast,
Above a term or two at most.
　The cringing knave, who seeks a place
Without success, thus tells his case:
Why should he longer mince the matter?
He fail'd, because he could not flatter;
He had not learn'd to turn his coat,
Nor for a party give his vote:
His crime he quickly understood;
Too zealous for the nation's good:
He found the ministers resent it,
Yet could not for his heart repent it.
　The Chaplain vows, he cannot fawn,
Though it would raise him to the lawn:
He pass'd his hours among his books;
You find it in his meagre looks:
He might, if he were worldly wise,
Preferment get, and spare his eyes;
But owns he had a stubborn spirit,
That made him trust alone to merit;
Would rise by merit to promotion;
Alas! a mere chimeric notion.
　The Doctor, if you will believe him,
Confess'd a sin; (and God forgive him!)
Call'd up at midnight, ran to save
A blind old beggar from the grave:
But see how Satan spreads his snares;
He quite forgot to say his prayers.
He cannot help it, for his heart,
Sometimes to act the parson's part:
Quotes from the Bible many a sentence,
That moves his patients to repentance;
And, when his medicines do no good,
Supports their minds with heavenly food:
At which, however well intended,
He hears the clergy are offended;
And grown so bold behind his back,
To call him hypocrite and quack.
In his own church he keeps a seat;
Says grace before and after meat;

And calls, without affecting airs,
His household twice a-day to prayers.
He shuns apothecaries' shops,
And hates to cram the sick with slops:
He scorns to make his art a trade;
Nor bribes my lady's favourite maid.
Old nurse-keepers would never hire,
To recommend him to the squire;
Which others, whom he will not name,
Have often practised to their shame.

The Statesman tells you, with a sneer,
His fault is to be too sincere;
And having no sinister ends,
Is apt to disoblige his friends.
The nation's good, his master's glory,
Without regard to Whig or Tory,
Were all the schemes he had in view,
Yet he was seconded by few:
Though some had spread a thousand lies,
'Twas he defeated the excise.
'Twas known, though he had borne aspersion,
That standing troops were his aversion:
His practice was, in every station,
To serve the king, and please the nation.
Though hard to find in every case
The fittest man to fill a place:
His promises he ne'er forgot,
But took memorials on the spot;
His enemies, for want of charity,
Said, he affected popularity:
'Tis true, the people understood,
That all he did was for their good;
Their kind affections he has tried;
No love is lost on either side.
He came to court with fortune clear,
Which now he runs out every year;
Must, at the rate that he goes on,
Inevitably be undone:
O! if his majesty would please
To give him but a writ of ease,

Would grant him license to retire,
As it has long been his desire,
By fair accounts it would be found,
He's poorer by ten thousand pound.
He owns, and hopes it is no sin,
He ne'er was partial to his kin;
He thought it base for men in stations,
To crowd the court with their relations:
His country was his dearest mother,
And every virtuous man his brother;
Through modesty or awkward shame,
(For which he owns himself to blame,)
He found the wisest man he could,
Without respect to friends or blood;
Nor ever acts on private views,
When he has liberty to choose.

   The Sharper swore he hated play,
Except to pass an hour away:
And well he might; for, to his cost,
By want of skill, he always lost;
He heard there was a club of cheats,
Who had contrived a thousand feats;
Could change the stock, or cog a die,
And thus deceive the sharpest eye:
Nor wonder how his fortune sunk,
His brothers fleece him when he's drunk.

   I own the moral not exact,
Besides, the tale is false, in fact;
And so absurd, that could I raise up,
From fields Elysian, fabling Æsop,
I would accuse him to his face,
For libelling the four-foot race.
Creatures of every kind but ours
Well comprehend their natural powers,
While we, whom reason ought to sway,
Mistake our talents every day.
The Ass was never known so stupid
To act the part of Tray or Cupid;
Nor leaps upon his master's lap,
There to be stroked, and fed with pap,

As Æsop would the world persuade;
He better understands his trade:
Nor comes whene'er his lady whistles,
But carries loads, and feeds on thistles.
Our author's meaning, I presume, is
A creature *bipes et implumis;*
Wherein the moralist design'd
A compliment on human kind;
For here he owns, that now and then
Beasts may degenerate into men.

AMBROSE PHILIPS [1675?–1749]

TO MISS CHARLOTTE PULTENEY, IN HER MOTHER'S ARMS

Timely blossom, Infant fair,
Fondling of a happy pair,
Every morn and every night
Their solicitous delight,
Sleeping, waking, still at ease,
Pleasing, without skill to please;
Little gossip, blithe and hale,
Tattling many a broken tale,
Singing many a tuneless song,
Lavish of a heedless tongue.
Simple maiden, void of art,
Babbling out the very heart,
Yet abandoned to thy will,
Yet imagining no ill,
Yet too innocent to blush,
Like the linnet in the bush,
To the mother-linnet's note
Moduling her slender throat,
Chirping forth thy pretty joys,
Wanton in the change of toys,
Like the linnet green, in May,
Flitting to each bloomy spray.

Wearied then, and glad of rest,
Like the linnet in the nest.
This thy present happy lot,
This, in time, will be forgot;
Other pleasures, other cares,
Ever-busy Time prepares;
And thou shalt in thy daughter see
This picture, once, resembled thee.

ALEXANDER POPE [1688–1744]

SOLITUDE

HAPPY the man, whose wish and care
A few paternal acres bound,
Content to breathe his native air
     In his own ground:

Whose herds with milk, whose fields with bread.
Whose flocks supply him with attire;
Whose trees in summer yield him shade,
     In winter fire:

Blest, who can unconcern'dly find
Hours, days, and years, slide soft away
In health of body, peace of mind,
     Quiet by day:

Sound sleep by night; study and ease
Together mixt, sweet recreation,
And innocence, which most does please
     With meditation.

Thus let me live, unseen, unknown;
Thus unlamented let me die;
Steal from the world, and not a stone
     Tell where I lie.

TRUE WIT

WHOEVER thinks a faultless piece to see,
Thinks what ne'er was, nor is, nor e'er shall be.
In every work regard the writer's end,
Since none can compass more than they intend;
And if the means be just, the conduct true,
Applause, in spite of trivial faults, is due;
As men of breeding, sometimes men of wit,
To avoid great errors, must the less commit:
Neglect the rules each verbal critic lays,
For not to know some trifles, is a praise.
Most critics, fond of some subservient art,
Still make the whole depend upon a part:
They talk of principles, but notions prize,
And all to one lov'd folly sacrifice.

Once on a time, La Mancha's knight, they say,
A certain bard encount'ring on the way,
Discours'd in terms as just, with looks as sage,
As e'er could Dennis of the Grecian stage;
Concluding all were desperate sots and fools,
Who durst depart from Aristotle's rules.
Our author, happy in a judge so nice,
Produc'd his play, and begg'd the knight's advice;
Made him observe the subject, and the plot,
The manners, passions, unities, what not?
All which, exact to rule, were brought about,
Were but a combat in the lists left out.
"What! leave the combat out?" exclaims the knight;
Yes, or we must renounce the Stagirite.
"Not so, by Heaven" (he answers in a rage),
"Knights, squires, and steeds, must enter on the stage."
So vast a throng the stage can ne'er contain.
"Then build a new, or act it in a plain."

Thus critics, of less judgment than caprice,
Curious not knowing, not exact but nice,
Form short ideas; and offend in arts
(As most in manners) by a love to parts.

Some to conceit alone their taste confine,
And glitt'ring thoughts struck out at every line;
Pleas'd with a work where nothing's just or fit;
One glaring chaos and wild heap of wit.
Poets like painters, thus unskill'd to trace
The naked nature and the living grace,
With gold and jewels cover every part,
And hide with ornaments their want of art.
True wit is nature to advantage dress'd,
What oft was thought, but ne'er so well express'd;
Something, whose truth convinc'd at sight we find,
That gives us back the image of our mind.
As shades more sweetly recommend the light,
So modest plainness set off sprightly wit.
For works may have more wit than does 'em good,
As bodies perish thro' excess of blood.

Others for language all their care express,
And value books, as women men, for dress:
Their praise is still,—" The style is excellent:"
The sense, they humbly take upon content.
Words are like leaves; and where they most abound,
Much fruit of sense beneath is rarely found;
False eloquence, like the prismatic glass,
Its gaudy colors spreads on every place;
The face of nature we no more survey,
All glares alike, without distinction gay:
But true expression, like th' unchanging sun,
Clears and improves whate'er it shines upon,
It gilds all objects, but it alters none.
Expression is the dress of thought, and still
Appears more decent, as more suitable;
A vile conceit in pompous words express'd,
Is like a clown in regal purple dress'd:
For different styles with different subjects sort,
As several garbs with country, town, and court.
Some by old words to fame have made pretense,
Ancients in phrase, mere moderns in their sense;
Such labour'd nothings, in so strange a style,
Amaze th' unlearn'd, and make the learnèd smile.

Unlucky, as Fungoso in the play,
These sparks with awkward vanity display
What the fine gentleman wore yesterday;
And but so mimic ancient wits at best
As apes our grandsires in their doublets dress'd.
In words, as fashions, the same rule will hold;
Alike fantastic, if too new, or old:
Be not the first by whom the new are tried,
Nor yet the last to lay the old aside.

  But most by numbers judge a poet's song;
And smooth or rough, with them, is right or wrong:
In the bright Muse, tho' thousand charms conspire,
Her voice is all these tuneful fools admire;
Who haunt Parnassus but to please their ear,
Not mend their minds; as some to church repair,
Not for the doctrine, but the music there.
These equal syllables alone require,
Though oft the ear the open vowels tire;
While expletives their feeble aid do join;
And ten low words oft creep in one dull line:
While they ring round the same unvary'd chimes,
With sure returns of still expected rhymes;
Where'er you find "the cooling western breeze,"
In the next line, it "whispers through the trees;"
If crystal streams "with pleasing murmurs creep,"
The reader's threaten'd (not in vain) with "sleep;"
Then, at the last and only couplet, fraught
With some unmeaning thing they call a thought,
A needless Alexandrine ends the song,
That, like a wounded snake, drags its slow length along.
Leave such to tune their own dull rhymes, and know
What's roundly smooth or languishingly slow;
And praise the easy vigor, of a line,
Where Denham's strength, and Waller's sweetness join.
True ease in writing comes from art, not chance,
As those move easiest who have learn'd to dance.
'Tis not enough no harshness gives offense,
The sound must seem an echo to the sense:
Soft is the strain when Zephyr gently blows,
And the smooth stream in smoother numbers flows;

But when loud surges lash the sounding shores,
The hoarse, rough verse should like the torrent roar:
When Ajax strives some rock's vast weight to throw,
The line, too, labours, and the words move slow;
Not so, when swift Camilla scours the plain,
Flies o'er th' unbending corn, and skims along the main.
Hear how Timotheus' vary'd lays surprise,
And bid alternate passions fall and rise!
While, at each change, the son of Libyan Jove
Now burns with glory, and then melts with love;
Now his fierce eyes with sparkling fury glow,
Now sighs steal out, and tears begin to flow:
Persians and Greeks like turns of nature found,
And the world's victor stood subdued by sound!
The power of music all our hearts allow,
And what Timotheus was, is Dryden now.
  Avoid extremes; and shun the fault of such,
Who still are pleas'd too little or too much.
At every trifle scorn to take offense,
That always shows great pride, or little sense;
Those heads, as stomachs, are not sure the best,
Which nauseate all, and nothing can digest.
Yet let not each gay turn thy rapture move;
For fools admire, but men of sense approve:
As things seem large which we through mists descry,
Dulness is ever apt to magnify.

[From Part II of An Essay on Criticism.]

AN ESSAY ON MAN

Awake, my St. John! leave all meaner things
To low ambition, and the pride of kings.
Let us (since life can little more supply
Than just to look about us, and to die)
Expatiate free o'er all this scene of man;
A mighty maze! but not without a plan;
A wild, where weeds and flow'rs promiscuous shoot;
Or garden, tempting with forbidden fruit.

Together let us beat this ample field,
Try what the open, what the covert yield!
The latent tracts, the giddy heights, explore
Of all who blindly creep, or sightless soar;
Eye nature's walks, shoot folly as it flies,
And catch the manners living as they rise:
Laugh where we must, be candid where we can;
But vindicate the ways of God to man.
Say first, of God above, or man below,
What can we reason, but from what we know?
Of man, what see we but his station here,
From which to reason, or to which refer?
Thro' worlds unnumber'd tho' the God be known,
'Tis ours to trace him only in our own.
He, who thro' vast immensity can pierce,
See worlds on worlds compose one universe,
Observe how system into system runs,
What other planets circle other suns,
What vary'd being peoples every star,
May tell why heav'n has made us as we are.
But of this frame the bearings and the ties,
The strong connections, nice dependencies,
Gradations just, has thy pervading soul
Look'd thro'? or can a part contain the whole?

Is the great chain, that draws all to agree,
And drawn support, upheld by God, or thee?
Presumptuous man! the reason wouldst thou find,
Why form'd so weak, so little, and so blind?
First, if thou canst, the harder reason guess,
Why form'd no weaker, blinder, and no less?
Ask of thy mother earth, why oaks are made
Taller or stronger than the weeds they shade?
Or ask of yonder argent fields above,
Why Jove's Satellites are less than Jove?

Of systems possible, if 'tis confest
That wisdom infinite must form the best,
Where all must full or not coherent be,
And all that rises, rise in due degree;
Then, in the scale of reas'ning life, 'tis plain,
There must be, somewhere, such a rank as man:

And all the question (wrangle e'er so long)
Is only this, if God has plac'd him wrong?
Respecting man whatever wrong we call,
May, must be right, as relative to all.
In human works, tho' labour'd on with pain,
A thousand movements scarce one purpose gain;
In God's, one single can its end produce;
Yet serves to second too some other use.
So man, who here seems principal alone,
Perhaps acts second to some sphere unknown,
Touches some wheel, or verges to some goal;
'Tis but a part we see, and not a whole.

When the proud steed shall know why man restrains
His fiery course, or drives him o'er the plains;
When the dull ox, why now he breaks the clod,
Is now a victim, and now Ægypt's god:
Then shall man's pride and dullness comprehend
His actions', passions', being's, use and end;
Why doing, suff'ring, check'd, impell'd; and why
This hour a slave, the next a deity.

Then say not man's imperfect, heav'n in fault;
Say rather, man's as perfect as he ought:
His knowledge measur'd to his state and place;
His time a moment, and a point his space.
If to be perfect in a certain sphere,
What matter, soon or late, or here or there?
The blest to-day is as completely so,
As who began a thousand years ago.

Heav'n from all creatures hides the book of fate,
All but the page prescrib'd, their present state:
From brutes what men, from men what spirits know:
Or who could suffer being here below?
The lamb thy riot dooms to bleed to-day,
Had he thy reason, would he skip and play?
Pleas'd to the last, he crops the flow'ry food,
And licks the hand just rais'd to shed his blood.
Oh blindness to the future! kindly giv'n,
That each may fill the circle mark'd by heav'n:
Who sees with equal eye, as God of all,
A hero perish, or a sparrow fall,

Atoms or systems into ruin hurl'd,
And now a bubble burst, and now a world.

Hope humbly then; with trembling pinions soar;
Wait the great teacher death, and God adore.
What future bliss, he gives not thee to know,
But gives that hope to be thy blessing now.
Hope springs eternal in the human breast:
Man never *is*, but always *to be* blest:
The soul, uneasy and confin'd from home,
Rests and expatiates in a life to come.

Lo, the poor Indian! whose untutor'd mind
Sees God in clouds, or hears him in the wind;
His soul, proud science never taught to stray
Far as the solar walk, or milky way;
Yet simple nature to his hope has giv'n,
Behind the cloud-topt hill, an humbler heav'n;
Some safer world in depth of woods embrac'd,
Some happier island in the wat'ry waste,
Where slaves once more their native land behold,
No fiends torment, no Christians thirst for gold.
To Be, contents his natural desire,
He asks no angel's wing, no seraph's fire;
But thinks admitted to that equal sky,
His faithful dog shall bear him company.

Go, wiser thou! and in thy scale of sense,
Weigh thy opinion against providence;
Call imperfection what thou fancy'st such,
Say, Here he gives too little, there too much:
Destroy all creatures for thy sport or gust,
Yet cry, If man's unhappy, God's unjust;
If man alone ingross not Heav'n's high care,
Alone made perfect here, immortal there:
Snatch from his hand the balance and the rod,
Re-judge his justice, be the God of God.
In pride, in reas'ning pride, our error lies;
All quit their sphere, and rush into the skies.
Pride still is aiming at the blest abodes;
Men would be angels, angels would be gods.
Aspiring to be gods if angels fell,
Aspiring to be angels men rebel;

And who but wishes to invert the laws
Of order, sins against th' eternal cause.

　Ask for what end the heav'nly bodies shine,
Earth for whose use? pride answers, "'Tis for mine:
For me kind nature wakes her genial pow'r,
Suckles each herb, and spreads out ev'ry flow'r;
Annual for me, the grape, the rose renew
The juice nectareous, and the balmy dew;
For me, the mine a thousand treasures brings;
For me, health gushes from a thousand springs;
Seas roll to waft me, suns to light me rise;
My foot-stool earth, my canopy the skies."

　But errs not nature from this gracious end,
From burning suns when livid deaths descend,
When earthquakes swallow, or when tempests sweep
Towns to one grave, whole nations to the deep?
"No ('tis reply'd) the first almighty cause
Acts not by partial, but by gen'ral laws;
Th' exceptions few; some change since all began:
And what created perfect?"—Why then man?
If the great end be human happiness,
Then nature deviates; and can man do less?
As much that end a constant course requires
Of show'rs and sun-shine, as of man's desires;
As much eternal springs and cloudless skies,
As men for ever temp'rate, calm, and wise.
If plagues or earthquakes break not Heav'n's design,
Why then a Borgia, or a Catiline?
Who knows but he, whose hand the light'ning forms,
Who heaves old ocean, and who wings the storms;
Pours fierce ambition in a Cæsar's mind,
Or turns young Ammon loose to scourge mankind?
From pride, from pride, our very reas'ning springs;
Account for moral as for nat'ral things:
Why charge we heav'n in those, in these acquit?
In both, to reason right is to submit.

　Better for us, perhaps, it might appear,
Were there all harmony, all virtue here;
That never air or ocean felt the wind,
That never passion discompos'd the mind.

But all subsists by elemental strife;
And passions are the elements of life.
The gen'ral order, since the whole began,
Is kept in nature, and is kept in man.

What would this man? Now upward will he soar,
And little less than angel, would be more;
Now looking downward, just as griev'd appears
To want the strength of bulls, the fur of bears.
Made for his use all creatures if he call,
Say what their use, had he the pow'rs of all;
Nature to these, without profusion, kind,
The proper organs, proper pow'rs assign'd;
Each seeming want compensated of course,
Here with degrees of swiftness, there of force;
All in exact proportion to the state;
Nothing to add, and nothing to abate.
Each beast, each insect, happy in its own:
Is Heav'n unkind to man, and man alone?
Shall he alone, whom rational we call
Be pleas'd with nothing, if not blest with all?

The bliss of man (could pride that blessing find)
Is not to act or think beyond mankind;
No pow'rs of body, or of soul to share,
But what his nature and his state can bear.
Why has not man a microscopic eye?
For this plain reason, man is not a fly.
Say what the use, were finer optics giv'n,
T' inspect a mite, not comprehend the heav'n?
Or touch, if tremblingly alive all o'er,
To smart and agonize at ev'ry pore?
Or quick effluvia darting thro' the brain,
Die of a rose in aromatic pain?
If nature thunder'd in his op'ning ears,
And stunn'd him with the music of the spheres,
How would he wish that heav'n had left him still
The whisp'ring zephyr, and the purling rill?
Who finds not Providence all good and wise,
Alike in what it gives, and what denies?

Far as creation's ample range extends,
The scale of sensual, mental pow'rs ascends:

Mark how it mounts to man's imperial race,
From the green myriads in the peopled grass:
What modes of sight betwixt each wide extreme,
The mole's dim curtain, and the lynx's beam:
Of smell, the headlong lioness between,
And hound sagacious on the tainted green:
Of hearing, from the life that fills the flood,
To that which warbles through the vernal wood?
The spider's touch, how exquisitely fine!
Feels at each thread, and lives along the line:
In the nice bee, what sense so subtly true
From pois'nous herbs extracts the healing dew:
How instinct varies in the grov'ling swine,
Compar'd, half reas'ning elephant, with thine!
'Twixt that, and reason, what a nice barrier?
For ever sep'rate, yet for ever near!
Remembrance and reflection how ally'd;
What thin partitions sense from thought divide?
And middle natures, how they long to join,
Yet never pass th' insuperable line!
Without this just gradation, could they be
Subjected, these to those, or all to thee?
The pow'rs of all subdu'd by thee alone,
Is not thy reason all these pow'rs in one?

See, thro' this air, this ocean, and this earth,
All matter quick, and bursting into birth.
Above, how high progressive life may go!
Around, how wide! how deep extend below!
Vast chain of being! which from God began,
Natures ethereal, human, angel, man,
Beast, bird, fish, insect, what no eye can see,
No glass can reach; from Infinite to thee,
From thee to nothing. On superior pow'rs
Were we to press, inferior might on ours;
Or in the full creation leave a void,
Where, one step broken, the great scale's destroy'd:
From Nature's chain whatever link you strike,
Tenth, or ten thousandth, breaks the chain alike.

And, if each system in gradation roll
Alike essential to th' amazing whole,

The least confusion but in one, not all
That system only, but the whole must fall.
Let earth unbalanc'd from her orbit fly,
Planets and suns run lawless thro' the sky;
Let ruling angels from their spheres be hurl'd,
Being on being wreck'd, and world on world;
Heav'n's whole foundations to their centre nod,
And nature tremble to the throne of God.
All this dread order break—for whom? for thee?
Vile worm!—oh madness! pride! impiety!

What if the foot, ordain'd the dust to tread,
Or hand, to toil, aspir'd to be the head?
What if the head, the eye, or ear repin'd
To serve mere engines to the ruling mind?
Just as absurd for any part to claim
To be another, in this gen'ral frame;
Just as absurd, to mourn the tasks or pains
The great directing Mind of all ordains.

All are but parts of one stupendous whole,
Whose body nature is, and God the soul;
That, chang'd thro' all, and yet in all the same,
Great in the earth, as in th' ethereal frame,
Warms in the sun, refreshes in the breeze,
Glows in the stars, and blossoms in the trees,
Lives thro' all life, extends thro' all extent,
Spreads undivided, operates unspent;
Breathes in our soul, informs our mortal part,
As full, as perfect, in a hair as heart;
As full, as perfect, in vile man that mourns,
As the rapt seraph that adores and burns:
To him no high, no low, no great, no small;
He fills, he bounds, connects, and equals all.

Cease then, nor order imperfection name:
Our proper bliss depends on what we blame.
Know thy own point: this kind, this due degree
Of blindness, weakness, Heav'n bestows on thee.
Submit. In this, or any other sphere,
Secure to be as blest as thou canst bear:
Safe in the hand of one disposing pow'r,
Or in the natal, or the mortal hour.

All nature is but art, unknown to thee;
All chance, direction which thou canst not see;
All discord, harmony not understood;
All partial evil, universal good.
And, spite of pride, in erring reason's spite,
One truth is clear, "Whatever is, is right."

[EPISTLE I.]

JOHN GAY [1685–1732]

THE HARE WITH MANY FRIENDS

FRIENDSHIP, like love, is but a name,
Unless to one you stint the flame.
The child whom many fathers share,
Hath seldom known a father's care.
'Tis thus in friendship; who depend
On many, rarely find a friend.

A Hare, who, in a civil way,
Complied with everything, like Gay,
Was known by all the bestial train,
Who haunt the wood, or graze the plain.
Her care was, never to offend,
And every creature was her friend.

As forth she went at early dawn,
To taste the dew-besprinkled lawn,
Behind she hears the hunter's cries,
And from the deep-mouthed thunder flies:
She starts, she stops, she pants for breath;
She hears the near advance of death;
She doubles, to mislead the hound,
And measures back her mazy round,
Till, fainting in the public way,
Half dead with fear she gasping lay.

What transport in her bosom grew,
When first the Horse appeared in view!
"Let me," says she, "your back ascend,
And owe my safety to a friend.

You know my feet betray my flight;
To friendship every burden's light."
The Horse replied: "Poor honest Puss,
It grieves my heart to see thee thus;
Be comforted; relief is near,
For all your friends are in the rear."

She next the stately Bull implored;
And thus replied the mighty lord.
"Since every beast alive can tell
That I sincerely wish you well,
I may, without offence, pretend,
To take the freedom of a friend;
Love calls me hence; a favourite cow
Expects me near yon barley-mow:
And when a lady's in the case,
You know, all other things give place.
To leave you thus might seem unkind;
But see, the Goat is just behind."

The Goat remarked her pulse was high,
Her languid head, her heavy eye;
"My back," says he, "may do you harm;
The Sheep's at hand, and wool is warm."

The Sheep was feeble, and complained
His sides a load of wool sustained:
Said he was slow, confessed his fears,
For hounds eat sheep as well as hares.

She now the trotting Calf addressed,
To save from death a friend distressed.
"Shall I," says he, "of tender age,
In this important care engage?
Older and abler passed you by;
How strong are those, how weak am I!
Should I presume to bear you hence,
Those friends of mine may take offence.
Excuse me, then. You know my heart.
But dearest friends, alas! must part!
How shall we all lament: Adieu!
For see, the hounds are just in view."

JAMES THOMSON [1700–1748]

THE CASTLE OF INDOLENCE

In lowly dale, fast by a river's side
With woody hill o'er hill encompassed round,
A most enchanting wizard did abide,
Than whom a fiend more fell is nowhere found.
It was, I ween, a lovely spot of ground;
And there a season atween June and May,
Half prankt with spring, with summer half imbrowned,
A listless climate made, where, sooth to say,
No living wight could work, ne cared for play.

Was nought around but images of rest:
Sleep-soothing groves, and quiet lawns between;
And flowery beds, that slumbrous influence kest,
From poppies breathed; and beds of pleasant green,
Where never yet was creeping creature seen.
Meantime unnumbered glittering streamlets played,
And hurlèd everywhere their waters sheen;
That, as they bickered through the sunny glade,
Though restless still themselves, a lulling murmur made.

Joined to the prattle of the purling rills,
Were heard the lowing herds along the vale,
And flocks loud bleating from the distant hills,
And vacant shepherds piping in the dale:
And now and then sweet Philomel would wail,
Or stock-doves plain amid the forest deep,
That drowsy rustled to the sighing gale;
And still a coil the grasshopper did keep:
Yet all the sounds yblent inclinèd all to sleep.

Full in the passage of the vale, above,
A sable, silent, solemn forest stood;
Where nought but shadowy forms were seen to move,
As Idless fancied in her dreaming mood:

And up the hills, on either side, a wood
  Of blackening pines, aye waving to and fro,
  Sent forth a sleepy horror through the blood;
  And where this valley winded out below,
The murmuring main was heard, and scarcely heard, to flow.

  A pleasing land of drowsy-head it was:
  Of dreams that wave before the half-shut eye;
  And of gay castles in the clouds that pass, ·
  Forever flushing round a summer-sky.
  There eke the soft delights, that witchingly
  Instil a wanton sweetness through the breast,
  And the calm pleasures, always hovered nigh;
  But whate'er smackt of noyance, or unrest,
Was far, far off expelled from this delicious nest.

  A certain music, never known before,
  Here lulled the pensive, melancholy mind;
  Full easily obtained. Behoves no more,
  But sidelong to the gently-waving wind
  To lay the well-tuned instrument reclined;
  From which, with airy flying fingers light,
  Beyond each mortal touch the most refined,
  The god of winds drew sounds of deep delight:
Whence, with just cause, the harp of Æolus it hight.

  Near the pavilions where we slept, still ran
  Soft-tinkling streams, and dashing waters fell,
  And sobbing breezes sighed, and oft began
  (So worked the wizard) wintry storms to swell,
  As heaven and earth they would together mell:
  At doors and windows, threatening, seemed to call
  The demons of the tempest, growling fell,
  Yet the least entrance found they none at all;
Whence sweeter grew our sleep, secure in massy hall.

  And hither Morpheus sent his kindest dreams,
  Raising a world of gayer tinct and grace;
  O'er which were shadowy cast Elysian gleams,

That played, in waving lights, from place to place,
And shed a roseate smile on Nature's face.
Not Titian's pencil e'er could so array,
So fleece with clouds, the pure ethereal space;
Ne could it e'er such melting forms display,
As loose on flowery beds all languishingly lay.

[From CANTO I of the poem of the same title.]

HYMN

THESE, as they change, Almighty Father, these,
Are but the varied God. The rolling year
Is full of Thee. Forth in the pleasing Spring
Thy beauty walks, thy tenderness and love.
Wide-flush the fields; the softening air is balm;
Echo the mountains round; the forest smiles;
And every sense, and every heart is joy.
Then comes thy glory in the summer-months,
With light and heart refulgent. Then thy sun
Shoots full perfection through the swelling year:
And oft thy voice in dreadful thunder speaks;
And oft at dawn, deep noon, or falling eve,
By brooks and groves, in hollow-whispering gales.
Thy bounty shines in autumn unconfined,
And spreads a common feast for all that lives.
In winter awful thou! with clouds and storms
Around thee thrown, tempest o'er tempest rolled
Majestic darkness! on the whirlwind's wing,
Riding sublime, thou bidst the world adore,
And humblest Nature with thy northern blast.

Mysterious round! what skill, what force Divine,
Deepfelt, in these appear! a simple train,
Yet so delightful mixed, with such kind art,
Such beauty and beneficence combined:
Shade, unperceived, so softening into shade;
And all so forming an harmonious whole;
That, as they still succeed, they ravish still.
But wandering oft, with brute unconscious gaze,

Man marks not Thee, marks not the mighty Hand,
That, ever-busy, wheels the silent spheres;
Works in the secret deep; shoots, steaming, thence
The fair profusion that o'erspreads the spring:
Flings from the sun direct the flaming day;
Feeds every creature; hurls the tempest forth;
And, as on earth this grateful change revolves,
With transport touches all the springs of life.
    Nature, attend! join every living soul,
Beneath the spacious temple of the sky,
In adoration join; and ardent raise
One general song! To Him, ye vocal gales,
Breathe soft, whose Spirit in your freshness breathes.
Oh, talk of Him in solitary glooms,
Where o'er the rock the scarcely waving pine
Fills the brown shade with a religious awe,
And ye, whose bolder note is heard afar,
Who shake the astonished world, lift high to heaven
The impetuous song, and say from whom you rage.
His praise, ye brooks, attune, ye trembling rills;
And let me catch it as I muse along.
Ye headlong torrents, rapid and profound;
Ye softer floods, that lead the humid maze
Along the vale; and thou, majestic main,
A secret world of wonders in thyself,
Sound His stupendous praise, whose greater voice
Or bids you roar, or bids your roarings fall.
So roll your incense, herbs, and fruits, and flowers,
In mingled clouds to Him, whose sun exalts,
Whose breath perfumes you, and whose pencil paints.
Ye forests, bend, ye harvests, wave to him;
Breathe your still song into the reaper's heart,
As home he goes beneath the joyous moon.
Ye that keep watch in Heaven, as earth asleep
Unconscious lies, effuse your mildest beams;
Ye constellations, while your angels strike,
Amid the spangled sky, the silver lyre.
Great source of day! blest image here below
Of thy Creator, ever pouring wide,

From world to world, the vital ocean round,
On nature write with every beam His praise.
The thunder rolls: be hushed the prostrate world,
While cloud to cloud returns the solemn hymn.
Bleat out afresh, ye hills; ye mossy rocks,
Retain the sound; the broad responsive low,
Ye valleys, raise; for the Great Shepherd reigns,
And his unsuffering kingdom yet will come.
Ye woodlands, all awake; a boundless song
Burst from the groves; and when the restless day,
Expiring, lays the warbling world asleep,
Sweetest of birds! sweet Philomela, charm
The listening shades, and teach the night His praise.
Ye chief, for whom the whole creation smiles;
At once the head, the heart, the tongue of all,
Crown the great hymn! in swarming cities vast,
Assembled men to the deep organ join
The long resounding voice, oft breaking clear,
At solemn pauses, through the swelling base;
And, as each mingling flame increases each,
In one united ardour rise to Heaven.
Or if you rather choose the rural shade,
And find a fane in every sacred grove,
There let the shepherd's lute, the virgin's lay,
The prompting seraph, and the poet's lyre,
Still sing the God of Seasons as they roll.
For me, when I forget the darling theme,
Whether the blossom blows, the Summer ray
Russets the plain, inspiring Autumn gleams,
Or Winter rises in the blackening east—
Be my tongue mute, my fancy paint no more,
And, dead to joy, forget my heart to beat.

Should Fate command me to the furthest verge
Of the green earth, to distant barbarous climes,
Rivers unknown to song; where first the sun
Gilds Indian mountains, or his setting beam
Flames on the Atlantic isles, 't is nought to me;
Since God is ever present, ever felt,
In the void waste as in the city full;

And where He vital breathes, there must be joy.
When even at last the solemn Hour shall come,
And wing my mystic flight to future worlds,
I cheerfully will obey; there with new powers,
Will rising wonders sing. I cannot go
Where Universal Love not smiles around,
Sustaining all yon orbs, and all their suns;
From seeming evil still educing good,
And better thence again, and better still,
In infinite progression. But I lose
Myself in Him, in Light ineffable!
Come, then, expressive silence, muse His praise.

[Postlude to THE SEASONS.]

JOHN DYER [1700–1758]

GRONGAR HILL

SILENT Nymph, with curious eye!
Who, the purple evening, lie
On the mountain's lonely van,
Beyond the noise of busy man;
Painting fair the form of things,
While the yellow linnet sings;
Or the tuneful nightingale
Charms the forest with her tale;
Come, with all thy various hues,
Come, and aid thy sister Muse;
Now while Phœbus riding high
Gives lustre to the land and sky!
Grongar Hill invites my song,
Draw the landskip bright and strong;
Grongar, in whose mossy cells
Sweetly musing Quiet dwells;
Grongar, in whose silent shade,
For the modest Muses made,
So oft I have, the evening still,
At the fountain of a rill,

Sate upon a flowery bed,
With my hand beneath my head;
While strayed my eyes o'er Towy's flood,
Over mead, and over wood,
From house to house, from hill to hill,
'Till Contemplation had her fill.

About his chequered sides I wind,
And leave his brooks and meads behind,
And groves, and grottoes where I lay,
And vistas shooting beams of day:
Wide and wider spreads the vale,
As circles on a smooth canal:
The mountains round—unhappy fate!
Sooner or later, of all height,
Withdraw their summits from the skies,
And lessen as the others rise:
Still the prospect wider spreads,
Adds a thousand woods and meads;
Still it widens, widens still,
And sinks the newly-risen hill.

Now I gain the mountain's brow,
What a landskip lies below!
No clouds, no vapours intervene,
But the gay, the open scene
Does the face of nature shew,
In all the hues of heaven's bow!
And, swelling to embrace the light,
Spreads around beneath the sight.

Old castles on the cliffs arise,
Proudly towering in the skies!
Rushing from the woods, the spires
Seem from hence ascending fires!
Half his beams Apollo sheds
On the yellow mountain-heads!
Gilds the fleeces of the flocks,
And glitters on the broken rocks!

Below me trees unnumbered rise,
Beautiful in various dyes:
The gloomy pine, the poplar blue,
The yellow beech, the sable yew,

The slender fir, that taper grows,
The sturdy oak with broad-spread boughs;
And beyond the purple grove,
Haunt of Phillis, queen of love!
Gaudy as the opening dawn,
Lies a long and level lawn
On which a dark hill, steep and high,
Holds and charms the wandering eye!
Deep are his feet in Towy's flood,
His sides are cloth'd with waving wood,
And ancient towers crown his brow,
That cast an aweful look below;
Whose ragged walls the ivy creeps,
And with her arms from falling keeps:
So both a safety from the wind
On mutual dependence find.

'Tis now the raven's bleak abode;
'Tis now th' apartment of the toad;
And there the fox securely feeds;
And there the poisonous adder breeds
Conceal'd in ruins, moss and weeds;
While, ever and anon, there falls
Huge heaps of hoary mouldered walls.
Yet time has seen, that lifts the low,
And level lays the lofty brow,
Has seen this broken pile compleat,
Big with the vanity of state;
But transient is the smile of fate!
A little rule, a little sway,
A sunbeam in a winter's day,
Is all the proud and mighty have
Between the cradle and the grave.

And see the rivers how they run,
Thro' woods and meads, in shade and sun,
Sometimes swift, sometimes slow,
Wave succeeding wave, they go
A various journey to the deep,
Like human life to endless sleep!
Thus is nature's vesture wrought,
To instruct our wandering thought;

Thus she dresses green and gay,
To disperse our cares away.
   Ever charming, ever new,
When will the landskip tire the view!
The fountain's fall, the river's flow,
The woody valleys, warm and low;
The windy summit, wild and high,
Roughly rushing on the sky;
The pleasant seat, the ruined tower,
The naked rock, the shady bower;
The town and village, dome and farm,
Each gives each a double charm,
As pearls upon an Æthiop's arm.
   See, on the mountain's southern side,
Where the prospect opens wide,
Where the evening gilds the tide;
How close and small the hedges lie!
What streaks of meadows cross the eye!
A step methinks may pass the stream,
So little distant dangers seem;
So we mistake the future's face,
Eyed thro' Hope's deluding glass;
As yon summits soft and fair
Clad in colours of the air,
Which to those who journey near,
Barren, brown, and rough appear;
Still we tread the same coarse way;
The present's still a cloudy day.
   O may I with myself agree,
And never covet what I see:
Content me with an humble shade,
My passions tamed, my wishes laid;
For while our wishes wildly roll,
We banish quiet from the soul:
'Tis thus the busy beat the air;
And misers gather wealth and care.
   Now, even now, my joys run high,
As on the mountain-turf I lie;
While the wanton Zephyr sings,
And in the vale perfumes his wings;

While the waters murmur deep;
While the shepherd charms his sheep;
While the birds unbounded fly,
And with music fill the sky,
Now, even now, my joys run high.
　　Be full, ye courts, be great who will;
Search for Peace with all your skill:
Open wide the lofty door,
Seek her on the marble floor,
In vain ye search, she is not there;
In vain ye search the domes of Care!
Grass and flowers Quiet treads,
On the meads, and mountain-heads,
Along with Pleasure, close allied,
Ever by each other's side:
And often, by the murmuring rill,
Hears the thrush, while all is still,
Within the groves of Grongar Hill.

EDWARD YOUNG [1681–1765]

MAN

How poor, how rich, how abject, how august,
How complicate, how wonderful, is man!
How passing wonder He, who made him such!
Who centred in our make such strange extremes!
From diff'rent natures marvellously mixt,
Connection exquisite of distant worlds!
Distinguish'd link in being's endless chain!
Midway from nothing to the deity!
A beam ethereal, sullied, and absorpt!
Tho' sullied, and dishonour'd, still divine!
Dim miniature of greatness absolute!
An heir of glory! a frail child of dust!
Helpless immortal! insect infinite!
A worm! a god!—I tremble at myself,
And in myself am lost! at home a stranger,

Thought wanders up and down, surpris'd, aghast,
And wond'ring at her own: how reason reels!
O what a miracle to man is man,
Triumphantly distress'd! what joy, what dread!
Alternately transported, and alarm'd!
What can preserve my life? or what destroy?
An angel's arm can't snatch me from the grave;
Legions of angels can't confine me there.

'Tis past conjecture; all things rise in proof:
While o'er my limbs sleep's soft dominion spreads:
What though my soul fantastic measures trod
O'er fairy fields; or mourn'd along the gloom
Of pathless woods; or down the craggy steep
Hurl'd headlong, swam with pain the mantled pool;
Or scal'd the cliff; or danc'd on hollow winds,
With antic shapes, wild natives of the brain?
Her ceaseless flight, tho' devious, speaks her nature
Of subtler essence than the trodden clod;
Active, aerial, tow'ring, unconfin'd,
Unfetter'd with her gross companion's fall.
Ev'n silent night proclaims eternal day.
For human weal, heaven husbands all events;
Dull sleep instructs, nor sport vain dreams in vain.

Why then their love deplore that are not lost?
Why wanders wretched thought their tombs around,
In infidel distress? Are angels there?
Slumbers, rak'd up in dust, ethereal fire?

They live! they greatly live a life on earth
Unkindled, unconceiv'd; and from an eye
Of tenderness let heavenly pity fall
On me, more justly number'd with the dead.
This is the desert, this the solitude:
How populous, how vital is the grave!
This is creation's melancholy vault,
The vale funereal, the sad cypress gloom;
The land of apparitions, empty shades!
All, all on earth, is shadow, all beyond
Is substance; the reverse is folly's creed;
How solid all, where change shall be no more!

This is the bud of being, the dim dawn,
The twilight of our day, the vestibule;
Life's theatre as yet is shut, and death,
Strong death alone can heave the massy bar,
This gross impediment of clay remove,
And make us embryos of existence free.
From real life, but little more remote
Is he, not yet a candidate for light,
The future embryo, slumb'ring in his sire.
Embryos we must be, till we burst the shell,
Yon ambient azure shell, and spring to life,
The life of gods, O transport! and of man.

Yet man, fool man! here buries all his thoughts;
Inters celestial hopes without one sigh.
Prisoner of earth, and pent beneath the moon,
Here pinions all his wishes; wing'd by heaven
To fly at infinite: and reach it there
Where seraphs gather immortality,
On life's fair tree, fast by the throne of God.
What golden joys ambrosial clust'ring glow
In his full beam, and ripen for the just,
Where momentary ages are no more!
Where time, and pain, and chance, and death expire!
And is it in the flight of threescore years
To push eternity from human thought,
And smother souls immortal in the dust?
A soul immortal, spending all her fires,
Wasting her strength in strenuous idleness,
Thrown into tumult, raptur'd, or alarm'd,
At aught this scene can threaten or indulge,
Resembles ocean into tempest wrought,
To waft a feather, or to drown a fly.

[From NIGHT I, NIGHT THOUGHTS.]

WILLIAM SHENSTONE [1714–1763]

THE DYING KID

A TEAR bedews my Delia's eye,
To think yon playful kid must die;
From crystal spring and flowery mead
Must, in his prime of life, recede.

Erewhile in sportive circles round
She saw him wheel, and frisk, and bound;
From rock to rock pursue his way,
And on the fearful margin play.

Pleased on his various freaks to dwell
She saw him climb my rustic cell;
Then eye my lawns with verdure bright,
And seem all ravished at the sight.

She tells with what delight he stood
To trace his features in the flood;
Then skipped aloof with quaint amaze
And then drew near again to gaze.

She tells me how with eager speed
He flew to hear my vocal reed;
And how with critic face profound,
And steadfast ear devoured the sound.

His every frolic light as air
Deserves the gentle Delia's care;
And tears bedew her tender eye,
To think the playful kid must die.

But knows my Delia, timely wise,
How soon this blameless era flies?
While violence and craft succeed,
Unfair design, and ruthless deed!

Soon would the vine his wounds deplore,
And yield her purple gifts no more;
Oh soon, erased from every grove
Were Delia's name, and Strephon's love.

No more those bowers might Strephon see,
Where first he fondly gazed on thee;
No more those beds of flowerets find
Which for thy charming brows he twined.

Each wayward passion soon would tear
His bosom, now so void of care.
And when they left his ebbing vein
What but insipid age remain?

Then mourn not the decrees of Fate
That gave his life so short a date;
And I will join thy tenderest sighs
To think that youth so swiftly flies.

THE SCHOOLMISTRESS

HER cap, far whiter than the driven snow,
Emblem right meet of decency does yield:
Her apron dyed in grain, as blue, I trow,
As is the harebell that adorns the field;
And in her hand, for sceptre, she does wield
Tway birchen sprays; with anxious fear entwined,
With dark distrust, and sad repentance filled;
And steadfast hate, and sharp affliction joined,
And fury uncontrolled, and chastisement unkind.

A russet stole was o'er her shoulders thrown;
A russet kirtle fenced the nipping air;
'T was simple russet, but it was her own;
'T was her own country bred the flock so fair!
'T was her own labour did the fleece prepare;

And, sooth to say, her pupils ranged around,
Through pious awe, did term it passing rare;
For they in gaping wonderment abound,
And think, no doubt, she been the greatest wight on ground.

Albeit ne flattery did corrupt her truth,
Ne pompous title did debauch her ear;
Goody, good woman, gossip, n'aunt, forsooth,
Or dame, the sole additions she did hear;
Yet these she challenged, these she held right dear;
Ne would esteem him act as mought behove,
Who should not honoured eld with these revere;
For never title yet so mean could prove,
But there was eke a mind which did that title love.

One ancient hen she took delight to feed,
The plodding pattern of the busy dame;
Which, ever and anon, impelled by need,
Into her school, begirt with chickens, came;
Such favour did her past deportment claim;
And, if neglect had lavished on the ground
Fragment of bread, she would collect the same;
For well she knew, and quaintly could expound,
What sin it were to waste the smallest crumb she found.

Herbs, too, she knew, and well of each could speak,
That in her garden sipped the silvery dew;
Where no vain flower disclosed a gaudy streak,
But herbs for use and physick, not a few,
Of grey renown, within those borders grew:
The tufted basil, pun-provoking thyme,
Fresh baum, and marygold of chearful hue:
The lowly gill, that never dares to climb;
And more I fain would sing, disdaining here to rhyme.

[From the poem of the same title.]

WILLIAM COLLINS [1721–1759]

ODE WRITTEN IN 1746

How sleep the Brave who sink to rest
By all their country's wishes blest!
When Spring, with dewy fingers cold,
Returns to deck their hallowed mould,
She there shall dress a sweeter sod
Than Fancy's feet have ever trod.

By fairy hands their knell is rung,
By forms unseen their dirge is sung:
There Honour comes, a pilgrim grey,
To bless the turf that wraps their clay;
And Freedom shall awhile repair
To dwell a weeping hermit there!

DIRGE [1]

To fair Fidele's grassy tomb
  Soft maids and village hinds shall bring
Each opening sweet of earliest bloom,
  And rifle all the breathing spring.

No wailing ghost shall dare appear
  To vex with shrieks this quiet grove;
But shepherd lads assembled here,
  And melting virgins own their love.

No withered witch shall here be seen;
  No goblins lead their nightly crew:
The female fays shall haunt the green,
  And dress thy grave with pearly dew!

[1] *Cf.* Shakspere's Dirge, page 96.

The redbreast oft, at evening hours,
  Shall kindly lend his little aid,
With hoary moss, and gathered flowers,
  To deck the ground where thou art laid.

When howling winds and beating rain,
  In tempests shake the sylvan cell;
Or 'midst the chase, on every plain,
  The tender thought on thee shall dwell;

Each lonely scene shall thee restore;
  For thee the tear be duly shed;
Beloved till life can charm no more,
  And mourned till pity's self be dead.

ODE TO EVENING

IF aught of oaten stop, or pastoral song,
May hope, chaste Eve! to soothe thy modest ear
    Like thy own solemn springs,
    Thy springs and dying gales:

O Nymph reserved! while now the bright-hair'd Sun
Sits in yon western tent, whose cloudy skirts
    With brede ethereal wove
    O'erhang his wavy bed

Now air is hush'd, save where the weak-eyed bat
With short, shrill shriek, flits by on leathern wing,
    Or where the beetle winds
    His small but sullen horn

As oft he rises 'midst the twilight path
Against the pilgrim borne in heedless hum—
    Now teach me, Maid composed!
    To breathe some softened strain

Whose numbers, stealing through thy darkening vale,
May not unseemly with its stillness suit,
    As musing slow I hail
    Thy genial loved return.

For when thy folding star arising shows
His paly circlet, at his warning lamp
    The fragrant Hours, and Elves
    Who slept in flowers the day,

And many a Nymph who wreathes her brows with sedge,
And sheds the freshening dew, and, lovelier still,
    The pensive Pleasures sweet,
    Prepare thy shadowy car.

Then let me rove some wild and heathy scene;
Or find some ruin, 'midst its dreary dells,
    Whose walls more awful nod
    By thy religious gleams.

Or, if chill blustering winds, or driving rain,
Prevent my willing feet, be mine the hut
    That, from the mountain's side,
    Views wilds, and swelling floods,

And hamlets brown, and dim-discovered spires;
And hears their simple bell; and marks o'er all
    Thy dewy fingers draw
    The gradual dusky veil,

While Spring shall pour his showers, as oft he wont,
And bathe thy breathing tresses, meekest Eve!
    While Summer loves to sport
    Beneath thy lingering light;

While sallow Autumn fills thy lap with leaves;
Or Winter, yelling through the troublous air,
    Affrights thy shrinking train,
    And rudely rends thy robes;

So long, sure-found beneath the sylvan shed,
Shall Fancy, Friendship, Science, smiling Peace,
    Thy gentlest influence own,
    And love thy fav'rite name!

ODE TO LIBERTY

Strophe

WHO shall awake the Spartan fife,
  And call in solemn sounds to life,
The youths, whose locks divinely spreading,
  Like vernal hyacinths in sullen hue,
At once the breath of fear and virtue shedding,
  Applauding freedom loved of old to view?
What new Alcæus, fancy-blest,
Shall sing the sword, in myrtles drest,
  At wisdom's shrine awhile its flame concealing,
(What place so fit to seal a deed renown'd?)
  Till she her brightest lightnings round revealing,
It leaped in glory forth, and dealt her prompted wound!
    O goddess, in that feeling hour,
      When most its sounds would court thy ears,
      Let not my shell's misguided power
      E'er draw thy sad, thy mindful tears.
No, freedom, no, I will not tell
How Rome, before thy weeping face,
With heaviest sound, a giant-statue, fell,
Pushed by a wild and artless race
From off its wide ambitious base,
When time his northern sons of spoil awoke,
  And all the blended work of strength and grace,
  With many a rude repeated stroke,
And many a barbarous yell, to thousand fragments broke.

Epode

  Yet, even where'er the least appeared,
  Th' admiring world thy hand revered;
  Still 'midst the scattered states around,
  Some remnants of her strength were found;
  They saw, by what escaped the storm,
  How wondrous rose her perfect form;

How in the great, the labour'd whole,
Each mighty master pour'd his soul!
For sunny Florence, seat of art,
Beneath her vines preserved a part,
Till they, whom science loved to name,
(O who could fear it?) quench'd her flame.
And lo, an humbler relic laid
In jealous Pisa's olive shade!
See small Marino joins the theme,
Tho' least, not last in thy esteem:
Strike, louder strike the ennobling strings
To those, whose merchant sons were kings;
To him, who, deck'd with pearly pride,
In Adria weds his green-haired bride;
Hail, port of glory, wealth, and pleasure,
Ne'er let me change this Lydian measure:
Nor e'er her former pride relate,
To sad Liguria's bleeding state.
Ah no! more pleased thy haunts I seek,
On wild Helvetia's mountains bleak:
(Where, when the favour'd of thy choice,
The daring archer heard thy voice;
Forth from his eyrie roused in dread,
The ravening eagle northward fled;)
Or dwell in willow'd meads more near,
With those to whom thy stork is dear:
Those whom the rod of Alva bruised,
Whose crown a British queen refused!
The magic works, thou feel'st the strains,
One holier name alone remains;
The perfect spell shall then avail,
Hail, nymph, adored by Britain, hail!

Antistrophe

Beyond the measure vast of thought,
The works the wizard Time has wrought!
The Gaul, 'tis held of antique story,
Saw Britain linked to his now adverse strand,

No sea between, nor cliff sublime and hoary,
He passed with unwet feet thro' all our land.
To the blown Baltic then, they say,
The wild waves found another way,
Where Orcas howls, his wolfish mountains rounding;
Till all the banded west at once 'gan rise,
A wide wild storm e'en nature's self confounding,
Withering her giant sons with strange uncouth surprise.
This pillared earth so firm and wide,
By winds and inward labours torn,
In thunders dread was pushed aside,
And down the shouldering billows borne.
And see, like gems, her laughing train,
The little isles on every side,
Mona, once hid from those who search the main,
Where thousand elfin shapes abide,
And Wight who checks the westering tide,
For thee consenting heaven has each bestowed,
A fair attendant on her sovereign pride:
To thee this blest divorce she owed,
For thou hast made her vales thy loved, thy last abode.

Second Epode

Then too, 'tis said, an hoary pile,
'Midst the green navel of our isle,
Thy shrine in some religious wood,
O soul-enforcing goddess, stood!
There oft the painted native's feet
Were wont thy form celestial meet:
Tho' now with hopeless toil we trace
Time's backward rolls, to find its place;
Whether the fiery-tressèd Dane,
Or Roman's self, o'erturned the fane,
Or in what heaven-left age it fell,
'Twere hard for modern song to tell.
Yet still, if truth those beams infuse,
Which guide at once, and charm the Muse,
Beyond yon braided clouds that lie,
Paving the light-embroidered sky,

Amidst the bright pavilioned plains,
The beauteous model still remains.
There, happier than in islands blest,
Or bowers by spring or Hebe drest,
The chiefs who fill our Albion's story,
In warlike weeds, retired in glory,
Hear their consorted Druids sing
Their triumphs to the immortal string.

How may the poet now unfold
What never tongue or numbers told?
How learn, delighted and amazed,
What hands unknown that fabric raised?
Even now before his favoured eyes,
In Gothic pride, it seems to rise!
Yet Græcia's graceful orders join,
Majestic through the mixed design:
The secret builder knew to choose
Each sphere-found gem of richest hues;
Whate'er heaven's purer mould contains,
When nearer suns emblaze its veins;
There on the walls the patriot's sight
May ever hang with fresh delight,
And, graved with some prophetic rage,
Read Albion's fame through every age.

Ye forms divine, ye laureat band,
That near her inmost altar stand!
Now soothe her to her blissful train
Blithe concord's social form to gain;
Concord, whose myrtle wand can steep
Even anger's bloodshot eyes in sleep;
Before whose breathing bosom's balm
Rage drops his steel, and storms grow calm:
Her let our sires and matrons hoar
Welcome to Britain's ravaged shore;
Our youths, enamoured of the fair,
Play with the tangles of her hair,
Till, in one loud applauding sound,
The nations shout to her around,
O how supremely art thou blest,
Thou, lady, thou shalt rule the west!

THOMAS GRAY [1716–1771]

ON A FAVOURITE CAT, DROWNED IN A TUB OF GOLD FISHES

'TWAS on a lofty vase's side,
Where China's gayest art had dyed
The azure flowers that blow,
Demurest of the tabby kind
The pensive Selina, reclined,
Gazed on the lake below.

Her conscious tail her joy declared:
The fair round face, the snowy beard,
The velvet of her paws,
Her coat that with the tortoise vies,
Her ears of jet, and emerald eyes—
She saw, and purr'd applause.

Still had she gazed, but 'midst the tide
Two angel forms were seen to glide,
The Genii of the stream:
Their scaly armour's Tyrian hue
Through richest purple, to the view
Betray'd a golden gleam.

The hapless Nymph with wonder saw:
A whisker first, and then a claw
With many an ardent wish
She stretch'd, in vain, to reach the prize—
What female heart can gold despise?
What Cat's averse to fish?

Presumptuous maid! with looks intent
Again she stretch'd, again she bent,
Nor knew the gulf between—
Malignant Fate sat by and smiled—
The slippery verge her feet beguiled;
She tumbled headlong in!

Eight times emerging from the flood
She mew'd to every watery God
   Some speedy aid to send:—
No Dolphin came, no Nereid stirr'd,
Nor cruel Tom nor Susan heard—
   A favourite has no friend!

From hence, ye Beauties! undeceived
Know one false step is ne'er retrieved,
   And be with caution bold:
Not all that tempts your wandering eyes
And heedless hearts, is lawful prize,
   Nor all that glisters, gold!

ODE ON THE SPRING

Lo! where the rosy-bosom'd Hours,
   Fair Venus' train appear,
Disclose the long-expecting flowers,
   And wake the purple year!
The Attic warbler pours her throat,
Responsive to the cuckow's note,
   The untaught harmony of spring:
While, whisp'ring pleasure as they fly,
Cool Zephyrs thro' the clear blue sky
   Their gather'd fragrance fling.

Where'er the oak's thick branches stretch
   A broader browner shade;
Where'er the rude and moss-grown beech
   O'er-canopies the glade
Beside some water's rushy brink
With me the Muse shall sit, and think
   (At ease reclin'd in rustic state)
How vain the ardour of the Crowd,
How low, how little are the Proud,
   How indigent the Great!

Still is the toiling hand of Care:
   The panting herds repose:
Yet hark, how thro' the peopled air
   The busy murmur glows!
The insect youth are on the wing,
Eager to taste the honied spring,
   And float amid the liquid noon:
Some lightly o'er the current skim,
Some shew their gaily-gilded trim
   Quick-glancing to the sun.

To Contemplation's sober eye
   Such is the race of Man:
And they that creep, and they that fly,
   Shall end where they began.
Alike the Busy and the Gay
But flutter thro' life's little day,
   In fortune's varying colours drest:
Brush'd by the hand of rough Mischance,
Or chill'd by age, their airy dance
   They leave, in dust to rest.

Methinks I hear in accents low
   The sportive kind reply:
"Poor moralist! and what art thou?
   A solitary fly!
Thy Joys no glittering female meets,
No hive hast thou of hoarded sweets,
   No painted plumage to display:
On hasty wings thy youth is flown;
Thy sun is set, thy spring is gone—
   We frolick, while 'tis May."

ELEGY

WRITTEN IN A COUNTRY CHURCHYARD

THE Curfew tolls the knell of parting day,
  The lowing herd winds slowly o'er the lea,
The plowman homeward plods his weary way,
  And leaves the world to darkness and to me.

Now fades the glimmering landscape on the sight,
  And all the air a solemn stillness holds,
Save where the beetle wheels his droning flight,
  And drowsy tinklings lull the distant folds;

Save that from yonder ivy-mantled tower
  The moping owl does to the moon complain
Of such, as wandering near her secret bower,
  Molest her ancient solitary reign.

Beneath those rugged elms, that yew-tree's shade,
  Where heaves the turf in many a mouldering heap,
Each in his narrow cell for ever laid,
  The rude Forefathers of the hamlet sleep.

The breezy call of incense-breathing Morn,
  The swallow twittering from the straw-built shed,
The cock's shrill clarion, or the echoing horn,
  No more shall rouse them from their lowly bed.

For them no more the blazing hearth shall burn,
  Or busy housewife ply her evening care:
No children run to lisp their sire's return,
  Or climb his knees the envied kiss to share.

Oft did the harvest to their sickle yield,
  Their furrow oft the stubborn glebe has broke;
How jocund did they drive their team afield!
  How bow'd the woods beneath their sturdy stroke!

Let not Ambition mock their useful toil,
  Their homely joys, and destiny obscure;
Nor Grandeur hear with a disdainful smile,
  The short and simple annals of the poor.

The boast of heraldry, the pomp of power,
  And all that beauty, all that wealth e'er gave,
Awaits alike th' inevitable hour.
  The paths of glory lead but to the grave.

Nor you, ye Proud, impute to These the fault,
  If Memory o'er their Tomb no Trophies raise,
Where through the long-drawn aisle and fretted vault
  The pealing anthem swells the note of praise.

Can storied urn or animated bust
  Back to its mansion call the fleeting breath?
Can Honour's voice provoke the silent dust,
  Or Flattery sooth the dull cold ear of Death?

Perhaps in this neglected spot is laid
  Some heart once pregnant with celestial fire;
Hands that the rod of empire might have sway'd,
  Or waked to ecstasy the living lyre.

But Knowledge to their eyes her ample page
  Rich with the spoils of time did ne'er unroll;
Chill Penury repress'd their noble rage,
  And froze the genial current of the soul.

Full many a gem of purest ray serene,
  The dark unfathom'd caves of ocean bear:
Full many a flower is born to blush unseen,
  And waste its sweetness on the desert air.

Some village-Hampden, that with dauntless breast
  The little Tyrant of his fields withstood;
Some mute inglorious Milton here may rest,
  Some Cromwell guiltless of his country's blood.

Th' applause of listening senates to command,
    The threats of pain and ruin to despise,
To scatter plenty o'er a smiling land,
    And read their history in a nation's eyes,

Their lot forbade: nor circumscribed alone
    Their growing virtues, but their crimes confin'd;
Forbade to wade through slaughter to a throne,
    And shut the gates of mercy on mankind,

The struggling pangs of conscious truth to hide,
    To quench the blushes of ingenuous shame,
Or heap the shrine of Luxury and Pride
    With incense kindled at the Muse's flame.

Far from the madding crowd's ignoble strife,
    Their sober wishes never learn'd to stray;
Along the cool sequester'd vale of life
    They kept the noiseless tenor of their way.

Yet even these bones from insult to protect,
    Some frail memorial still erected nigh,
With uncouth rhymes and shapeless sculpture deck't,
    Implores the passing tribute of a sigh.

Their name, their years, spelt by th' unletter'd Muse,
    The place of fame and elegy supply:
And many a holy text around she strews,
    That teach the rustic moralist to die.

For who to dumb Forgetfulness a prey,
    This pleasing anxious being e'er resign'd,
Left the warm precincts of the cheerful day,
    Nor cast one longing lingering look behind?

On some fond breast the parting soul relies,
    Some pious drops the closing eye requires;
Ev'n from the tomb the voice of Nature cries,
    Ev'n in our Ashes live their wonted Fires.

For thee, who mindful of the unhonour'd Dead
  Dost in these lines their artless tale relate,
If chance, by lonely Contemplation led,
  Some kindred spirit shall inquire thy fate,

Haply some hoary-headed Swain may say,
  Oft have we seen him at the peep of dawn
Brushing with hasty steps the dews away
  To meet the sun upon the upland lawn.

"Hard by yon wood, now smiling as in scorn,
  Muttering his wayward fancies he would rove;
Now drooping, woeful-wan, like one forlorn,
  Or crazed with care, or cross'd in hopeless love.

"One morn I miss'd him on the custom'd hill,
  Along the heath, and near his favourite tree;
Another came; nor yet beside the rill,
  Nor up the lawn, nor at the wood was he;

"The next with dirges due in sad array
  Slow through the church-way path we saw him borne,—
Approach and read (for thou canst read) the lay
  Graved on the stone beneath yon agèd thorn."

THE EPITAPH

Here rests his head upon the lap of Earth
  A youth, to Fortune and to Fame unknown;
Fair Science frown'd not on his humble birth
  And Melancholy mark'd him for her own.

Large was his bounty, and his soul sincere;
  Heaven did a recompense as largely send:
He gave to Misery (all he had) a tear,
  He gain'd from Heaven ('twas all he wish'd) a friend.

No farther seek his merits to disclose,
  Or draw his frailties from their dread abode
(There they alike in trembling hope repose)
  The bosom of his Father and his God.

THE BARD [1]

A PINDARIC ODE

I

Strophe

"RUIN seize thee, ruthless King!
Confusion on thy banners wait,
Though fann'd by Conquest's crimson wing
They mock the air with idle state.
Helm, nor hauberk's twisted mail,
Nor e'en thy virtues, Tyrant, shall avail
To save thy secret soul from nightly fears,
From Cambria's curse, from Cambria's tears!"
  Such were the sounds, that o'er the crested pride
Of the first Edward scatter'd wild dismay,
As down the steep of Snowdon's shaggy side
He wound with toilsome march his long array.
Stout Gloster stood aghast in speechless trance;
To arms! cried Mortimer, and couch'd his quivering lance.

Antistrophe

On a rock, whose haughty brow
Frowns o'er old Conway's foaming flood,
Robed in the sable garb of woe,
With haggard eyes the Poet stood
(Loose his beard, and hoary hair
Streamed, like a meteor, to the troubled air)
And with a Master's hand, and Prophet's fire,
Struck the deep sorrows of his lyre:
  "Hark, how each giant-oak, and desert cave,
Sighs to the torrent's awful voice beneath!
O'er thee, O King! their hundred arms they wave,
Revenge on thee in hoarser murmurs breathe;
Vocal no more, since Cambria's fatal day,
To high-born Hoel's harp, or soft Llewellyn's lay.

---

[1] Founded on the tradition that Edward I, having conquered Wales, ordered that the bards be put to death.

Epode

"Cold is Cadwallo's tongue,
That hush'd the stormy main;
Brave Urien sleeps upon his craggy bed:
Mountains, ye mourn in vain
Modred, whose magic song
Made huge Plinlimmon bow his cloud-topped head.
On dreary Arvon's shore they lie,
Smear'd with gore, and ghastly pale:
Far, far aloof the affrighted ravens sail;
The famish'd Eagle screams, and passes by.

Dear lost companions of my tuneful art,
Dear, as the light that visits these sad eyes,
Dear, as the ruddy drops that warm my heart,
Ye died amidst your dying country's cries—
No more I weep. They do not sleep.
On yonder cliffs, a grisly band,
I see them sit, they linger yet,
Avengers of their native land:
With me in dreadful harmony they join,
And weave with bloody hands the tissue of thy line:—

II

Strophe

"Weave the warp, and weave the woof,
The winding sheet of Edward's race.
Give ample room, and verge enough
The characters of hell to trace.
Mark the year, and mark the night,
When Severn shall re-echo with affright
The shrieks of death, through Berkley's roofs that ring,
Shrieks of an agonizing King!
She-Wolf of France, with unrelenting fangs,
That tear'st the bowels of thy mangled Mate,
From thee be born, who o'er thy country hangs

The scourge of Heav'n. What Terrors round him wait!
Amazement in his van, with Flight combined,
And Sorrow's faded form, and Solitude behind.

Antistrophe

"Mighty Victor, mighty Lord,
Low on his funeral couch he lies!
No pitying heart, no eye, afford
A tear to grace his obsequies.
  Is the sable Warrior fled?
Thy son is gone. He rests among the Dead.
The Swarm, that in thy noon-tide beam were born?
Gone to salute the rising Morn.
Fair laughs the Morn, and soft the Zephyr blows,
While proudly riding o'er the azure realm
In gallant trim the gilded Vessel goes;
Youth on the prow, and Pleasure at the helm;
Regardless of the sweeping Whirlwind's sway,
That, hush'd in grim repose, expects his evening-prey.

Epode

"Fill high the sparkling bowl,
The rich repast prepare;
Reft of a crown, he yet may share the feast.
Close by the regal chair
Fell Thirst and Famine scowl
A baleful smile upon their baffled Guest.
  Heard ye the din of battle bray,
Lance to lance, and horse to horse?
Long Years of havoc urge their destin'd course,
And through the kindred squadrons mow their way.
Ye Towers of Julius, London's lasting shame,
With many a foul and midnight murther fed,
Revere his Consort's faith, his Father's fame,
And spare the meek Usurper's holy head.
Above, below, the rose of snow,
Twin'd with her blushing foe, we spread:

The bristled Boar in infant-gore
Wallows beneath the thorny shade.
Now, brothers, bending o'er the accursed loom
Stamp we our vengeance deep, and ratify his doom.

III

Strophe

" ' Edward, lo! to sudden fate
(Weave we the woof. The thread is spun).
Half of thy heart we consecrate.
(The web is wove. The work is done.) '
  Stay, oh stay! nor thus forlorn
Leave me unbless'd, unpitied, here to mourn!
In yon bright track, that fires the western skies,
They melt, they vanish from my eyes.
  But oh! what solemn scenes on Snowdon's height
Descending slow their glittering skirts unroll?
Visions of glory, spare my aching sight,
Ye unborn Ages, crowd not on my soul!
No more our long-lost Arthur we bewail.
All-hail, ye genuine Kings, Britannia's Issue, hail!

Antistrophe

"Girt with many a baron bold
Sublime their starry fronts they rear;
And gorgeous Dames, and Statesmen old
In bearded majesty, appear.
In the midst a Form divine!
Her eye proclaims her of the Briton-Line;
Her lion-port, her awe-commanding face,
Attemper'd sweet to virgin-grace.
What strings symphonious tremble in the air,
What strains of vocal transport round her play!
Hear from the grave, great Taliessin,[1] hear;
They breathe a soul to animate thy clay.
Bright Rapture calls, and soaring, as she sings,
Waves in the eye of Heaven her many-colour'd wings.

[1] A noted Welsh bard of the 6th century.

Epode

"The verse adorn again
Fierce War, and faithful Love,
And Truth severe, by fairy Fiction drest.
In buskin'd measures move
Pale Grief, and pleasing Pain,
With Horror, Tyrant of the throbbing breast.
A Voice, as of the Cherub-Choir,
Gales from blooming Eden bear;
And distant warblings lessen on my ear,
That lost in long futurity expire.
 Fond impious Man, think'st thou, yon sanguine cloud,
Raised by thy breath, has quench'd the Orb of day?
To-morrow he repairs the golden flood,
And warms the nations with redoubled ray.
 Enough for me: With joy I see
The different doom our Fates assign.
Be thine Despair, and sceptred Care,
To triumph, and to die, are mine."—
 He spoke, and headlong from the mountain's height
Deep in the roaring tide he plunged to endless night.

OLIVER GOLDSMITH [1728–1774]

SONG

WHEN lovely woman stoops to folly,
 And finds too late that men betray,
What charm can soothe her melancholy?
 What art can wash her guilt away?

The only art her guilt to cover,
 To hide her shame from every eye,
To give repentance to her lover,
 And wring his bosom, is—to die.

THE DESERTED VILLAGE

SWEET Auburn! loveliest village of the plain;
Where health and plenty cheered the labouring swain,
Where smiling spring its earliest visit paid,
And parting summer's lingering blooms delayed:
Dear lovely bowers of innocence and ease,
Seats of my youth, when every sport could please,
How often have I loitered o'er thy green,
Where humble happiness endeared each scene!
How often have I paused on every charm,
The sheltered cot, the cultivated farm,
The never-failing brook, the busy mill,
The decent church that topt the neighbouring hill,
The hawthorn bush, with seats beneath the shade
For talking age and whispering lovers made!
How often have I blest the coming day,
When toil remitting lent its turn to play,
And all the village train, from labour free,
Led up their sports beneath the spreading tree,
While many a pastime circled in the shade,
The young contending as the old surveyed;
And many a gambol frolicked o'er the ground,
And sleights of art and feats of strength went round.
And still, as each repeated pleasure tired,
Succeeding sports the mirthful band inspired;
The dancing pair that simply sought renown
By holding out to tire each other down;
The swain mistrustless of his smutted face,
While secret laughter tittered round the place;
The bashful virgin's side-long looks of love,
The matron's glance that would those looks reprove:
These were thy charms, sweet village! sports like these,
With sweet succession, taught even toil to please:
These round thy bowers their cheerful influence shed:
These were thy charms—but all these charms are fled.
  Sweet smiling village, loveliest of the lawn,
Thy sports are fled, and all thy charms withdrawn

Amidst thy bowers the tyrant's hand is seen,
And desolation saddens all thy green:
One only master grasps the whole domain,
And half a tillage stints thy smiling plain.
No more thy glassy brook reflects the day,
But, choked with sedges, works its weedy way;
Along the glades, a solitary guest,
The hollow sounding bittern guards its nest;
Amidst thy desert walks the lapwing flies,
And tires their echoes with unvaried cries;
Sunk are thy bowers in shapeless ruin all,
And the long grass o'ertops the mouldering wall;
And trembling, shrinking from the spoiler's hand,
Far, far away thy children leave the land.

Ill fares the land, to hastening ills a prey,
Where wealth accumulates, and men decay:
Princes and lords may flourish, or may fade;
A breath can make them, as a breath has made:
But a bold peasantry, their country's pride,
When once destroyed, can never be supplied.

A time there was, ere England's griefs began,
When every rood of ground maintained its man;
For him light labour spread her wholesome store,
Just gave what life required, but gave no more:
His best companions, innocence and health;
And his best riches, ignorance of wealth.

But times are altered; trade's unfeeling train
Usurp the land and dispossess the swain;
Along the lawn, where scattered hamlets rose,
Unwieldy wealth and cumbrous pomp repose,
And every want to opulence allied,
And every pang that folly pays to pride.
These gentle hours that plenty bade to bloom,
Those calm desires that asked but little room,
Those healthful sports that graced the peaceful scene,
Lived in each look, and brightened all the green;
These, far departing, seek a kinder shore,
And rural mirth and manners are no more.

Sweet Auburn! parent of the blissful hour,
Thy glades forlorn confess the tyrant's power.

Here, as I take my solitary rounds
Amidst thy tangling walks and ruined grounds,
And, many a year elapsed, return to view
Where once the cottage stood, the hawthorn grew,
Remembrance wakes with all her busy train,
Swells at my breast, and turns the past to pain.
    In all my wanderings round this world of care,
In all my griefs—and God has given my share—
I still had hopes, my latest hours to crown,
Amidst these humble bowers to lay me down;
To husband our life's taper at the close,
And keep the flame from wasting by repose:
I still had hopes, for pride attends us still,
Amidst the swains to show my book-learned skill,
Around my fire an evening group to draw,
And tell of all I felt, and all I saw;
And, as an hare whom hounds and horns pursue
Pants to the place from whence at first she flew,
I still had hopes, my long vexations past,
Here to return—and die at home at last.
    O blest retirement, friend to life's decline,
Retreats from care, that never must be mine,
How happy he who crowns in shades like these
A youth of labour with an age of ease;
Who quits a world where strong temptations try,
And, since 'tis hard to combat, learns to fly!
For him no wretches, born to work and weep,
Explore the mine, or tempt the dangerous deep;
No surly porter stands in guilty state,
To spurn imploring famine from the gate;
But on he moves to meet his latter end,
Angels around befriending Virtue's friend;
Bends to the grave with unperceived decay,
While resignation gently slopes the way;
And, all his prospects brightening to the last,
His heaven commences ere the world be past!
    Sweet was the sound, when oft at evening's close
Up yonder hill the village murmur rose.
There, as I passed with careless steps and slow,
The mingling notes came softened from below;

The swain responsive as the milk-maid sung,
The sober herd that lowed to meet their young,
The noisy geese that gabbled o'er the pool,
The playful children just let loose from school,
The watch-dog's voice that bayed the whispering wind,
And the loud laugh that spoke the vacant mind;—
These all in sweet confusion sought the shade,
And filled each pause the nightingale had made.
But now the sounds of population fail,
No cheerful murmurs fluctuate in the gale,
No busy steps the grass-grown foot-way tread,
For all the bloomy flush of life is fled.
All but yon widowed, solitary thing,
That feebly bends beside the plashy spring:
She, wretched matron, forced in age, for bread,
To strip the brook with mantling cresses spread,
To pick her wintry faggot from the thorn,
To seek her nightly shed, and weep till morn;
She only left of all the harmless train,
The sad historian of the pensive plain.

Near yonder copse, where once the garden smiled,
And still where many a garden flower grows wild;
There, where a few torn shrubs the place disclose,
The village preacher's modest mansion rose.
A man he was to all the country dear,
And passing rich with forty pounds a year;
Remote from towns he ran his godly race,
Nor e'er had changed, nor wished to change his place;
Unpractised he to fawn, or seek for power,
By doctrines fashioned to the varying hour;
Far other aims his heart had learned to prize,
More skilled to raise the wretched than to rise.
His house was known to all the vagrant train;
He chid their wanderings but relieved their pain:
The long-remembered beggar was his guest,
Whose beard descending swept his aged breast;
The ruined spendthrift, now no longer proud,
Claimed kindred there, and had his claims allowed;
The broken soldier, kindly bade to stay,
Sat by the fire, and talked the night away,

Wept o'er his wounds, or, tales of sorrow done,
Shouldered his crutch and showed how fields were won.
Pleased with his guests, the good man learned to glow,
And quite forgot their vices in their woe;
Careless their merits or their faults to scan,
His pity gave ere charity began.

Thus to relieve the wretched was his pride,
And e'en his failings leaned to Virtue's side;
But in his duty prompt at every call,
He watched and wept, he prayed and felt for all;
And, as a bird each fond endearment tries
To tempt its new-fledged offspring to the skies,
He tried each art, reproved each dull delay,
Allured to brighter worlds, and led the way.

Beside the bed where parting life was laid,
And sorrow, guilt, and pain by turns dismayed,
The reverend champion stood. At his control
Despair and anguish fled the struggling soul;
Comfort came down the trembling wretch to raise,
And his last faltering accents whispered praise.

At church, with meek and unaffected grace,
His looks adorned the venerable place;
Truth from his lips prevailed with double sway,
And fools, who came to scoff, remained to pray.
The service past, around the pious man,
With steady zeal, each honest rustic ran;
Even children followed with endearing wile,
And plucked his gown to share the good man's smile.
His ready smile a parent's warmth exprest;
Their welfare pleased him, and their cares distrest:
To them his heart, his love, his griefs were given,
But all his serious thoughts had rest in heaven.
As some tall cliff that lifts its awful form,
Swells from the vale, and midway leaves the storm,
Tho' round its breast the rolling clouds are spread,
Eternal sunshine settles on its head.

Beside yon straggling fence that skirts the way,
With blossom'd furze unprofitably gay,
There, in his noisy mansion, skill'd to rule,
The village master taught his little school.

A man severe he was, and stern to view;
I knew him well, and every truant knew;
Well had the boding tremblers learned to trace
The day's disasters in his morning face;
Full well they laughed with counterfeited glee
At all his jokes, for many a joke had he;
Full well the busy whisper circling round
Conveyed the dismal tidings when he frowned.
Yet he was kind, or, if severe in aught,
The love he bore to learning was in fault;
The village all declared how much he knew:
'Twas certain he could write, and cipher too;
Lands he could measure, terms and tides presage,
And even the story ran that he could gauge;
In arguing, too, the parson owned his skill,
For, even tho' vanquished, he could argue still;
While words of learned length and thundering sound
Amazed the gazing rustics ranged around;
And still they gazed, and still the wonder grew,
That one small head could carry all he knew.

    But past is all his fame. The very spot
Where many a time he triumphed is forgot.
Near yonder thorn, that lifts its head on high,
Where once the sign-post caught the passing eye,
Low lies that house where nut-brown draughts inspired,
Where graybeard mirth and smiling toil retired,
Where village statesmen talked with looks profound,
And news much older than their ale went round.
Imagination fondly stoops to trace
The parlour splendours of that festive place:
The white-washed wall, the nicely sanded floor,
The varnished clock that clicked behind the door;
The chest contrived a double debt to pay,
A bed by night, a chest of drawers by day;
The pictures placed for ornament and use,
The twelve good rules, the royal game of goose;
The hearth, except when winter chill'd the day,
With aspen boughs and flowers and fennel gay;
While broken tea-cups, wisely kept for show,
Ranged o'er the chimney, glistened in a row.

Vain transitory splendours! could not all
Reprieve the tottering mansion from its fall?
Obscure it sinks, nor shall it more impart
An hour's importance to the poor man's heart.
Thither no more the peasant shall repair
To sweet oblivion of his daily care;
No more the farmer's news, the barber's tale,
No more the woodman's ballad shall prevail;
No more the smith his dusky brow shall clear,
Relax his ponderous strength, and lean to hear;
The host himself no longer shall be found
Careful to see the mantling bliss go round;
Nor the coy maid, half willing to be prest,
Shall kiss the cup to pass it to the rest.

Yes! let the rich deride, the proud disdain,
These simple blessings of the lowly train;
To me more dear, congenial to my heart,
One native charm, than all the gloss of art.
Spontaneous joys, where Nature has its play,
The soul adopts, and owns their first born sway;
Lightly they frolic o'er the vacant mind,
Unenvied, unmolested, unconfined.
But the long pomp, the midnight masquerade,
With all the freaks of wanton wealth arrayed—
In these, ere triflers half their wish obtain,
The toiling pleasure sickens into pain;
And, e'en while fashion's brightest arts decoy,
The heart distrusting asks if this be joy.

Ye friends to truth, ye statesmen who survey
The rich man's joy increase, the poor's decay,
'Tis yours to judge, how wide the limits stand
Between a splendid and an happy land.
Proud swells the tide with loads of freighted ore,
And shouting Folly hails them from her shore;
Hoards e'en beyond the miser's wish abound,
And rich men flock from all the world around.
Yet count our gains! This wealth is but a name
That leaves our useful products still the same.
Not so the loss. The man of wealth and pride
Takes up a space that many poor supplied;

Space for his lake, his park's extended bounds,
Space for his horses, equipage, and hounds:
The robe that wraps his limbs in silken sloth
Has robbed the neighbouring fields of half their growth;
His seat, where solitary sports are seen,
Indignant spurns the cottage from the green:
Around the world each needful product flies,
For all the luxuries the world supplies;
While thus the land adorned for pleasure all
In barren splendour feebly waits the fall.

As some fair female unadorned and plain,
Secure to please while youth confirms her reign,
Slights every borrowed charm that dress supplies,
Nor shares with art the triumph of her eyes;
But when those charms are past, for charms are frail,
When time advances, and when lovers fail,
She then shines forth, solicitous to bless,
In all the glaring impotence of dress.
Thus fares the land by luxury betrayed:
In nature's simplest charms at first arrayed,
But verging to decline, its splendours rise,
Its vistas strike, its palaces surprise;
While, scourged by famine from the smiling land
The mournful peasant leads his humble band,
And while he sinks, without one arm to save,
The country blooms—a garden and a grave.

Where then, ah! where, shall poverty reside,
To 'scape the pressure of contiguous pride?
If to some common's fenceless limits strayed,
He drives his flock to pick the scanty blade,
Those fenceless fields the sons of wealth divide,
And even the bare-worn common is denied.

If to the city sped—what waits him there?
To see profusion that he must not share;
To see ten thousand baneful arts combined
To pamper luxury, and thin mankind;
To see those joys the sons of pleasure know
Extorted from his fellow-creature's woe.
Here while the courtier glitters in brocade,
There the pale artist plies the sickly trade;

Here while the proud their long-drawn pomps display,
There the black gibbet glooms beside the way.
The dome where pleasure holds her midnight reign
Here, richly deckt, admits the gorgeous train:
Tumultuous grandeur crowds the blazing square,
The rattling chariots clash, the torches glare.
Sure scenes like these no troubles e'er annoy!
Sure these denote one universal joy!
Are these thy serious thoughts?—Ah, turn thine eyes
Where the poor houseless shivering female lies.
She once, perhaps, in village plenty blest,
Has wept at tales of innocence distrest;
Her modest looks the cottage might adorn,
Sweet as the primrose peeps beneath the thorn:
Now lost to all; her friends, her virtue fled,
Near her betrayer's door she lays her head,
And, pinch'd with cold, and shrinking from the shower,
With heavy heart deplores that luckless hour,
When idly first, ambitious of the town,
She left her wheel and robes of country brown.

Do thine, sweet Auburn,—thine, the loveliest train,—
Do thy fair tribes participate her pain?
Even now, perhaps, by cold and hunger led,
At proud men's doors they ask a little bread!
Ah, no! To distant climes, a dreary scene,
Where half the convex world intrudes between,
Through torrid tracts with fainting steps they go,
Where wild Altama murmurs to their woe.
Far different there from all that charmed before
The various terrors of that horrid shore;
Those blazing suns that dart a downward ray,
And fiercely shed intolerable day;
Those matted woods, where birds forget to sing,
But silent bats in drowsy clusters cling;
Those poisonous fields with rank luxuriance crowned,
Where the dark scorpion gathers death around;
Where at each step the stranger fears to wake
The rattling terrors of the vengeful snake;
Where crouching tigers wait their hapless prey,
And savage men more murderous still than they;

While oft in whirls the mad tornado flies,
Mingling the ravaged landscape with the skies.
Far different these from every former scene,
The cooling brook, the grassy vested green,
The breezy covert of the warbling grove,
That only sheltered thefts of harmless love.

Good Heaven! what sorrows gloomed that parting day,
That called them from their native walks away;
When the poor exiles, every pleasure past,
Hung round the bowers, and fondly looked their last,
And took a long farewell, and wished in vain
For seats like these beyond the western main,
And shuddering still to face the distant deep,
Returned and wept, and still returned to weep.
The good old sire the first prepared to go
To new found worlds, and wept for others' woe;
But for himself, in conscious virtue brave,
He only wished for worlds beyond the grave.
His lovely daughter, lovelier in her tears,
The fond companion of his helpless years,
Silent went next, neglectful of her charms,
And left a lover's for a father's arms.
With louder plaints the mother spoke her woes,
And blest the cot where every pleasure rose,
And kist her thoughtless babes with many a tear
And claspt them close, in sorrow doubly dear,
Whilst her fond husband strove to lend relief
In all the silent manliness of grief.

O luxury! thou curst by Heaven's decree,
How ill exchanged are things like these for thee!
How do thy potions, with insidious joy,
Diffuse their pleasure only to destroy!
Kingdoms by thee, to sickly greatness grown,
Boast of a florid vigour not their own.
At every draught more large and large they grow,
A bloated mass of rank unwieldy woe;
Till sapped their strength, and every part unsound,
Down, down, they sink, and spread a ruin round.

Even now the devastation is begun,
And half the business of destruction done;

Even now, methinks, as pondering here I stand,
I see the rural virtues leave the land.
Down where yon anchoring vessel spreads the sail,
That idly waiting flaps with every gale,
Downward they move, a melancholy band,
Pass from the shore, and darken all the strand.
Contented Toil, and hospitable Care,
And kind connubial tenderness, are there;
And piety with wishes placed above,
And steady loyalty, and faithful love.
And thou, sweet Poetry, thou loveliest maid,
Still first to fly where sensual joys invade;
Unfit in these degenerate times of shame
To catch the heart, or strike for honest fame;
Dear charming nymph, neglected and decried,
My shame in crowds, my solitary pride;
Thou source of all my bliss, and all my woe,
That found'st me poor at first, and keep'st me so;
Thou guide by which the nobler arts excel,
Thou nurse of every virtue, fare thee well!
Farewell, and oh! where'er thy voice be tried,
On Torno's cliffs, or Pambamarca's side,
Whether where equinoctial fervours glow,
Or winter wraps the polar world in snow,
Still let thy voice, prevailing over time,
Redress the rigours of the inclement clime;
Aid slighted truth with thy persuasive strain;
Teach erring man to spurn the rage of gain;
Teach him, that states of native strength possest,
Tho' very poor, may still be very blest;
That trade's proud empire hastes to swift decay,
As ocean sweeps the laboured mole away;
While self-dependent power can time defy,
As rocks resist the billows and the sky.

JANE ELLIOT [1727–1805]

THE FLOWERS OF THE FOREST

A Lament for Flodden.

I'VE heard them lilting, at our ewe-milking,
Lasses a-lilting, before the dawn of day;
But now they are moaning, on ilka green loaning[1];
The Flowers of the Forest are a' wede away.

At bughts[2] in the morning nae blythe lads are scorning[3];
The lasses are lanely, and dowie, and wae;
Nae daffing[4], nae gabbing, but sighing and sabbing,
Ilk ane lifts her leglin[5], and hies her away.

In hairst[6], at the shearing, nae youths now are jeering,
The bandsters[7] are lyart,[8] and runkled and gray;
At fair or at preaching, nae wooing, nae fleeching[9]—
The Flowers of the Forest are a' wede away.

At e'en, in the gloaming, nae swankies[10] are roaming
'Bout stacks wi' the lasses at bogle to play;
But ilk ane sits eerie, lamenting her dearie—
The Flowers of the Forest are a' wede away.

Dool and wae for the order sent our lads to the Border!
The English, for ance, by guile wan the day;
The Flowers of the Forest, that fought aye the foremost,
The prime of our land, lie cauld in the clay.

We'll hear nae more lilting at our ewe-milking,
Women and bairns are heartless and wae;
Sighing and moaning on ilka green loaning,
The Flowers of the Forest are a' wede away.

---

[1] a grass path through corn-fields for the use of cattle.   [2] sheep-pens.
[3] teasing   [4] jesting.   [5] pail.   [6] harvest.
[7] men who bind up the sheaves.   [8] hoary.   [9] coaxing.   [10] strapping lads.

THOMAS WARTON [1728–1790]

DEATH OF KING ARTHUR

O'ER Cornwall's cliffs the tempest roared,
High the screaming sea-mew soared;
On Tintagell's topmost tower
Darksome fell the sleety shower;
Round the rough castle shrilly sung
The whirling blast, and wildly flung
On each tall rampart's thundering side
The surges of the tumbling tide:
When Arthur ranged his red-cross ranks
On conscious Camlan's crimsoned banks:
By Mordred's faithless guile decreed
Beneath a Saxon spear to bleed!
Yet in vain a paynim foe
Armed with fate the mighty blow;
For when he fell an Elfin Queen
All in secret, and unseen,
O'er the fainting hero threw
Her mantle of ambrosial blue;
And bade her spirits bear him far,
In Merlin's agate-axled car,
To her green isle's enamelled steep
Far in the navel of the deep.
O'er his wounds she sprinkled dew
From flowers that in Arabia grew:
On a rich enchanted bed
She pillowed his majestic head;
O'er his brow, with whispers bland,
Thrice she waved an opiate wand;
And to soft music's airy sound,
Her magic curtains closed around.
There, renewed the vital spring,
Again he reigns a mighty king;
And many a fair and fragrant clime,
Blooming in immortal prime,

By gales of Eden ever fanned,
Owns the monarch's high command:
Thence to Britain shall return
(If right prophetic rolls I learn),
Borne on Victory's spreading plume,
His ancient sceptre to resume;
Once more, in old heroic pride,
His barbèd courser to bestride;
His Knightly table to restore,
And brave the tournaments of yore.

[From THE GRAVE OF KING ARTHUR.]

WILLIAM COWPER [1731–1800]

EPITAPH ON A HARE

HERE lies, whom hound did ne'er pursue,
   Nor swifter greyhound follow,
Whose foot ne'er tainted morning dew,
   Nor ear heard huntsman's halloo;

Old Tiney, surliest of his kind,
   Who, nursed with tender care,
And to domestic bounds confined,
   Was still a wild Jack hare.

Though duly from my hand he took
   His pittance every night,
He did it with a jealous look,
   And, when he could, would bite.

His diet was of wheaten bread,
   And milk, and oats, and straw;
Thistles, or lettuces instead,
   With sand to scour his maw.

On twigs of hawthorn he regaled,
  On pippins' russet peel,
And, when his juicy salads failed,
  Sliced carrot pleased him well.

A Turkey carpet was his lawn,
  Whereon he loved to bound,
To skip and gambol like a fawn,
  And swing his rump around.

His frisking was at evening hours,
  For then he lost his fear,
But most before approaching showers,
  Or when a storm drew near.

Eight years and five round-rolling moons
  He thus saw steal away,
Dozing out all his idle noons,
  And every night at play.

I kept him for his humour's sake,
  For he would oft beguile
My heart of thoughts that made it ache,
  And force me to a smile.

But now beneath this walnut shade
  He finds his long last home,
And waits, in snug concealment laid,
  Till gentler Puss shall come.

He, still more agèd, feels the shocks
  From which no care can save,
And, partner once of Tiney's box,
  Must soon partake his grave.

EVENING IN WINTER

Oh, Winter, ruler of the inverted year,
Thy scattered hair with sleet-like ashes filled,
Thy breath congealed upon thy lips, thy cheeks
Fringed with a beard made white with other snows
Than those of age, thy forehead wrapped in clouds.—
A leafless branch thy sceptre, and thy throne
A sliding car indebted to no wheels,
But urged by storms along the slippery way,—
I love thee, all unlovely as thou seem'st,
And dreaded as thou art. Thou hold'st the sun
A prisoner in the yet undawning East,
Shortening his journey between morn and noon,
And hurrying him, impatient of his stay,
Down to the rosy west; but kindly still
Compensating his loss with added hours
Of social converse and instructive ease,
And gathering at short notice in one group
The family dispersed, and fixing thought
Not less dispersed by daylight and its cares.
I crown the king of intimate delights,
Fire-side enjoyments, home-born happiness,
And all the comforts that the lowly roof
Of undisturbed retirement, and the hours
Of long uninterrupted evening know.
No rattling wheels stop short before these gates;
No powdered, pert proficients in the art
Of sounding an alarm, assault these doors
Till the street rings; no stationary steeds
Cough their own knell, while heedless of the sound
The silent circle fan themselves, and quake:
But here the needle plies its busy task,
The pattern grows, the well-depicted flower,
Wrought patiently into the snowy lawn,
Unfolds its bosom; buds and leaves and sprigs
And curly tendrils, gracefully disposed,
Follow the nimble finger of the fair;

A wreath that cannot fade, of flowers that blow
With most success when all besides decay.
The poet's or historian's page, by one
Made vocal for the amusement of the rest;
The sprightly lyre, whose treasure of sweet sounds
The touch from many a trembling chord shakes out;
And the clear voice symphonious, yet distinct,
And in the charming strife triumphant still;
Beguile the night, and set a keener edge
On female industry; the threaded steel
Flies swiftly, and unfelt the task proceeds.
The volume closed, the customary rites
Of the last meal commence: a Roman meal,
Such as the mistress of the world once found
Delicious, when her patriots of high note,
Perhaps by moonlight, at their humble doors,
And under an old oak's domestic shade,
Enjoyed—spare feast!—a radish and an egg.
Discourse ensues, not trivial, yet not dull,
Nor such as with a frown forbids the play
Of fancy, or prescribes the sound of mirth;
Nor do we madly, like an impious world,
Who deem religion frenzy, and the God
That made them an intruder on their joys,
Start at his awful name, or deem his praise
A jarring note; themes of a graver tone
Exciting oft our gratitude and love,
While we retrace with memory's pointing wand
That calls the past to our exact review,
The dangers we have 'scaped, the broken snare,
The disappointed foe, deliverance found
Unlooked for, life preserved and peace restored,
Fruits of omnipotent eternal love:—
Oh, evenings worthy of the gods! exclaimed
The Sabine bard. Oh, evenings, I reply,
More to be prized and coveted than yours,
As more illumined and with nobler truths,
That I, and mine, and those we love, enjoy.

[From Book IV, The Task.]

TO MARY

THE twentieth year is well-nigh past,
Since first our sky was overcast;
Ah, would that this might be the last!
     My Mary!

Thy spirits have a fainter flow,
I see thee daily weaker grow;
'Twas my distress that brought thee low,
     My Mary!

Thy needles, once a shining store,
For my sake restless heretofore,
Now rust disused, and shine no more,
     My Mary!

For though thou gladly wouldst fulfil
The same kind office for me still,
Thy sight now seconds not thy will,
     My Mary!

But well thou playedst the housewife's part,
And all thy threads with magic art
Have wound themselves about this heart,
     My Mary!

Thy indistinct expressions seem
Like language uttered in a dream;
Yet me they charm, whate'er the theme,
     My Mary!

Thy silver locks, once auburn bright,
Are still more lovely in my sight
Than golden beams of orient light,
     My Mary!

For, could I view nor them nor thee,
What sight worth seeing could I see?
The sun would rise in vain for me,
     My Mary!

Partakers of thy sad decline,
Thy hands their little force resign;
Yet, gently prest, press gently mine,
            My Mary!

Such feebleness of limbs thou provest,
That now at every step thou movest
Upheld by two, yet still thou lovest,
            My Mary!

And still to love, though prest with ill,
In wintry age to feel no chill,
With me is to be lovely still,
            My Mary!

But ah! by constant heed I know,
How oft the sadness that I show
Transforms thy smiles to looks of woe,
            My Mary!

And should my future lot be cast
With much resemblance of the past,
Thy worn-out heart will break at last,
            My Mary!

ON THE RECEIPT OF MY MOTHER'S PICTURE

OH, that those lips had language! Life has passed
With me but roughly since I heard thee last.
Those lips are thine—thy own sweet smile I see,
The same that oft in childhood solaced me;
Voice only fails, else how distinct they say,
"Grieve not, my child, chase all thy fears away!"
The meek intelligence of those dear eyes
(Blessed be the art that can immortalize,
The art that baffles Time's tyrannic claim
To quench it) here shines on me still the same.
  Faithful remembrancer of one so dear,
O welcome guest, though unexpected here!

Who bidst me honour with an artless song,
Affectionate, a mother lost so long,
I will obey, not willingly alone,
But gladly, as the precept were her own:
And, while that face renews my filial grief,
Fancy shall weave a charm for my relief,
Shall steep me in Elysian reverie,
A momentary dream that thou art she.

My mother! when I learnt that thou wast dead,
Say, wast thou conscious of the tears I shed?
Hovered thy spirit o'er thy sorrowing son,
Wretch even then life's journey just begun?
Perhaps thou gavest me, though unfelt, a kiss:
Perhaps a tear, if souls can weep in bliss—
Ah, that maternal smile! It answers—Yes.
I heard the bell tolled on thy burial day,
I saw the hearse that bore thee slow away,
And, turning from my nursery window, drew
A long, long sigh, and wept a last adieu!
But was it such?—It was.—Where thou art gone
Adieus and farewells are a sound unknown.
May I but meet thee on that peaceful shore,
The parting word shall pass my lips no more!
Thy maidens, grieved themselves at my concern,
Oft gave me promise of thy quick return.
What ardently I wished I long believed,
And, disappointed still, was still deceived.
By expectation every day beguiled,
Dupe of *to-morrow* even from a child.
Thus many a sad to-morrow came and went,
Till, all my stock of infant sorrow spent,
I learned at last submission to my lot;
But, though I less deplored thee, ne'er forgot.

Where once we dwelt our name is heard no more,
Children not thine have trod my nursery floor;
And where the gardener Robin, day by day,
Drew me to school along the public way,
Delighted with my bauble coach, and wrapped
In scarlet mantle warm, and velvet capped,

'Tis now become a history little known,
That once we called the pastoral house our own.
Short-lived possession! but the record fair
That memory keeps, of all thy kindness there,
Still outlives many a storm that has effaced
A thousand other themes less deeply traced.
Thy nightly visits to my chamber made,
That thou mightst know me safe and warmly laid;
Thy morning bounties ere I left my home,
The biscuit, or confectionery plum;
The fragrant waters on my cheek bestowed
By thy own hand, till fresh they shone and glowed;
All this, and more endearing still than all,
Thy constant flow of love, that knew no fall,
Ne'er roughened by those cataracts and brakes
That humour interposed too often makes;
All this still legible in memory's page,
And still to be so to my latest age,
Adds joy to duty, makes me glad to pay
Such honours to thee as my numbers may;
Perhaps a frail memorial, but sincere,
Not scorned in heaven, though little noticed here.
    Could Time, his flight reversed, restore the hours,
When, playing with thy vesture's tissued flowers,
The violet, the pink, and jessamine,
I pricked them into paper with a pin
(And thou wast happier than myself the while,
Wouldst softly speak, and stroke my head and smile),
Could those few pleasant days again appear,
Might one wish bring them, would I wish them here?
I would not trust my heart—the dear delight
Seems so to be desired, perhaps I might.—
But no—what here we call our life is such
So little to be loved, and thou so much,
That I should ill requite thee to constrain
Thy unbound spirit into bonds again.
    Thou, as a gallant bark from Albion's coast
(The storms all weathered and the ocean crossed)
Shoots into port at some well-havened isle,
Where spices breathe, and brighter seasons smile,

There sits quiescent on the floods that show
Her beauteous form reflected clear below,
While airs impregnated with incense play
Around her, fanning light her streamers gay;
So thou, with sails how swift! hast reached the shore,
"Where tempests never beat nor billows roar."
And thy loved consort on the dangerous tide
Of life long since has anchored by thy side.
But me, scarce hoping to attain that rest,
Always from port withheld, always distressed—
Me howling blasts drive devious, tempest tost,
Sails ripped, seams opening wide, and compass lost,
And day by day some current's thwarting force
Sets me more distant from a prosperous course.
Yet, oh, the thought that thou art safe, and he!
That thought is joy, arrive what may to me.
My boast is not, that I deduce my birth
From loins enthroned and rulers of the earth;
But higher far my proud pretensions rise—
The son of parents passed into the skies!
And now, farewell—Time unrevoked has run
His wonted course, yet what I wished is done.
By contemplation's help, not sought in vain,
I seem to have lived my childhood o'er again;
To have renewed the joys that once were mine,
Without the sin of violating thine:
And, while the wings of Fancy still are free,
And I can view this mimic show of thee,
Time has but half succeeded in his theft—
Thyself removed, thy power to soothe me left.

LOSS OF THE ROYAL GEORGE

Toll for the Brave!
The brave that are no more!
All sunk beneath the wave
Fast by their native shore!

Eight hundred of the brave
Whose courage well was tried,
Had made the vessel heel
And laid her on her side.

A land-breeze shook the shrouds
And she was overset;
Down went the Royal George,
With all her crew complete.

Toll for the brave!
Brave Kempenfelt is gone;
His last sea-fight is fought,
His work of glory done.

It was not in the battle;
No tempest gave the shock;
She sprang no fatal leak,
She ran upon no rock.

His sword was in its sheath,
His fingers held the pen,
When Kempenfelt went down
With twice four hundred men.

—Weigh the vessel up
Once dreaded by our foes!
And mingle with our cup
The tears that England owes.

Her timbers yet are sound,
And she may float again
Full charged with England's thunder,
And plough the distant main:

But Kempenfelt is gone,
His victories are o'er;
And he and his eight hundred
Shall plough the wave no more.

THOMAS CHATTERTON [1752–1770]

MYNSTRELLES SONGE

O! SYNGE untoe mie roundelaie,
O! droppe the brynie teare wythe mee,
Daunce ne moe atte hallie daie,
Lycke a reynynge[1] ryver bee;
  Mie love ys dedde,
  Gon to hys death-bedde,
  Al under the wyllowe tree.

Blacke hys cryne[2] as the wyntere nyghte,
Whyte hys rode[3] as the sommer snowe,
Rodde hys face as the mornynge lyghte,
Cale he lyes ynne the grave belowe;

Swote hys tyngue as the throstles note,
Quycke ynn daunce as thoughte canne bee,
Defte hys taboure, codgelle stote,
O! hee lyes bie the wyllowe tree:

Harke! the ravenne flappes hys wynge,
In the briered delle belowe;
Harke! the dethe-owle loude dothe synge,
To the nyghte-mares as heie goe;

See! the whyte moone sheenes onne hie;
Whyterre ys mie true loves shroude;
Whyterre yanne the mornynge skie,
Whyterre yanne the evenynge cloude;

Heere, uponne mie true loves grave,
Schalle the baren fleurs be layde,
Nee one hallie Seyncte to save
Al the celness of a mayde.

---

[1] running.   [2] hair.   [3] complexion.

Wythe mie hondes I'lle dente the brieres
Rounde his hallie corse to gre,
Ouphante fairie lyghte youre fyres,
Heere mie boddie stylle schalle bee.

Comme, wythe acorne-coppe & thorne,
Drayne mie hartys blodde awaie;
Lyfe & all yttes goode I scorne,
Daunce bie nete, or feaste bie daie.

Waterre wytches, crownede wythe reytes,[4]
Bere mee to yer leathalle tyde.
I die; I comme; mie true love waytes.
Thos the damselle spake, and dyed.
      Mie love ys dedde, etc.

                  [From ÆLLA.]

GEORGE CRABBE [1754–1832]

VILLAGE LIFE

"As Truth will paint it, and as Bards will not."

HERE, wandering long, amid these frowning fields,
I sought the simple life that Nature yields;
Rapine and Wrong and Fear usurped her place,
And a bold, artful, surly, savage race;
Who, only skilled to take the finny tribe,
The yearly dinner, or septennial bribe,
Wait on the shore, and, as the waves run high,
On the tossed vessel bend their eager eye,
Which to their coast directs its vent'rous way;
Theirs or the ocean's miserable prey.
  As on their neighbouring beach yon swallows stand,
And wait for favouring winds to leave the land;
While still for flight the ready wing is spread:
So waited I the favouring hour, and fled;
Fled from these shores where guilt and famine reign,
And cried, "Ah! hapless they who still remain:

    [4] water-flags

Who still remain to hear the ocean roar,
Whose greedy waves devour the lessening shore;
Till some fierce tide, with more imperious sway
Sweeps the low hut and all it holds away;
When the sad tenant weeps from door to door,
And begs a poor protection from the poor "!

But these are scenes where Nature's niggard hand
Gave a spare portion to the famished land;
Hers is the fault, if here mankind complain
Of fruitless toil and labour spent in vain;
But yet in other scenes more fair in view,
When Plenty smiles—alas! she smiles for few—
And those who taste not, yet behold her store,
Are as the slaves that dig the golden ore—
The wealth around them makes them doubly poor.
Or will you deem them amply paid in health,
Labour's fair child, that languishes with wealth?
Go, then! and see them rising with the sun,
Through a long course of daily toil to run;
See them beneath the Dog-star's raging heat,
When the knees tremble and the temples beat;
Behold them, leaning on their scythes, look o'er
The labour past, and toils to come explore;
See them alternate suns and showers engage,
And hoard up aches and anguish for their age;
Through fens and marshy moors their steps pursue,
When their warm pores imbibe the evening dew;
Then own that labour may as fatal be
To these thy slaves, as thine excess to thee.

Amid this tribe too oft a manly pride
Strives in strong toil the fainting heart to hide;
There may you see the youth of slender frame
Contend with weakness, weariness, and shame;
Yet, urged along, and proudly loth to yield,
He strives to join his fellows of the field;
Till long-contending nature droops at last,
Declining health rejects his poor repast,
His cheerless spouse the coming danger sees,
And mutual murmurs urge the slow disease.

Yet grant them health, 't is not for us to tell,
Though the head droops not, that the heart is well;
Or will you praise that homely, healthy fare,
Plenteous and plain, that happy peasants share!
Oh! trifle not with wants you cannot feel,
Nor mock the misery of a stinted meal;
Homely, not wholesome, plain, not plenteous, such
As you who praise, would never deign to touch.

Ye gentle souls, who dream of rural ease,
Whom the smooth stream and smoother sonnet please;
Go! if the peaceful cot your praises share,
Go look within, and ask if peace be there;
If peace be his, that drooping weary sire;
Or theirs, that offspring round their feeble fire;
Or hers, that matron pale, whose trembling hand
Turns on the wretched hearth the expiring brand.

Nor yet can Time itself obtain for these
Life's latest comforts, due respect and ease;
For yonder see that hoary swain, whose age
Can with no cares except its own engage;
Who, propped on that rude staff, looks up to see
The bare arms broken from the withering tree,
On which, a boy, he climbed the loftiest bough,
Then his first joy, but his sad emblem now.

He once was chief in all the rustic trade;
His steady hand the straightest furrow made;
Full many a prize he won, and still is proud
To find the triumphs of his youth allowed;
A transient pleasure sparkles in his eyes,
He hears and smiles, then thinks again and sighs;
For now he journeys to his grave in pain;
The rich disdain him; nay, the poor disdain:
Alternate masters now their slave command,
Urge the weak efforts of his feeble hand,
And, when his age attempts its task in vain,
With ruthless taunts, of lazy poor complain.

Oft may you see him, when he tends the sheep,
His winter charge, beneath the hillock weep;
Oft hear him murmur to the winds that blow
O'er his white locks and bury them in snow,

When, roused by rage and muttering in the morn,
He mends the broken hedge with icy thorn:—
"Why do I live, when I desire to be
At once from life and life's long labour free?
Like leaves in spring, the young are blown away,
Without the sorrows of a slow decay;
I, like yon withered leaf, remain behind,
Nipped by the frost, and shivering in the wind;
There it abides till younger buds come on
As I, now all my fellow-swains are gone;
Then from the rising generation thrust,
It falls, like me, unnoticed to the dust.

"These fruitful fields, these numerous flocks I see,
Are others' gain, but killing cares to me;
To me the children of my youth are lords,
Cool in their looks, but hasty in their words:
Wants of their own demand their care; and who
Feels his own want and succours others too?
A lonely, wretched man, in pain I go,
None need my help, and none relieve my woe;
Then let my bones beneath the turf be laid,
And men forget the wretch they would not aid."

Thus groan the old, till by disease oppressed,
They taste a final woe, and then they rest

Theirs is yon House that holds the parish poor,
Whose walls of mud scarce bear the broken door;
There, where the putrid vapours, flagging, play,
And the dull wheel hums doleful through the day;
There children dwell who know no parents' care;
Parents, who know no children's love, dwell there!
Heart-broken matrons on their joyless bed,
Forsaken wives, and mothers never wed;
Dejected widows with unheeded tears,
And crippled age with more than childhood fears;
The lame, the blind, and, far the happiest they!
The moping idiot, and the madman gay.

Here too the sick their final doom receive,
Here brought, amid the scenes of grief, to grieve,
Where the loud groans from some sad chamber flow,
Mixed with the clamors of the crowd below;

Here, sorrowing, they each kindred sorrow scan.
And the cold charities of man to man:
Whose laws indeed for ruined age provide,
And strong compulsion plucks the scrap from pride;
But still that scrap is bought with many a sigh,
And pride embitters what it can't deny.

    Say, ye, oppressed by some fantastic woes,
Some jarring nerve that baffles your repose;
Who press the downy couch, while slaves advance
With timid eye to read the distant glance;
Who with sad prayers the weary doctor tease
To name the nameless, ever-new, disease;
Who with mock patience dire complaints endure
Which real pain, and that alone, can cure;
How would ye bear in real pain to lie,
Despised, neglected, left alone to die?
How would ye bear to draw your latest breath
When all that's wretched paves the way for death?

[From Book I, The Village.]

ROBERT BURNS [1759–1796]

BONIE LESLEY

    O, saw ye bonie Lesley
      As she gaed o'er the Border?
    She's gane, like Alexander,
      To spread her conquests farther!

    To see her is to love her,
      And love but her forever;
    For Nature made her what she is,
      And never made anither!

    Thou art a queen, fair Lesley—
      Thy subjects, we before thee:
    Thou art divine, fair Lesley,—
      The hearts o' men adore thee,

The Deil he could na scaith thee,
  Or aught that wad belang thee:
He'd look into thy bonie face,
  And say: "I canna wrang thee!"

The Powers aboon will tent[1] thee,
  Misfortune sha' na steer[2] thee:
Thou'rt like themsel' sae lovely,
  That ill they'll ne'er let near thee.

Return again, fair Lesley,
  Return to Caledonie!
That we may brag we hae a lass
  There's nane again sae bonie.

AE FOND KISS

Ae fond kiss, and then we sever!
Ae fareweel, and then forever!
Deep in heart-wrung tears I'll pledge thee,
Warring sighs and groans I'll wage thee.
Who shall say that Fortune grieves him,
While the star of hope she leaves him?
Me, nae cheerfu' twinkle lights me,
Dark despair around benights me.

I'll ne'er blame my partial fancy:
Naething could resist my Nancy!
But to see her was to love her,
Love but her, and love forever.
Had we never lov'd sae kindly,
Had we never lov'd sae blindly,
Never met—or never parted—
We had ne'er been broken-hearted.

Fare-thee-weel, thou first and fairest!
Fare-thee-weel, thou best and dearest!

[1] tend.   [2] molest.

Thine be ilka[1] joy and treasure,
Peace, Enjoyment, Love, and Pleasure!
Ae fond kiss, and then we sever!
Ae fareweel, alas, forever!
Deep in heart-wrung tears I'll pledge thee,
Warring sighs and groans I'll wage thee.

MY LUVE IS LIKE A RED, RED ROSE

O, MY luve is like a red, red rose,
That's newly sprung in June.
O, my luve is like the melodie
That's sweetly play'd in tune.

As fair art thou, my bonie lass,
So deep in luve am I,
And I will luve thee still, my dear,
Till a' the seas gang dry.

Till a' the seas gang dry, my dear,
And the rocks melt wi' the sun!
I will luve thee still, my dear,
While the sands o' life shall run.

And fare thee weel, my only luve,
And fare thee weel awhile!
And I will come again, my luve,
Tho' it were ten thousand mile.

THE BANKS O' DOON

YE banks and braes o' bonie Doon,
How can ye bloom sae fresh and fair?
How can ye chant, ye little birds,
And I sae weary fu' o' care!

[1] every.

Thou'lt break my heart, thou warbling bird,
    That wantons thro' the flowering thorn!
Thou minds me o' departed joys,
    Departed—never to return.

Aft hae I rov'd by bonie Doon
    To see the rose and woodbine twine,
And ilka bird sang o' its luve,
    And fondly sae did I o' mine.
Wi' lightsome heart I pu'd a rose,
    Fu' sweet upon its thorny tree!
And my fause luver staw[1] my rose—
    But ah! he left the thorn wi' me.

SCOTS, WHA HAE

Scots, wha hae wi' Wallace bled,
Scots, wham Bruce has aften led,
Welcome to your gory bed
    Or to victorie!

Now's the day, and now's the hour:
See the front o' battle lour,
See approach proud Edward's power—
    Chains and slaverie!

Wha will be a traitor knave?
Wha can fill a coward's grave?
Wha sae base as be a slave?
    Let him turn, and flee!

Wha for Scotland's King and Law
Freedom's sword will strongly draw,
Free-man stand or free-man fa'?
    Let him follow me!

[1] stole.

By Oppression's woes and pains,
By your sons in servile chains,
We will drain our dearest veins
   But they shall be free!

Lay the proud usurpers low!
Tyrants fall in every foe!
Liberty's in every blow!
   Let us do, or die!

TAM GLEN

My heart is a-breaking, dear tittie[1],
  Some counsel unto me come len',
To anger them a' is a pity;
  But what will I do wi' Tam Glen?

I'm thinking, wi' sic a braw fellow
  In poortith[2] I might mak a fen'[3].
What care I in riches to wallow,
  If I maunna marry Tam Glen?

There's Lowrie the laird o' Dumeller,
  "Guid-day to you,"—brute! he comes ben[4].
He brags and he blaws o' his siller,
  But when will he dance like Tam Glen?

My minnie does constantly deave[5] me,
  And bids me beware o' young men.
They flatter, she says, to deceive me—
  But wha can think sae o' Tam Glen?

My daddie says, gin I'll forsake him,
  He'll gie me guid hunder marks ten.
But if it's ordained I maun take him,
  O wha will I get but Tam Glen?

[1] sister.   [2] poverty.   [3] shift.   [4] into the parlour.   [5] deafen.

Yestreen at the valentine's dealing,
   My heart to my mou gied a sten[1]:
For thrice I drew ane without failing,
   And thrice it was written, "Tam Glen!"

The last Halloween I was waukin[2]
   My droukit[3] sark-sleeve, as ye ken—
His likeness cam up the house staukin,
   And the very grey breeks o' Tam Glen!

Come counsel, dear tittie, don't tarry!
   I'll gie ye my bonie black hen,
Gif ye will advise me to marry
   The lad I lo'e dearly, Tam Glen.

AULD LANG SYNE

SHOULD auld acquaintance be forgot,
   And never brought to mind?
Should auld acquaintance be forgot,
   And auld lang syne!

   For auld lang syne, my dear,
     For auld lang syne,
   We'll tak a cup o' kindness yet
     For auld lang syne!

And surely ye'll be your pint-stowp,
   And surely I'll be mine,
And we'll tak a cup of kindness yet
   For auld lang syne!

We twa hae run about the braes,
   And pu'd the gowans[4] fine,
But we've wander'd monie a weary fit
   Sin' auld lang syne.

[1] leap.   [2] watching.   [3] wet.   [4] daisies.

We twa hae paidl'd [1] i' the burn
  Frae morning sun till dine;
But seas between us braid hae roar'd
  Sin' auld lang syne.

And there's a hand, my trusty fiere[2],
  And gie's a hand o' thine,
And we'll tak a right guid-willie waught,[3]
  For auld lang syne.
        For auld, &c.

HIGHLAND MARY

YE banks and braes and streams around
  The castle o' Montgomery,
Green be your woods, and fair your flowers,
  Your waters never drumlie!
There summer first unfald her robes,
  And there the langest tarry!
For there I took the last fareweel
  O' my sweet Highland Mary!

How sweetly bloom'd the gay green birk,
  How rich the hawthorn's blossom,
As underneath their fragrant shade
  I clasp'd her to my bosom!
The golden hours on angel wings
  Flew o'er me and my dearie:
For dear to me as light and life
  Was my sweet Highland Mary.

Wi' monie a vow, and lock'd embrace,
  Our parting was fu' tender;
And, pledging aft to meet again,
  We tore oursels asunder.

[1] paddled.   [2] companion.   [3] draught.

But O, fell Death's untimely frost,
    That nipt my flower sae early!
Now green's the sod, and cauld's the clay
    That wraps my Highland Mary!

O pale, pale now, those rosy lips
    I aft hae kiss'd sae fondly;
And clos'd for ay the sparkling glance
    That dwelt on me sae kindly;
And mouldering now in silent dust
    That heart that lo'ed me dearly!
But still within my bosom's core
    Shall live my Highland Mary.

TO A MOUSE, ON TURNING HER UP IN HER NEST, WITH THE PLOUGH

Wee, sleekit, cowrin, tim'rous beastie,
O, what a panic's in thy breastie!
Thou need na start awa sae hasty,
          Wi' bickerin brattle[1]!
I wad be laith to rin an' chase thee,
          Wi' murd'ring pattle[2]!

I'm truly sorry man's dominion
Has broken Nature's social union,
An' justifies that ill opinion,
          Which makes thee startle
At me, thy poor, earth-born companion,
          An' fellow-mortal!

I doubt na, whyles, but thou may thieve;
What then? poor beastie, thou maun live!
A daimen-icker in a thrave[3]
          'S a sma' request:
I'll get a blessing wi' the lave[4],
          And never miss't!

---

[1] hurry.   [2] hand-stick for clearing the plough.
[3] an occasional ear of corn in twenty-four sheaves.   [4] rest.

Thy wee bit housie, too, in ruin!
Its silly wa's the win's are strewin!
An' naething, now, to big[1] a new ane,
   O' foggage green!
An' bleak December's winds ensuin,
   Baith snell[2] an' keen!

Thou saw the fields laid bare an' waste,
An' weary winter comin' fast,
An' cozie here, beneath the blast,
   Thou thought to dwell,
Till, crash! the cruel coulter past
   Out thro' thy cell.

That wee bit heap o' leaves an' stibble
Has cost thee monie a weary nibble!
Now thou's turned out, for a' thy trouble,
   But[3] house or hald[4],
To thole[5] the winter's sleety dribble,
   An' cranreuch[6] cauld!

But, Mousie, thou art no thy lane[7]
In proving foresight may be vain:
The best-laid schemes o' mice an' men
   Gang aft agley,[8]
An' lea'e us nought but grief and pain
   For promised joy.

Still, thou art blest, compared wi' me!
The present only toucheth thee:
But, och! I backward cast my e'e
   On prospects drear!
An' forward, tho' I canna see,
   I guess an' fear!

[1] build.   [2] bitter.   [3] without.   [4] holding.
[5] endure.   [6] hoar-frost.   [7] not alone.   [8] awry.

JOHN ANDERSON, MY JO

John Anderson my jo, John,
    When we were first acquent,
Your locks were like the raven,
    Your bonie brow was brent [1];
But now your brow is beld, John,
    Your locks are like the snaw;
But blessings on your frosty pow,
    John Anderson my jo!

John Anderson my jo, John,
    We clamb the hill thegither;
And monie a cantie day, John,
    We've had wi' ane anither:
Now we maun totter down, John,
    But hand in hand we'll go,
And sleep thegither at the foot,
    John Anderson my jo!

O, WERT THOU IN THE CAULD BLAST

O, wert thou in the cauld blast
    On yonder lea, on yonder lea,
My plaidie to the angry airt', [2]
    I'd shelter thee, I'd shelter thee.
Or did Misfortune's bitter storms
    Around thee blaw, around thee blaw,
Thy bield [3] should be my bosom,
    To share it a', to share it a'.

Or were I in the wildest waste,
    Sae black and bare, sae black and bare,
The desert were a Paradise,
    If thou wert there, if thou wert there.

[1] smooth.   [2] wind.   [3] shelter.

Or were I monarch o' the globe,
  Wi' thee to reign, wi' thee to reign,
The brightest jewel in my crown
  Wad be my queen, wad be my queen.

IS THERE FOR HONEST POVERTY

A MAN'S A MAN FOR A' THAT

Is there for honest poverty
  That hings his head, and a' that?
The coward-slave, we pass him by—
  We dare be poor for a' that!
    For a' that, and a' that,
      Our toils obscure, and a' that,
      The rank is but the guinea stamp,
      The man's the gowd for a' that.

What tho' on hamely fare we dine,
  Wear hoddin-grey[1], and a' that?
Gie fools their silks, and knaves their wine—
  A man's a man for a' that.
    For a' that, and a' that,
      Their tinsel show, and a' that,
      The honest man, tho' e'er sae poor,
      Is king o' men for a' that.

Ye see yon birkie[2] ca'd a lord,
  Wha struts, and stares, and a' that?
Tho' hundreds worship at his word,
  He's but a cuif [3] for a' that.
    For a' that, an' a' that,
      His riband, star, and a' that,
      The man o' independent mind,
      He looks and laughs at a' that.

A prince can mak a belted knight,
  A marquis, duke, and a' that!

---

[1] coarse woollen cloth.   [2] conceited fellow.   [3] blockhead.

But an honest man's aboon[1] his might—
   Guid faith, he mauna fa'[2] that!
     For a' that, and a' that,
       Their dignities and a' that,
     The pith o' sense and pride o' worth
     Are higher rank than a' that.

Then let us pray that come it may
   (As come it will for a' that)
That Sense and Worth o'er a' the earth,
   Shall bear the gree[3] and a' that!
     For a' that, and a' that,
       It's coming yet, for a' that,
     That man to man the world o'er
     Shall brithers be for a' that.

WILLIAM BLAKE [1757–1827]

TO THE MUSES

Whether on Ida's shady brow,
   Or in the chambers of the East,
The chambers of the Sun that now
   From ancient melody have ceased;

Whether in Heaven ye wander fair,
   Or the green corners of the Earth,
Or the blue regions of the air,
   Where the melodious winds have birth·

Whether on crystal rocks ye rove
   Beneath the bosom of the sea,
Wandering in many a coral grove;
   Fair Nine, forsaking Poetry:

How have you left your ancient love
   That bards of old enjoyed in you!
The languid strings do scarcely move,
   The sound is forced, the notes are few.

[1] above.   [2] claim.   [3] i. e., have the first place.

LOVE'S SECRET

Never seek to tell thy love
  Love that never told can be;
For the gentle wind doth move
  Silently, invisibly.

I told my love, I told my love,
  I told her all my heart,
Trembling, cold, in ghastly fears:—
  Ah! she did depart.

Soon after she was gone from me
  A traveller came by,
Silently, invisibly:
  He took her with a sigh.

AH, SUNFLOWER

Ah, Sunflower, weary of time,
Who countest the steps of the sun,
Seeking after that sweet golden clime
Where the traveller's journey is done—

Where the youth pined away with desire,
And the pale virgin, shrouded in snow,
Arise from their graves, and aspire
Where my sunflower wishes to go!

AUGURIES OF INNOCENCE

To see the world in a grain of sand,
  And a heaven in a wild flower;
Hold infinity in the palm of your hand,
  And eternity in an hour.

THE LAMB

LITTLE lamb, who made thee?
Dost thou know who made thee,
Gave thee life and bade thee feed
By the stream and o'er the mead;
Gave thee clothing of delight,
Softest clothing, woolly, bright;
Gave thee such a tender voice,
Making all the vales rejoice?
      Little lamb, who made thee?
      Dost thou know who made thee?

Little lamb, I'll tell thee;
Little lamb, I'll tell thee.
He is callèd by thy name,
For He calls himself a Lamb;
He is meek and He is mild,
He became a little child.
I a child and thou a lamb,
We are callèd by His name.
      Little lamb, God bless thee!
      Little lamb, God bless thee!

THE TIGER

TIGER! Tiger! burning bright
In the forests of the night,
What immortal hand or eye
Could frame thy fearful symmetry?

In what distant deeps or skies
Burnt the fire of thine eyes?
On what wings dare he aspire?
What the hand dare seize the fire?

And what shoulder, and what art,
Could twist the sinews of thy heart?
And when thy heart began to beat,
What dread hand? and what dread feet?

What the hammer? what the chain?
In what furnace was thy brain?
What the anvil? what dread grasp
Dare its deadly terrors clasp?

When the stars threw down their spears,
And watered heaven with their tears,
Did he smile his work to see?
Did he who made the Lamb make thee?

Tiger! Tiger! burning bright
In the forests of the night,
What immortal hand or eye
Dare frame thy fearful symmetry?

WILLIAM WORDSWORTH [1770–1850]

LINES COMPOSED A FEW MILES ABOVE TINTERN ABBEY

FIVE years have past; five summers, with the length
Of five long winters! and again I hear
These waters, rolling from their mountain-springs
With a soft inland murmur.—Once again
Do I behold these steep and lofty cliffs,
That on a wild secluded scene impress
Thoughts of more deep seclusion; and connect
The landscape with the quiet of the sky.
The day is come when I again repose
Here, under this dark sycamore, and view
These plots of cottage-ground, these orchard-tufts,
Which at this season, with their unripe fruits,
Are clad in one green hue, and lose themselves

'Mid groves and copses. Once again I see
These hedge-rows, hardly hedge-rows, little lines
Of sportive wood run wild: these pastoral farms,
Green to the very door; and wreaths of smoke
Sent up, in silence, from among the trees!
With some uncertain notice, as might seem
Of vagrant dwellers in the houseless woods,
Or of some Hermit's cave, where by his fire
The Hermit sits alone.
                        These beauteous forms,
Through a long absence, have not been to me
As is a landscape to a blind man's eye:
But oft, in lonely rooms, and 'mid the din
Of towns and cities, I have owed to them
In hours of weariness, sensations sweet,
Felt in the blood, and felt along the heart;
And passing even into my purer mind,
With tranquil restoration:—feelings too
Of unremembered pleasure: such, perhaps,
As have no slight or trivial influence
On that best portion of a good man's life,
His little, nameless, unremembered acts
Of kindness and of love. Nor less, I trust,
To them I may have owed another gift,
Of aspect more sublime; that blessed mood,
In which the burthen of the mystery,
In which the heavy and the weary weight
Of all this unintelligible world,
Is lightened:—that serene and blessed mood,
In which the affections gently lead us on,—
Until, the breath of this corporeal frame
And even the motion of our human blood
Almost suspended, we are laid asleep
In body, and become a living soul:
While with an eye made quiet by the power
Of harmony, and the deep power of joy,
We see into the life of things.
                                If this
Be but a vain belief, yet, oh! how oft—

In darkness and amid the many shapes
Of joyless daylight; when the fretful stir
Unprofitable, and the fever of the world,
Have hung upon the beatings of my heart—
How oft, in spirit, have I turned to thee,
O sylvan Wye! thou wanderer thro' the woods,
How often has my spirit turned to thee!

    And now, with gleams of half-extinguished thought,
With many recognitions dim and faint,
And somewhat of a sad perplexity,
The picture of the mind revives again:
While here I stand, not only with the sense
Of present pleasure, but with pleasing thoughts
That in this moment there is life and food
For future years. And so I dare to hope,
Though changed, no doubt, from what I was when first
I came among these hills; when like a roe
I bounded o'er the mountains, by the sides
Of the deep rivers, and the lonely streams,
Wherever nature led: more like a man
Flying from something that he dreads, than one
Who sought the thing he loved. For nature then
(The coarser pleasures of my boyish days,
And their glad animal movements all gone by)
To me was all in all.—I cannot paint
What then I was. The sounding cataract
Haunted me like a passion: the tall rock,
The mountain, and the deep and gloomy wood,
Their colours and their forms, were then to me
An appetite; a feeling and a love,
That had no need of a remoter charm,
By thought supplied, nor any interest
Unborrowed from the eye.—That time is past,
And all its aching joys are now no more,
And all its dizzy raptures. Not for this
Faint I, nor mourn nor murmur; other gifts
Have followed; for such loss, I would believe,
Abundant recompense. For I have learned
To look on nature, not as in the hour

Of thoughtless youth; but hearing oftentimes
The still, sad music of humanity,
Nor harsh nor grating, though of ample power
To chasten and subdue. And I have felt
A presence that disturbs me with the joy
Of elevated thoughts; a sense sublime
Of something far more deeply interfused,
Whose dwelling is the light of setting suns,
And the round ocean, and the living air,
And the blue sky, and in the mind of man;
A motion and a spirit, that impels
All thinking things, all objects of all thought,
And rolls through all things. Therefore am I still
A lover of the meadows and the woods,
And mountains; and of all that we behold
From this green earth; of all the mighty world
Of eye, and ear,—both what they half create,
And what perceive; well pleased to recognize
In nature and the language of the sense,
The anchor of my purest thoughts, the nurse,
The guide, the guardian of my heart, and soul
Of all my moral being.

                Nor perchance,
If I were not thus taught, should I the more
Suffer my genial spirits to decay:
For thou art with me here upon the banks
Of this fair river; thou my dearest Friend,
My dear, dear Friend; and in thy voice I catch
The language of my former heart, and read
My former pleasures in the shooting lights
Of thy wild eyes. Oh! yet a little while
May I behold in thee what I was once,
My dear, dear Sister! and this prayer I make,
Knowing that Nature never did betray
The heart that loved her; 'tis her privilege,
Through all the years of this our life, to lead
From joy to joy: for she can so inform
The mind that is within us, so impress
With quietness and beauty, and so feel

With lofty thoughts, that neither evil tongues,
Rash judgments, nor the sneers of selfish men,
Nor greetings where no kindness is, nor all
The dreary intercourse of daily life
Shall e'er prevail against us, or disturb
Our cheerful faith, that all which we behold
Is full of blessings. Therefore let the moon
Shine on thee in thy solitary walk;
And let the misty mountain-winds be free
To blow against thee: and, in after years,
When these wild ecstasies shall be matured
Into a sober pleasure; when thy mind
Shall be a mansion for all lovely forms,
Thy memory be as a dwelling-place
For all sweet sounds and harmonies; oh! then,
If solitude, or fear, or pain, or grief,
Should be thy portion, with what healing thoughts
Of tender joy wilt thou remember me,
And these my exhortations! Nor, perchance—
If I should be where I no more can hear
Thy voice, nor catch from thy wild eyes these gleams
Of past existence—wilt thou then forget
That on the banks of this delightful stream
We stood together; and that I, so long
A worshipper of Nature, hither came
Unwearied in that service: rather say
With warmer love—oh! with far deeper zeal
Of holier love. Nor wilt thou then forget,
That after many wanderings, many years
Of absence, these steep woods and lofty cliffs,
And this green pastoral landscape, were to me
More dear, both for themselves and for thy sake!

SHE DWELT AMONG THE UNTRODDEN WAYS

SHE dwelt among the untrodden ways
    Beside the springs of Dove,
A Maid whom there were none to praise
    And very few to love:

A violet by a mossy stone
  Half hidden from the eye!
Fair as a star, when only one
  Is shining in the sky.

She lived unknown, and few could know
  When Lucy ceased to be;
But she is in her grave, and, oh,
  The difference to me!

A SLUMBER DID MY SPIRIT SEAL

A SLUMBER did my spirit seal;
  I had no human fears:
She seemed a thing that could not feel
  The touch of earthly years.

No motion has she now, no force;
  She neither hears nor sees;
Rolled round in earth's diurnal course,
  With rocks, and stones, and trees.

TO THE CUCKOO

O BLITHE New-comer! I have heard,
I hear thee and rejoice.
O Cuckoo! shall I call thee Bird,
Or but a wandering Voice?

While I am lying on the grass
Thy twofold shout I hear,
From hill to hill it seems to pass,
At once far off, and near.

Though babbling only to the Vale,
Of sunshine and of flowers,
Thou bringest unto me a tale
Of visionary hours.

Thrice welcome, darling of the Spring!
Even yet thou art to me
No bird, but an invisible thing,
A voice, a mystery;

The same whom in my school-boy days
I listened to; that Cry
Which made me look a thousand ways
In bush, and tree, and sky.

To seek thee did I often rove
Through woods and on the green;
And thou wert still a hope, a love;
Still longed for, never seen.

And I can listen to thee yet;
Can lie upon the plain
And listen, till I do beget
That golden time again.

O blessèd Bird! the earth we pace
Again appears to be
An unsubstantial, faery place;
That is fit home for Thee!

THE SOLITARY REAPER

BEHOLD her, single in the field,
Yon solitary Highland Lass!
Reaping and singing by herself;
Stop here, or gently pass!
Alone she cuts and binds the grain,
And sings a melancholy strain;
O listen! for the Vale profound
Is overflowing with the sound.

No Nightingale did ever chant
More welcome notes to weary bands

Of travellers in some shady haunt,
Among Arabian sands:
A voice so thrilling ne'er was heard
In spring-time from the Cuckoo-bird,
Breaking the silence of the seas
Among the farthest Hebrides.

Will no one tell me what she sings?—
Perhaps the plaintive numbers flow
For old, unhappy, far-off things,
And battles long ago:
Or is it some more humble lay,
Familiar matter of to-day?
Some natural sorrow, loss, or pain,
That has been, and may be again?

Whate'er the theme, the maiden sang
As if her song could have no ending;
I saw her singing at her work,
And o'er the sickle bending;—
I listened, motionless and still;
And, as I mounted up the hill,
The music in my ear I bore
Long after it was heard no more.

I WANDERED LONELY AS A CLOUD

I WANDERED lonely as a cloud
That floats on high o'er vales and hills,
When all at once I saw a crowd,
A host, of golden daffodils;
Beside the lake, beneath the trees,
Fluttering and dancing in the breeze.

Continuous as the stars that shine
And twinkle on the milky way,
They stretched in never-ending line
Along the margin of a bay:

Ten thousand saw I at a glance,
Tossing their heads in sprightly dance.

The waves beside them danced; but they
Out-did the sparkling waves in glee:
A poet could not but be gay,
In such a jocund company:
I gazed—and gazed—but little thought
What wealth the show to me had brought:

For oft, when on my couch I lie
In vacant or in pensive mood,
They flash upon that inward eye
Which is the bliss of solitude;
And then my heart with pleasure fills,
And dances with the daffodils.

SHE WAS A PHANTOM OF DELIGHT

She was a Phantom of delight
When first she gleamed upon my sight;
A lovely Apparition sent
To be a moment's ornament;
Her eyes as stars of Twilight fair;
Like Twilight's, too, her dusky hair;
But all things else about her drawn
From May-time and the cheerful Dawn;
A dancing Shape, an Image gay,
To haunt, to startle, and way-lay.

I saw her upon nearer view,
A Spirit, yet a Woman too!
Her household motions light and free,
And steps of virgin-liberty;
A countenance in which did meet
Sweet records, promises as sweet;
A Creature not too bright or good
For human nature's daily food;

For transient sorrows, simple wiles,
Praise, blame, love, kisses, tears and smiles.

And now I see with eye serene
The very pulse of the machine;
A Being breathing thoughtful breath,
A Traveller between life and death;
The reason firm, the temperate will,
Endurance, foresight, strength, and skill;
A perfect Woman, nobly planned,
To warn, to comfort, and command;
And yet a Spirit still, and bright
With something of angelic light.

ELEGIAC STANZAS

SUGGESTED BY A PICTURE OF PEELE CASTLE IN A STORM
PAINTED BY SIR GEORGE BEAUMONT

I was thy neighbour once, thou rugged Pile!
Four summer weeks I dwelt in sight of thee:
I saw thee every day; and all the while
Thy Form was sleeping on a glassy sea.

So pure the sky, so quiet was the air;
So like, so very like, was day to day!
Whene'er I looked thy Image still was there;
It trembled, but it never passed away.

How perfect was the calm! it seemed no sleep;
No mood which season takes away or brings:
I could have fancied that the mighty Deep
Was even the gentlest of all gentle Things.

Ah! then, if mine had been the Painter's hand,
To express what then I saw; and add the gleam
The light that never was on sea or land,
The consecration and the Poet's dream;

I would have planted thee, thou hoary Pile!
Amid a world how different from this!
Beside a sea that could not cease to smile;
On tranquil land, beneath a sky of bliss.

Thou should'st have seemed a treasure-house divine
Of peaceful years; a chronicle of heaven;—
Of all the sunbeams that did ever shine
The very sweetest had to thee been given.

A Picture had it been of lasting ease,
Elysian quiet, without toil or strife;
No motion but the moving tide, a breeze,
Or merely silent Nature's breathing life.

Such, in the fond illusion of my heart,
Such Picture would I at that time have made:
And seen the soul of truth in every part;
A steadfast peace that might not be betrayed.

So once it would have been,—'tis so no more;
I have submitted to a new control:
A power is gone, which nothing can restore;
A deep distress hath humanized my Soul.

Not for a moment could I now behold
A smiling sea, and be what I have been:
The feeling of my loss will ne'er be old;
This, which I know, I speak with mind serene.

Then, Beaumont, Friend! who would have been the Friend,
If he had lived, of Him whom I deplore,
This work of thine I blame not, but commend;
This sea in anger, and that dismal shore.

Oh, 'tis a passionate Work!—yet wise and well;
Well chosen is the spirit that is here;
That Hulk which labours in the deadly swell,
This rueful sky, this pageantry of fear!

And this huge Castle, standing here sublime,
I love to see the look with which it braves,
Cased in the unfeeling armour of old time
The lightning, the fierce wind, and trampling waves.

Farewell, farewell, the heart that lives alone,
Housed in a dream, at distance from the Kind!
Such happiness, wherever it be known,
Is to be pitied; for 'tis surely blind.

But welcome fortitude, and patient cheer,
And frequent sights of what is to be borne!
Such sights, or worse, as are before me here.—
Not without hope we suffer and we mourn.

THE WORLD IS TOO MUCH WITH US

THE world is too much with us; late and soon,
Getting and spending, we lay waste our powers:
Little we see in Nature that is ours;
We have given our hearts away, a sordid boon!
The Sea that bares her bosom to the moon;
The winds that will be howling at all hours,
And are up-gathered now like sleeping flowers;
For this, for everything, we are out of tune;
It moves us not.—Great God! I'd rather be
A Pagan, suckled in a creed outworn,
So might I, standing on this pleasant lea,
Have glimpses that would make me less forlorn;
Have sight of Proteus rising from the sea;
Or hear old Triton blow his wreathèd horn.

COMPOSED UPON WESTMINSTER BRIDGE

EARTH has not anything to show more fair:
Dull would he be of soul who could pass by
A sight so touching in its majesty:
This City now doth, like a garment, wear
The beauty of the morning; silent, bare,
Ships, towers, domes, theatres and temples lie
Open unto the fields, and to the sky;
All bright and glittering in the smokeless air.
Never did sun more beautifully steep
In his first splendour, valley, rock, or hill;
Ne'er saw I, never felt, a calm so deep!
The river glideth at his own sweet will:
Dear God! the very houses seem asleep;
And all that mighty heart is lying still!

IT IS A BEAUTEOUS EVENING

IT is a beauteous evening, calm and free,
The holy time is quiet as a Nun
Breathless with adoration; the broad sun
Is sinking down in its tranquillity;
The gentleness of heaven broods o'er the Sea:
Listen! the mighty Being is awake,
And doth with his eternal motion make
A sound like thunder—everlastingly.
Dear Child! dear Girl! that walkest with me here,
If thou appear untouched by solemn thought,
Thy nature is not therefore less divine:
Thou liest in Abraham's bosom all the year;
And worship'st at the Temple's inner shrine,
God being with thee when we know it not.

LONDON 1802

MILTON! thou shouldst be living at this hour:
England hath need of thee; she is a fen
Of stagnant waters: altar, sword, and pen,
Fireside, the heroic wealth of hall and bower,
Have forfeited their ancient English dower
Of inward happiness. We are selfish men;
Oh! raise us up, return to us again;
And give us manners, virtue, freedom, power.
Thy soul was like a Star, and dwelt apart:
Thou hadst a voice whose sound was like the sea:
Pure as the naked heavens, majestic, free,
So didst thou travel on life's common way,
In cheerful godliness; and yet thy heart
The lowliest duties on herself did lay.

ODE TO DUTY

STERN Daughter of the Voice of God!
O Duty! if that name thou love
Who art a light to guide, a rod
To check the erring, and reprove;
Thou, who art victory and law
When empty terrors overawe:
From vain temptations dost set free:
And calm'st the weary strife of frail humanity!

There are who ask not if thine eye
Be on them; who, in love and truth,
Where no misgiving is, rely
Upon the genial sense of youth:
Glad Hearts! without reproach or blot
Who do thy work, and know it not:
Oh! if through confidence misplaced
They fail, thy saving arms, dread Power!
            Around them cast.

Serene will be our days and bright,
And happy will our nature be,
When love is an unerring light,
And joy its own security.
And they a blissful course may hold
Even now, who, not unwisely bold,
Live in the spirit of this creed;
Yet seek thy firm support, according to their need.

I, loving freedom, and untried,
No sport of every random gust,
Yet being to myself a guide,
Too blindly have reposed my trust:
And oft, when in my heart was heard
Thy timely mandate, I deferred
The task, in smoother walks to stray;
But thee I now would serve more strictly, if I may.

Through no disturbance of my soul,
Or strong compunction in me wrought,
I supplicate for thy control;
But in the quietness of thought:
Me this unchartered freedom tires;
I feel the weight of chance-desires:
My hopes no more must change their name,
I long for a repose that ever is the same.

Stern Lawgiver! yet thou dost wear
The Godhead's most benignant grace;
Nor know we anything so fair
As is the smile upon thy face:
Flowers laugh before thee on their beds
And fragrance in thy footing treads;
Thou dost preserve the stars from wrong;
And the most ancient heavens, through thee,
    Are fresh and strong.

To humbler functions, awful Power!
I call thee: I myself commend

Unto thy guidance from this hour;
Oh, let my weakness have an end!
Give unto me, made lowly wise,
The spirit of self-sacrifice;
The confidence of reason give;
And in the light of truth thy Bondman let me live!

ODE ON INTIMATIONS OF IMMORTALITY FROM RECOLLECTIONS OF EARLY CHILDHOOD

THERE was a time when meadow, grove, and stream,
The earth, and every common sight,
        To me did seem
        Apparelled in celestial light,
The glory and the freshness of a dream.
It is not now as it hath been of yore;—
        Turn whereso'er I may,
        By night or day,
The things which I have seen I now can see no more.

        The Rainbow comes and goes,
        And lovely is the Rose,
        The Moon doth with delight
Look round her when the heavens are bare;
        Waters on a starry night
        Are beautiful and fair;
    The sunshine is a glorious birth;
    But yet I know, where'er I go,
That there hath past away a glory from the earth.

Now, while the birds thus sing a joyous song,
        And while the young lambs bound
        As to the tabor's sound,
To me alone there came a thought of grief;
A timely utterance gave that thought relief,
        And I again am strong:
The cataracts blow their trumpets from the steep;

No more shall grief of mine the season wrong;
I hear the Echoes through the mountains throng,
The Winds come to me from the fields of sleep,
  And all the earth is gay;
   Land and sea
  Give themselves up to jollity,
   And with the heart of May
  Doth every Beast keep holiday;—
   Thou Child of Joy,
Shout round me, let me hear thy shouts,
   Thou happy Shepherd-boy!

Ye blessèd Creatures, I have heard the call
  Ye to each other make; I see
The heavens laugh with you in your jubilee;
  My heart is at your festival,
  My head hath its coronal,
The fulness of your bliss, I feel—I feel it all.
  O evil day! if I were sullen
  While Earth herself is adorning,
   This sweet May-morning,
  And the Children are culling
   On every side,
  In a thousand valleys far and wide,
  Fresh flowers; while the sun shines warm,
And the Babe leaps up on his Mother's arm:—
  I hear, I hear, with joy I hear!
  —But there's a Tree, of many, one,
A single Field which I have looked upon,
Both of them speak of something that is gone:
  The Pansy at my feet
  Doth the same tale repeat:
Whither is fled the visionary gleam?
Where is it now, the glory and the dream?

Our birth is but a sleep and a forgetting:
The Soul that rises with us, our life's Star,
  Hath had elsewhere its setting,
   And cometh from afar:

Not in entire forgetfulness,
  And not in utter nakedness,
But trailing clouds of glory do we come
  From God, who is our home:
Heaven lies about us in our infancy!
Shades of the prison-house begin to close
  Upon the growing Boy,
But he beholds the light, and whence it flows,
  He sees it in his joy;
The Youth, who daily farther from the east
  Must travel, still is Nature's Priest,
  And by the vision splendid
  Is on his way attended;
At length the Man perceives it die away,
And fade into the light of common day.

Earth fills her lap with pleasures of her own;
Yearnings she hath in her own natural kind,
And, even with something of a Mother's mind,
  And no unworthy aim,
  The homely Nurse doth all she can
To make her Foster-child, her Inmate Man,
  Forget the glories he hath known,
And that imperial palace whence he came.

Behold the Child among his new-born blisses,
A six years' Darling of a pigmy size!
See, where 'mid work of his own hand he lies,
Fretted by sallies of his mother's kisses,
With light upon him from his father's eyes!
See, at his feet, some little plan or chart,
Some fragment from his dream of human life,
Shaped by himself with newly-learnèd art;
  A wedding or a festival,
  A mourning or a funeral;
    And this hath now his heart,
  And unto this he frames his song:
    Then will he fit his tongue
To dialogues of business, love, or strife;

But it will not be long
Ere this be thrown aside,
And with new joy and pride
The little Actor cons another part;
Filling from time to time his "humourous stage"
With all the Persons, down to palsied Age,
That Life brings with her in her equipage;
As if his whole vocation
Were endless imitation.

Thou, whose exterior semblance doth belie
Thy Soul's immensity;
Thou best Philosopher, who yet dost keep
Thy heritage, thou Eye among the blind,
That, deaf and silent, read'st the eternal deep,
Haunted for ever by the eternal mind,—
Mighty Prophet! Seer blest!
On whom those truths do rest,
Which we are toiling all our lives to find,
In darkness lost, the darkness of the grave;
Thou, over whom thy Immortality
Broods like the Day, a Master o'er a Slave,
A Presence which is not to be put by;
Thou little Child, yet glorious in the might
Of heaven-born freedom on thy being's height,
Why with such earnest pains dost thou provoke
The years to bring the inevitable yoke,
Thus blindly with thy blessedness at strife?
Full soon thy Soul shall have her earthly freight,
And custom lie upon thee with a weight,
Heavy as frost, and deep almost as life!

O joy! that in our embers
Is something that doth live,
That nature yet remembers
What was so fugitive!
The thought of our past years in me doth breed
Perpetual benediction: not indeed

For that which is most worthy to be blest—
Delight and liberty, the simple creed
Of Childhood, whether busy or at rest,
With new-fledged hope still fluttering in his breast:—
  Not for these I raise
   The song of thanks and praise;
 But for those obstinate questionings
 Of sense and outward things,
 Fallings from us, vanishings;
 Blank misgivings of a Creature
Moving about in worlds not realized,
High instincts before which our mortal Nature
Did tremble like a guilty Thing surprised:
  But for those first affections,
   Those shadowy recollections,
  Which, be they what they may,
Are yet the fountain light of all our day,
Are yet a master light of all our seeing;
 Uphold us, cherish, and have power to make
Our noisy years seem moments in the being
Of the eternal Silence: truths that wake,
  To perish never;
Which neither listlessness, nor mad endeavour,
  Nor Man nor Boy,
Nor all that is at enmity with joy,
Can utterly abolish or destroy!
  Hence in a season of calm weather
  Though inland far we be,
Our Souls have sight of that immortal sea
  Which brought us hither,
  Can in a moment travel thither,
And see the Children sport upon the shore,
And hear the mighty waters rolling evermore.

Then sing, ye Birds, sing, sing a joyous song!
  And let the young Lambs bound
  As to the tabor's sound!
We in thought will join your throng,
  Ye that pipe and ye that play,

Ye that through your hearts to-day
Feel the gladness of the May!
What though the radiance which was once so bright
Be now forever taken from my sight,
  Though nothing can bring back the hour
Of splendour in the grass, of glory in the flower;
  We will grieve not, rather find
  Strength in what remains behind;
  In the primal sympathy
  Which having been must ever be;
  In the soothing thoughts that spring
  Out of human suffering;
  In the faith that looks through death,
In years that bring the philosophic mind.

And O ye Fountains, Meadows, Hills, and Groves,
Forebode not any severing of our loves!
Yet in my heart of hearts I feel your might;
I only have relinquished one delight
To live beneath your more habitual sway.
I love the Brooks which down their channels fret,
Even more than when I tripped lightly as they;
The innocent brightness of a new-born Day
          Is lovely yet;
The Clouds that gather round the setting sun
Do take a sober colouring from an eye
That hath kept watch o'er man's mortality;
Another race hath been, and other palms are won.
Thanks to the human heart by which we live,
Thanks to its tenderness, its joys, and fears,
To me the meanest flower that blows can give
Thoughts that do often lie too deep for tears.

SAMUEL TAYLOR COLERIDGE [1772–1834]

KUBLA KHAN

In Xanadu did Kubla Khan
A stately pleasure-dome decree:
Where Alph, the sacred river, ran
Through caverns measureless to man
  Down to a sunless sea.
So twice five miles of fertile ground
With walls and towers were girdled round:
And here were gardens bright with sinuous rills,
Where blossomed many an incense-bearing tree;
And here were forests ancient as the hills,
Enfolding sunny spots of greenery.
But oh! that deep romantic chasm which slanted
Down the green hill athwart a cedarn cover!
A savage place! as holy and enchanted
As e'er beneath a waning moon was haunted
By woman wailing for her demon-lover!
And from this chasm, with ceaseless turmoil seething,
As if this earth in fast thick pants were breathing,
A mighty fountain momently was forced:
Amid whose swift half-intermitted burst
Huge fragments vaulted like rebounding hail,
Or chaffy grain beneath the thresher's flail;
And 'mid these dancing rocks at once and ever
It flung up momently the sacred river.
Five miles meandering with a mazy motion
Through wood and dale the sacred river ran,
Then reached the caverns measureless to man,
And sank in tumult to a lifeless ocean:
And 'mid this tumult Kubla heard from far
Ancestral voices prophesying war!

    The shadow of the dome of pleasure
    Floated midway on the waves;
    Where was heard the mingled measure
    From the fountain and the caves.

It was a miracle of rare device,
A sunny pleasure-dome with caves of ice!
    A damsel with a dulcimer
    In a vision once I saw:
    It was an Abyssinian maid,
    And on her dulcimer she played,
    Singing of Mount Abora.
    Could I revive within me
    Her symphony and song,
    To such a deep delight 'twould win me,
That with music loud and long,
I would build that dome in air,
That sunny dome! those caves of ice!
And all who heard should see them there,
And all should cry, " Beware! Beware!
His flashing eyes, his floating hair!
Weave a circle round him thrice,
And close your eyes with holy dread,
For he on honey-dew hath fed,
And drunk the milk of Paradise."

THE RIME OF THE ANCIENT MARINER

ARGUMENT[1]

How a Ship having passed the Line was driven by storms to the cold
Country toward the South Pole; and how from thence she made her
course to the tropical Latitude of the Great Pacific Ocean; and of the
strange things that befell; and in what manner the Ancyent Marinere
came back to his own Country.

PART I

An ancient
mariner meeteth
three gallants
bidden to a
wedding-feast,
and detaineth
one.

It is an ancient Mariner,
And he stoppeth one of three.
"By thy long gray beard and glittering eye,
Now wherefore stopp'st thou me?

[1] The Argument was prefixed to the first Edition of " The Ancient Mariner," 1798.
The syllabus was added in 1829, when Coleridge considerably revised the poem. The
text given is that of the edition of 1829.

The Bridegroom's doors are opened wide,
And I am next of kin;
The guests are met, the feast is set:
May'st hear the merry din."

He holds him with his skinny hand,
"There was a ship," quoth he.
"Hold off! unhand me, gray-beard loon!"
Eftsoons his hand dropt he.

He holds him with his glittering eye—
The Wedding-Guest stood still,
And listens like a three years' child:
The Mariner hath his will.

The Wedding-Guest sat on a stone:
He cannot choose but hear;
And thus spake on that ancient man,
The bright-eyed Mariner.

"The ship was cheered, the harbor cleared,
Merrily did we drop
Below the kirk, below the hill,
Below the lighthouse top.

The sun came up upon the left,
Out of the sea came he!
And he shone bright, and on the right
Went down into the sea.

Higher and higher every day,
Till over the mast at noon—"
The Wedding-Guest here beat his breast,
For he heard the loud bassoon.

The bride hath paced into the hall,
Red as a rose is she;
Nodding their heads before her goes
The merry minstrelsy.

The Wedding-Guest he beat his breast,
Yet he cannot choose but hear;
And thus spake on that ancient man,
The bright-eyed Mariner.

The ship drawn by a storm toward the south pole.

"And now the Storm-blast came, and he
Was tyrannous and strong:
He struck with his o'ertaking wings,
And chased us south along.

With sloping masts and dipping prow,
As who pursued with yell and blow
Still treads the shadow of his foe,
And forward bends his head,
The ship drove fast, loud roared the blast,
And southward aye we fled.

And now there came both mist and snow,
And it grew wondrous cold:
And ice, mast-high, came floating by,
As green as emerald.

The land of ice, and of fearful sounds, where no living thing was to be seen.

And through the drifts the snowy clifts
Did send a dismal sheen:
Nor shapes of men nor beasts we ken—
The ice was all between.

The ice was here, the ice was there,
The ice was all around:
It cracked and growled, and roared and howled,
Like voices in a swound!

Till a great sea-bird called the Albatross came through the snow-fog, and was received with great joy and hospitality.

At length did cross an Albatross,
Thorough the fog it came;
As if it had been a Christian soul,
We hailed it in God's name.

It ate the food it ne'er had eat,
And round and round it flew.

The ice did split with a thunder-fit;
The helmsman steered us through!

And a good south wind sprung up behind;
The Albatross did follow,
And every day, for food or play,
Came to the mariner's hollo!

In mist or cloud, on mast or shroud,
It perched for vespers nine;
While all the night, through fog-smoke white,
Glimmered the white moon-shine."

"God save thee, ancient Mariner!
From the fiends, that plague thee thus!—
Why look'st thou so."—"With my cross-bow
I shot the Albatross."

PART II

"The Sun now rose upon the right:
Out of the sea came he,
Still hid in mist, and on the left
Went down into the sea.

And the good south wind still blew behind,
But no sweet bird did follow,
Nor any day for food or play
Came to the mariners' hollo!

And I had done an hellish thing,
And it would work 'em woe:
For all averred, I had killed the bird,
That made the breeze to blow.
Ah wretch! said they, the bird to slay,
That made the breeze to blow!

Nor dim nor red, like God's own head,
The glorious Sun uprist:
Then all averred, I had killed the bird
That brought the fog and mist.
'Twas right, said they, such birds to slay,
That bring the fog and mist.

The fair breeze blew, the white foam flew,
The furrow followed free;
We were the first that ever burst
Into that silent sea.

Down dropt the breeze, the sails dropt down,
'Twas sad as sad could be;
And we did speak only to break
The silence of the sea!

All in a hot and copper sky,
The bloody Sun, at noon,
Right up above the mast did stand,
No bigger than the Moon.

Day after day, day after day,
We stuck, nor breath nor motion;
As idle as a painted ship
Upon a painted ocean.

Water, water, everywhere,
And all the boards did shrink;
Water, water, everywhere,
Nor any drop to drink.

The very deep did rot: O Christ!
That ever this should be!
Yea, slimy things did crawl with legs
Upon the slimy sea.

About, about, in reel and rout
The death-fires danced at night;

The water, like a witch's oils,
Burnt green, and blue and white.

And some in dreams assured were
Of the Spirit that plagued us so;
Nine fathom deep he had followed us
From the land of mist and snow.

And every tongue, through utter drought,
Was withered at the root;
We could not speak, no more than if
We had been choked with soot.

Ah! well-a-day! what evil looks
Had I from old and young!
Instead of the cross, the Albatross
About my neck was hung.

PART III

"There passed a weary time. Each throat
Was parched, and glazed each eye.
A weary time! a weary time!
How glazed each weary eye!—
When looking westward, I beheld
A something in the sky.

At first it seemed a little speck,
And then it seemed a mist;
It moved and moved, and took at last
A certain shape, I wist.

A speck, a mist, a shape, I wist!
And still it neared and neared:
As if it dodged a water-sprite,
It plunged and tacked and veered.

At its nearer
approach, it
seemeth him to
be a ship; and
at a dear ransom
he freeth his
speech from the
bonds of thirst.

With throats unslaked, with black lips baked,
We could nor laugh nor wail;
Through utter drought all dumb we stood!
I bit my arm, I sucked the blood,
And cried, A sail! a sail!

With throats unslaked, with black lips baked,
Agape they heard me call:
Gramercy! they for joy did grin,
And all at once their breath drew in,
As they were drinking all.

See! see! (I cried) she tacks no more!
Hither to work us weal,
Without a breeze, without a tide,
She steadies with upright keel!

The western wave was all aflame.
The day was well-nigh done!
Almost upon the western wave
Rested the broad bright Sun;
When that strange shape drove suddenly
Betwixt us and the Sun.

It seemeth him
but the skeleton
of a ship.

And straight the Sun was flecked with bars,
(Heaven's Mother send us grace!)
As if through a dungeon-grate he peered
With broad and burning face.

Alas! (thought I, and my heart beat loud)
How fast she nears and nears!
Are those her sails that glance in the Sun,
Like restless gossameres?

And its ribs are
seen as bars on
the face of the
setting Sun.

The Spectre
Woman and her
Death-mate, and
no other on board the skeleton-ship.

Are those her ribs through which the Sun
Did peer, as through a grate?
And is that Woman all her crew?
Is that a Death? and are there two?
Is Death that woman's mate?

Like vessel, like crew!

Her lips were red, her looks were free,
Her locks were yellow as gold:
Her skin was as white as leprosy,
The Night-mare Life-in-Death was she,
Who thicks man's blood with cold.

Death and Life-in-Death have diced for the ship's crew, and she (the latter) winneth the ancient Mariner.

The naked hulk alongside came,
And the twain were casting dice;
'The game is done! I've won! I've won!'
Quoth she, and whistles thrice.

The Sun's rim dips; the stars rush out.
At one stride comes the dark;
With far-heard whisper, o'er the sea,
Off shot the spectre-bark.

We listened and looked sideways up!
Fear at my heart, as at a cup,
My life-blood seemed to sip!
The stars were dim, and thick the night,
The steersman's face by his lamp gleamed white;
From the sails the dew did drip—
Till clomb above the eastern bar
The hornèd Moon, with one bright star
Within the nether tip.

One after one, by the star-dogged Moon,
Too quick for groan or sigh,
Each turned his face with a ghastly pang,
And cursed me with his eye.

His shipmates drop down dead.

Four times fifty living men,
(And I heard nor sigh nor groan)
With heavy thump, a lifeless lump,
They dropped down one by one.

But Life-in-Death begins her work on the ancient Mariner.

The souls did from their bodies fly,—
They fled to bliss or woe!
And every soul, it passed by me,
Like the whizz of my cross-bow—!"

PART IV

"I fear thee, ancient Mariner!
I fear thy skinny hand
And thou art long, and lank, and brown,
As is the ribbed sea-sand.

I fear thee and thy glittering eye.
And thy skinny hand, so brown."—

"Fear not, fear not, thou Wedding-Guest!
This body dropt not down.

Alone, alone, all, all alone,
Alone on a wide wide sea!
And never a saint took pity on
My soul in agony.

The many men, so beautiful!
And they all dead did lie:
And a thousand, thousand slimy things
Lived on; and so did I.

I looked upon the rotting sea,
And drew my eyes away;
I looked upon the rotting deck,
And there the dead men lay.

I looked to heaven, and tried to pray;
But or ever a prayer had gusht,
A wicked whisper came, and made
My heart as dry as dust.

I closed my lids, and kept them close,
And the balls like pulses beat;
For the sky and the sea, and the sea and the sky
Lay like a load on my weary eye,
And the dead were at my feet.

But the curse
liveth for him in
the eye of the
dead men.

The cold sweat melted from their limbs,
Nor rot nor reek did they:
The look with which they looked on me
Had never passed away.

An orphan's curse would drag to hell
A spirit from on high;
But oh! more horrible than that
Is a curse in a dead man's eye!
Seven days, seven nights, I saw that curse,
And yet I could not die.

The moving Moon went up the sky,
And nowhere did abide:
Softly she was going up,
And a star or two beside—
Her beams bemocked the sultry main,
Like April hoar-frost spread;
But where the ship's huge shadow lay,
The charmèd water burnt alway
A still and awful red.

By the light of
the Moon he
beholdeth God's
creatures of the
great calm.

Beyond the shadow of the ship,
I watched the water-snakes:
They moved in tracks of shining white,
And when they reared, the elfish light
Fell off in hoary flakes.

Within the shadow of the ship
I watched their rich attire:
Blue, glossy green, and velvet black,
They coiled and swam; and every track
Was a flash of golden fire.

O happy living things! no tongue
Their beauty might declare:
A spring of love gushed from my heart,
And I blessed them unaware:
Sure my kind saint took pity on me,
And I blessed them unaware.

He blesseth
them in his
heart.

The selfsame moment I could pray;
And from my neck so free
The Albatross fell off, and sank
Like lead into the sea.

Part V

"Oh sleep! it is a gentle thing,
Beloved from pole to pole!
To Mary Queen the praise be given!
She sent the gentle sleep from Heaven,
That slid into my soul.

By grace of the holy Mother, the ancient Mariner is refreshed with rain.

The silly buckets on the deck,
That had so long remained,
I dreamt that they were filled with dew;
And when I awoke, it rained.

My lips were wet, my throat was cold,
My garments all were dank;
Sure I had drunken in my dreams,
And still my body drank.

I moved, and could not feel my limbs:
I was so light—almost
I thought that I had died in sleep,
And was a blessed ghost.

He heareth sounds and seeth strange sights and commotions in the sky and the element.

And soon I heard a roaring wind:
It did not come anear;
But with its sound it shook the sails,
That were so thin and sere.

The upper air burst into life!
And a hundred fire-flags sheen,
To and fro they were hurried about!
And to and fro, and in and out,
The wan stars danced between.

And the coming wind did roar more loud,
And the sails did sigh like sedge;
And the rain poured down from one black cloud;
The Moon was at its edge.

The thick black cloud was cleft, and still
The Moon was at its side:
Like waters shot from some high crag,
The lightning fell with never a jag,
A river steep and wide.

The bodies of the ship's crew are inspired, and the ship moves on;

The loud wind never reached the ship,
Yet now the ship moved on!
Beneath the lightning and the Moon
The dead men gave a groan.

They groaned, they stirred, they all uprose,
Nor spake, nor moved their eyes;
It had been strange, even in a dream,
To have seen those dead men rise.

The helmsman steered, the ship moved on;
Yet never a breeze up blew;
The mariners all 'gan work the ropes,
Where they were wont to do;
They raised their limbs like lifeless tools—
We were a ghastly crew.

The body of my brother's son
Stood by me, knee to knee:
The body and I pulled at one rope
But he said nought to me."—

But not by the souls of the men, nor by demons of earth or middle air, but by a blessed troop of angelic spirits, sent down by the invocation of the guardian saint.

"I fear thee, ancient Mariner!"—
"Be calm, thou Wedding-Guest!
'Twas not those souls that fled in pain,
Which to their corses came again,
But a troop of spirits blest:

For when it dawned—they dropped their arms,
And clustered round the mast;
Sweet sounds rose slowly through their mouths,
And from their bodies passed.

Around, around, flew each sweet sound,
Then darted to the Sun;
Slowly the sounds came back again,
Now mixed, now one by one.

Sometimes a-dropping from the sky
I heard the sky-lark sing;
Sometimes all little birds that are,
How they seemed to fill the sea and air
With their sweet jargoning!

And now 'twas like all instruments,
Now like a lonely flute;
And now it is an angel's song,
That makes the heavens be mute.

It ceased; yet still the sails made on
A pleasant noise till noon,
A noise like of a hidden brook
In the leafy month of June,
That to the sleeping woods all night
Singeth a quiet tune.

Till noon we quietly sailed on,
Yet never a breeze did breathe:
Slowly and smoothly went the ship,
Moved onward from beneath.

The lonesome Spirit from the south-pole carries on the ship as far as the Line, in obedience to the angelic troop, but still requireth vengeance.

Under the keel nine fathom deep,
From the land of mist and snow,
The spirit slid: and it was he
That made the ship to go.
The sails at noon left off their tune,
And the ship stood still also.

The Sun, right up above the mast,
Had fixed her to the ocean:
But in a minute she 'gan stir,
With a short uneasy motion—
Backwards and forwards half her length
With a short uneasy motion.

Then like a pawing horse let go,
She made a sudden bound:
It flung the blood into my head,
And I fell down in a swound.

The Polar
Spirit's fellow-
demons, the
invisible inhabit-
ants of the
element, take
part in his
wrong; and two
of them relate one to the other, that penance long and heavy for the ancient Mariner hath
been accorded to the Polar Spirit, who returneth southward.

How long in that same fit I lay,
I have not to declare;
But ere my living life returned,
I heard and in my soul discerned
Two voices in the air.

'Is it he?' quoth one, 'Is this the man?
By him who died on cross,
With his cruel bow he laid full low
The harmless Albatross.

The spirit who bideth by himself
In the land of mist and snow,
He loved the bird that loved the man
Who shot him with his bow.'

The other was a softer voice,
As soft as honey-dew:
Quoth he, 'The man hath penance done,
And penance more will do.'

PART VI

First Voice—

"'But tell me, tell me! speak again,
Thy soft response renewing—
What makes that ship drive on so fast?
What is the ocean doing?'

Second Voice—

'Still as a slave before his lord,
The ocean hath no blast;
His great bright eye most silently
Up to the Moon is cast—

If he may know which way to go;
For she guides him smooth or grim.
See, brother, see! how graciously
She looketh down on him.'

First Voice—

The Mariner
hath been cast
into a trance;
'But why drives on that ship so fast,
Without or wave or wind?'

for the angelic power causeth the vessel to drive northward faster than human life could endure.

Second Voice—

'The air is cut away before,
And closes from behind.
Fly, brother, fly! more high, more high!
Or we shall be belated:
For slow and slow that ship will go,
When the Mariner's trance is abated.'

The supernatural
motion is
retarded; the
Mariner awakes,
and his penance
begins anew.
I woke, and we were sailing on
As in a gentle weather:
'Twas night, calm night, the Moon was high,
The dead men stood together.

All stood together on the deck,
For a charnel-dungeon fitter:
All fixed on me their stony eyes,
That in the Moon did glitter.

The pang, the curse, with which they died,
Had never passed away:
I could not draw my eyes from theirs,
Nor turn them up to pray.

The curse is
finally expiated.

And now this spell was snapt: once more
I viewed the ocean green,
And looked far forth, yet little saw
Of what had else been seen—

Like one, that on a lonesome road
Doth walk in fear and dread,
And having once turned round walks on,
And turns no more his head;
Because he knows, a frightful fiend
Doth close behind him tread.

But soon there breathed a wind on me,
Nor sound nor motion made:
Its path was not upon the sea,
In ripple or in shade.

It raised my hair, it fanned my cheek
Like a meadow-gale of spring—
It mingled strangely with my fears,
Yet it felt like a welcoming.

Swiftly, swiftly flew the ship,
Yet she sailed softly too:
Sweetly, sweetly blew the breeze—
On me alone it blew.

And the ancient
Mariner be-
holdeth his
native country.

Oh! dream of joy! is this indeed
The light-house top I see?
Is this the hill? is this the kirk?
Is this mine own countree?

We drifted o'er the harbour-bar,
And I with sobs did pray—
'O let me be awake, my God!
Or let me sleep alway.'

The harbour-bay was clear as glass,
So smoothly it was strewn!
And on the bay the moonlight lay,
And the shadow of the Moon.

The rock shone bright, the kirk no less,
That stands above the rock:
The moonlight steeped in silentness
The steady weathercock.

And the bay was white with silent light
Till rising from the same,
Full many shapes, that shadows were,
In crimson colours came.

The angelic spirits leave the dead bodies,

And appear in their own forms of light.

A little distance from the prow
Those crimson shadows were:
I turned my eyes upon the deck—
Oh, Christ! what saw I there!

Each corse lay flat, lifeless and flat,
And, by the holy rood!
A man all light, a seraph-man,
On every corse there stood.

This seraph-band, each waved his hand:
It was a heavenly sight!
They stood as signals to the land,
Each one a lovely light;

This seraph-band, each waved his hand,
No voice did they impart—
No voice; but oh! the silence sank
Like music on my heart.

But soon I heard the dash of oars,
I heard the Pilot's cheer;
My head was turned perforce away,
And I saw a boat appear.

The Pilot and the Pilot's boy,
I heard them coming fast:
Dear Lord in Heaven! it was a joy
The dead men could not blast.

I saw a third—I heard his voice:
It is the Hermit good!
He singeth loud his godly hymns
That he makes in the wood.
He'll shrieve my soul, he'll wash away
The Albatross's blood.

Part VII

The Hermit of
the Wood,

"This Hermit good lives in that wood
Which slopes down to the sea.
How loudly his sweet voice he rears!
He loves to talk with marineres
That come from a far countree.

He kneels at morn, and noon, and eve—
He hath a cushion plump:
It is the moss that wholly hides
The rotted old oak-stump.

The skiff-boat neared: I heard them talk,
'Why, this is strange, I trow!
Where are those lights so many and fair,
That signal made but now?'

Approacheth
the ship with
wonder.

'Strange, by my faith!' the Hermit said—
'And they answered not our cheer!
The planks looked warped! and see those sails,
How thin they are and sere!
I never saw aught like to them,
Unless perchance it were

Brown skeletons of leaves that lag
My forest-brook along;
When the ivy-tod is heavy with snow,
And the owlet whoops to the wolf below,
That eats the she-wolf's young.'

'Dear Lord! it hath a fiendish look'—
(The Pilot made reply)
'I am a-feared.'—'Push on, push on!'
Said the Hermit cheerily.

The boat came closer to the ship,
But I nor spake nor stirred;
The boat came close beneath the ship,
And straight a sound was heard.

The ship suddenly sinketh.

Under the water it rumbled on,
Still louder and more dread:
It reached the ship, it split the bay;
The ship went down like lead.

The ancient Mariner is saved in the Pilot's boat.

Stunned by that loud and dreadful sound,
Which sky and ocean smote,
Like one that hath been seven days drowned
My body lay afloat;
But swift as dreams, myself I found
Within the Pilot's boat.

Upon the whirl, where sank the ship,
The boat spun round and round;
And all was still, save that the hill
Was telling of the sound.

I moved my lips—the Pilot shrieked
And fell down in a fit;
The Holy Hermit raised his eyes,
And prayed where he did sit.

I took the oars: The Pilot's boy
Who now doth crazy go
Laughed loud and long, and all the while
His eyes went to and fro.
'Ha! ha!' quoth he, 'full plain I see,
The Devil knows how to row.'

And now, all in my own countree,
I stood on the firm land!
The Hermit stepped forth from the boat,
And scarcely he could stand.

The ancient Mariner earnestly entreateth the Hermit to shrieve him; and the penance of life falls on him.

'O shrieve me, shrieve me, holy man!'
The Hermit crossed his brow.
'Say quick,' quoth he, 'I bid thee say—
What manner of man art thou?'

Forthwith this frame of mine was wrenched
With a woful agony,
Which forced me to begin my tale;
And then it left me free.

And ever and anon throughout his future life an agony constraineth him to travel from land to land,

Since then, at an uncertain hour,
That agony returns:
And till my ghastly tale is told,
This heart within me burns.

I pass, like night, from land to land;
I have strange power of speech;
That moment that his face I see,
I know the man that must hear me:
To him my tale I teach.

What loud uproar bursts from that door!
The wedding-guests are there:
But in the garden-bower the bride
And bride-maids singing are:
And hark the little vesper bell,
Which biddeth me to prayer!

O Wedding-Guest! this soul hath been
Alone on a wide wide sea:
So lonely, 'twas, that God himself
Scarce seemed there to be.

O sweeter than the marriage-feast,
'Tis sweeter far to me,
To walk together to the kirk,
With a goodly company!—

To walk together to the kirk,
And all together pray.
While each to his great Father bends,
Old men, and babes, and loving friends
And youths and maidens gay!

And to teach,
by his own
example, love
and reverence to
all things that
God made and
loveth.

Farewell, farewell! but this I tell
To thee, thou Wedding-Guest!
He prayeth well, who loveth well
Both man and bird and beast.

He prayeth best, who loveth best
All things both great and small;
For the dear God who loveth us,
He made and loveth all."

The Mariner, whose eye is bright,
Whose beard with age is hoar,
Is gone; and now the Wedding-Guest
Turned from the bridegroom's door.

He went like one that hath been stunned,
And is of sense forlorn:
A sadder and a wiser man,
He rose the morrow morn.

THE KNIGHT'S TOMB

WHERE is the grave of Sir Arthur O'Kellyn?
Where may the grave of that good man be?—
By the side of a spring, on the breast of Hevellyn,
Under the twigs of a young birch tree!
The oak that in summer was sweet to hear,
And rustled its leaves in the fall of the year,
And whistled and roared in the winter alone,
Is gone,—and the birch in its stead is grown—
The Knight's bones are dust,
And his good sword rust;
His soul is with the saints, I trust.

SIR WALTER SCOTT [1771–1832]

BONNY DUNDEE

To the Lords of Convention 't was Claver'se who spoke,
"Ere the King's crown shall fall there are crowns to be broke;
So let each Cavalier who loves honour and me,
Come follow the bonnet of Bonny Dundee.
 Come fill up my cup, come fill up my can,
 Come saddle your horses and call up your men;
 Come open the West Port and let me gang free,
 And it 's room for the bonnets of Bonny Dundee!"

Dundee he is mounted, he rides up the street,
The bells are rung backward, the drums they are beat;
But the Provost, douce man, said, "Just e'en let him be,
The Gude Town is weel quit of that Deil of Dundee."

As he rode down the sanctified bends of the Bow
Ilk carline was flyting and shaking her pow;
But the young plants of grace they looked couthie and slee,
Thinking luck to thy bonnet, thou Bonny Dundee!

With sour-featured Whigs the Grass-market was crammed,
As if half the West had set tryst to be hanged;
There was spite in each look, there was fear in each e'e,
As they watched for the bonnets of Bonny Dundee.

These cowls of Kilmarnock had spits and had spears,
And lang-hafted gullies to kill cavaliers;
But they shrunk to close-heads and the causeway was free,
At the toss of the bonnet of Bonny Dundee.

He spurred to the foot of the proud Castle rock,
And with the gay Gordon he gallantly spoke;
"Let Mons Meg and her marrows speak twa words or three,
For the love of the bonnet of Bonny Dundee."

The Gordon demands of him which way he goes—
"Where'er shall direct me the shade of Montrose!
Your Grace in short space shall hear tidings of me,
Or that low lies the bonnet on Bonny Dundee.

"There are hills beyond Pentland and lands beyond Forth,
If there's lords in the Lowlands, there's chiefs in the North;
There are wild Duniewassals three thousand times three,
Will cry *hoigh!* for the bonnet of Bonny Dundee.

"There's brass on the target of barkened bull-hide;
There's steel in the scabbard that dangles beside;
The brass shall be burnished, the steel shall flash free,
At a toss of the bonnet of Bonny Dundee.

"Away to the hills, to the caves, to the rocks—
Ere I own an usurper, I'll couch with the fox;
And tremble, false Whigs, in the midst of your glee,
You have not seen the last of my bonnet and me!"

He waved his proud hand and the trumpets were blown,
The kettle-drums clashed and the horsemen rode on,
Till on Ravelston's cliffs and on Clermiston's lee
Died away the wild war-notes of Bonny Dundee.

Come fill up my cup, come fill up my can,
Come saddle the horses and call up the men,
Come open your gates and let me gae free,
For it's up with the bonnets of Bonny Dundee!

[From THE DOOM OF DEVORGOIL.]

THE FIGHT ON FLODDEN FIELD

BLOUNT and Fitz-Eustace rested still
With Lady Clare upon the hill,
On which—for far the day was spent—
The western sunbeams now were bent;
The cry they heard, its meaning knew,
Could plain their distant comrades view:
  Sadly to Blount did Eustace say,
"Unworthy office here to stay!
No hope of gilded spurs to-day.—
But see! look up—on Flodden bent
The Scottish foe has fired his tent."
  And sudden, as he spoke,
From the sharp ridges of the hill,
All downward to the banks of Till,
  Was wreathed in sable smoke.
Volumed and vast, and rolling far,
The cloud enveloped Scotland's war
  As down the hill they broke;
Nor martial shout, nor minstrel tone,
Announced their march; their tread alone,
At times one warning trumpet blown,
  At times a stifled hum,
Told England, from his mountain-throne
  King James did rushing come.
Scarce could they hear or see their foes
Until at weapon-point they close.—
They close in clouds of smoke and dust,
With sword-sway and with lance's thrust;
  And such a yell was there,
Of sudden and portentous birth,
As if men fought upon the earth,

And fiends in upper air:
Oh! life and death were in the shout,
Recoil and rally, charge and rout,
    And triumph and despair.
Long looked the anxious squires; their eye
Could in the darkness nought descry.

At length the freshening western blast
Aside the shroud of battle cast;
And first the ridge of mingled spears
Above the brightening cloud appears,
And in the smoke the pennons flew,
As in the storm the white seamew.
Then marked they, dashing broad and far,
The broken billows of the war,
And plumèd crests of chieftains brave
Floating like foam upon the wave;
    But nought distinct they see:
Wide raged the battle on the plain;
Spears shook and falchions flashed amain;
Fell England's arrow-flight like rain;
Crests rose, and stooped, and rose again,
    Wild and disorderly.
Amid the scene of tumult, high
They saw Lord Marmion's falcon fly;
The stainless Tunstall's banner white,
And Edmund Howard's lion bright,
Still bear them bravely in the fight,
    Although against them come
Of gallant Gordons many a one,
And many a stubborn Badenoch-man,
And many a rugged Border clan,
    With Huntly and with Home.—
Far on the left, unseen the while,
Stanley broke Lennox and Argyle,
Though there the western mountaineer
Rushed with bare bosom on the spear,
And flung the feeble targe aside,
And with both hands the broadsword plied.

'Twas vain.—But Fortune, on the right,
With fickle smile cheered Scotland's fight.
Then fell that spotless banner white,
  The Howard's lion fell;
Yet still Lord Marmion's falcon flew
With wavering flight, while fiercer grew
  Around the battle-yell.
The Border Slogan rent the sky!
A Home! a Gordon! was the cry:
  Loud were the clanging blows;
Advanced,—forced back, now low, now high,
  The pennon sunk and rose;
As bends the bark's mast in the gale,
When rent are rigging, shrouds and sail,
  It wavered mid the foes.

[From Canto **VI**, Marmion.]

ROBERT SOUTHEY [1774-1843]

THE BATTLE OF BLENHEIM

It was a summer evening,
  Old Kaspar's work was done,
And he before his cottage door
  Was sitting in the sun,
And by him sported on the green
His little grandchild Wilhelmine.

She saw her brother Peterkin
  Roll something large and round,
Which he beside the rivulet
  In playing there had found;
He came to ask what he had found,
That was so large, and smooth, and round.

Old Kaspar took it from the boy,
  Who stood expectant by;

And then the old man shook his head,
 And with a natural sigh,
"'Tis some poor fellow's skull," said he,
"Who fell in the great victory.

"I find them in the garden
 For there's many here about;
And often when I go to plough,
 The ploughshare turns them out!
For many thousand men," said he,
"Were slain in that great victory."

"Now tell me what 'twas all about,"
 Young Peterkin, he cries;
And little Wilhelmine looks up
 With wonder-waiting eyes;
"Now tell us all about the war,
And what they fought each other for."

"It was the English," Kaspar cried,
 "Who put the French to rout;
But what they fought each other for,
 I could not well make out;
But everybody said," quoth he,
"That 'twas a famous victory.

"My father lived at Blenheim then,
 Yon little stream hard by;
They burnt his dwelling to the ground,
 And he was forced to fly;
So with his wife and child he fled,
Nor had he where to rest his head.

"With fire and sword the country round
 Was wasted far and wide,
And many a childing mother then,
 And new-born baby died;
But things like that, you know, must be
At every famous victory.

"They say it was a shocking sight
      After the field was won;
For many thousand bodies here
      Lay rotting in the sun;
But things like that, you know, must be
After a famous victory.

"Great praise the Duke of Marlbro' won,
      And our good Prince Eugene."
"Why 'twas a very wicked thing!"
      Said little Wilhelmine.
"Nay, nay, my little girl," quoth he,
"It was a famous victory.

"And everybody praised the Duke
      Who this great fight did win."
"But what good came of it at last?"
      Quoth little Peterkin.
"Why that I cannot tell," said he,
"But 'twas a famous victory."

CHARLES LAMB [1775–1834]

THE OLD FAMILIAR FACES

I HAVE had playmates, I have had companions,
In my days of childhood, in my joyful school-days;
All, all are gone, the old familiar faces.

I have been laughing, I have been carousing,
Drinking late, sitting late, with my bosom cronies;
All, all are gone, the old familiar faces.

I loved a Love once, fairest among women:
Closed are her doors on me, I must not see her—
All, all are gone, the old familiar faces.

I have a friend, a kinder friend has no man:
Like an ingrate, I left my friend abruptly;
Left him, to muse on the old familiar faces.

Ghost-like I paced round the haunts of my childhood,
Earth seem'd a desert I was bound to traverse,
Seeking to find the old familiar faces.

Friend of my bosom, thou more than a brother,
Why wert not thou born in my father's dwelling?
So might we talk of the old familiar faces.

How some they have died, and some they have left me,
And some are taken from me; all are departed;
All, all are gone, the old familiar faces.

WALTER SAVAGE LANDOR [1775–1864]

ROSE AYLMER

Ah what avails the sceptred race,
    Ah what the form divine!
What every virtue, every grace!
    Rose Aylmer, all were thine.

Rose Aylmer, whom these wakeful eyes
    May weep, but never see,
A night of memories and of sighs
    I consecrate to thee.

DIRCE

Stand close around, ye Stygian set,
    With Dirce in one boat conveyed,
Or Charon, seeing, may forget
    That he is old, and she a shade.

THE DEATH OF ARTEMIDORA

"ARTEMIDORA! Gods invisible,
While thou art lying faint along the couch,
Have tied the sandal to thy slender feet
And stand beside thee, ready to convey
Thy weary steps where other rivers flow.
Refreshing shades will waft thy weariness
Away, and voices like thy own come near
And nearer, and solicit an embrace."
  Artemidora sigh'd, and would have pressed
The hand now pressing hers, but was too weak.
Iris stood over her dark hair unseen
While thus Elpenor spake. He looked into
Eyes that had given light and life ere-while
To those above them, but now dim with tears
And wakefulness. Again he spake of joy
Eternal. At that word, that sad word, *joy*,
Faithful and fond her bosom heav'd once more:
Her head fell back; and now a loud deep sob
Swell'd thro' the darken'd chamber; 'twas not hers.

TO IANTHE

PAST ruin'd Ilion Helen lives,
  Alcestis rises from the shades;
Verse calls them forth; 'tis verse that gives
  Immortal youth to mortal maids.

Soon shall Oblivion's deepening veil
  Hide all the peopled hills you see,
The gay, the proud, while lovers hail
  These many summers you and me.

ON LUCRETIA BORGIA'S HAIR

BORGIA, thou once wert almost too august
And high for adoration; now thou'rt dust;
All that remains of thee these plaits unfold,
Calm hair meandering in pellucid gold.

IPHIGENEIA AND AGAMEMNON

IPHIGENEIA, when she heard her doom
At Aulis, and when all beside the King
Had gone away, took his right hand, and said,
"O father! I am young and very happy.
I do not think the pious Calchas heard
Distinctly what the Goddess spake. Old-age
Obscures the senses. If my nurse, who knew
My voice so well, sometimes misunderstood
While I was resting on her knee both arms
And hitting it to make her mind my words,
And looking in her face, and she in mine,
Might he not also hear one word amiss,
Spoken from so far off, even from Olympus?"
The father placed his cheek upon her head,
And tears dropped down it, but the king of men
Replied not. Then the maiden spake once more.
"O father! sayst thou nothing? Hear'st thou not
Me, whom thou ever hast, until this hour,
Listened to fondly, and awakened me
To hear my voice amid the voice of birds,
When it was inarticulate as theirs,
And the down deadened it within the nest?"
He moved her gently from him, silent still,
And this, and this alone, brought tears from her,
Although she saw fate nearer: then with sighs,
"I thought to have laid down my hair before
Benignant Artemis, and not have dimmed
Her polished altar with my virgin blood;

I thought to have selected the white flowers
To please the Nymphs, and to have asked of each
By name, and with no sorrowful regret,
Whether, since both my parents willed the change,
I might at Hymen's feet bend my clipped brow;
And (after those who mind us girls the most,)
Adore our own Athena, that she would
Regard me mildly with her azure eyes,
But father! to see you no more, and see
Your love, O father! go ere I am gone . . ."
Gently he moved her off, and drew her back,
Bending his lofty head far over hers,
And the dark depths of nature heaved and burst.
He turn'd away; not far, but silent still.
She now first shuddered; for in him, so nigh,
So long a silence seemed the approach of death,
And like it. Once again she raised her voice.
"O father! if the ships are now detained,
And all your vows move not the Gods above,
When the knife strikes me there will be one prayer
The less to them: and purer can there be
Any, or more fervent than the daughter's prayer
For her dear father's safety and success?"
A groan that shook him shook not his resolve.
An aged man now entered, and without
One word, stepped slowly on, and took the wrist
Of the pale maiden. She looked up and saw
The fillet of the priest and calm cold eyes.
Then turned she where her parent stood, and cried
"O father! grieve no more: the ships can sail."

ON HIS SEVENTY-FIFTH BIRTHDAY

I STROVE with none; for none was worth my strife,
    Nature I loved, and next to Nature, Art;
I warmed both hands before the fire of life,
    It sinks, and I am ready to depart.

THOMAS CAMPBELL [1777–1844]

YE MARINERS OF ENGLAND

A NAVAL ODE

YE mariners of England
That guard our native seas,
Whose flag has braved a thousand years
The battle and the breeze!
Your glorious standard launch again
To match another foe,
And sweep through the deep,
While the stormy winds do blow;
While the battle rages loud and long,
And the stormy winds do blow.

The spirits of your fathers
Shall start from every wave!—
For the deck it was their field of fame
And Ocean was their grave:
Where Blake and mighty Nelson fell
Your manly hearts shall glow,
As ye sweep through the deep,
While the stormy winds do blow;
While the battle rages loud and long,
And the stormy winds do blow.

Britannia needs no bulwark,
No towers along the steep;
Her march is o'er the mountain waves,
Her home is on the deep.
With thunders from her native oak
She quells the floods below—
As they roar on the shore,
When the stormy winds do blow;
When the battle rages loud and long,
And the stormy winds do blow.

The meteor flag of England
Shall yet terrific burn,
Till danger's troubled night depart
And the star of peace return.
Then, then, ye ocean-warriors!
Our song and feast shall flow
To the fame of your name,
When the storm has ceased to blow;
When the fiery fight is heard no more,
And the storm has ceased to blow.

THOMAS MOORE [1779–1852]

PRO PATRIA MORI

WHEN he, who adores thee, has left but the name
Of his fault and his sorrows behind,
Oh! say wilt thou weep, when they darken the fame
Of a life that for thee was resigned?
Yes, weep, and however my foes may condemn,
Thy tears shall efface their decree;
For Heaven can witness, though guilty to them,
I have been but too faithful to thee.

With thee were the dreams of my earliest love;
Every thought of my reason was thine;
In my last humble prayer to the Spirit above,
Thy name shall be mingled with mine.
Oh! blest are the lovers and friends who shall live
The days of thy glory to see;
But the next dearest blessing that Heaven can give
Is the pride of thus dying for thee.

GEORGE NOEL GORDON, LORD BYRON
[1788–1824]

MAID OF ATHENS, ERE WE PART

Ζωή μου, σᾶς ἀγαπῶ.

Maid of Athens, ere we part,
Give, oh, give me back my heart!
Or, since that has left my breast,
Keep it now, and take the rest!
Hear my vow before I go,
Ζωή μου, σᾶς ἀγαπῶ.

By those tresses unconfined,
Woo'd by each Ægean wind;
By those lids whose jetty fringe
Kiss thy soft cheeks' blooming tinge;
By those wild eyes like the roe,
Ζωή μου, σᾶς ἀγαπῶ.

By that lip I long to taste;
By that zone-encircled waist;
By all the token-flowers that tell
What words can never speak so well;
By love's alternate joy and woe,
Ζωή μου, σᾶς ἀγαπῶ.

Maid of Athens! I am gone:
Think of me, sweet! when alone.
Though I fly to Istambol,
Athens holds my heart and soul;
Can I cease to love thee? No!
Ζωή μου, σᾶς ἀγαπῶ.

WHEN WE TWO PARTED

WHEN we two parted
  In silence and tears,
Half broken-hearted
  To sever for years,
Pale grew thy cheek and cold,
  Colder thy kiss;
Truly that hour foretold
  Sorrow to this.

The dew of the morning
  Sunk chill on my brow—
It felt like the warning
  Of what I feel now.
Thy vows are all broken,
  And light is thy fame:
I hear thy name spoken,
  And share in its shame.

They name thee before me,
  A knell to mine ear;
A shudder comes o'er me—
  Why wert thou so dear?
They know not I knew thee,
  Who knew thee too well:
Long, long shall I rue thee,
  Too deeply to tell.

In secret we met—
  In silence I grieve
That thy heart could forget,
  Thy spirit deceive.
If I should meet thee
  After long years,
How should I greet thee?—
  With silence and tears.

SHE WALKS IN BEAUTY

SHE walks in beauty, like the night
  Of cloudless climes and starry skies;
And all that's best of dark and bright
  Meet in her aspect and her eyes:
Thus mellow'd to that tender light
  Which heaven to gaudy day denies.

One shade the more, one ray the less,
  Had half impair'd the nameless grace
Which waves in every raven tress,
  Or softly lightens o'er her face;
Where thoughts serenely sweet express
  How pure, how dear their dwelling-place.

And on that cheek, and o'er that brow,
  So soft, so calm, yet eloquent,
The smiles that win, the tints that glow,
  But tell of days in goodness spent,
A mind at peace with all below,
  A heart whose love is innocent!

SONNET ON CHILLON

ETERNAL Spirit of the chainless mind!
Brightest in dungeons, Liberty! thou art,
For there thy habitation is the heart—
The heart which love of thee alone can bind;
And when thy sons to fetters are consign'd—
To fetters, and the damp vault's dayless gloom,
Their country conquers with their martyrdom,
And Freedom's fame finds wings on every wind.
Chillon! thy prison is a holy place,
And thy sad floor an altar—for 'twas trod,
Until his very steps have left a trace
Worn, as if thy cold pavement were a sod,
By Bonnivard! May none those marks efface!
For they appeal from tyranny to God.

STANZAS FOR MUSIC

THERE be none of Beauty's daughters
   With a magic like thee;
And like music on the waters
   Is thy sweet voice to me:
When, as if its sound were causing
The charmed ocean's pausing,
The waves lie still and gleaming,
And the lull'd winds seem dreaming;

And the midnight moon is weaving
   Her bright chain o'er the deep;
Whose breast is gently heaving,
   As an infant's asleep:
So the spirit bows before thee,
To listen and adore thee;
With a full but soft emotion,
Like the swell of Summer's ocean.

ON THE FIELD OF WATERLOO

AND Harold stands upon this place of skulls,
The grave of France, the deadly Waterloo!
How in an hour the power which gave annuls
Its gifts, transferring fame as fleeting too;
In "pride of place" here last the eagle flew,
Then tore with bloody talon the rent plain,
Pierced by the shaft of banded nations through;
Ambition's life and labours all were vain;
He wears the shatter'd links of the world's broken chain.

Fit retribution! Gaul may champ the bit
And foam in fetters;—but is Earth more free?
Did nations combat to make *One* submit;
Or league to teach all kings true sovereignty?
What! shall reviving Thraldom again be
The patch'd-up idol of enlighten'd days?

Shall we, who struck the Lion down, shall we
Pay the Wolf homage? proffering lowly gaze
And servile knees to thrones? No; *prove* before ye praise!

If not, o'er one fallen despot boast no more!
In vain fair cheeks were furrow'd with hot tears
For Europe's flowers long rooted up before
The trampler of her vineyards; in vain years
Of death, depopulation, bondage, fears,
Have all been borne, and broken by the accord
Of roused-up millions; all that most endears
Glory, is when the myrtle wreathes a sword
Such as Harmodius drew on Athens' tyrant lord.

There was a sound of revelry by night,
And Belgium's capital had gather'd then
Her Beauty and her Chivalry, and bright
The lamps shone o'er fair women and brave men;
A thousand hearts beat happily; and when
Music arose with its voluptuous swell,
Soft eyes look'd love to eyes which spake again,
And all went merry as a marriage bell;
But hush! hark! a deep sound strikes like a rising knell!

Did ye not hear it?—No; 'twas but the wind,
Or the car rattling o'er the stony street;
On with the dance! let joy be unconfin'd;
No sleep till morn, when Youth and Pleasure meet
To chase the glowing Hours with flying feet—
But hark!—that heavy sound breaks in once more,
As if the clouds its echo would repeat;
And nearer, clearer, deadlier than before!
Arm! Arm! it is—it is—the cannon's opening roar!

Within a window'd niche of that high hall
Sate Brunswick's fated chieftain; he did hear
That sound the first amidst the festival,
And caught its tone with Death's prophetic ear;
And when they smiled because he deem'd it near,
His heart more truly knew that peal too well

Which stretch'd his father on a bloody bier,
And roused the vengeance blood alone could quell;
He rush'd into the field, and, foremost fighting, fell.

Ah! then and there was hurrying to and fro,
And gathering tears, and tremblings of distress,
And cheeks all pale, which but an hour ago
Blush'd at the praise of their own loveliness;
And there were sudden partings, such as press
The life from out young hearts, and choking sighs
Which ne'er might be repeated; who could guess
If ever more should meet those mutual eyes,
Since upon night so sweet such awful morn could rise!

And there was mounting in hot haste: the steed,
The mustering squadron, and the clattering car,
Went pouring forward with impetuous speed,
And swiftly forming in the ranks of war;
And the deep thunder peal on peal afar;
And near, the beat of the alarming drum
Roused up the soldier ere the morning star;
While throng'd the citizens with terror dumb,
Or whispering, with white lips—"The foe, they come!
    they come!"

And wild and high the "Cameron's gathering" rose!
The war-note of Lochiel, which Albyn's hills
Have heard, and heard, too, have her Saxon foes:—
How in the noon of night that pibroch thrills,
Savage and shrill! But with the breath which fills
Their mountain-pipe, so fill the mountaineers
With the fierce native daring which instils
The stirring memory of a thousand years,
And Evan's, Donald's fame rings in each clansman's ears!

And Ardennes waves above them her green leaves,
Dewy with nature's tear-drops as they pass,
Grieving, if aught inanimate e'er grieves,
Over the unreturning brave,—alas!

Ere evening to be trodden like the grass
Which now beneath them, but above shall grow
In its next verdure, when this fiery mass
Of living valour, rolling on the foe
And burning with high hope shall moulder cold and low.

Last noon beheld them full of lusty life,
Last eve in Beauty's circle proudly gay,
The midnight brought the signal-sound of strife.
The morn the marshalling in arms,—the day
Battle's magnificently stern array!
The thunder-clouds close o'er it, which when rent
The earth is cover'd thick with other clay,
Which her own clay shall cover, heap'd and pent,
Rider and horse,—friend, foe,—in one red burial blent!

[From CHILDE HAROLD'S PILGRIMAGE.]

THE ISLES OF GREECE

THE isles of Greece, the isles of Greece!
  Where burning Sappho loved and sung,
Where grew the arts of war and peace,—
  Where Delos rose, and Phœbus sprung!
Eternal summer gilds them yet,
But all, except their sun, is set.

The Scian and the Teian muse,
  The hero's harp, the lover's lute,
Have found the fame your shores refuse:
  Their place of birth alone is mute
To sounds which echo further west
Than your sires' "Islands of the Blest."

The mountains look on Marathon—
  And Marathon looks on the sea;
And musing there an hour alone,
  I dream'd that Greece might still be free;

For standing on the Persians' grave,
I could not deem myself a slave.

A king sate on the rocky brow
  Which looks o'er sea-born Salamis;
And ships, by thousands, lay below,
  And men in nations;—all were his!
He counted them at break of day—
And when the sun set, where were they?

And where are they? and where art thou,
  My country? On thy voiceless shore
The heroic lay is tuneless now—
  The heroic bosom beats no more!
And must thy lyre, so long divine,
Degenerate into hands like mine?

'Tis something, in the dearth of fame,
  Though link'd among a fetter'd race,
To feel at least a patriot's shame,
  Even as I sing, suffuse my face;
For what is left the poet here?
For Greeks a blush—for Greece a tear.

Must *we* but weep o'er days more blest?
  Must *we* but blush?—Our fathers bled.
Earth! render back from out thy breast
  A remnant of our Spartan dead!
Of the three hundred grant but three,
To make a new Thermopylæ!

What, silent still? and silent all?
  Ah! no;—the voices of the dead
Sound like a distant torrent's fall,
  And answer, "Let one living head,
But one arise,—we come, we come!"
'Tis but the living who are dumb.

In vain—in vain: strike other chords;
  Fill high the cup with Samian wine!

Leave battles to the Turkish hordes,
  And shed the blood of Scio's vine!
Hark! rising to the ignoble call—
How answers each bold Bacchanal!

You have the Pyrrhic dance as yet;
  Where is the Pyrrhic phalanx gone?
Of two such lessons, why forget
  The nobler and the manlier one?
You have the letters Cadmus gave—
Think ye he meant them for a slave?

Fill high the bowl with Samian wine!
  We will not think of themes like these!
It made Anacreon's song divine;
  He served—but served Polycrates—
A tyrant; but our masters then
Were still, at least, our countrymen.

The tyrant of the Chersonese
  Was freedom's best and bravest friend;
That tyrant was Miltiades!
  Oh! that the present hour would lend
Another despot of the kind!
Such chains as his were sure to bind.

Fill high the bowl with Samian wine!
  On Suli's rock, and Parga's shore,
Exists the remnant of a line
  Such as the Doric mothers bore;
And there, perhaps, some seed is sown,
The Heracleidan blood might own.

Trust not for freedom to the Franks,
  They have a king who buys and sells;
In native swords and native ranks,
  The only hope of courage dwells:
But Turkish force, and Latin fraud,
Would break your shield, however broad.

Fill high the bowl with Samian wine!
  Our virgins dance beneath the shade—
I see their glorious black eyes shine;
  But gazing on each glowing maid,
My own the burning tear-drop laves,
To think such breasts must suckle slaves.

Place me on Sunium's marbled steep,
  Where nothing, save the waves and I,
May hear our mutual murmurs sweep;
  There, swan-like, let me sing and die:
A land of slaves shall ne'er be mine—
Dash down yon cup of Samian wine!

                         [From Canto III, DON JUAN.]

DON JUAN SOLILOQUIZES

MILTON's the prince of poets—so we say;
  A little heavy, but no less divine:
An independent being in his day—
  Learn'd, pious, temperate in love and wine;
But his life falling into Johnson's way,
  We're told this great high priest of all the Nine
Was whipt at college—a harsh sire—odd spouse,
For the first Mrs. Milton left his house.

All these are, *certes*, entertaining facts,
  Like Shakspere's stealing deer, Lord Bacon's bribes;
Like Titus' youth, and Cæsar's earliest acts;
  Like Burns (whom Doctor Currie well describes);
Like Cromwell's pranks;—but although truth exacts
  These amiable descriptions from the scribes,
As most essential to their hero's story,
They do not much contribute to his glory.

All are not moralists, like Southey, when
  He prated to the world of "Pantisocrasy:"

Or Wordsworth unexcised, unhired, who then
    Season'd his pedlar poems with democracy;
Or Coleridge, long before his flighty pen
    Let to the Morning Post its aristocracy;
When he and Southey, following the same path,
Espoused two partners (milliners of Bath).

Such names at present cut a convict figure,
    The very Botany Bay in moral geography;
Their royal treason, renegado rigor,
    Are good manure for their more bare biography.
Wordsworth's last quarto, by the way, is bigger
    Than any since the birthday of typography;
A drowsy frowzy poem, call'd the "Excursion,"
Writ in a manner which is my aversion.

He there builds up a formidable dyke
    Between his own and others' intellect;
But Wordsworth's poem, and his followers, like
    Joanna Southcote's Shiloh, and her sect,
Are things which in this century don't strike
    The public mind,—so few are the elect;
And the new births of both their stale virginities
Have proved but dropsies, taken for divinities.

But let me to my story: I must own,
    If I have any fault, it is digression,
Leaving my people to proceed alone,
    While I soliloquize beyond expression:
But these are my addresses from the throne,
    Which put off business to the ensuing session:
Forgetting each omission is a loss to
The world, not quite so great as Ariosto.

I know that what our neighbors call "*longueurs*,"
    (We've not so good a *word*, but have the *thing*,
In that complete perfection which insures
    An epic from Bob Southey every Spring—)

Form not the true temptation which allures
    The reader; but 'twould not be hard to bring
Some fine examples of the *epopée*,
To prove its grand ingredient is *ennui*.

We learn from Horace, "Homer sometimes sleeps;"
    We feel without him, Wordsworth sometimes wakes,—
To show with what complacency he creeps,
    With his dear "*Wagoners,*" around his lakes.
He wishes for "a boat" to sail the deeps—
    Of ocean?—No, of air; and then he makes
Another outcry for "a little boat,"
And drivels seas to set it well afloat.

If he must fain sweep o'er the ethereal plain,
    And Pegasus runs restive in his "Wagon,"
Could he not beg the loan of Charles's Wain?
    Or pray Medea for a single dragon?
Or if, too classic for his vulgar brain,
    He fear'd his neck to venture such a nag on,
And he must needs mount nearer to the moon,
Could not the blockhead ask for a balloon?

"Pedlars," and "Boats," and "Wagons!" Oh! ye shades
    Of Pope and Dryden, are we come to this?
That trash of such sort not alone evades
    Contempt, but from the bathos' vast abyss
Floats scumlike uppermost, and these Jack Cades
    Of sense and song above your graves may hiss—
The "little boatman" and his "Peter Bell"
Can sneer at him who drew "Achitophel!"

[From Canto III, Don Juan.]

CHARLES WOLFE [1791–1823]

THE BURIAL OF SIR JOHN MOORE AT CORUNNA

Not a drum was heard, not a funeral note,
 As his corse to the rampart we hurried;
Not a soldier discharged his farewell shot
 O'er the grave where our hero we buried.

We buried him darkly at dead of night,
 The sods with our bayonets turning;
By the struggling moonbeam's misty light,
 And the lantern dimly burning.

No useless coffin enclosed his breast,
 Not in sheet nor in shroud we wound him;
But he lay like a warrior taking his rest
 With his martial cloak around him.

Few and short were the prayers we said,
 And we spoke not a word of sorrow;
But we stedfastly gazed on the face that was dead,
 And we bitterly thought of the morrow.

We thought as we hollowed his narrow bed,
 And smoothed down his lonely pillow,
That the foe and the stranger would tread o'er his head,
 And we far away on the billow!

Lightly they'll talk of the spirit that's gone,
 And o'er his cold ashes upbraid him,—
But little he'll reck, if they let him sleep on
 In the grave where a Briton has laid him.

But half of our weary task was done
 When the clock struck the hour for retiring;
And we heard the distant and random gun
 That the foe was sullenly firing.

Slowly and sadly we laid him down,
From the field of his fame fresh and gory;
We carved not a line, and we raised not a stone—
But we left him alone with his glory.

JOHN KEATS [1795–1821]

ON FIRST LOOKING INTO CHAPMAN'S HOMER

MUCH have I travell'd in the realms of gold,
And many goodly states and kingdoms seen;
Round many western islands have I been
Which bards in fealty to Apollo hold.
Oft of one wide expanse had I been told
That deep-browed Homer ruled as his demesne;
Yet did I never breathe its pure serene
Till I heard Chapman speak out loud and bold:
Then felt I like some watcher of the skies
When a new planet swims into his ken;
Or like stout Cortez when with eagle eyes
He star'd at the Pacific—and all his men
Look'd at each other with a wild surmise—
Silent, upon a peak in Darien.

ODE

BARDS of Passion and of Mirth,
Ye have left your souls on earth!
Have ye souls in heaven too,
Double-lived in regions new?
Yes, and those of heaven commune
With the spheres of sun and moon;
With the noise of fountains wond'rous,
And the parle of voices thund'rous,
With the whisper of heaven's trees
And one another, in soft ease
Seated on Elysian lawns
Brows'd by none but Dian's fawns;

Underneath large blue-bells tented,
Where the daisies are rose-scented,
And the rose herself has got
Perfume which on earth is not;
Where the nightingale doth sing
Not a senseless, tranced thing,
But divine melodious truth;
Philosophic numbers smooth;
Tales and golden histories
Of heaven and its mysteries.

Thus ye live on high, and then
On the earth ye live again;
And the souls ye lift behind you
Teach us, here, the way to find you,
Where your other souls are joying,
Never slumber'd, never cloying.
Here, your earth-born souls still speak
To mortals, of their little week;
Of their sorrows and delights;
Of their passions and their spites;
Of their glory and their shame;
What doth strengthen and what maim.
Thus ye teach us, every day,
Wisdom, though fled far away.

Bards of Passion and of Mirth,
Ye have left your souls on earth!
Ye have souls in heaven too,
Double-lived in regions new!

WHEN I HAVE FEARS

WHEN I have fears that I may cease to be
Before my pen has glean'd my teeming brain,
Before high pilèd books, in charact'ry,
Hold like rich garners the full-ripen'd grain;
When I behold, upon the night's starr'd face,
Huge cloudy symbols of a high romance,
And think that I may never live to trace
Their shadows, with the magic hand of chance;

And when I feel, fair creature of an hour!
That I shall never look upon thee more,
Never have relish in the faery power
Of unreflecting love!—then on the shore
Of the wide world I stand alone, and think
Till Love and Fame to nothingness do sink.

THE EVE OF ST. AGNES

St. Agnes' Eve—Ah, bitter chill it was!
The owl, for all his feathers, was a-cold;
The hare limp'd trembling through the frozen grass,
And silent was the flock in woolly fold:
Numb were the Beadsman's fingers, while he told
His rosary, and while his frosted breath,
Like pious incense from a censer old,
Seem'd taking flight for heaven, without a death,
Past the sweet Virgin's picture, while his prayer he saith.

His prayer he saith, this patient, holy man
Then takes his lamp, and riseth from his knees,
And back returneth, meagre, barefoot, wan,
Along the chapel aisle by slow degrees:
The sculptur'd dead, on each side, seem to freeze,
Emprison'd in black, purgatorial rails:
Knights, ladies, praying in dumb orat'ries,
He passeth by; and his weak spirit fails
To think how they may ache in icy hoods and mails.

Northward he turneth through a little door,
And scarce three steps, ere Music's golden tongue
Flatter'd to tears this aged man and poor;
But no—already had his deathbell rung;
The joys of all his life were said and sung:
His was harsh penance on St. Agnes' Eve:
Another way he went, and soon among
Rough ashes sat he for his soul's reprieve,
And all night kept awake, for sinners' sake to grieve.

That ancient Beadsman heard the prelude soft;
And so it chanc'd, for many a door was wide,
From hurry to and fro. Soon, up aloft,
The silver, snarling trumpets 'gan to chide:
The level chambers, ready with their pride,
Were glowing to receive a thousand guests:
The carved angels, ever eager-eyed,
Star'd where upon their heads the cornice rests,
With hair blown back, and wings put cross-wise on their breasts.

At length burst in the argent revelry,
With plume, tiara, and all rich array,
Numerous as shadows haunting fairily
The brain, new stuff'd, in youth, with triumphs gay
Of old romance. These let us wish away,
And turn, sole-thoughted, to one Lady there,
Whose heart had brooded, all that wintry day,
On love, and wing'd St. Agnes' saintly care,
As she had heard old dames full many times declare.

They told her how, upon St. Agnes' Eve,
Young virgins might have visions of delight,
And soft adorings from their loves receive
Upon the honey'd middle of the night
If ceremonies due they did aright;
As, supperless to bed they must retire,
And couch supine their beauties, lily white;
Nor look behind, nor sideways, but require
Of Heaven with upward eyes for all that they desire.

Full of this whim was thoughtful Madeline;
The music, yearning like a God in pain,
She scarcely heard: her maiden eyes divine,
Fix'd on the floor, saw many a sweeping train
Pass by—she heeded not at all: in vain
Came many a tiptoe, amourous cavalier,
And back retir'd; not cool'd by high disdain,
But she saw not: her heart was otherwhere:
She sigh'd for Agnes' dreams, the sweetest of the year.

She danc'd along with vague, regardless eyes,
Anxious her lips, her breathing quick and short:
The hallow'd hour was near at hand: she sighs
Amid the timbrels, and the throng'd resort
Of whisperings in anger, or in sport;
'Mid looks of love, defiance, hate, and scorn,
Hoodwink'd with faery fancy; all amort,
Save to St. Agnes and her lambs unshorn,
And all the bliss to be before to-morrow morn.

So, purposing each moment to retire,
She linger'd still. Meantime, across the moors,
Had come young Porphyro, with heart on fire
For Madeline. Beside the portal doors,
Buttress'd from moonlight, stands he, and implores
All saints to give him sight of Madeline,
But for one moment in the tedious hours,
That he might gaze and worship all unseen;
Perchance speak, kneel, touch, kiss—in sooth such things have
        been.

He ventures in: let no buzz'd whisper tell:
All eyes be muffled, or a hundred swords
Will storm his heart, Love's fev'rous citadel:
For him, those chambers held barbarian hordes,
Hyena foemen, and hot-blooded lords,
Whose very dogs would execrations howl
Against his lineage: not one breast affords
Him any mercy, in that mansion foul,
Save one old beldame, weak in body and in soul.

Ah, happy chance! the aged creature came,
Shuffling along with ivory-headed wand,
To where he stood, hid from the torch's flame,
Behind a broad hall-pillar, far beyond
The sound of merriment and chorus bland.
He startled her; but soon she knew his face,
And grasp'd his fingers in her palsied hand,
Saying, "Mercy, Porphyro! hie thee from this place;
They are all here to-night, the whole blood-thirsty race!

" Get hence! get hence! there's dwarfish Hildebrand;
He had a fever late, and in the fit
He cursed thee and thine, both house and land:
Then there's that old Lord Maurice, not a whit
More tame for his gray hairs—Alas me! flit!
Flit like a ghost away."—"Ah, Gossip dear,
We're safe enough; here in this arm-chair sit,
And tell me how"—"Good Saints! not here, not here;
Follow me, child, or else these stones will be thy bier."

He follow'd through a lowly arched way,
Brushing the cobwebs with his lofty plume;
And as she mutter'd "Well-a—Well-a-day!"
He found him in a little moonlight room,
Pale, lattic'd, chill, and silent as a tomb.
"Now tell me where is Madeline," said he,
"O tell me, Angela, by the holy loom
Which none but secret sisterhood may see,
When they St. Agnes' wool are weaving piously."

"St. Agnes! Ah! it is St. Agnes' Eve—
Yet men will murder upon holy days:
Thou must hold water in a witch's sieve,
And be liege-lord of all the Elves and Fays,
To venture so: it fills me with amaze
To see thee, Porphyro!—St. Agnes' Eve!
God's help! my lady fair the conjurer plays
This very night; good angels her deceive!
But let me laugh awhile, I've mickle time to grieve."

Feebly she laugheth in the languid moon,
While Porphyro upon her face doth look,
Like puzzled urchin on an aged crone
Who keepeth clos'd a wond'rous riddle-book,
As spectacled she sits in chimney nook.
But soon his eyes grew brilliant, when she told
His lady's purpose; and he scarce could brook
Tears, at the thought of those enchantments cold,
And Madeline asleep in lap of legends old.

Sudden a thought came like a full-blown rose,
Flushing his brow, and in his pained heart
Made purple riot: then doth he propose
A stratagem, that makes the beldame start:
"A cruel man and impious thou art:
Sweet lady, let her pray, and sleep, and dream
Alone with her good angels, far apart
From wicked men like thee. Go, go!—I deem
Thou canst not surely be the same that thou didst seem."

"I will not harm her, by all saints I swear,"
Quoth Porphyro: "O may I ne'er find grace
When my weak voice shall whisper its last prayer,
If one of her soft ringlets I displace,
Or look with ruffian passion in her face:
Good Angela, believe me by these tears;
Or I will, even in a moment's space,
Awake, with horrid shout, my foemen's ears,
And beard them, though they be more fang'd than wolves and
        bears."

"Ah! why wilt thou affright a feeble soul?
A poor, weak, palsy-stricken church-yard thing,
Whose passing-bell may ere the midnight toll;
Whose prayers for thee, each morn and evening,
Were never miss'd." Thus plaining, doth she bring
A gentler speech from burning Porphyro;
So woful, and of such deep sorrowing,
That Angela gives promise she will do
Whatever he shall wish, betide her weal or woe.

Which was, to lead him, in close secrecy,
Even to Madeline's chamber, and there hide
Him in a closet, of such privacy
That he might see her beauty unespied,
And win perhaps that night a peerless bride,
While legion'd fairies pac'd the coverlet,
And pale enchantment held her sleepy-eyed.
Never on such a night have lovers met,
Since Merlin paid his Demon all the monstrous debt.

"It shall be as thou wishest," said the Dame:
"All cates and dainties shall be stored there
Quickly on this feast-night: by the tambour frame
Her own lute thou wilt see: no time to spare,
For I am slow and feeble, and scarce dare
On such a catering trust my dizzy head.
Wait here, my child, with patience; kneel in prayer
The while: Ah! thou must needs the lady wed,
Or may I never leave my grave among the dead."

So saying, she hobbled off with busy fear.
The lover's endless minutes slowly pass'd;
The dame return'd, and whisper'd in his ear
To follow her; with aged eyes aghast
From fright of dim espial. Safe at last,
Through many a dusky gallery, they gain
The maiden's chamber, silken, hush'd, and chaste;
Where Porphyro took covert, pleas'd amain.
His poor guide hurried back with agues in her brain.

Her falt'ring hand upon the balustrade
Old Angela was feeling for the stair,
When Madeline, St. Agnes' charmed maid,
Rose, like a mission'd spirit, unaware:
With silver taper's light, and pious care,
She turn'd, and down the aged gossip led
To a safe level matting. Now prepare,
Young Porphyro, for gazing on that bed;
She comes, she comes again, like ring-dove fray'd and fled.

Out went the taper as she hurried in;
Its little smoke, in pallid moonshine, died:
She clos'd the door, she panted, all akin
To spirits of the air, and visions wide:
No uttered syllable, or, woe betide!
But to her heart, her heart was voluble,
Paining with eloquence her balmy side;
As though a tongueless nightingale should swell
Her throat in vain, and die, heart-stifled, in her dell.

A casement high and triple arch'd there was,
All garlanded with carven imag'ries
Of fruits, and flowers, and bunches of knot-grass.
And diamonded with panes of quaint device,
Innumerable of stains and splendid dyes,
As are the tiger-moth's deep-damask'd wings;
And in the midst, 'mong thousand heraldries,
And twilight saints, and dim emblazonings,
A shielded scutcheon blush'd with blood of queens and kings.

Full on this casement shone the wintry moon,
And threw warm gules on Madeline's fair breast,
As down she knelt for heaven's grace and boon;
Rose-bloom fell on her hands, together prest,
And on her silver cross soft amethyst,
And on her hair a glory, like a saint:
She seem'd a splendid angel, newly drest,
Save wings, for heaven: Porphyro grew faint:
She knelt, so pure a thing, so free from mortal taint.

Anon his heart revives: her vespers done,
Of all its wreathed pearls her hair she frees;
Unclasps her warmed jewels one by one
Loosens her fragrant bodice; by degrees
Her rich attire creeps rustling to her knees;
Half-hidden, like a mermaid in seaweed,
Pensive awhile she dreams awake, and sees,
In fancy, fair St. Agnes in her bed,
But dares not look behind, or all the charm is fled.

Soon, trembling in her soft and chilly nest,
In sort of wakeful swoon, perplex'd she lay.
Until the poppied warmth of sleep oppress'd
Her soothed limbs, and soul fatigued away;
Flown, like a thought, until the morrow-day;
Blissfully haven'd both from joy and pain;
Clasp'd like a missal where swart Paynims pray;
Blinded alike from sunshine and from rain,
As though a rose should shut, and be a bud again.

Stol'n to this paradise, and so entranced,
Porphyro gazed upon her empty dress,
And listen'd to her breathing, if it chanced
To wake into a slumberous tenderness;
Which when he heard, that minute did he bless,
And breath'd himself: then from the closet crept,
Noiseless as fear in a wide wilderness,
And over the hush'd carpet, silent, stepped,
And 'tween the curtains peep'd, where, lo!—how fast she slept.

Then by the bedside, where the faded moon
Made a dim, silver twilight, soft he set
A table, and, half-anguish'd, threw thereon
A cloth of woven crimson, gold, and jet:—
O for some drowsy Morphean amulet!
The boisterous, midnight, festive clarion,
The kettle-drum, and far-heard clarionet,
Affray his ears, though but in dying tone:—
The hall door shuts again, and all the noise is gone.

And still she slept an azure-lidded sleep,
In blanched linen, smooth, and lavender'd,
While he from forth the closet brought a heap
Of candied apple, quince, and plum, and gourd;
With jellies soother than the creamy curd,
And lucent syrops, tinct with cinnamon;
Manna and dates, in argosy transferr'd
From Fez; and spiced dainties, every one,
From silken Samarcand to cedar'd Lebanon.

These delicates he heap'd with glowing hand
On golden dishes and in baskets bright
Of wreathed silver: sumptuous they stand
In the retired quiet of the night,
Filling the chilly room with perfume light.—
"And now, my love, my seraph fair, awake!
Thou art my heaven, and I thine eremite:
Open thine eyes, for meek St. Agnes' sake,
Or I shall drowse beside thee, so my soul doth ache."

Thus whispering, his warm, unnerved arm
Sank in her pillow. Shaded was her dream
By the dusk curtains:—'twas a midnight charm
Impossible to melt as iced stream:
The lustrous salvers in the moonlight gleam:
Broad golden fringe upon the carpet lies:
It seem'd he never, never could redeem
From such a stedfast spell his lady's eyes;
So mus'd awhile, entoil'd in woofed phantasies.

Awakening up, he took her hollow lute,—
Tumultuous,—and, in chords that tenderest be,
He play'd an ancient ditty, long since mute,
In Provence call'd, "La belle dame sans merci:"
Close to her ear touching the melody:—
Wherewith disturb'd, she utter'd a soft moan:
He ceased—she panted quick—and suddenly
Her blue affrayed eyes wide open shone:
Upon his knees he sank, pale as smooth-sculptured stone.

Her eyes were open, but she still beheld,
Now wide awake, the vision of her sleep:
There was a painful change, that nigh expell'd
The blisses of her dream so pure and deep
At which fair Madeline began to weep,
And moan forth witless words with many a sigh;
While still her gaze on Porphyro would keep;
Who knelt, with joined hands and piteous eye,
Fearing to move or speak, she look'd so dreamingly.

"Ah, Porphyro!" said she, "but even now
Thy voice was at sweet tremble in mine ear,
Made tunable with every sweetest vow:
And those sad eyes were spiritual and clear.
How chang'd thou art! how pallid, chill, and drear!
Give me that voice again, my Porphyro,
Those looks immortal, those complainings dear!
Oh leave me not in this eternal woe,
For if thou diest, my Love, I know not where to go."

Beyond a mortal man impassion'd far
At these voluptuous accents, he arose,
Ethereal, flush'd, and like a throbbing star
Seen mid the sapphire heaven's deep repose;
Into her dream he melted, as the rose
Blendeth its odour with the violet,—
Solution sweet: meantime the frost wind blows
Like Love's alarum pattering the sharp sleet
Against the window-panes; St. Agnes' moon hath set.

'Tis dark: quick pattereth the flaw-blown sleet:
"This is no dream, my bride, my Madeline!"
'Tis dark: the iced gusts still rave and beat:
"No dream, alas! alas! and woe is mine!
Porphyro will leave me here to fade and pine.—
Cruel! what traitor could thee hither bring?
I curse not, for my heart is lost in thine,
Though thou forsakest a deceived thing;—
A dove forlorn and lost with sick unpruned wing."

"My Madeline! sweet dreamer! lovely bride!
Say, may I be for aye thy vassal blest?
Thy beauty's shield, heart-shap'd and vermeil dyed?
Ah, silver shrine, here will I take my rest
After so many hours of toil and quest,
A famish'd pilgrim,—saved by miracle.
Though I have found, I will not rob thy nest
Saving of thy sweet self; if thou think'st well
To trust, fair Madeline, to no rude infidel.

"Hark! 'tis an elfin-storm from faery land,
Of haggard seeming, but a boon indeed:
Arise—arise! the morning is at hand;—
The bloated wassaillers will never heed:—
Let us away, my love, with happy speed;
There are no ears to hear, or eyes to see,—
Drown'd all in Rhenish and the sleepy mead:
Awake! arise! my love, and fearless be,
For o'er the southern moors I have a home for thee."

She hurried at his words, beset with fears,
For there were sleeping dragons all around,
At glaring watch, perhaps, with ready spears—
Down the wide stairs a darkling way they found.—
In all the house was heard no human sound.
A chain-droop'd lamp was flickering by each door;
The arras, rich with horseman, hawk, and hound,
Flutter'd in the besieging wind's uproar;
And the long carpets rose along the gusty floor.

They glide, like phantoms, into the wide hall;
Like phantoms, to the iron porch, they glide;
Where lay the Porter, in uneasy sprawl,
With a huge empty flagon by his side:
The wakeful bloodhound rose, and shook his hide,
But his sagacious eye an inmate owns:
By one, and one, the bolts full easy slide:—
The chains lie silent on the footworn stones;—
The key turns, and the door upon its hinges groans.

And they are gone: ay, ages long ago
These lovers fled away into the storm.
That night the Baron dreamt of many a woe,
And all his warrior-guests, with shade and form
Of witch, and demon, and large coffin-worm,
Were long be-nightmar'd. Angela the old
Died palsy-twitch'd, with meagre face deform;
The Beadsman, after thousand aves told,
For aye unsought for slept among his ashes cold.

ODE ON A GRECIAN URN

THOU still unravish'd bride of quietness,
    Thou foster-child of silence and slow time,
Sylvan historian, who canst thus express
    A flowery tale more sweetly than our rhyme:
What leaf-fring'd legend haunts about thy shape

Of deities or mortals, or of both,
  In Tempe or the dales of Arcady?
What men or gods are these? What maidens loth?
What mad pursuit? What struggle to escape?
  What pipes and timbrels? What wild ecstasy?

Heard melodies are sweet, but those unheard
  Are sweeter; therefore, ye soft pipes, play on;
Not to the sensual ear, but, more endear'd,
  Pipe to the spirit ditties of no tone:
Fair youth, beneath the trees, thou canst not leave
  Thy song, nor ever can those trees be bare;
    Bold Lover, never, never canst thou kiss
Though winning near the goal—yet, do not grieve;
  She cannot fade, though thou hast not thy bliss,
    For ever wilt thou love, and she be fair!

Ah, happy, happy boughs! that cannot shed
  Your leaves, nor ever bid the Spring adieu;
And, happy melodist, unwearied,
  For ever piping songs for ever new;
More happy love! more happy, happy love!
  For ever warm and still to be enjoy'd,
    For ever panting, and for ever young;
All breathing human passion far above,
  That leaves a heart high-sorrowful and cloy'd,
    A burning forehead, and a parching tongue.

Who are these coming to the sacrifice?
  To what green altar, O mysterious priest,
Lead'st thou that heifer lowing at the skies,
  And all her silken flanks with garlands dressed?
What little town by river or sea shore,
  Or mountain-built with peaceful citadel,
    Is emptied of this folk, this pious morn?
And, little town, thy streets for evermore
  Will silent be; and not a soul to tell
    Why thou art desolate, can e'er return.

O Attic shape! Fair attitude! with brede
    Of marble men and maidens over wrought,
With forest branches and the trodden weed;
    Thou, silent form, dost tease us out of thought
As doth eternity: Cold Pastoral!
    When old age shall this generation waste,
        Thou shalt remain, in midst of other woe
Than ours, a friend to man, to whom thou say'st,
    "Beauty is truth, truth beauty,"—that is all
        Ye know on earth, and all ye need to know.

ODE TO A NIGHTINGALE

My heart aches, and a drowsy numbness pains
    My sense, as though of hemlock I had drunk,
Or emptied some dull opiate to the drains
    One minute past, and Lethe-wards had sunk:
'Tis not through envy of thy happy lot,
    But being too happy in thine happiness.—
        That thou, light wingèd Dryad of the trees,
            In some melodious plot
    Of beechen green, and shadows numberless,
        Singest of summer in full-throated ease.

O, for a draught of vintage! that hath been
    Cool'd a long age in the deep-delvèd earth,
Tasting of Flora and the country green,
    Dance, and Provençal song, and sunburnt mirth!
O for a beaker full of the warm South,
    Full of the true, the blushful Hippocrene,
        With beaded bubbles winking at the brim,
            And purple-stainèd mouth;
    That I might drink, and leave the world unseen,
        And with thee fade away into the forest dim:

Fade far away, dissolve, and quite forget
    What thou amongst the leaves hast never known,
The weariness, the fever, and the fret
    Here, where men sit and hear each other groan;

Where palsy shakes a few, sad, last gray hairs,
  Where youth grows pale, and spectre-thin, and dies;
    Where but to think is to be full of sorrow
      And leaden-eyed despairs,
  Where Beauty cannot keep her lustrous eyes,
    Or new Love pine at them beyond to-morrow.

Away! away! for I will fly to thee,
  Not charioted by Bacchus and his pards,
But on the viewless wings of Poesy,
  Though the dull brain perplexes and retards:
Already with thee! tender is the night,
  And haply the Queen-Moon is on her throne,
    Cluster'd around by all her starry Fays;
      But here there is no light,
  Save what from heaven is with the breezes blown
    Through verdurous glooms and winding mossy ways.

I cannot see what flowers are at my feet,
  Nor what soft incense hangs upon the boughs,
But, in embalmèd darkness, guess each sweet
  Wherewith the seasonable month endows
The grass, the thicket, and the fruit-tree wild;
  White hawthorn, and the pastoral eglantine;
    Fast fading violets cover'd up in leaves;
      And mid-May's eldest child,
  The coming musk-rose, full of dewy wine,
    The murmurous haunt of flies on summer eves.

Darkling I listen; and, for many a time
  I have been half in love with easeful Death,
Call'd him soft names in many a musèd rhyme,
  To take into the air my quiet breath;
Now more than ever seems it rich to die,
  To cease upon the midnight with no pain,
    While thou art pouring forth thy soul abroad
      In such an ecstasy!
  Still wouldst thou sing, and I have ears in vain—
    To thy high requiem become a sod.

Thou wast not born for death, immortal Bird!
  No hungry generations tread thee down;
The voice I hear this passing night was heard
  In ancient days by emperor and clown:
Perhaps the self-same song that found a path
    Through the sad heart of Ruth, when, sick for home,
      She stood in tears amid the alien corn;
        The same that oft-times hath
    Charm'd magic casements, opening on the foam
      Of perilous seas, in faery lands forlorn.

Forlorn! the very word is like a bell
  To toll me back from thee to my sole self!
Adieu! the fancy cannot cheat so well
  As she is fam'd to do, deceiving elf.
Adieu! adieu! thy plaintive anthem fades
    Past the near meadows, over the still stream,
      Up the hill-side; and now 'tis buried deep
        In the next valley-glades:
    Was it a vision, or a waking dream?
      Fled is that music:—Do I wake or sleep?

LA BELLE DAME SANS MERCI

BALLAD

O WHAT can ail thee, knight-at-arms,
  Alone and palely loitering!
The sedge has wither'd from the lake,
  And no birds sing.

O what can ail thee, knight-at-arms!
  So haggard and so woe-begone?
The squirrel's granary is full,
  And the harvest's done.

I see a lily on thy brow
  With anguish moist and fever dew,
And on thy cheeks a fading rose
  Fast withereth too.

I met a lady in the meads,
  Full beautiful—a faery's child,
Her hair was long, her foot was light,
  And her eyes were wild.

I made a garland for her head,
  And bracelets too, and fragrant zone;
She look'd at me as she did love,
  And made sweet moan.

I set her on my pacing steed,
  And nothing else saw all day long.
For sidelong would she bend, and sing
  A faery's song.

She found me roots of relish sweet,
  And honey wild, and manna dew,
And sure in language strange she said—
  "I love thee true."

She took me to her elfin grot,
  And there she wept, and sigh'd full sore,
And there I shut her wild wild eyes
  With kisses four.

And there she lullèd me asleep,
  And there I dream'd—Ah! woe betide!
The latest dream I ever dream'd
  On the cold hill's side.

I saw pale kings and princes too,
  Pale warriors, death-pale were they all;
They cried—"La Belle Dame sans Merci
  Hath thee in thrall!"

I saw their starv'd lips in the gloom,
  With horrid warning gapèd wide,
And I awoke and found me here,
  On the cold hill's side.

And this is why I sojourn here,
  Alone and palely loitering,
Though the sedge is wither'd from the lake
  And no birds sing.

BRIGHT STAR

BRIGHT star! would I were steadfast as thou art—
Not in lone splendour hung aloft the night,
And watching, with eternal lids apart,
Like Nature's patient sleepless Eremite,
The moving waters at their priestlike task
Of pure ablution round earth's human shores,
Or gazing on the new soft fallen mask
Of snow upon the mountains and the moors—
No—yet still steadfast, still unchangeable,
Pillow'd upon my fair love's ripening breast,
To feel for ever its soft fall and swell,
Awake for ever in a sweet unrest,
Still, still to hear her tender-taken breath,
And so live ever—or else swoon to death.

PERCY BYSSHE SHELLEY [1792–1822]

MUSIC, WHEN SOFT VOICES DIE

MUSIC, when soft voices die,
Vibrates in the memory—
Odours, when sweet violets sicken,
Live within the sense they quicken,

Rose leaves, when the rose is dead,
Are heaped for the beloved's bed;
And so thy thoughts, when thou art gone
Love itself shall slumber on.

OZYMANDIAS

I MET a traveller from an antique land
Who said: Two vast and trunkless legs of stone
Stand in the desert. Near them, on the sand,
Half sunk, a shattered visage lies, whose frown,
And wrinkled lip, and sneer of cold command,
Tell that its sculptor well those passions read
Which yet survive, stamped on these lifeless things,
The hand that mocked them and the heart that fed:
And on the pedestal these words appear:
"My name is Ozymandias, king of kings:
Look on my works, ye Mighty, and despair!"
Nothing beside remains. Round the decay
Of that colossal wreck, boundless and bare
The lone and level sands stretch far away.

TO A SKYLARK

HAIL to thee, blithe spirit!
   Bird thou never wert,
That from heaven, or near it,
   Pourest thy full heart
In profuse strain of unpremeditated art.

Higher still and higher
   From the earth thou springest
Like a cloud of fire;
   The blue deep thou wingest,
And singing still dost soar, and soaring ever singest.

In the golden lightning
   Of the sunken sun,
O'er which clouds are brightning,
   Thou dost float and run;
Like an unbodied joy whose race is just begun.

The pale purple even
    Melts around thy flight;
Like a star of heaven,
    In the broad daylight
Thou art unseen, but yet I hear thy shrill delight,

Keen as are the arrows
    Of that silver sphere,
Whose intense lamp narrows
    In the white dawn clear,
Until we hardly see, we feel that it is there.

All the earth and air
    With thy voice is loud,
As, when night is bare,
    From one lonely cloud
The moon rains out her beams, and heaven is overflowed.

What thou art we know not;
    What is most like thee?
From rainbow clouds there flow not
    Drops so bright to see,
As from thy presence showers a rain of melody.

Like a poet hidden
    In the light of thought,
Singing hymns unbidden,
    Till the world is wrought
To sympathy with hopes and fears it heeded not:

Like a high-born maiden
    In a palace-tower,
Soothing her love-laden
    Soul in secret hour
With music sweet as love, which overflows her bower:

Like a glow-worm golden
    In a dell of dew,
Scattering unbeholden
    Its aërial hue
Among the flowers and grass, which screen it from the view:

Like a rose embowered
   In its own green leaves,
By warm winds deflowered,
   Till the scent it gives
Makes faint with too much sweet these heavy-wingèd thieves:

Sound of vernal showers
   On the twinkling grass,
Rain-awakened flowers,
   All that ever was
Joyous, and clear, and fresh, thy music doth surpass:

Teach us, sprite or bird,
   What sweet thoughts are thine:
I have never heard
   Praise of love or wine
That panted forth a flood of rapture so divine.

Chorus Hymeneal,
   Or triumphal chaunt,
Matched with thine would be all
   But an empty vaunt,
A thing wherein we feel there is some hidden want.

What objects are the fountains
   Of thy happy strain?
What fields, or waves, or mountains?
   What shapes of sky or plain?
What love of thine own kind? what ignorance of pain?

With thy clear keen joyance
   Languor cannot be:
Shadow of annoyance
   Never came near thee:
Thou lovest; but ne'er knew love's sad satiety.

Waking or asleep,
   Thou of death must deem
Things more true and deep
   Than we mortals dream,
Or how could thy notes flow in such a crystal stream?

We look before and after,
    And pine for what is not:
Our sincerest laughter
    With some pain is fraught;
Our sweetest songs are those that tell of saddest thought.

Yet if we could scorn
    Hate, and pride, and fear:
If we were things born
    Not to shed a tear,
I know not how thy joy we ever should come near.

Better than all measures
    Of delightful sound,
Better than all treasures
    That in books are found,
Thy skill to poet were, thou scorner of the ground!

Teach me half the gladness
    That thy brain must know,
Such harmonious madness
    From my lips would flow,
The world should listen then, as I am listening now.

THE CLOUD

I BRING fresh showers for the thirsting flowers,
    From the seas and the streams;
I bear light shade for the leaves when laid
    In their noonday dreams.
From my wings are shaken the dews that waken
    The sweet buds every one,
When rocked to rest on their mother's breast,
    As she dances about the sun.
I wield the flail of the lashing hail,
    And whiten the green plains under,
And then again I dissolve it in rain,
    And laugh as I pass in thunder.

I sift the snow on the mountains below,
And their great pines groan aghast,
And all the night 'tis my pillow white,
While I sleep in the arms of the blast.
Sublime on the towers of my skiey bowers,
Lightning, my pilot, sits,
In a cavern under is fettered the thunder,
It struggles and howls at fits;
Over earth and ocean, with gentle motion,
This pilot is guiding me,
Lured by the love of the genii that move
In the depths of the purple sea;
Over the rills, and the crags, and the hills,
Over the lakes and the plains,
Wherever he dream, under mountain or stream,
The Spirit he loves remains;
And I all the while bask in heaven's blue smile,
Whilst he is dissolving in rains.

The sanguine sunrise, with his meteor eyes,
And his burning plumes outspread,
Leaps on the back of my sailing rack,
When the morning star shines dead,
As on the jag of a mountain crag,
Which an earthquake rocks and swings,
An eagle alit one moment may sit
In the light of its golden wings.
And when sunset may breathe, from the lit sea beneath,
Its ardours of rest and of love,
And the crimson pall of eve may fall
From the depth of heaven above,
With wings folded I rest, on mine airy nest,
As still as a brooding dove.

That orbèd maiden with white fire laden,
Whom mortals call the moon,
Glides glimmering o'er my fleece-like floor,
By the midnight breezes strewn;

And wherever the beat of her unseen feet,
    Which only the angels hear,
May have broken the woof of my tent's thin roof,
    The stars peep behind her and peer;
And I laugh to see them whirl and flee,
    Like a swarm of golden bees,
When I widen the rent in my wind-built tent,
    Till the calm rivers, lakes, and seas,
Like strips of the sky fallen through me on high,
    Are each paved with the moon and these.

I bind the sun's throne with a burning zone,
    And the moon's with a girdle of pearl;
The volcanoes are dim, and the stars reel and swim,
    When the whirlwinds my banner unfurl.
From cape to cape, with a bridge-like shape,
    Over a torrent sea,
Sunbeam-proof, I hang like a roof,
    The mountains its columns be.
The triumphal arch through which I march
    With hurricane, fire, and snow,
When the powers of the air are chained to my chair,
    Is the million-coloured bow;
The sphere-fire above its soft colours wove,
    While the moist earth was laughing below.

I am the daughter of earth and water,
    And the nursling of the sky;
I pass through the pores of the ocean and shores;
    I change, but I cannot die.
For after the rain, when with never a stain
    The pavilion of heaven is bare,
And the winds and sunbeams, with their convex gleams,
    Build up the blue dome of air,
I silently laugh at my own cenotaph,
    And out of the caverns of rain,
Like a child from the womb, like a ghost from the tomb,
    I arise and unbuild it again.

ODE TO THE WEST WIND

I

O WILD West Wind, thou breath of Autumn's being,
Thou, from whose unseen presence the leaves dead
Are driven, like ghosts from an enchanter fleeing,

Yellow, and black, and pale, and hectic red,
Pestilence-stricken multitudes: O thou,
Who chariotest to their dark wintry bed

The wingèd seeds, where they lie cold and low,
Each like a corpse within its grave, until
Thine azure sister of the spring shall blow

Her clarion o'er the dreaming earth, and fill
(Driving sweet buds like flocks to feed in air)
With living hues and odours plain and hill;

Wild Spirit, which art moving everywhere;
Destroyer and preserver; hear, Oh hear!

II

Thou on whose stream, 'mid the steep sky's commotion,
Loose clouds like earth's decaying leaves are shed,
Shook from the tangled boughs of Heaven and Ocean,

Angels of rain and lightning: there are spread
On the blue surface of thine airy surge,
Like the bright hair uplifted from the head

Of some fierce Mænad, even from the dim verge
Of the horizon to the zenith's height
The locks of the approaching storm. Thou dirge

Of the dying year, to which this closing night
Will be the dome of a vast sepulchre,
Vaulted with all thy congregated might

Of vapours, from whose solid atmosphere
Black rain, and fire, and hail will burst: Oh hear!

III

Thou who didst waken from his summer dreams
The blue Mediterranean, where he lay,
Lulled by the coil of his crystalline streams,

Beside a pumice isle in Baiæ's bay,
And saw in sleep old palaces and towers
Quivering within the wave's intenser day,

All overgrown with azure moss and flowers
So sweet, the sense faints picturing them! Thou
For whose path the Atlantic's level powers

Cleave themselves into chasms, while far below
The sea-blooms and the oozy woods which wear
The sapless foliage of the ocean, know

Thy voice, and suddenly grow gray with fear,
And tremble and despoil themselves: Oh hear!

IV

If I were a dead leaf thou mightest bear;
If I were a swift cloud to fly with thee;
A wave to pant beneath thy power, and share

The impulse of thy strength, only less free
Than thou, O uncontrollable! If even
I were as in my boyhood, and could be

The comrade of thy wanderings over heaven,
As then, when to outstrip thy skiey speed
Scarce seemed a vision; I would ne'er have striven

As thus with thee in prayer in my sore need.
Oh lift me as a wave, a leaf, a cloud!
I fall upon the thorns of life! I bleed!

A heavy weight of hours has chained and bowed
One too like thee: tameless, and swift, and proud.

v

Make me thy lyre, even as the forest is:
What if my leaves are falling like its own!
The tumult of thy mighty harmonies

Will take from both a deep, autumnal tone,
Sweet though in sadness. Be thou, spirit fierce,
My spirit! Be thou me, impetuous one!

Drive my dead thoughts over the universe
Like withered leaves to quicken a new birth!
And, by the incantation of this verse,

Scatter, as from an unextinguished hearth
Ashes and sparks, my words among mankind!
Be through my lips to unawakened earth

The trumpet of a prophecy! O, wind,
If Winter comes, can Spring be far behind?

TO NIGHT

SWIFTLY walk over the western wave,
  Spirit of Night!
Out of thy misty eastern cave,
 Where all the long and lone daylight,
Thou wovest dreams of joy and fear,
Which make thee terrible and dear,—
  Swift be thy flight!

Wrap thy form in a mantle gray,
    Star-inwrought!
Blind with thine hair the eyes of Day;
Kiss her until she be wearied out,
Then wander o'er city, and sea, and land
Touching all with thine opiate wand—
    Come, long sought!

When I arose and saw the dawn,
    I sighed for thee;
When light rode high, and the dew was gone,
And noon lay heavy on flower and tree,
And the weary Day turned to his rest,
Lingering like an unloved guest,
    I sighed for thee.

Thy brother Death came, and cried,
    Wouldst thou me?
Thy sweet child Sleep, the filmy-eyed,
Murmured like a noontide bee,
Shall I nestle near thy side?
Wouldst thou me?—And I replied,
    No, not thee!

Death will come when thou art dead
    Soon, too soon—
Sleep will come when thou art fled;
Of neither would I ask the boon
I ask of thee, belovèd Night—
Swift be thine approaching flight,
    Come soon, soon!

LINES TO AN INDIAN AIR

I ARISE from dreams of thee
In the first sweet sleep of night,
When the winds are breathing low,
And the stars are shining bright:

I arise from dreams of thee,
And a spirit in my feet
Hath led me—who knows how?
To thy chamber window, Sweet!

The wandering airs they faint
On the dark, the silent stream—
The champak odours fail
Like sweet thoughts in a dream;
The nightingale's complaint
It dies upon her heart,
As I must die on thine,
O belovèd as thou art!

O lift me from the grass!
I die, I faint, I fail!
Let thy love in kisses rain
On my lips and eyelids pale.
My cheek is cold and white, alas!
My heart beats loud and fast;
Oh! press it close to thine again,
Where it will break at last.

ADONAIS

AN ELEGY ON THE DEATH OF JOHN KEATS

Ἀστὴρ πρὶν μέν ἔλαμπες ἐνὶ ζωοῖσιν Ἑῷος.
Νῦν δε θανὼν λάμπεις Ἕσπερος ἐν φθιμένοις.

PLATO.

I WEEP for Adonais—he is dead!
Oh weep for Adonais! though our tears
Thaw not the frost which binds so dear a head!
And thou, sad Hour, selected from all years
To mourn our loss, rouse thy obscure compeers,
And teach them thine own sorrow! Say: "With me
Died Adonais; till the Future dares
Forget the Past, his fate and fame shall be
An echo and a light unto eternity!"

Where wert thou, mighty Mother, when he lay,
When thy Son lay, pierced by the shaft which flies
In darkness? where was lorn Urania
When Adonais died? With veilèd eyes,
'Mid listening Echoes, in her Paradise
She sate, while one, with soft enamoured breath,
Rekindled all the fading melodies
With which, like flowers that mock the corse beneath,
He had adorned and hid the coming bulk of death.

Oh weep for Adonais—he is dead!
Wake, melancholy Mother, wake and weep!
Yet wherefore? Quench within their burning bed
Thy fiery tears, and let thy lov'd heart keep,
Like his, a mute and uncomplaining sleep;
For he is gone, where all things wise and fair
Descend;—oh, dream not that the amourous Deep
Will yet restore him to the vital air;
Death feeds on his mute voice, and laughs at our despair.

Most musical of mourners, weep again
Lament anew, Urania!—He died,
Who was the Sire of an immortal strain,
Blind, old, and lonely, when his country's pride,
The priest, the slave, and the liberticide,
Trampled and mocked with many a loathèd rite
Of lust and blood; he went, unterrified,
Into the gulf of death; but his clear Sprite
Yet reigns o'er earth; the third among the sons of light.

Most musical of mourners, weep anew!
Not all to that bright station dared to climb;
And happier they their happiness who knew,
Whose tapers yet burn through that night of time
In which suns perished; others more sublime,
Struck by the envious wrath of man or God,
Have sunk, extinct in their refulgent prime;
And some yet live, treading the thorny road,
Which leads, through toil and hate, to Fame's serene abode.

But now, thy youngest, dearest one has perished,
The nursling of thy widowhood, who grew,
Like a pale flower by some sad maiden cherished,
And fed with true love tears, instead of dew;
Most musical of mourners, weep anew!
Thy extreme hope, the loveliest and the last,
The bloom, whose petals nipt before they blew
Died on the promise of the fruit, is waste;
The broken lily lies—the storm is overpast.

To that high Capital, where kingly Death
Keeps his pale court in beauty and decay,
He came; and bought, with price of purest breath,
A grave among the eternal.—Come away!
Haste, while the vault of blue Italian day
Is yet his fitting charnel-roof! while still
He lies, as if in dewy sleep he lay;
Awake him not! surely he takes his fill
Of deep and liquid rest, forgetful of all ill.

He will awake no more, oh, never more!—
Within the twilight chamber spreads apace,
The shadow of white Death, and at the door
Invisible Corruption waits to trace
His extreme way to her dim dwelling-place;
The eternal Hunger sits, but pity and awe
Soothe her pale rage, nor dares she to deface
So fair a prey, till darkness, and the law
Of change shall o'er his sleep the mortal curtain draw.

Oh weep for Adonais!—The quick Dreams,
The passion-wingèd Ministers of thought,
Who were his flocks, whom near the living streams
Of his young spirit he fed, and whom he taught
The love which was its music, wander not,—
Wander no more, from kindling brain to brain,
But droop there, whence they sprung; and mourn their lot
Round the cold heart, where, after their sweet pain,
They ne'er will gather strength, or find a home again.

And one with trembling hands clasps his cold head,
And fans him with her moonlight wings, and cries;
"Our love, our hope, our sorrow, is not dead;
See, on the silken fringe of his faint eyes,
Like dew upon a sleeping flower, there lies
A tear some Dream has loosened from his brain."
Lost Angel of a ruined Paradise!
She knew not 'twas her own; as with no stain
She faded, like a cloud which had outwept its rain.

One from a lucid urn of starry dew
Washed his light limbs as if embalming them;
Another clipt her profuse locks, and threw
The wreath upon him, like an anadem,
Which frozen tears instead of pearls begem;
Another in her wilful grief would break
Her bow and wingèd reeds, as if to stem
A greater loss with one which was more weak;
And dull the barbèd fire against his frozen cheek.

Another Splendour on his mouth alit,
That mouth, whence it was wont to draw the breath
Which gave it strength to pierce the guarded wit,
And pass into the panting heart beneath
With lightning and with music: the damp death
Quenched its caress upon his icy lips;
And, as a dying meteor stains a wreath
Of moonlight vapour, which the cold night clips,
It flushed through his pale limbs, and passed to its eclipse.

And others came . . . Desires and Adorations,
Wingèd Persuasions and veilèd Destinies,
Splendours and Glooms, and glimmering Incarnations
Of hopes and fears, and twilight Phantasies;
And Sorrow, with her family of Sighs,
And Pleasure, blind with tears, led by the gleam
Of her own dying smile instead of eyes,
Came in slow pomp;—the moving pomp might seem
Like pageantry of mist on an autumnal stream.

All he had loved, and moulded into thought,
From shape, and hue, and odour, and sweet sound,
Lamented Adonais. Morning sought
Her eastern watchtower, and her hair unbound,
Wet with the tears which should adorn the ground,
Dimmed the aërial eyes that kindle day;
Afar the melancholy thunder moaned,
Pale Ocean in unquiet slumber lay,
And the wild winds flew round, sobbing in their dismay.

Lost Echo sits amid the voiceless mountains,
And feeds her grief with his remembered lay,
And will no more reply to winds or fountains,
Or amourous birds perched on the young green spray,
Or herdsman's horn, or bell at closing day;
Since she can mimic not his lips, more dear
Than those for whose disdain she pined away
Into a shadow of all sounds:—a drear
Murmur, between their songs, is all the woodmen hear.

Grief made the young Spring wild, and she threw down
Her kindling buds, as if she Autumn were,
Or they dead leaves; since her delight is flown
For whom should she have waked the sullen year?
To Phœbus was not Hyacinth so dear
Nor to himself Narcissus, as to both
Thou Adonais: wan they stand and sere
Amid the faint companions of their youth,
With dew all turned to tears; odour, to sighing ruth.

Thy spirit's sister, the lorn nightingale,
Mourns not her mate with such melodious pain;
Not so the eagle, who like thee could scale
Heaven, and could nourish in the sun's domain
Her mighty youth with morning, doth complain,
Soaring and screaming round her empty nest,
As Albion wails for thee; the curse of Cain
Light on his head who pierced thy innocent breast
And scared the angel soul that was its earthly guest!

Ah woe is me! Winter is come and gone,
But grief returns with the revolving year;
The airs and streams renew their joyous tone:
The ants, the bees, the swallows reappear;
Fresh leaves and flowers deck the dead Season's bier;
The amourous birds now pair in every brake,
And build their mossy homes in field and brere;
And the green lizard, and the golden snake,
Like unimprisoned flames, out of their trance awake.

Through wood and stream and field and hill and Ocean
A quickening life from the Earth's heart has burst
As it has ever done, with change and motion,
From the great morning of the world when first
God dawned on Chaos; in its stream immersed
The lamps of Heaven flash with a softer light;
All baser things pant with life's sacred thirst;
Diffuse themselves; and spend in love's delight,
The beauty and the joy of their renewèd might.

The leprous corpse touched by this spirit tender
Exhales itself in flowers of gentle breath;
Like incarnations of the stars, when splendour
Is changed to fragrance, they illumine death
And mock the merry worm that wakes beneath;
Nought we know, dies. Shall that alone which knows
Be as a sword consumed before the sheath
By sightless lightning?—th' intense atom glows
A moment, then is quenched in a most cold repose.

Alas! that all we loved of him should be
But for our grief, as if it had not been,
And grief itself be mortal! Woe is me!
Whence are we, and why are we? of what scene
The actors or spectators? Great and mean
Meet massed in death, who lends what life must borrow.
As long as skies are blue, and fields are green,
Evening must usher night, night urge the morrow,
Month follow month with woe, and year wake year to sorrow.

He will awake no more, oh, never more!
"Wake thou," cried Misery, "childless Mother, rise
Out of thy sleep, and slake, in thy heart's core,
A wound more fierce than his with tears and sighs."
And all the Dreams that watched Urania's eyes,
And all the Echoes whom their sister's song
Had held in holy silence, cried: "Arise!"
Swift as a Thought by the snake Memory stung,
From her ambrosial rest the fading Splendour sprung.

She rose like an autumnal Night, that springs
Out of the East, and follows wild and drear
The golden Day, which, on eternal wings,
Even as a ghost abandoning a bier,
Had left the Earth a corpse. Sorrow and fear
So struck, so roused, so rapt Urania;
So saddened round her like an atmosphere
Of stormy mist; so swept her on her way
Even to the mournful place where Adonais lay.

Out of her secret Paradise she sped,
Through camps and cities rough with stone, and steel,
And human hearts, which to her airy tread
Yielding not, wounded the invisible
Palms of her tender feet where'er they fell:
And barbèd tongues, and thoughts more sharp than they
Rent the soft Form they never could repel,
Whose sacred blood, like the young tears of May,
Paved with eternal flowers that undeserving way.

In the death chamber for a moment Death
Shamed by the presence of that living Might
Blushed to annihilation, and the breath
Revisited those lips, and life's pale light
Flashed through those limbs, so late her dear delight.
"Leave me not wild and drear and comfortless,
As silent lightning leaves the starless night!
Leave me not!" cried Urania: her distress
Roused Death: Death rose and smiled, and met her vain caress.

"Stay yet awhile! speak to me once again;
Kiss me, so long but as a kiss may live;
And in my heartless breast and burning brain
That word, that kiss, shall all thoughts else survive,
With food of saddest memory kept alive,
Now thou art dead, as if it were a part
Of thee, my Adonais! I would give
All that I am to be as thou now art!
But I am chained to Time, and cannot thence depart!

"O gentle child, beautiful as thou wert,
Why didst thou leave the trodden paths of men
Too soon, and with weak hands though mighty heart
Dare the unpastured dragon in his den?
Defenceless as thou wert, oh where was then
Wisdom the mirrored shield, or scorn the spear?
Or hadst thou waited the full cycle, when
Thy spirit should have filled its crescent sphere,
The monsters of life's waste had fled from thee like deer.

"The herded wolves, bold only to pursue;
The obscene ravens, clamourous o'er the dead;
The vultures to the conqueror's banner true
Who feed where Desolation first has fed,
And whose wings rain contagion;—how they fled,
When like Apollo, from his golden bow,
The Pythian of the age one arrow sped
And smiled!—The spoilers tempt no second blow,
They fawn on the proud feet that spurn them lying low.

"The sun comes forth, and many reptiles spawn;
He sets, and each ephemeral insect then
Is gathered into death without a dawn,
And the immortal stars awake again;
So is it in the world of living men:
A godlike mind soars forth, in its delight
Making earth bare and veiling heaven, and when
It sinks, the swarms that dimmed or shared its light
Leave to its kindred lamps the spirit's awful night."

Thus ceased she: and the mountain shepherds came,
Their garlands sere, their magic mantles rent;
The Pilgrim of Eternity, whose fame
Over his living head like Heaven is bent,
An early but enduring monument,
Came, veiling all the lightnings of his song
In sorrow; from her wilds Ierne sent
The sweetest lyrist of her saddest wrong,
And love taught grief to fall like music from his tongue.

Midst others of less note, came one frail Form,
A phantom among men; companionless
As the last cloud of an expiring storm
Whose thunder is its knell; he, as I guess,
Had gazed on Nature's naked loveliness,
Actæon-like, and now he fled astray
With feeble steps o'er the world's wilderness,
And his own thoughts, along that rugged way,
Pursued, like raging hounds, their father and their prey.

A pardlike Spirit beautiful and swift—
A Love in desolation masked;—a Power
Girt round with weakness;—it can scarce uplift
The weight of the superincumbent hour;
It is a dying lamp, a falling shower,
A breaking billow;—even whilst we speak
Is it not broken? On the withering flower
The killing sun smiles brightly: on a cheek
The life can burn in blood, even while the heart may break.

His head was bound with pansies over-blown,
And faded violets, white, and pied, and blue;
And a light spear topped with a cypress cone,
Round whose rude shaft dark ivy tresses grew
Yet dripping with the forest's noonday dew,
Vibrated, as the ever-beating heart
Shook the weak hand that grasped it; of that crew
He came the last, neglected and apart;
A herd-abandoned deer struck by the hunter's dart.

All stood aloof, and at his partial moan
Smiled through their tears; well knew that gentle band
Who in another's fate now wept his own;
As in the accents of an unknown land,
He sung new sorrow; sad Urania scanned
The Stranger's mien, and murmured: "Who art thou?"
He answered not, but with a sudden hand
Made bare his branded and ensanguined brow,
Which was like Cain's or Christ's—oh, that it should be so!

What softer voice is hushed over the dead?
Athwart what brow is that dark mantle thrown?
What form leans sadly o'er the white deathbed,
In mockery of monumental stone,
The heavy heart heaving without a moan?
If it be He, who, gentlest of the wise,
Taught, soothed, loved, honoured the departed one;
Let me not vex, with inharmonious sighs
The silence of that heart's accepted sacrifice.

Our Adonais has drunk poison—oh!
What deaf and viperous murderer could crown
Life's early cup with such a draught of woe?
The nameless worm would now itself disown:
It felt, yet could escape the magic tone
Whose prelude held all envy, hate, and wrong,
But what was howling in one breast alone,
Silent with expectation of the song,
Whose master's hand is cold, whose silver lyre unstrung.

Live thou, whose infamy is not thy fame!
Live! fear no heavier chastisement from me,
Thou noteless blot on a remembered name!
But be thyself, and know thyself to be!
And ever at thy season be thou free
To spill the venom when thy fangs o'erflow:
Remorse and Self-contempt shall cling to thee;
Hot Shame shall burn upon thy secret brow,
And like a beaten hound tremble thou shalt—as now.

Nor let us weep that our delight is fled
Far from these carrion kites that scream below;
He wakes or sleeps with the enduring dead;
Thou canst not soar where he is sitting now.—
Dust to the dust! but the pure spirit shall flow
Back to the burning fountain whence it came,
A portion of the Eternal, which must glow
Through time and change, unquenchably the same,
Whilst thy cold embers choke the sordid hearth of shame.

Peace, peace! he is not dead, he doth not sleep—
He hath awakened from the dream of life—
'Tis we, who lost in stormy visions, keep
With phantoms an unprofitable strife,
And in mad trance, strike with our spirit's knife
Invulnerable nothings.—We decay
Like corpses in a charnel; fear and grief
Convulse us and consume us day by day,
And cold hopes swarm like worms within our living clay.

He has outsoared the shadow of our night;
Envy and calumny and hate and pain,
And that unrest which men miscall delight,
Can touch him not and torture not again;
From the contagion of the world's slow stain
He is secure, and now can never mourn
A heart grown cold, a head grown gray in vain;
Nor, when the spirit's self has ceased to burn,
With sparkless ashes load an unlamented urn.

He lives, he wakes—'tis Death is dead, not he;
Mourn not for Adonais,—Thou young Dawn
Turn all thy dew to splendour, for from thee
The spirit thou lamentest is not gone;
Ye caverns and ye forests, cease to moan!
Cease ye faint flowers and fountains, and thou Air
Which like a mourning veil thy scarf hadst thrown
O'er the abandoned Earth, now leave it bare
Even to the joyous stars which smile on its despair!

He is made one with Nature: there is heard
His voice in all her music, from the moan
Of thunder to the song of night's sweet bird;
He is a presence to be felt and known
In darkness and in light, from herb and stone,
Spreading itself where'er that Power may move
Which has withdrawn his being to its own;
Which wields the world with never wearied love,
Sustains it from beneath, and kindles it above.

He is a portion of the loveliness
Which once he made more lovely: he doth bear
His part, while the one Spirit's plastic stress
Sweeps through the dull dense world, compelling there
All new successions to the forms they wear;
Torturing th' unwilling dross that checks its flight
To its own likeness, as each mass may bear;
And bursting in its beauty and its might
From trees and beasts and men into the Heaven's light.

The splendours of the firmament of time
May be eclipsed, but are extinguished not;
Like stars to their appointed height they climb
And death is a low mist which cannot blot
The brightness it may veil. When lofty thought
Lifts a young heart above its mortal lair,
And love and life contend in it, for what
Shall be its earthly doom, the dead live there
And move like winds of light on dark and stormy air.

The inheritors of unfulfilled renown
Rose from their thrones, built beyond mortal thought,
Far in the Unapparent. Chatterton
Rose pale, his solemn agony had not
Yet faded from him; Sidney, as he fought
And as he fell and as he lived and loved
Sublimely mild, a Spirit without spot,
Arose; and Lucan, by his death approved:
Oblivion as they rose shrank like a thing reproved.

And many more, whose names on Earth are dark
But whose transmitted effluence cannot die
So long as fire outlives the parent spark,
Rose, robed in dazzling immortality.
"Thou art become as one of us," they cry,
"It was for thee yon kingless sphere has long
Swung blind in unascended majesty,
Silent alone amid an Heaven of Song.
Assume thy wingèd throne, thou Vesper of our throng!"

Who mourns for Adonais? Oh come forth
Fond wretch! and know thyself and him aright.
Clasp with thy panting soul the pendulous Earth;
As from a centre, dart thy spirit's light
Beyond all worlds, until its spacious might
Satiate the void circumference: then shrink
Even to a point within our day and night;
And keep thy heart light lest it make thee sink
When hope has kindled hope, and lured thee to the brink.

Or go to Rome, which is the sepulchre
Oh! not of him, but of our joy: 'tis nought
That ages, empires, and religions there
Lie buried in the ravage they have wrought;
For such as he can lend,—they borrow not
Glory from those who made the world their prey;
And he is gathered to the kings of thought
Who waged contention with their time's decay,
And of the past are all that cannot pass away.

Go thou to Rome,—at once the Paradise,
The grave, the city, and the wilderness;
And where its wrecks like shattered mountains rise,
And flowering weeds, and fragrant copses dress
The bones of Desolation's nakedness,
Pass, till the Spirit of the spot shall lead
Thy footsteps to a slope of green access
Where, like an infant's smile, over the dead
A light of laughing flowers along the grass is spread.

And gray walls moulder round, on which dull Time
Feeds, like slow fire upon a hoary brand;
And one keen pyramid with wedge sublime,
Pavilioning the dust of him who planned
This refuge for his memory, doth stand
Like flame transformed to marble; and beneath,
A field is spread, on which a newer band
Have pitched in Heaven's smile their camp of death
Welcoming him we lose with scarce extinguished breath.

Here pause: these graves are all too young as yet
To have outgrown the sorrow which consigned
Its charge to each; and if the seal is set,
Here, on one fountain of a mourning mind,
Break it not thou! too surely shalt thou find
Thine own well full, if thou returnest home,
Of tears and gall. From the world's bitter wind
Seek shelter in the shadow of the tomb.
What Adonais is, why fear we to become?

The One remains, the many change and pass;
Heaven's light forever shines, Earth's shadows fly;
Life, like a dome of many-coloured glass,
Stains the white radiance of Eternity,
Until Death tramples it to fragments.—Die,
If thou wouldst be with that which thou dost seek!
Follow where all is fled!—Rome's azure sky,
Flowers, ruins, statues, music, words, are weak
The glory they transfuse with fitting truth to speak.

Why linger, why turn back, why shrink, my Heart?
Thy hopes are gone before: from all things here
They have departed; thou shouldst now depart!
A light is past from the revolving year,
And man, and woman; and what still is dear
Attracts to crush, repels to make thee wither.
The soft sky smiles,—the low wind whispers near;
'Tis Adonais calls! oh, hasten thither,
No more let Life divide what Death can join together.

That Light whose smile kindles the Universe,
That Beauty in which all things work and move,
That Benediction which the eclipsing Curse
Of birth can quench not, that sustaining Love
Which through the web of being blindly wove
By man and beast and earth and air and sea,
Burns bright or dim, as each are mirrors of
The fire for which all thirst; now beams on me,
Consuming the last clouds of cold mortality.

The breath whose might I have invoked in song
Descends on me; my spirit's bark is driven,
Far from the shore, far from the trembling throng
Whose sails were never to the tempest given;
The massy earth and spherèd skies are riven!
I am borne darkly, fearfully, afar;
Whilst burning through the inmost veil of Heaven,
The soul of Adonais, like a star,
Beacons from the abode where the Eternal are.

DIRGE

ROUGH wind, that moanest loud
    Grief too sad for song;
Wild wind, when sullen cloud
    Knells all the night long;
Sad storm, whose tears are vain,
Bare woods, whose branches strain,
Deep caves and dreary main,
    Wail, for the world's wrong!

THOMAS HOOD [1798–1845]

FAIR INES

O saw ye not fair Ines?
She's gone into the West,
To dazzle when the sun is down,
And rob the world of rest:
She took our daylight with her,
The smiles that we love best,
With morning blushes on her cheek,
And pearls upon her breast.

O turn again, fair Ines,
Before the fall of night,
For fear the Moon should shine alone,
And stars unrivaled bright;
And blessèd will the lover be
That walks beneath their light,
And breathes the love against thy cheek
I dare not even write!

Would I had been, fair Ines,
That gallant cavalier,
Who rode so gaily by thy side,
And whispered thee so near!—
Were there no bonny dames at home
Or no true lovers here,
That he should cross the seas to win
The dearest of the dear?

I saw thee, lovely Ines,
Descend along the shore,
With bands of noble gentlemen,
And banners waved before;
And gentle youth and maidens gay,
And snowy plumes they wore;—
It would have been a beauteous dream,
—If it had been no more!

Alas, alas! fair Ines,
She went away with song,
With Music waiting on her steps,
And shoutings of the throng;
But some were sad and felt no mirth,
But only Music's wrong,
In sounds that sang Farewell, Farewell
To her you've loved so long.

Farewell, farewell, fair Ines!
That vessel never bore
So fair a lady on its deck,
Nor danced so light before,—
Alas for pleasure on the sea,
And sorrow on the shore!
The smile that blest one lover's heart
Has broken many more!

ALFRED, LORD TENNYSON [1809–1892]

THE LADY OF SHALOTT

PART I

On either side the river lie
Long fields of barley and of rye,
That clothe the wold and meet the sky;
And thro' the field the road runs by
          To many-tower'd Camelot;
And up and down the people go,
Gazing where the lilies blow
Round an island there below,
          The island of Shalott.

Willows whiten, aspens quiver,
Little breezes dusk and shiver
Thro' the wave that runs for ever
By the island in the river
          Flowing down to Camelot.

Four gray walls, and four gray towers,
Overlook a space of flowers.
And the silent isle imbowers
    The Lady of Shalott.

By the margin, willow-veil'd,
Slide the heavy barges trail'd
By slow horses; and unhail'd
The shallop flitteth silken-sail'd
    Skimming down to Camelot;
But who hath seen her wave her hand?
Or at the casement seen her stand?
Or is she known in all the land,
    The Lady of Shalott?

Only reapers, reaping early
In among the bearded barley,
Hear a song that echoes cheerly
From the river winding clearly,
    Down to tower'd Camelot;
And by the moon the reaper weary,
Piling sheaves in uplands airy,
Listening, whispers "'T is the fairy
    Lady of Shalott."

PART II

There she weaves by night and day
A magic web with colours gay.
She has heard a whisper say,
A curse is on her if she stay
    To look down to Camelot.
She knows not what the curse may be,
And so she weaveth steadily,
And little other care hath she,
    The Lady of Shalott.

And moving thro' a mirror clear
That hangs before her all the year,

Shadows of the world appear.
There she sees the highway near
    Winding down to Camelot;
There the river eddy whirls,
And there the surly village-churls,
And the red cloaks of market girls,
    Pass onward from Shalott.

Sometimes a troop of damsels glad,
An abbot on an ambling pad,
Sometimes a curly shepherd-lad,
Or long-hair'd page in crimson clad,
    Goes by to tower'd Camelot;
And sometimes thro' the mirror blue
The knights come riding two and two:
She hath no loyal knight and true,
    The Lady of Shalott.

But in her web she still delights
To weave the mirror's magic sights,
For often thro' the silent nights
A funeral, with plumes and lights
    And music, went to Camelot;
Or when the moon was overhead,
Came two young lovers lately wed:
"I am half sick of shadows," said
    The Lady of Shalott.

PART III

A bow-shot from her bower-eaves,
He rode between the barley-sheaves,
The sun came dazzling thro' the leaves,
And flamed upon the brazen greaves
    Of bold Sir Lancelot.
A red-cross knight for ever kneel'd
To a lady in his shield,
That sparkled on the yellow field,
    Beside remote Shalott.

The gemmy bridle glitter'd free,
Like to some branch of stars we see
Hung in the golden Galaxy.
The bridle bells rang merrily
      As he rode down to Camelot;
And from his blazon'd baldric slung
A mighty silver bugle hung,
And as he rode his armour rung,
      Beside remote Shalott.

All in the blue unclouded weather
Thick-jewell'd shone the saddle-leather,
The helmet and the helmet-feather
Burn'd like one burning flame together,
      As he rode down to Camelot;
As often thro' the purple night,
Below the starry clusters bright,
Some bearded meteor, trailing light,
      Moves over still Shalott.

His broad clear brow in sunlight glow'd;
On burnish'd hooves his war-horse trode;
From underneath his helmet flow'd
His coal-black curls as on he rode,
      As he rode down to Camelot.
From the bank and from the river
He flash'd into the crystal mirror,
"Tirra lirra," by the river
      Sang Sir Lancelot.

She left the web, she left the loom,
She made three paces thro' the room,
She saw the water-lily bloom,
She saw the helmet and the plume,
      She look'd down to Camelot.
Out flew the web and floated wide;
The mirror crack'd from side to side;
"The curse is come upon me," cried
      The Lady of Shalott.

PART IV

In the stormy east-wind straining,
The pale yellow woods were waning,
The broad stream in his banks complaining,
Heavily the low sky raining
      Over tower'd Camelot;
Down she came and found a boat
Beneath a willow left afloat,
And round about the prow she wrote
      The Lady of Shalott.

And down the river's dim expanse
Like some bold seër in a trance,
Seeing all his own mischance—
With a glassy countenance
      Did she look to Camelot.
And at the closing of the day
She loosed the chain, and down she lay;
The broad stream bore her far away,
      The Lady of Shalott.

Lying, robed in snowy white
That loosely flew to left and right—
The leaves upon her falling light—
Thro' the noises of the night
      She floated dòwn to Camelot;
And as the boat-head wound along
The willowy hills and fields among,
They heard her singing her last song,
      The Lady of Shalott.

Heard a carol, mournful, holy,
Chanted loudly, chanted lowly,
Till her blood was frozen slowly
And her eyes were darken'd wholly
      Turn'd to tower'd Camelot.
For ere she reach'd upon the tide
The first house by the water-side,
Singing in her song she died,
      The Lady of Shalott.

Under tower and balcony,
By garden-wall and gallery,
A gleaming shape she floated by,
Dead-pale between the houses high,
    Silent into Camelot.
Out upon the wharfs they came,
Knight and burgher, lord and dame,
And round the prow they read her name,
    The Lady of Shalott.

Who is this? and what is here?
And in the lighted palace near
Died the sound of royal cheer,
And they cross'd themselves for fear,
    All the Knights at Camelot:
But Lancelot mused a little space;
He said, "She has a lovely face;
God in his mercy lend her grace,
    The Lady of Shalott."

THE LOTOS–EATERS

"Courage!" he said, and pointed toward the land,
"This mounting wave will roll us shoreward soon."
In the afternoon they came unto a land
In which it seemed always afternoon.
All round the coast the languid air did swoon,
Breathing like one that hath a weary dream.
Full-faced above the valley stood the moon;
And, like a downward smoke, the slender stream
Along the cliff to fall and pause and fall did seem.

A land of streams! some, like a downward smoke,
Slow-dropping veils of thinnest lawn, did go;
And some thro' wavering lights and shadows broke,
Rolling a slumbrous sheet of foam below.
They saw the gleaming river seaward flow
From the inner land; far off, three mountain-tops,
Three silent pinnacles of aged snow,

Stood sunset-flush'd; and, dew'd with showery drops,
Up-clomb the shadowy pine above the woven copse.

The charmed sunset linger'd low adown
In the red West; thro' mountain clefts the dale
Was seen far inland, and the yellow down
Border'd with palm, and many a winding vale
And meadow, set with slender galingale;
A land where all things always seem'd the same!
And round about the keel with faces pale,
Dark faces pale against that rosy flame,
The mild-eyed melancholy Lotos-eaters came.

Branches they bore of that enchanted stem,
Laden with flower and fruit, whereof they gave
To each, but whoso did receive of them
And taste, to him the gushing of the wave
Far far away did seem to mourn and rave
On alien shores; and if his fellow spake,
His voice was thin, as voices from the grave;
And deep-asleep he seem'd, yet all awake,
And music in his ears his beating heart did make.

They sat them down upon the yellow sand,
Between the sun and moon upon the shore;
And sweet it was to dream of Fatherland,
Of child, and wife and slave; but evermore
Most weary seem'd the sea, weary the oar,
Weary the wandering fields of barren foam.
Then some one said, "We will return no more;"
And all at once they sang, "Our island home
Is far beyond the wave; we will no longer roam."

CHORIC SONG

There is sweet music here that softer falls
Than petals from blown roses on the grass,
Or night-dews on still waters between walls
Of shadowy granite, in a gleaming pass;

Music that gentlier on the spirit lies,
Than tired eyelids upon tired eyes;
Music that brings sweet sleep down from the blissful skies.
Here are cool mosses deep,
And thro' the moss the ivies creep,
And in the stream the long-leaved flowers weep,
And from the craggy ledge the poppy hangs in sleep.

Why are we weigh'd upon with heaviness,
And utterly consumed with sharp distress,
While all things else have rest from weariness?
All things have rest: why should we toil alone,
We only toil, who are the first of things,
And make perpetual moan,
Still from one sorrow to another thrown;
Nor ever fold our wings,
And cease from wanderings,
Nor steep our brows in slumber's holy balm;
Nor harken what the inner spirit sings,
"There is no joy but calm!"—
Why should we only toil, the roof and crown of things?

Lo! in the middle of the wood,
The folded leaf is woo'd from out the bud
With winds upon the branch, and there
Grows green and broad, and takes no care,
Sun-steep'd at noon, and in the moon
Nightly dew-fed; and turning yellow
Falls, and floats adown the air.
Lo! sweeten'd with the summer light,
The full-juiced apple, waxing over-mellow,
Drops in a silent autumn night.
All its allotted length of days
The flower ripens in its place,
Ripens and fades, and falls, and hath no toil,
Fast-rooted in the fruitful soil.

Hateful is the dark-blue sky,
Vaulted o'er the dark-blue sea.

Death is the end of life; ah, why
Should life all labour be?
Let us alone. Time driveth onward fast,
And in a little while our lips are dumb.
Let us alone. What is it that will last?
All things are taken from us, and become
Portions and parcels of the dreadful past.
Let us alone. What pleasure can we have
To war with evil? Is there any peace
In ever climbing up the climbing wave?
All things have rest, and ripen toward the grave
In silence—ripen, fall, and cease:
Give us long rest or death, dark death, or dreamful ease.

How sweet it were, hearing the downward stream,
With half-shut eyes ever to seem
Falling asleep in a half-dream!
To dream and dream, like yonder amber light,
Which will not leave the myrrh-bush on the height;
To hear each other's whisper'd speech;
Eating the Lotos day by day,
To watch the crisping ripples on the beach,
And tender curving lines of creamy spray;
To lend our hearts and spirits wholly
To the influence of mild-minded melancholy;
To muse and brood and live again in memory,
With those old faces of our infancy
Heap'd over with a mound of grass,
Two handfuls of white dust, shut in an urn of brass!

Dear is the memory of our wedded lives,
And dear the last embraces of our wives
And their warm tears; but all hath suffer'd change;
For surely now our household hearths are cold,
Our sons inherit us, our looks are strange,
And we should come like ghosts to trouble joy.
Or else the island princes over-bold
Have eat our substance, and the minstrel sings
Before them of the ten years' war in Troy,

And our great deeds, as half-forgotten things.
Is there confusion in the little isle?
Let what is broken so remain.
The Gods are hard to reconcile;
'T is hard to settle order once again.
There *is* confusion worse than death,
Trouble on trouble, pain on pain,
Long labour unto aged breath,
Sore task to hearts worn out by many wars
And eyes grown dim with gazing on the pilot-stars.
But, propped on beds of amaranthe and moly,
How sweet—while warm airs lull us, blowing lowly—
With half-dropped eyelid still,
Beneath a heaven dark and holy,
To watch the long bright river drawing slowly
His waters from the purple hill—
To hear the dewy echoes calling
From cave to cave thro' the thick-twined vine—
To watch the emerald-colour'd water falling
Thro' many a woven acanthus-wreath divine!
Only to hear and see the far-off sparkling brine,
Only to hear were sweet, stretch'd out beneath the pine.

The Lotos blooms below the barren peak,
The Lotos blows by every winding creek;
All day the wind breathes low with mellower tone;
Thro' every hollow cave and alley lone
Round and round the spicy downs the yellow Lotos-dust is blown.
We have had enough of action, and of motion we,
Roll'd to starboard, roll'd to larboard, when the surge was
    seething free,
Where the wallowing monster spouted his foam-fountains in
    the sea.
Let us swear an oath, and keep it with an equal mind,
In the hollow Lotos-land to live and lie reclined
On the hills like Gods together, careless of mankind.
For they lie beside their nectar, and the bolts are hurl'd
Far below them in the valleys, and the clouds are lightly curl'd
Round their golden houses, girdled with the gleaming world;

Where they smile in secret, looking over wasted lands,
Blight and famine, plague and earthquake, roaring deeps and
    fiery sands,
Clanging fights, and flaming towns, and sinking ships, and
    praying hands.
But they smile, they find a music centred in a doleful song
Steaming up, a lamentation and an ancient tale of wrong,
Like a tale of little meaning tho' the words are strong;
Chanted from an ill-used race of men that cleave the soil,
Sow the seed, and reap the harvest with enduring toil,
Storing yearly little dues of wheat, and wine and oil;
Till they perish and they suffer—some, 't is whisper'd—down
    in hell
Suffer endless anguish, others in Elysian valleys dwell,
Resting weary limbs at last on beds of asphodel.
Surely, surely, slumber is more sweet than toil, the shore
Than labour in the deep mid-ocean, wind and wave and oar;
O, rest ye, brother mariners, we will not wander more.

ULYSSES

It little profits that an idle king,
By this still hearth, among these barren crags,
Match'd with an agèd wife, I mete and dole
Unequal laws unto a savage race,
That hoard, and sleep, and feed, and know not me.
I cannot rest from travel: I will drink
Life to the lees: all times I have enjoy'd
Greatly, have suffer'd greatly, both with those
That loved me, and alone; on shore, and when
Thro' scudding drifts the rainy Hyades
Vext the dim sea; I am become a name;
For always roaming with a hungry heart
Much have I seen and known; cities of men,
And manners, climates, councils, governments,
Myself not least, but honour'd of them all;
And drunk delight of battle with my peers,
Far on the ringing plains of windy Troy.
I am a part of all that I have met.

Yet all experience is an arch where-thro'
Gleans that untravell'd world, whose margin fades
Forever and forever when I move.
How dull it is to pause, to make an end,
To rust unburnish'd, not to shine in use!
As tho' to breathe were life. Life piled on life
Were all too little, and of one to me
Little remains: but every hour is saved
From that eternal silence, something more,
A bringer of new things; and vile it were
For some three suns to store and hoard myself,
And this grey spirit yearning in desire
To follow knowledge like a sinking star,
Beyond the utmost bound of human thought.

   This is my son, mine own Telemachus,
To whom I leave the sceptre and the isle—
Well-loved of me, discerning to fulfil
This labour, by slow prudence to make mild
A rugged people, and thro' soft degrees
Subdue them to the useful and the good.
Most blameless is he, centred in the sphere
Of common duties, decent not to fail
In offices of tenderness, and pay
Meet adoration to my household gods,
When I am gone. He works his work, I mine.

   There lies the port; the vessel puffs her sail:
There gloom the dark broad seas. My mariners,
Souls that have toil'd, and wrought, and thought with me—
That ever with a frolic welcome took
The thunder and the sunshine, and opposed
Free hearts, free foreheads—you and I are old;
Old age hath yet his honour and his toil;
Death closes all: but something ere the end,
Some work of noble note, may yet be done,
Not unbecoming men that strove with Gods.
The lights begin to twinkle from the rocks:
The long day wanes: the slow moon climbs: the deep
Moans round with many voices. Come, my friends
'Tis not too late to seek a newer world.
Push off, and sitting well in order smite

The sounding furrows; for my purpose holds
To sail beyond the sunset, and the baths
Of all the western stars, until I die.
It may be that the gulfs will wash us down:
It may be we shall touch the Happy Isles,
And see the great Achilles, whom we knew.
Tho' much is taken, much abides; and tho'
We are not now that strength which in old days
Moved earth and heaven; that which we are, we are;
One equal temper of heroic hearts,
Made weak by time and fate, but strong in will
To strive, to seek, to find, and not to yield.

TEARS, IDLE TEARS

TEARS, idle tears, I know not what they mean,
Tears from the depth of some divine despair
Rise in the heart, and gather to the eyes,
In looking on the happy autumn-fields,
And thinking of the days that are no more.

Fresh as the first beam glittering on a sail,
That brings our friends up from the underworld,
Sad as the last which reddens over one
That sinks with all we love below the verge;
So sad, so fresh, the days that are no more.

Ah, sad and strange as in dark summer dawns
The earliest pipe of half-awaken'd birds
To dying ears, when unto dying eyes
The casement slowly grows a glimmering square;
So sad, so strange, the days that are no more.

Dear as remember'd kisses after death,
And sweet as those by hopeless fancy feign'd
On lips that are for others; deep as love,
Deep as first love, and wild with all regret;
O Death in Life, the days that are no more!

[Song from THE PRINCESS.]

BREAK, BREAK, BREAK

Break, break, break,
  On thy cold grey stones, O Sea!
And I would that my tongue could utter
  The thoughts that arise in me.

O well for the fisherman's boy,
  That he shouts with his sister at play!
O well for the sailor lad,
  That he sings in his boat on the bay!

And the stately ships go on
  To their haven under the hill;
But O for the touch of a vanish'd hand,
  And the sound of a voice that is still!

Break, break, break,
  At the foot of thy crags, O Sea!
But the tender grace of a day that is dead
  Will never come back to me.

MORTE D'ARTHUR

So all day long the noise of battle roll'd
Among the mountains by the winter sea;
Until King Arthur's table, man by man,
Had fallen in Lyonness about their Lord,
King Arthur: then, because his wound was deep,
The bold Sir Bedivere uplifted him,
Sir Bedivere, the last of all his knights,
And bore him to a chapel nigh the field,
A broken chancel with a broken cross,
That stood on a dark strait of barren land.
On one side lay the Ocean, and on one
Lay a great water, and the moon was full.
  Then spake King Arthur to Sir Bedivere:
"The sequel of to-day unsolders all

The goodliest fellowship of famous knights
Whereof this world holds record. Such a sleep
They sleep—the men I loved. I think that we
Shall nevermore, at any future time,
Delight our souls with talk of knightly deeds,
Walking about the gardens and the halls
Of Camelot, as in the days that were.
I perish by this people which I made,—
Tho' Merlin sware that I should come again
To rule once more—but let what will be, be,
I am so deeply smitten thro' the helm
That without help I cannot last till morn.
Thou therefore take my brand Excalibur,
Which was my pride: for thou rememberest how
In those old days, one summer noon, an arm
Rose up from out the bosom of the lake,
Clothed in white samite, mystic, wonderful,
Holding the sword—and how I row'd across
And took it, and have worn it like a king:
And, wheresoever I am sung or told
In aftertime, this also shall be known:
But now delay not: take Excalibur,
And fling him far into the middle mere:
Watch what thou seest, and lightly bring me word."
    To him replied the bold Sir Bedivere:
"It is not meet, Sir King, to leave thee thus,
Aidless, alone, and smitten thro' the helm.
A little thing may harm a wounded man.
Yet I thy hest will all perform at full,
Watch what I see, and lightly bring thee word."
    So saying, from the ruin'd shrine he stept
And in the moon athwart the place of tombs,
Where lay the mighty bones of ancient men,
Old knights, and over them the sea-wind sang
Shrill, chill, with flakes of foam. He, stepping down
By zig-zag paths, and juts of pointed rock,
Came on the shining levels of the lake.
    There drew he forth the brand Excalibur,
And o'er him, drawing it, the winter moon,

Brightening the skirts of a long cloud, ran forth
And sparkled keen with frost against the hilt:
For all the haft twinkled with diamond sparks,
Myriads of topaz-lights, and jacinth-work
Of subtlest jewellery. He gazed so long
That both his eyes were dazzled, as he stood,
This way and that dividing the swift mind,
In act to throw: but at the last it seem'd
Better to leave Excalibur conceal'd
There in the many-knotted water-flags,
That whistled stiff and dry about the marge.
So strode he back slow to the wounded King.

    Then spake King Arthur to Sir Bedivere:
"Hast thou perform'd my mission which I gave?
What is it thou hast seen? or what hast heard?"

    And answer made the bold Sir Bedivere:
"I heard the ripple washing in the reeds,
And the wild water lapping on the crag."

    To whom replied King Arthur, faint and pale:
"Thou hast betray'd thy nature and thy name,
Not rendering true answer, as beseem'd
Thy fealty, nor like a noble knight:
For surer sign had followed, either hand,
Or voice, or else a motion of the mere.
This is a shameful thing for men to lie.
Yet now, I charge thee, quickly go again
As thou art lief and dear, and do the thing
I bade thee, watch, and lightly bring me word."

    Then went Sir Bedivere the second time
Across the ridge, and paced beside the mere,
Counting the dewy pebbles, fix'd in thought;
But when he saw the wonder of the hilt,
How curiously and strangely chased, he smote
His palms together, and he cried aloud,

    "And if indeed I cast the brand away,
Surely a precious thing, one worthy note,
Should thus be lost forever from the earth,
Which might have pleased the eyes of many men.
What good should follow this, if this were done?

What harm, undone? deep harm to disobey,
Seeing obedience is the bond of rule.
Were it well to obey then, if a king demand
An act unprofitable, against himself?
The King is sick, and knows not what he does.
What record, or what relic of my lord
Should be to aftertime, but empty breath
And rumours of a doubt? but were this kept,
Stored in some treasure-house of mighty kings,
Some one might show it at a joust of arms,
Saying, 'King Arthur's sword, Excalibur,
Wrought by the lonely maiden of the Lake.
Nine years she wrought it, sitting in the deeps
Upon the hidden bases of the hills.'
So might some old man speak in the aftertime
To all the people, winning reverence.
But now much honour and much fame were lost."

   So spake he, clouded with his own conceit,
And hid Excalibur the second time,
And so strode back slow to the wounded King.

   Then spoke King Arthur, breathing heavily:
"What is it thou hast seen? or what hast heard?"
And answer made the bold Sir Bedivere:
"I heard the water lapping on the crag,
And the long ripple washing in the reeds."

   To whom replied King Arthur, much in wrath:
"Ah, miserable and unkind, untrue,
Unknightly, traitor-hearted! Woe is me!
Authority forgets a dying king,
Laid widow'd of the power in his eye
That bow'd the will. I see thee what thou art,
For thou, the latest-left of all my knights,
In whom should meet the offices of all,
Thou wouldst betray me for the precious hilt;
Either from lust of gold, or like a girl
Valuing the giddy pleasure of the eyes.
Yet, for a man may fail in duty twice,
And the third time may prosper, get thee hence:
But, if thou spare to fling Excalibur,

I will arise and slay thee with my hands."
  Then quickly rose Sir Bedivere, and ran,
And, leaping down the ridges lightly, plunged
Among the bulrush-beds, and clutch'd the sword,
And strongly wheel'd and threw it. The great brand
Made lightnings in the splendour of the moon,
And flashing round and round, and whirl'd in an arch,
Shot like a streamer of the northern morn,
Seen where the moving isles of winter shock
By night, with noises of the northern sea.
So flash'd and fell the brand Excalibur:
But ere he dipt the surface, rose an arm
Clothed in white samite, mystic, wonderful,
And caught him by the hilt, and brandish'd him
Three times, and drew him under in the mere.
And lightly went the other to the King.

  Then spoke King Arthur, drawing thicker breath:
"Now see I by thine eyes that this is done.
Speak out: what is it thou hast heard, or seen?"

  And answer made the bold Sir Bedivere:
"Sir King, I closed mine eyelids, lest the gems
Should blind my purpose, for I never saw,
Nor shall see, here or elsewhere, till I die,
Not tho' I live three lives of mortal men,
So great a miracle as yonder hilt.
Then with both hands I flung him, wheeling him;
But when I look'd again, behold an arm,
Clothed in white samite, mystic, wonderful,
That caught him by the hilt, and brandish'd him
Three times, and drew him under in the mere."

  And answer made King Arthur, breathing hard:
"My end draws nigh; 'tis time that I were gone.
Make broad thy shoulders to receive my weight,
And bear me to the margin; yet I fear
My wound hath taken cold, and I shall die."

  So saying, from the pavement he half rose,
Slowly, with pain, reclining on his arm,
And looking wistfully with wide blue eyes
As in a picture. Him Sir Bedivere

Remorsefully regarded thro' his tears,
And would have spoken, but he found not words,
Then took with care, and kneeling on one knee,
O'er both his shoulders drew the languid hands,
And rising bore him thro' the place of tombs.

But, as he walk'd, King Arthur panted hard,
Like one that feels a nightmare on his bed
When all the house is mute. So sigh'd the King,
Muttering and murmuring at his ear, "Quick, quick!
I fear it is too late, and I shall die."
But the other swiftly strode from ridge to ridge,
Clothed with his breath, and looking, as he walk'd,
Larger than human on the frozen hills.
He heard the deep behind him, and a cry
Before. His own thought drove him, like a goad.
Dry clash'd his harness in the icy caves
And barren chasms, and all to left and right
The bare black cliff clang'd round him, as he based
His feet on juts of slippery crag that rang
Sharp-smitten with the dint of armèd heels—
And on a sudden, lo! the level lake,
And the long glories of the winter moon.

Then saw they how there hove a dusky barge,
Dark as a funeral scarf from stem to stern,
Beneath them; and descending they were ware
That all the decks were dense with stately forms
Black-stoled, black-hooded, like a dream—by these
Three Queens with crowns of gold—and from them rose
A cry that shiver'd to the tingling stars,
And, as it were one voice, an agony
Of lamentation, like a wind, that shrills
All night in a waste land, where no one comes,
Or hath come, since the making of the world.

Then murmur'd Arthur, "Place me in the barge,"
And to the barge they came. There those three Queens
Put forth their hands, and took the King, and wept.
But she, that rose the tallest of them all
And fairest, laid his head upon her lap,
And loosed the shatter'd casque, and chafed his hands,

And call'd him by his name, complaining loud,
And dropping bitter tears against his brow
Striped with dark blood: for all his face was white
And colourless, and like the wither'd moon
Smote by the fresh beam of the springing east;
And all his greaves and cuisses dash'd with drops
Of onset; and the light and lustrous curls—
That made his forehead like a rising sun
High from the dais-throne—were parch'd with dust;
Or, clotted into points and hanging loose,
Mix'd with the knightly growth that fringed his lips.
So like a shatter'd column lay the King;
Not like that Arthur who, with lance in rest,
From spur to plume a star of tournament,
Shot thro' the lists at Camelot, and charged
Before the eyes of ladies and of kings.

Then loudly cried the bold Sir Bedivere,
"Ah! my Lord Arthur, whither shall I go?
Where shall I hide my forehead and my eyes?
For now I see the true old times are dead,
When every morning brought a noble chance,
And every chance brought out a noble knight.
Such times have been not since the light that led
The holy Elders with the gift of myrrh.
But now the whole Round Table is dissolved
Which was an image of the mighty world;
And I, the last, go forth companionless,
And the days darken round me, and the years,
Among new men, strange faces, other minds."

And slowly answered Arthur from the barge:
"The old order changeth, yielding place to new,
And God fulfils Himself in many ways,
Lest one good custom should corrupt the world.
Comfort thyself: what comfort is in me?
I have lived my life, and that which I have done
May He within Himself make pure! but thou,
If thou shouldst never see my face again,
Pray for my soul. More things are wrought by prayer
Than this world dreams of. Wherefore, let thy voice

Rise like a fountain for me night and day.
For what are men better than sheep or goats
That nourish a blind life within the brain,
If, knowing God, they lift not hands of prayer
Both for themselves and those who call them friend?
For so the whole round earth is every way
Bound by gold chains about the feet of God.
But now farewell. I am going a long way,
With these thou seëst—if indeed I go—
(For all my mind is clouded with a doubt)
To the island-valley of Avilion;
Where falls not hail, or rain, or any snow,
Nor ever wind blows loudly; but it lies
Deep-meadow'd, happy, fair with orchard-lawns
And bowery hollows crown'd with summer sea,
Where I will heal me of my grievous wound."

So said he, and the barge with oar and sail
Moved from the brink, like some full-breasted swan
That, fluting a wild carol ere her death,
Ruffles her pure cold plume, and takes the flood
With swarthy webs. Long stood Sir Bedivere
Revolving many memories, till the hull
Look'd one black dot against the verge of dawn,
And on the mere the wailing died away.

IN MEMORIAM A. H. H.

OBIIT MDCCCXXXIII

STRONG Son of God, immortal Love,
    Whom we, that have not seen thy face,
    By faith, and faith alone, embrace,
Believing where we cannot prove;

Thine are these orbs of light and shade;
    Thou madest Life in man and brute;
    Thou madest Death; and lo, thy foot
Is on the skull which thou hast made.

Thou wilt not leave us in the dust:
  Thou madest man, he knows not why,
  He thinks he was not made to die;
And thou hast made him: thou art just.

Thou seemest human and divine,
  The highest, holiest manhood, thou.
  Our wills are ours, we know not how;
Our wills are ours, to make them thine.

Our little systems have their day;
  They have their day and cease to be;
  They are but broken lights of thee,
And thou, O Lord, art more than they.

We have but faith: we cannot know,
  For knowledge is of things we see;
  And yet we trust it comes from thee,
A beam in darkness: let it grow.

Let knowledge grow from more to more,
  But more of reverence in us dwell;
  That mind and soul, according well,
May make one music as before,

But vaster. We are fools and slight;
  We mock thee when we do not fear:
  But help thy foolish ones to bear;
Help thy vain worlds to bear thy light.

Forgive what seem'd my sin in me,
  What seem'd my worth since I began;
  For merit lives from man to man,
And not from man, O Lord, to thee.

Forgive my grief for one removed,
  Thy creature, whom I found so fair.
  I trust he lives in Thee, and there
I find him worthier to be loved.

Forgive these wild and wandering cries,
 Confusions of a wasted youth;
 Forgive them where they fail in truth,
And in thy wisdom make me wise.

CALM is the morn without a sound,
 Calm as to suit a calmer grief.
 And only thro' the faded leaf
The chestnut pattering to the ground;

Calm and deep peace on this high wold,
 And on these dews that drench the furze,
 And all the silvery gossamers
That twinkle into green and gold;

Calm and still light on yon great plain
 That sweeps with all its autumn bowers,
 And crowded farms and lessening towers,
To mingle with the bounding main;

Calm and deep peace in this wide air,
 These leaves that redden to the fall,
 And in my heart, if calm at all,
If any calm, a calm despair;

Calm on the seas, and silver sleep,
 And waves that sway themselves in rest,
 And dead calm in that noble breast
Which heaves but with the heaving deep.

O, YET we trust that somehow good
 Will be the final goal of ill,
 To pangs of nature, sins of will,
Defects of doubt, and taints of blood;

That nothing walks with aimless feet;
 That not one life shall be destroy'd,
 Or cast as rubbish to the void,
When God hath made the pile complete;

That not a worm is cloven in vain;
  That not a moth with vain desire
  Is shrivell'd in a fruitless fire,
Or but subserves another's gain.

Behold, we know not anything;
  I can but trust that good shall fall
  At last—far off—at last, to all,
And every winter change to spring.

So runs my dream; but what am I?
  An infant crying in the night;
  An infant crying for the light,
And with no language but a cry.

THE wish, that of the living whole
  No life may fail beyond the grave,
  Derives it not from what we have
The likest God within the soul?

Are God and Nature then at strife,
  That Nature lends such evil dreams?
  So careful of the type she seems,
So careless of the single life,

That I, considering everywhere
  Her secret meaning in her deeds,
  And finding that of fifty seeds
She often brings but one to bear,

I falter where I firmly trod,
  And falling with my weight of cares
  Upon the great world's altar-stairs
That slope thro' darkness up to God,

I stretch lame hands of faith, and grope,
  And gather dust and chaff, and call
  To what I feel is Lord of all,
And faintly trust the larger hope.

"So careful of the type?" but no.
  From scarped cliff and quarried stone
  She cries: "A thousand types are gone;
I care for nothing, all shall go.

"Thou makest thine appeal to me:
  I bring to life, I bring to death;
  The spirit does but mean the breath:
I know no more." And he, shall he,

Man, her last work, who seem'd so fair,
  Such splendid purpose in his eyes,
  Who roll'd the psalm to wintry skies,
Who built him fanes of fruitless prayer,

Who trusted God was love indeed
  And love Creation's final law—
  Tho' Nature, red in tooth and claw
With ravine, shriek'd against his creed—

Who loved, who suffer'd countless ills,
  Who battled for the True, the Just,
  Be blown about the desert dust,
Or seal'd within the iron hills?

No more? A monster then, a dream,
  A discord. Dragons of the prime,
  That tear each other in their slime,
Were mellow music match'd with him.

O life as futile, then, as frail!
  O for thy voice to soothe and bless!
  What hope of answer, or redress?
Behind the veil, behind the veil.

DEAR friend, far off, my lost desire,
  So far, so near in woe and weal,
  O loved the most, when most I feel
There is a lower and a higher;

Known and unknown, human, divine;
 Sweet human hand and lips and eye;
 Dear heavenly friend that canst not die,
Mine, mine, for ever, ever mine;

Strange friend, past, present, and to be;
 Loved deeplier, darklier understood;
 Behold, I dream a dream of good,
And mingle all the world with thee.

THY voice is on the rolling air;
 I hear thee where the waters run;
 Thou standest in the rising sun,
And in the setting thou art fair.

What art thou then? I cannot guess;
 But tho' I seem in star and flower
 To feel thee some diffusive power,
I do not therefore love thee less.

My love involves the love before;
 My love is vaster passion now;
 Tho' mix'd with God and Nature thou,
I seem to love thee more and more.

Far off thou art, but ever nigh;
 I have thee still, and I rejoice;
 I prosper, circled with thy voice;
I shall not lose thee tho' I die.

O LIVING will that shalt endure
 When all that seems shall suffer shock,
 Rise in the spiritual rock,
Flow thro' our deeds and make them pure,

That we may lift from out of dust
 A voice as unto him that hears,
 A cry above the conquer'd years
To one that with us works, and trust,

With faith that comes of self-control,
  The truths that never can be proved
Until we close with all we loved,
And all we flow from, soul in soul.

[From In Memoriam A. H. H.]

ODE ON THE DEATH OF THE DUKE OF WELLINGTON

Bury the Great Duke
  With an empire's lamentation;
Let us bury the Great Duke
  To the noise of the mourning of a mighty nation;
Mourning when their leaders fall,
Warriors carry the warrior's pall,
And sorrow darkens hamlet and hall.

Where shall we lay the man whom we deplore?
Here, in streaming London's central roar.
Let the sound of those he wrought for,
And the feet of those he fought for,
Echo around his bones for evermore.

Lead out the pageant: sad and slow,
As fits an universal woe,
Let the long, long procession go,
And let the sorrowing crowd about it grow,
And let the mournful martial music blow;
The last great Englishman is low.

Mourn, for to us he seems the last,
Remembering all his greatness in the past,
No more in soldier fashion will he greet
With lifted hand the gazer in the street.
O friends, our chief state-oracle is mute!
Mourn for the man of long-enduring blood,
The statesman-warrior, moderate, resolute,
Whole in himself, a common good.
Mourn for the man of amplest influence,

Yet clearest of ambitious crime,
Our greatest yet with least pretence,
Great in council and great in war,
Foremost captain of his time,
Rich in saving common-sense,
And, as the greatest only are,
In his simplicity sublime.
O good gray head which all men knew,
O voice from which their omens all men drew,
O iron nerve to true occasion true,
O fallen at length that tower of strength
Which stood four-square to all the winds that blew!
Such was he whom we deplore.
The long self-sacrifice of life is o'er.
The great World-victor's victor will be seen no more.

All is over and done,
Render thanks to the Giver,
England, for thy son.
Let the bell be toll'd.
Render thanks to the Giver,
And render him to the mould.
Under the cross of gold
That shines over city and river,
There he shall rest forever
Among the wise and the bold.
Let the bell be toll'd,
And a reverent people behold
The towering car, the sable steeds.
Bright let it be with its blazon'd deeds,
Dark in its funeral fold.
Let the bell be toll'd,
And a deeper knell in the heart be knoll'd;
And the sound of the sorrowing anthem roll'd
Thro' the dome of the golden cross;
And the volleying cannon thunder his loss;
He knew their voices of old.
For many a time in many a clime
His captain's-ear has heard them boom

Bellowing victory, bellowing doom.
When he with those deep voices wrought,
Guarding realms and kings from shame,
With those deep voices our dead captain taught
The tyrant, and asserts his claim
In that dread sound to the great name
Which he has worn so pure of blame,
In praise and in dispraise the same,
A man of well-attemper'd frame.
O civic muse, to such a name,
To such a name for ages long,
To such a name,
Preserve a broad approach of fame,
And ever-echoing avenues of song!

"Who is he that cometh, like an honour'd guest,
With banner and with music, with soldier and with priest,
With a nation weeping, and breaking on my rest?"—
Mighty Seaman, this is he
Was great by land as thou by sea.
Thine island loves thee well, thou famous man,
The greatest sailor since our world began.
Now, to the roll of muffled drums,
To thee the greatest soldier comes;
For this is he
Was great by land as thou by sea.
His foes were thine; he kept us free;
O, give him welcome, this is he
Worthy of our gorgeous rites,
And worthy to be laid by thee;
For this is England's greatest son,
He that gain'd a hundred fights,
Nor ever lost an English gun;
This is he that far away
Against the myriads of Assaye
Clash'd with his fiery few and won;
And underneath another sun,
Warring on a later day,
Round affrighted Lisbon drew

The treble works, the vast designs
Of his labour'd rampart-lines,
Where he greatly stood at bay,
Whence he issued forth anew,
And ever great and greater grew,
Beating from the wasted vines
Back to France her banded swarms,
Back to France with countless blows,
Till o'er the hills her eagles flew
Beyond the Pyrenean pines,
Follow'd up in valley and glen
With blare of bugle, clamour of men,
Roll of cannon and clash of arms,
And England pouring on her foes,
Such a war had such a close.
Again their ravening eagle rose
In anger, wheel'd on Europe-shadowing wings,
And barking for the throne of kings;
Till one that sought but Duty's iron crown
On that loud Sabbath shook the spoiler down;
A day of onsets of despair!
Dash'd on every rocky square,
Their surging charges foam'd themselves away;
Last, the Prussian trumpet blew;
Thro' the long-tormented air
Heaven flash'd a sudden jubilant ray,
And down we swept and charged and overthrew.
So great a soldier taught us there
What long-enduring hearts could do
In that world-earthquake, Waterloo!
Mighty Seaman, tender and true,
And pure as he from taint of craven guile,
O saviour of the silver-coasted isle,
O shaker of the Baltic and the Nile,
If aught of things that here befall
Touch a spirit among things divine,
If love of country move thee there at all,
Be glad, because his bones are laid by thine!
And thro' the centuries let a people's voice

In full acclaim,
A people's voice,
The proof and echo of all human fame,
A people's voice, when they rejoice
At civic revel and pomp and game,
Attest their great commander's claim
With honour, honour, honour, honour to him,
Eternal honour to his name.

A people's voice! we are a people yet.
Tho' all men else their nobler dreams forget,
Confused by brainless mobs and lawless Powers,
Thank Him who isled us here, and roughly set
His Briton in blown seas and storming showers,
We have a voice with which to pay the debt
Of boundless love and reverence and regret
To those great men who fought, and kept it ours.
And keep it ours, O God, from brute control!
O Statesmen, guard us, guard the eye, the soul
Of Europe, keep our noble England whole,
And save the one true seed of freedom sown
Betwixt a people and their ancient throne,
That sober freedom out of which there springs
Our loyal passion for our temperate kings!
For, saving that, ye help to save mankind
Till public wrong be crumbled into dust,
And drill the raw world for the march of mind,
Till crowds at length be sane and crowns be just.
But wink no more in slothful overtrust.
Remember him who led your hosts;
He bade you guard the sacred coasts.
Your cannons moulder on the seaward wall;
His voice is silent in your council-hall
For ever; and whatever tempests lour
For ever silent; even if they broke
In thunder, silent; yet remember all
He spoke among you, and the Man who spoke;
Who never sold the truth to serve the hour,
Nor palter'd with Eternal God for power;

Who let the turbid streams of rumour flow
Thro' either babbling world of high and low;
Whose life was work, whose language rife
With rugged maxims hewn from life;
Who never spoke against a foe;
Whose eighty winters freeze with one rebuke
All great self-seekers trampling on the right.
Truth-teller was our England's Alfred named;
Truth-lover was our English Duke!
Whatever record leap to light
He never shall be shamed.

Lo! the leader in these glorious wars
Now to glorious burial slowly borne,
Follow'd by the brave of other lands,
He, on whom from both her open hands
Lavish Honour shower'd all her stars,
And affluent Fortune emptied all her horn.
Yea, let all good things await
Him who cares not to be great
But as he saves or serves the state.
Not once or twice in our rough island-story
The path of duty was the way to glory.
He that walks it, only thirsting
For the right, and learns to deaden
Love of self, before his journey closes,
He shall find the stubborn thistle bursting
Into glossy purples, which out-redden
All voluptuous garden-roses.
Not once or twice in our fair island-story
The path of duty was the way to glory.
He, that ever following her commands,
On with toil of heart and knees and hands,
Thro' the long gorge to the far light has won
His path upward, and prevail'd,
Shall find the toppling crags of Duty scaled
Are close upon the shining table-lands
To which our God Himself is moon and sun.
Such was he: his work is done.

But while the races of mankind endure
Let his great example stand
Colossal, seen of every land,
And keep the soldier firm, the statesman pure;
Till in all lands and thro' all human story
The path of duty be the way to glory.
And let the land whose hearths he saved from shame
For many and many an age proclaim
At civic revel and pomp and game,
And when the long-illumined cities flame,
Their ever-loyal iron leader's fame,
With honour, honour, honour, honour to him,
Eternal honour to his name.

Peace, his triumph will be sung
By some yet unmoulded tongue
Far on in summers that we shall not see.
Peace, it is a day of pain
For one about whose patriarchal knee
Late the little children clung.
O peace, it is a day of pain
For one upon whose hand and heart and brain
Once the weight and fate of Europe hung.
Ours the pain, be his the gain!
More than is of man's degree
Must be with us, watching here
At this, our great solemnity.
Whom we see not we revere;
We revere, and we refrain
From talk of battles loud and vain,
And bawling memories all too free
For such a wise humility
As befits a solemn fane:
We revere, and while we hear
The tides of Music's golden sea
Setting toward eternity,
Uplifted high in heart and hope are we,
Until we doubt not that for one so true
There must be other nobler work to do

Than when he fought at Waterloo,
And victor he must ever be.
For tho' the Giant Ages heave the hill
And break the shore, and evermore
Make and break, and work their will,
Tho' world on world in myriad myriads roll
Round us, each with different powers,
And other forms of life than ours,
What know we greater than the soul?
On God and Godlike men we build our trust.
Hush, the Dead March wails in the people's ears;
The dark crowd moves, and there are sobs and tears;
The black earth yawns; the mortal disappears;
Ashes to ashes, dust to dust;
He is gone who seem'd so great.—
Gone, but nothing can bereave him
Of the force he made his own
Being here, and we believe him
Something far advanced in State,
And that he wears a truer crown
Than any wreath that man can weave him.
Speak no more of his renown,
Lay your earthly fancies down,
And in the vast cathedral leave him,
God accept him, Christ receive him!

FLOWER IN THE CRANNIED WALL

FLOWER in the crannied wall,
I pluck you out of the crannies,
I hold you here, root and all, in my hand,
Little flower—but *if* I could understand
What you are, root and all, and all in all,
I should know what God and man is.

CROSSING THE BAR

SUNSET and evening star,
    And one clear call for me!
And may there be no moaning of the bar,
    When I put out to sea,

But such a tide as moving seems asleep,
    Too full for sound and foam,
When that which drew from out the boundless deep
    Turns again home

Twilight and evening bell,
    And after that the dark!
And may there be no sadness of farewell,
    When I embark;

For tho' from out our bourne of Time and Place
    The flood may bear me far,
I hope to see my Pilot face to face
    When I have crost the bar.

EDWARD FITZGERALD [1809–1883]

THE LOQUACIOUS VESSELS

As under cover of departing Day
Slunk hunger-stricken Ramazán away,
    Once more within the Potter's house alone
I stood, surrounded by the Shapes of Clay.

Shapes of all Sorts and Sizes, great and small,
That stood along the floor and by the wall;
    And some loquacious Vessels were; and some
Listen'd perhaps, but never talk'd at all.

Said one among them—"Surely not in vain
My substance of the common Earth was ta'en
  And to this Figure moulded, to be broke,
Or trampled back to shapeless Earth again."

Then said a Second—"Ne'er a peevish Boy
Would break the Bowl from which he drank in joy;
  And He that with his hand the Vessel made
Will surely not in after Wrath destroy."

After a momentary silence spake
Some Vessel of a more ungainly Make;
  "They sneer at me for leaning all awry:
What! did the Hand then of the Potter shake?"

Whereat some one of the loquacious Lot—
I think a Súfi pipkin—waxing hot—
  "All this of Pot and Potter—Tell me then,
Who is the Potter, pray, and who the Pot?"

"Why," said another, "Some there are who tell
Of one who threatens he will toss to Hell
  The luckless Pots he marr'd in making—Pish!
He's a Good Fellow, and 't will all be well."

"Well," murmur'd one. "Let whoso make or buy,
My Clay with long Oblivion is gone dry:
  But fill me with the old familiar Juice,
Methinks I might recover by and by."

So while the Vessels one by one were speaking,
The little Moon look'd in that all were seeking:
  And then they jogg'd each other, "Brother! Brother!
Now for the Porter's shoulder-knot a-creaking!"

[From The Rubáiyát of Omar Khayyam.]

ELIZABETH BARRETT BROWNING
[1806–1861]

SONNETS

Go from me. Yet I feel that I shall stand
Henceforward in thy shadow. Nevermore
Alone upon the threshold of my door
Of individual life, I shall command
The uses of my soul, nor lift my hand
Serenely in the sunshine as before,
Without the sense of that which I forbore—
Thy touch upon the palm. The widest land
Doom takes to part us, leaves thy heart in mine
With pulses that beat double. What I do
And what I dream include thee, as the wine
Must taste of its own grapes. And when I sue
God for myself, He hears that name of thine,
And sees within my eyes the tears of two.

If I leave all for thee, wilt thou exchange
And be all to me? Shall I never miss
Home-talk and blessing and the common kiss
That comes to each in turn, nor count it strange,
When I look up, to drop on a new range
Of walls and floors, another home than this?
Nay, wilt thou fill that place by me which is
Filled by dead eyes too tender to know change?
That's hardest. If to conquer love, has tried,
To conquer grief, tries more, as all things prove;
For grief indeed is love and grief beside.
Alas, I have grieved so I am hard to love.
Yet love me—wilt thou? Open thine heart wide,
And fold within the wet wings of thy dove.

How do I love thee? Let me count the ways.
I love thee to the depth and breadth and height

My soul can reach, when feeling out of sight
For the ends of Being and ideal Grace,
I love thee to the level of everyday's
Most quiet need, by sun and candle-light.
I love thee freely, as men strive for Right;
I love thee purely, as they turn from Praise.
I love thee with the passion put to use
In my old griefs, and with my childhood's faith.
I love thee with a love I seemed to lose
With my lost saints,—I love thee with the breath,
Smiles, tears, of all my life!—and, if God choose,
I shall but love thee better after death.

[From SONNETS FROM THE PORTUGUESE.]

ROBERT BROWNING [1812–1889]

TWO SONGS

I

HEAP cassia, sandal-buds and stripes
Of labdanum, and aloe-balls,
Smeared with dull nard an Indian wipes
    From out her hair: such balsam falls
    Down sea-side mountain pedestals,
From tree-tops where tired winds are fain,
Spent with the vast and howling main,
To treasure half their island-gain.

And strew faint sweetness from some old
    Egyptian's fine worm-eaten shroud
Which breaks to dust when once unrolled;
    Or shredded perfume, like a cloud
From closet long to quiet vowed,
With mothed and dropping arras hung,
Mouldering her lute and books among,
As when a queen, long dead, was young.

[From PARACELSUS.]

II

The year's at the spring
And day's at the morn;
Morning's at seven;
The hill-side's dew-pearled;
The lark's on the wing;
The snail's on the thorn:
God's in his heaven—
All's right with the world!

[From PIPPA PASSES.]

HOME–THOUGHTS, FROM ABROAD

OH, to be in England
Now that April's there,
And whoever wakes in England
Sees, some morning, unaware,
That the lowest boughs and the brushwood sheaf
Round the elm-tree bole are in tiny leaf,
While the chaffinch sings on the orchard bough
In England—now!

And after April, when May follows,
And the whitethroat builds, and all the swallows!
Hark, where my blossomed pear-tree in the hedge
Leans to the field and scatters on the clover
Blossoms and dewdrops—at the bent spray's edge—
That's the wise thrush; he sings each song twice over,
Lest you should think he never could recapture
The first fine careless rapture!
And though the fields look rough with hoary dew,
All will be gay when noontide wakes anew
The buttercups, the little children's dower
—Far brighter than this gaudy melon-flower!

MY LAST DUCHESS

FERRARA

THAT'S my last Duchess painted on the wall,
Looking as if she were alive. I call
That piece a wonder, now: Fra Pandolf's hands
Worked busily a day, and there she stands.
Will't please you sit and look at her? I said
"Fra Pandolf" by design, for never read
Strangers like you that pictured countenance,
The depth and passion of its earnest glance,
But to myself they turned (since none puts by
The curtain I have drawn for you, but I)
And seemed as they would ask me, if they durst,
How such a glance came there; so, not the first
Are you to turn and ask thus. Sir, 'twas not
Her husband's presence only, called that spot
Of joy into the Duchess' cheek: perhaps
Fra Pandolf chanced to say, "Her mantle laps
Over my lady's wrist too much," or "Paint
Must never hope to reproduce the faint
Half-flush that dies along her throat:" such stuff
Was courtesy, she thought, and cause enough
For calling up that spot of joy. She had
A heart—how shall I say?—too soon made glad,
Too easily impressed: she liked whate'er
She looked on, and her looks went everywhere.
Sir, 'twas all one! My favour at her breast,
The dropping of the daylight in the West,
The bough of cherries some officious fool
Broke in the orchard for her, the white mule
She rode with round the terrace—all and each
Would draw from her alike the approving speech,
Or blush, at least. She thanked men,—good! but thanked
Somehow—I know not how—as if she ranked
My gift of a nine-hundred-years-old name
With anybody's gift. Who'd stoop to blame

This sort of trifling? Even had you skill
In speech—(which I have not)—to make your will
Quite clear to such an one, and say, "Just this
Or that in you disgusts me; here you miss,
Or there exceed the mark"—and if she let
Herself be lessoned so, nor plainly set
Her wits to yours, forsooth, and made excuse,
—E'en then would be some stooping; and I choose
Never to stoop. Oh sir, she smiled, no doubt,
Whene'er I passed her; but who passed without
Much the same smile? This grew; I gave commands;
Then all smiles stopped together. There she stands
As if alive. Will't please you rise? We'll meet
The company below, then. I repeat,
The Count your master's known munificence
Is ample warrant that no just pretence
Of mine for dowry will be disallowed;
Though his fair daughter's self, as I avowed
At starting, is my object. Nay, we'll go
Together down, sir. Notice Neptune, though,
Taming a sea-horse, thought a rarity,
Which Claus of Innsbruck cast in bronze for me!

MEETING AT NIGHT

The grey sea and the long black land;
And the yellow half-moon large and low;
And the startled little waves that leap
In fiery ringlets from their sleep,
As I gain the cove with pushing prow,
And quench its speed i' the slushy sand.

Then a mile of warm sea-scented beach;
Three fields to cross till a farm appears;
A tap at the pane, the quick sharp scratch
And blue spurt of a lighted match,
And a voice less loud, through its joys and fears,
Than the two hearts beating each to each!

THE LAST RIDE TOGETHER

I SAID—Then, dearest, since 'tis so,
Since now at length my fate I know,
Since nothing all my love avails,
Since all my life seemed meant for, fails,
    Since this was written and needs must be—
My whole heart rises up to bless
Your name in pride and thankfulness!
Take back the hope you gave,—I claim
Only a memory of the same,
—And this beside, if you will not blame,
    Your leave for one more last ride with me.

My mistress bent that brow of hers;
Those deep dark eyes where pride demurs
When pity would be softening through,
Fixed me a breathing-while or two
    With life or death in the balance: right!
The blood replenished me again;
My last thought was at least not vain:
I and my mistress, side by side
Shall be together, breathe and ride,
So, one day more am I deified.
    Who knows but the world may end to-night?

Hush! if you saw some western cloud
All billowy-bosomed, over-bowed
By many benedictions—sun's
And moon's and evening-star's at once—
    And so, you, looking and loving best,
Conscious grew, your passion drew
Cloud, sunset, moonrise, star-shine too,
Down on you, near and yet more near,
Till flesh must fade for heaven was here!—
Thus leant she and lingered—joy and fear!
    Thus lay she a moment on my breast.

Then we began to ride. My soul
Smoothed itself out, a long-cramped scroll
Freshening and fluttering in the wind.
Past hopes already lay behind.
    What need to strive with a life awry?
Had I said that, had I done this,
So might I gain, so might I miss.
Might she have loved me? just as well
She might have hated, who can tell!
Where had I been now if the worst befell?
    And here we are riding, she and I.

Fail I alone, in words and deeds?
Why, all men strive, and who succeeds?
We rode; it seemed my spirit flew,
Saw other regions, cities new,
    As the world rushed by on either side.
I thought,—All labour, yet no less
Bear up beneath their unsuccess.
Look at the end of work, contrast
The petty done, the undone vast,
This present of theirs with the hopeful past!
    I hoped she would love me; here we ride.

What hand and brain went ever paired?
What heart alike conceived and dared?
What act proved all its thought had been?
What will but felt the fleshly screen?
    We ride and I see her bosom heave.
There's many a crown for who can reach.
Ten lines, a statesman's life in each!
The flag stuck on a heap of bones,
A soldier's doing! what atones?
They scratch his name on the Abbey-stones.
    My riding is better, by their leave.

What does it all mean, poet? Well,
Your brains beat into rhythm, you tell

What we felt only; you expressed
You hold things beautiful the best,
 And place them in rhyme so, side by side.
'Tis something, nay 'tis much: but then,
Have you yourself what's best for men?
Are you—poor, sick, old ere your time—
Nearer one whit your own sublime
Than we who never have turned a rhyme?
 Sing, riding's a joy! For me, I ride.

And you, great sculptor—so, you gave
A score of years to Art, her slave,
And that's your Venus, whence we turn
To yonder girl that fords the burn!
 You acquiesce, and shall I repine?
What, man of music, you grown grey
With notes and nothing else to say,
Is this your sole praise from a friend,
"Greatly his opera's strains intend,
But in music we know how fashions end!"
 I gave my youth; but we ride, in fine.

Who knows what's fit for us? Had fate
Proposed bliss here should sublimate
My being—had I signed the bond—
Still one must lead some life beyond,
 Have a bliss to die with, dim-descried.
This foot once planted on the goal,
This glory-garland round my soul,
Could I descry such? Try and test!
I sink back shuddering from the quest.
Earth being so good, would heaven seem best?
 Now, heaven and she are beyond this ride.

And yet—she has not spoke so long!
What if heaven be that, fair and strong
At life's best, with our eyes upturned
Whither life's flower is first discerned,
 We, fixed so, ever should so abide?

What if we still ride on, we two,
With life forever old yet new,
Changed not in kind but in degree,
The instant made eternity,—
And heaven just prove that I and she
   Ride, ride together, forever ride?

A TOCCATA OF GALUPPI'S

OH Galuppi, Baldassare, this is very sad to find!
I can hardly misconceive you; it would prove me deaf and blind;
But although I take your meaning, 'tis with such a heavy mind!

Here you come with your old music, and here's all the good it
   brings.
What, they lived once thus at Venice where the merchants
   were the kings,
Where St. Mark's is, where the Doges used to wed the sea with
   rings?

Ay, because the sea's the street there; and 'tis arched by . . .
   what you call
. . . Shylock's bridge with houses on it, where they kept the
   carnival:
I was never out of England—it's as if I saw it all.

Did young people take their pleasure when the sea was warm
   in May?
Balls and masks begun at midnight, burning ever to mid-day,
When they made up fresh adventures for the morrow, do you
   say?

Was a lady such a lady, cheeks so round and lips so red,—
On her neck the small face buoyant, like a bell-flower on its
   bed,
O'er the breast's superb abundance where a man might base
   his head?

Well, and it was graceful of them—they'd break talk off and afford
—She, to bite her mask's black velvet—he, to finger on his sword,
While you sat and played Toccatas, stately at the clavichord?

What? Those lesser thirds so plaintive, sixths diminished, sigh on sigh,
Told them something? Those suspensions, those solutions—
"Must we die?"
Those commiserating sevenths—"Life might last! we can but try!"

"Were you happy?"—"Yes."—"And are you still as happy?"
—"Yes. And you?"
—"Then, more kisses!"—"Did *I* stop them, when a million seemed so few?"
Hark, the dominant's persistence till it must be answered to!

So, an octave struck the answer. Oh, they praised you, I dare say!
"Brave Galuppi! that was music! good alike at grave and gay!
I can always leave off talking when I hear a master play!"

Then they left you for their pleasure: till in due time, one by one,
Some with lives that came to nothing, some with deeds as well undone,
Death stepped tacitly and took them where they never see the sun.

But when I sit down to reason, think to take my stand nor swerve,
While I triumph o'er a secret wrung from nature's close reserve,
In you come with your cold music till I creep through every nerve.

Yes, you, like a ghostly cricket, creaking where a house was
    burned:
"Dust and ashes, dead and done with, Venice spent what Ven-
    ice earned.
The soul, doubtless, is immortal—where a soul can be dis-
    cerned.

"Yours for instance: you know physics, something of geology,
Mathematics are your pastime; souls shall rise in their degree;
Butterflies may dread extinction,—you'll not die, it cannot be!

"As for Venice and her people, merely born to bloom and drop,
Here on earth they bore their fruitage, mirth and folly were
    the crop:
What of soul was left, I wonder, when the kissing had to stop?

"Dust and ashes!" So you creak it, and I want the heart to
    scold.
Dear dead women, with such hair, too—what's become of all
    the gold
Used to hang and brush their bosoms? I feel chilly and grown
    old.

ABT VOGLER

(AFTER HE HAS BEEN EXTEMPORIZING UPON THE MUSICAL
    INSTRUMENT OF HIS INVENTION)

WOULD that the structure brave, the manifold music I build,
    Bidding my organ obey, calling its keys to their work,
Claiming each slave of the sound, at a touch, as when Solomon
    willed
    Armies of angels that soar, legions of demons that lurk,
Man, brute, reptile, fly,—alien of end and of aim,
    Adverse, each from the other heaven-high, hell-deep re-
        moved,—
Should rush into sight at once as he named the ineffable Name,
    And pile him a palace straight, to pleasure the princess he
        loved!

Would it might tarry like his, the beautiful building of mine,
  This which my keys in a crowd pressed and importuned to
    raise!
Ah, one and all, how they helped, would disport now and now
    combine,
  Zealous to hasten the work, heighten their master his praise!
And one would bury his brow with a blind plunge down to
    hell,
  Burrow awhile and build, broad on the roots of things,
Then up again swim into sight, having based me my palace
    well,
  Founded it, fearless of flame, flat on the nether springs.

And another would mount and march, like the excellent min-
    ion he was,
  Ay, another and yet another, one crowd but with many a
    crest,
Raising my rampired walls of gold as transparent as glass,
  Eager to do and die, yield each his place to the rest:
For higher still and higher (as a runner tips with fire,
  When a great illumination surprises a festal night—
Outlined round and round Rome's dome from space to spire)
  Up, the pinnacled glory reached, and the pride of my soul
    was in sight.

In sight? Not half! for it seemed, it was certain, to match
    man's birth,
  Nature in turn conceived, obeying an impulse as I;
And the emulous heaven yearned down, made effort to reach
    the earth,
  As the earth has done her best, in my passion, to scale the
    sky:
Novel splendours burst forth, grew familiar and dwelt with
    mine,
  Not a point nor peak but found and fixed its wandering
    star;
Meteor-moons, balls of blaze: and they did not pale nor pine,
  For earth had attained to heaven, there was no more near
    nor far.

Nay more; for there wanted not who walked in the glare and
    glow,
    Presences plain in the place; or, fresh from the Protoplast,
Furnished for ages to come, when a kindlier wind should blow,
    Lured now to begin and live, in a house to their liking at
      last;
Or else the wonderful Dead who have passed through the body
    and gone,
    But were back once more to breathe in an old world worth
      their new:
What never had been, was now; what was, as it shall be anon;
And what is,—shall I say, matched both? for I was made per-
    fect too.

All through my keys that gave their sounds to a wish of my
    soul,
    All through my soul that praised as its wish flowed visibly
      forth,
All through music and me! For think, had I painted the
    whole,
    Why, there it had stood, to see, nor the process so wonder-
      worth:
Had I written the same, made verse—still, effect proceeds
    from cause,
    Ye know why the forms are fair, ye hear how the tale is
      told;
It is all triumphant art, but art in obedience to laws,
    Painter and poet are proud in the artist-list enrolled:—

But here is the finger of God, a flash of the will that can,
    Existent behind all laws, that made them and, lo, they are!
And I know not if, save in this, such gift be allowed to man,
    That out of three sounds he frame, not a fourth sound, but
      a star.
Consider it well: each tone of our scale in itself is naught:
    It is everywhere in the world—loud, soft, and all is said:
Give it to me to use! I mix it with two in my thought:
    And there! Ye have heard and seen: consider and bow the
      head!

Well, it is gone at last, the palace of music I reared;
　Gone! and the good tears start, the praises that come too slow;
For one is assured at first, one scarce can say that he feared,
　That he even gave it a thought, the gone thing was to go.
Never to be again! But many more of the kind
　As good, nay, better, perchance: is this your comfort to me?
To me, who must be saved because I cling with my mind
　To the same, same self, same love, same God: ay, what was,
　　shall be.

Therefore to whom turn I but to thee, the ineffable Name?
　Builder and maker, thou, of houses not made with hands!
What, have fear of change from thee who art ever the same?
　Doubt that thy power can fill the heart that thy power ex-
　　pands?
There shall never be one lost good! What was, shall live as
　before;
　The evil is null, is naught, is silence implying sound;
What was good shall be good, with, for evil, so much good
　more;
　On the earth the broken arcs; in the heaven a perfect round.

All we have willed or hoped or dreamed of good shall exist;
　Not its semblance, but itself; no beauty, nor good, nor power
Whose voice has gone forth, but each survives for the melo-
　dist
　When eternity affirms the conception of an hour,
The high that proved too high, the heroic for earth too hard,
　The passion that left the ground to lose itself in the sky,
Are music sent up to God by the lover and the bard;
　Enough that he heard it once: we shall hear it by and by.

And what is our failure here but a triumph's evidence
　For the fulness of the days? Have we withered or ago-
　　nized?
Why else was the pause prolonged but that singing might issue
　thence?
　Why rushed the discords in, but that harmony should be
　　prized?

Sorrow is hard to bear, and doubt is slow to clear,
 Each sufferer says his say, his scheme of the weal and woe:
But God has a few of us whom he whispers in the ear;
 The rest may reason and welcome; 'tis we musicians know.

Well, it is earth with me; silence resumes her reign:
 I will be patient and proud, and soberly acquiesce.
Give me the keys. I feel for the common chord again,
 Sliding by semitones till I sink to the minor,—yes,
And I blunt it into a ninth, and I stand on alien ground,
 Surveying awhile the heights I rolled from into the deep;
Which, hark, I have dared and done, for my resting-place is found,
 The C Major of this life: so, now I will try to sleep.

RABBI BEN EZRA

GROW old along with me!
The best is yet to be,
The last of life, for which the first was made:
Our times are in his hand
Who saith, "A whole I planned,
Youth shows but half; trust God: see all, nor be afraid!"

Not that, amassing flowers,
Youth sighed, "Which rose make ours,
Which lily leave and then as best recall?"
Not that, admiring stars,
It yearned, "Nor Jove, nor Mars;
Mine be some figured flame which blends, transcends them all!"

Not for such hopes and fears
Annulling youth's brief years,
Do I remonstrate: folly wide the mark!
Rather I prize the doubt
Low kinds exist without,
Finished and finite clods, untroubled by a spark.

Poor vaunt of life indeed,
Were man but formed to feed
On joy, to solely seek and find and feast:
Such feasting ended, then
As sure an end to men;
Irks care the crop-full bird? Frets doubt the maw-crammed
    beast?

Rejoice we are allied
To that which doth provide
And not partake, effect and not receive!
A spark disturbs our clod;
Nearer we hold of God
Who gives, than of his tribes that take, I must believe.

Then, welcome each rebuff
That turns earth's smoothness rough,
Each sting that bids nor sit nor stand but go!
Be our joys three-parts pain!
Strive, and hold cheap the strain;
Learn, nor account the pang; dare, never grudge the throe!

For thence,—a paradox
Which comforts while it mocks,—
Shall life succeed in that it seems to fail:
What I aspired to be,
And was not, comforts me:
A brute I might have been, but would not sink i' the scale.

What is he but a brute
Whose flesh has soul to suit,
Whose spirit works lest arms and legs want play?
To man, propose this test—
Thy body at its best,
How far can that project thy soul on its lone way?

Yet gifts should prove their use:
I own the Past profuse
Of power each side, perfection every turn:

Eyes, ears took in their dole,
Brain treasured up the whole;
Should not the heart beat once "How good to live and learn"?

Not once beat "Praise be thine!
I see the whole design,
I, who saw power, see now love perfect too:
Perfect I call thy plan:
Thanks that I was a man!
Maker, remake, complete,—I trust what thou shalt do!"

For pleasant is this flesh;
Our soul, in its rose-mesh
Pulled ever to the earth, still yearns for rest:
Would we some prize might hold
To match those manifold
Possessions of the brute,—gain most, as we did best!

Let us not always say,
"Spite of this flesh to-day
I strove, made head, gained ground upon the whole!"
As the bird wings and sings,
Let us cry, "All good things
Are ours, nor soul helps flesh more, now, than flesh helps soul!"

Therefore I summon age
To grant youth's heritage,
Life's struggle having so far reached its term:
Thence shall I pass, approved
A man, for aye removed
From the developed brute; a god, though in the germ.

And I shall thereupon
Take rest, ere I be gone
Once more on my adventure brave and new:
Fearless and unperplexed,
When I wage battle next,
What weapons to select, what armour to indue.

Youth ended, I shall try
My gain or loss thereby;
Leave the fire ashes, what survives is gold:
And I shall weigh the same,
Give life its praise or blame:
Young, all lay in dispute; I shall know, being old.

For note, when evening shuts,
A certain moment cuts
The deed off, calls the glory from the grey:
A whisper from the west
Shoots—"Add this to the rest,
Take it and try its worth: here dies another day."

So, still within this life,
Though lifted o'er its strife,
Let me discern, compare, pronounce at last,
"This rage was right i' the main,
That acquiescence vain:
The Future I may face now I have proved the Past."

For more is not reserved
To man, with soul just nerved
To act to-morrow what he learns to-day:
Here, work enough to watch
The Master work, and catch
Hints of the proper craft, tricks of the tool's true play.

As it was better, youth
Should strive, through acts uncouth,
Toward making, than repose on aught found made:
So, better, age, exempt
From strife, should know, than tempt
Further. Thou waitedst age: wait death nor be afraid!

Enough now, if the Right
And Good and Infinite
Be named here, as thou callest thy hand thine own,

With knowledge absolute,
Subject to no dispute
From fools that crowded youth, nor let thee feel alone.

Be there, for once and all,
Severed great minds from small,
Announced to each his station in the Past!
Was I, the world arraigned,
Were they, my soul disdained,
Right? Let age speak the truth and give us peace at last!

Now, who shall arbitrate?
Ten men love what I hate,
Shun what I follow, slight what I receive;
Ten, who in ears and eyes
Match me: we all surmise,
They this thing, and I that: whom shall my soul believe?

Not on the vulgar mass
Called "work," must sentence pass,
Things done, that took the eye and had the price;
O'er which, from level stand,
The low world laid its hand,
Found straightway to its mind, could value in a trice:

But all the world's coarse thumb
And finger failed to plumb,
So passed in making up the main account;
All instincts immature,
All purposes unsure,
That weighed not as his work, yet swelled the man's amount:

Thoughts hardly to be packed
Into a narrow act,
Fancies that broke through language and escaped;
All I could never be,
All, men ignored in me,
This, I was worth to God, whose wheel the pitcher shaped.

Ay, note that Potter's wheel,
That metaphor! and feel
Why time spins fast, why passive lies our clay,—
Thou, to whom fools propound,
When the wine makes its round,
"Since life fleets, all is change; the Past gone, seize to-day!"

Fool! All that is, at all,
Lasts ever, past recall;
Earth changes, but thy soul and God stand sure:
What entered into thee,
That was, is, and shall be:
Time's wheel runs back or stops: Potter and clay endure.

He fixed thee 'mid this dance
Of plastic circumstance,
This Present, thou, forsooth, wouldst fain arrest:
Machinery just meant
To give thy soul its bent,
Try thee and turn thee forth, sufficiently impressed.

What though the earlier grooves,
Which ran the laughing loves
Around thy base, no longer pause and press?
What though, about thy rim,
Skull-things in order grim
Grow out, in graver mood, obey the sterner stress?

Look not thou down but up!
To uses of a cup,
The festal board, lamp's flash and trumpet's peal,
The new wine's foaming flow,
The Master's lips aglow!
Thou, heaven's consummate cup, what needst thou with earth's
      wheel?

But I need, now as then,
Thee, God, who mouldest men;
And since, not even while the whirl was worst,

Did I—to the wheel of life
With shapes and colours rife,
Bound dizzily—mistake my end, to slake thy thirst:

So, take and use thy work:
Amend what flaws may lurk,
What strain o' the stuff, what warpings past the aim!
My times be in thy hand!
Perfect the cup as planned!
Let age approve of youth, and death complete the same!

PROSPICE

FEAR death?—to feel the fog in my throat,
  The mist in my face,
When the snows begin, and the blasts denote
  I am nearing the place,
The power of the night, the press of the storm,
  The post of the foe;
Where he stands, the Arch Fear in a visible form,
  Yet the strong man must go;
For the journey is done and the summit attained,
  And the barriers fall,
Though a battle's to fight ere the guerdon be gained,
  The reward of it all.
I was ever a fighter, so—one fight more,
  The best and the last!
I would hate that death bandaged my eyes, and forebore,
  And bade me creep past.
No! let me taste the whole of it, fare like my peers
  The heroes of old,
Bear the brunt, in a minute pay glad life's arrears
  Of pain, darkness and cold.
For sudden the worst turns the best to the brave,
  The black minute's at end,
And the elements' rage, the fiend-voices that rave,
  Shall dwindle, shall blend,

Shall change, shall become first a peace out of pain,
  Then a light, then thy breast,
O thou soul of my soul! I shall clasp thee again,
  And with God be the rest!

EPILOGUE

At the midnight in the silence of the sleep-time,
  When you set your fancies free,
Will they pass to where—by death, fools think, imprisoned—
Low he lies who once so loved you, whom you loved so,
        —Pity me?

Oh to love so, be so loved, yet so mistaken!
  What had I on earth to do
With the slothful, with the mawkish, the unmanly?
Like the aimless, helpless, hopeless did I drivel
        —Being—who?

One who never turned his back but marched breast forward,
  Never doubted clouds would break,
Never dreamed, though right were worsted, wrong would
    triumph,
Held we fall to rise, are baffled to fight better,
        Sleep to wake.

No, at noonday in the bustle of man's work-time
  Greet the unseen with a cheer!
Bid him forward, breast and back as either should be,
"Strive and thrive!" cry "Speed,—fight on, fare ever
        There as here!"

[Asolando.]

ARTHUR HUGH CLOUGH [1819–1861]

SAY NOT THE STRUGGLE NOUGHT AVAILETH

SAY not the struggle nought availeth,
   The labour and the wounds are vain,
The enemy faints not, nor faileth,
   And as things have been they remain.

If hopes were dupes, fears may be liars;
   It may be, in yon smoke concealed,
Your comrades chase e'en now the fliers,
   And, but for you, possess the field.

For while the tired waves, vainly breaking,
   Seem here no painful inch to gain,
Far back, through creeks and inlets making,
   Comes silent, flooding in, the main.

And not by eastern windows only,
   When daylight comes, comes in the light,
In front, the sun climbs slow, how slowly,
   But westward, look, the land is bright.

QUI LABORAT, ORAT

O ONLY Source of all our light and life,
   Whom as our truth, our strength, we see and feel,
But whom the hours of mortal moral strife
   Alone aright reveal!

Mine inmost soul, before Thee inly brought,
   Thy presence owns ineffable, divine;
Chastised each rebel self-encentred thought,
   My will adoreth Thine.

With eye down-dropped, if then this earthly mind
　　Speechless remain, or speechless e'en depart;
Nor seek to see—for what of earthly kind
　　Can see Thee as Thou art?—

If well-assured 'tis but profanely bold
　　In thought's abstractest forms to seem to see,
It dare not dare the dread communion hold
　　In ways unworthy Thee,

O not unowned, thou shalt unnamed forgive,
　　In worldly walks the prayerless heart prepare;
And if in work its life it seem to live,
　　Shalt make that work be prayer.

Nor times shall lack, when while the work it plies,
　　Unsummoned powers the blinding film shall part,
And scarce by happy tears made dim, the eyes
　　In recognition start.

But, as thou willest, give or e'en forbear
　　The beatific supersensual sight,
So, with Thy blessing blessed, that humbler prayer
　　Approach Thee morn and night.

WHERE LIES THE LAND?

WHERE lies the land to which the ship would go?
Far, far ahead, is all her seamen know.
And where the land she travels from? Away,
Far, far behind, is all that they can say.

On sunny noons upon the deck's smooth face,
Linked arm in arm, how pleasant here to pace;
Or, o'er the stern reclining, watch below
The foaming wake far widening as we go.

On stormy nights when wild northwesters rave,
How proud a thing to fight with wind and wave!

The dripping sailor on the reeling mast
Exults to bear, and scorns to wish it past.

Where lies the land to which the ship would go?
Far, far ahead, is all her seamen know.
And where the land she travels from? Away,
Far, far behind, is all that they can say.

CHARLES KINGSLEY [1819–1875]

THE SANDS OF DEE

"O Mary, go and call the cattle home,
 And call the cattle home,
 And call the cattle home,
 Across the sands of Dee:"
The western wind was wild and dank with foam,
 And all alone went she.

The western tide crept up along the sand,
 And o'er and o'er the sand,
 And round and round the sand,
 As far as eye could see:
The rolling mist came down and hid the land,
 And never home came she.

"Oh! is it weed, or fish, or floating hair,
 A tress of golden hair,
 A drownèd maiden's hair
 Above the nets at sea?
Was never salmon yet that shone so fair
 Among the stakes at Dee."

They rowed her in across the rolling foam,
 The cruel crawling foam,
 The cruel hungry foam
 To her grave beside the sea:
But still the boatmen hear her call the cattle home
 Across the sands of Dee.

MATTHEW ARNOLD [1822–1888]

REQUIESCAT

Strew on her roses, roses,
　And never a spray of yew!
In quiet she reposes;
　Ah, would that I did too!

Her mirth the world required;
　She bathed it in smiles of glee,
But her heart was tired, tired,
　And now they let her be.

Her life was turning, turning,
　In mazes of heat and sound.
But for peace her soul was yearning,
　And now peace laps her round.

Her cabin'd, ample spirit,
　It flutter'd and fail'd for breath.
To-night it doth inherit
　The vasty hall of death.

THE FUTURE

A wanderer is man from his birth.
He was born in a ship
On the breast of the river of Time;
Brimming with wonder and joy
He spreads out his arms to the light,
Rivets his gaze on the banks of the stream.

As what he sees is, so have his thoughts been.
Whether he wakes
Where the snowy mountainous pass,
Echoing the screams of the eagles,

Hems in its gorges the bed
Of the new-born clear flowing stream;
Whether he first sees light
Where the river in gleaming rings
Sluggishly winds through the plain;
Whether in sound of the swallowing sea—
As is the world on the banks,
So is the mind of the man.

   Vainly does each, as he glides,
Fable and dream
Of the lands which the river of Time
Had left ere he woke on its breast,
Or shall reach when his eyes have been closed.
Only the tract where he sails
He wots of; only the thoughts,
Raised by the objects he passes, are his.

Who can see the green earth any more
As she was by the sources of Time?
Who imagines her fields as they lay
In the sunshine, unworn by the plough?
Who thinks as they thought,
The tribes who then roam'd on her breast,
Her vigourous, primitive sons?
What girl
Now reads in her bosom as clear
As Rebekah read, when she sate
At eve by the palm-shaded well?
Who guards in her breast
As deep, as pellucid a spring
Of feeling, as tranquil, as sure?

   What bard,
At the height of his vision, can deem
Of God, of the world, of the soul,
With a plainness as near,
As flashing as Moses felt
When he lay in the night by his flock

On the starlit Arabian waste?
Can rise and obey
The beck of the Spirit like him?

This tract which the river of Time
Now flows through with us, is the plain.
Gone is the calm of its earlier shore.
Border'd by cities and hoarse
With a thousand cries is its stream.
And we on its breast, our minds
Are confused as the cries which we hear,
Changing and shot as the sights which we see.

And we say that repose has fled
For ever the course of the river of Time.
That cities will crowd to its edge
In a blacker, incessanter line;
That the din will be more on its banks,
Denser the trade on its stream,
Flatter the plain where it flows,
Fiercer the sun overhead.
That never will those on its breast
See an ennobling sight,
Drink of the feeling of quiet again.

But what was before us we know not,
And we know not what shall succeed.

Haply, the river of Time—
As it grows, as the towns on its marge
Fling their wavering lights
On a wider, statelier stream—
May acquire, if not the calm
Of its early mountainous shore,
Yet a solemn peace of its own.

And the width of the waters, the hush
Of the gray expanse where he floats,
Freshening its current and spotted with foam

As it draws to the Ocean, may strike
Peace to the soul of the man on its breast—
As the pale waste widens around him,
As the banks fade dimmer away,
As the stars come out, and the night-wind
Brings up the stream
Murmurs and scents of the infinite sea.

THE FORSAKEN MERMAN

COME, dear children, let us away;
Down and away below!
Now my brothers call from the bay,
Now the great winds shoreward blow,
Now the salt tides seaward flow;
Now the wild white horses play,
Champ and chafe and toss in the spray.
Children dear, let us away!
This way, this way!

Call her once before you go—
Call once yet!
In a voice that she will know:
"Margaret! Margaret!"
Children's voices should be dear
(Call once more) to a mother's ear;
Children's voices, wild with pain—
Surely she will come again!
Call her once and come away;
This way, this way!
"Mother dear, we cannot stay!
The wild white horses foam and fret."
Margaret! Margaret!

Come, dear children, come away down;
Call no more!
One last look at the white-wall'd town,
And the little gray church on the windy shore,

Then come down!
She will not come though you call all day;
Come away, come away!

Children dear, was it yesterday
We heard the sweet bells over the bay?
In the caverns where we lay,
Through the surf and through the swell,
The far-off sound of a silver bell?
Sand-strewn caverns, cool and deep,
Where the winds are all asleep;
Where the spent lights quiver and gleam,
Where the salt weed sways in the stream,
Where the sea-beasts, ranged all round,
Feed in the ooze of their pasture-ground;
Where the sea-snakes coil and twine,
Dry their mail and bask in the brine;
Where great whales come sailing by,
Sail and sail, with unshut eye,
Round the world for ever and aye?
When did music come this way?
Children dear, was it yesterday?

Children dear, was it yesterday
(Call yet once) that she went away?
Once she sate with you and me,
On a red gold throne in the heart of the sea,
And the youngest sate on her knee.
She comb'd its bright hair, and she tended it well,
When down swung the sound of a far-off bell.
She sigh'd, she look'd up through the clear green sea;
She said: "I must go, for my kinsfolk pray
In the little gray church on the shore to-day.
'Twill be Easter-time in the world—ah me!
And I lose my poor soul, Merman! here with thee."
I said: "Go up, dear heart, through the waves;
Say thy prayer, and come back to the kind sea-caves!"
She smiled, she went up through the surf in the bay.
Children dear, was it yesterday?

Children dear, were we long alone?
"The sea grows stormy, the little ones moan;
Long prayers," I said, "In the world they say;
Come!" I said; and we rose through the surf in the bay.
We went up the beach, by the sandy down
Where the sea-stocks bloom, to the white-wall'd town;
Through the narrow paved streets, where all was still,
To the little gray church on the windy hill.
From the church came a murmur of folk at their prayers,
But we stood without in the cold blowing airs.
We climb'd on the graves, on the stones worn with rains,
And we gazed up the aisle through the small leaded panes.
She sate by the pillar; we saw her clear:
"Margaret, hist! come quick, we are here!
Dear heart," I said, "we are long alone;
The sea grows stormy, the little ones moan."
But, ah, she gave me never a look,
For her eyes were seal'd to the holy book!
Loud prays the priest; shut stands the door.
Come away, children, call no more!
Come away, come down, call no more!

Down, down, down!
Down to the depths of the sea!
She sits at her wheel in the humming town,
Singing most joyfully.
Hark what she sings: "O joy, O joy,
For the humming street, and the child with its toy!
For the priest and the bell, and the holy well;
For the wheel where I spun,
And the blessed light of the sun!"
And so she sings her fill,
Singing most joyfully,
Till the spindle drops from her hand,
And the whizzing wheel stands still.
She steals to the window, and looks at the sand,
And over the sand at the sea;
And her eyes are set in a stare;
And anon there breaks a sigh,

And anon there drops a tear,
From a sorrow-clouded eye,
And a heart sorrow-laden,
A long, long sigh;
For the cold strange eyes of a little Mermaiden
And the gleam of her golden hair.

Come away, away children;
Come children, come down!
The hoarse wind blows coldly;
Lights shine in the town.
She will start from her slumber
When gusts shake the door;
She will hear the winds howling,
Will hear the waves roar.
We shall see, while above us
The waves roar and whirl,
A ceiling of amber,
A pavement of pearl.
Singing: "Here came a mortal,
But faithless was she!
And alone dwell for ever
The kings of the sea."

But, children, at midnight,
When soft the winds blow,
When clear falls the moonlight,
When spring tides are low;
When sweet airs come seaward
From heaths starr'd with broom,
And high rocks throw mildly
On the blanch'd sands a gloom;
Up the still, glistening beaches,
Up the creeks we will hie,
Over banks of bright seaweed
The ebb-tide leaves dry.
We will gaze, from the sand-hills,
At the white, sleeping town;
At the church on the hill-side—

And then come back down.
Singing: "There dwells a loved one,
But cruel is she!
She left lonely for ever
The kings of the sea."

DOVER BEACH

THE sea is calm to-night,
The tide is full, the moon lies fair
Upon the straits;—on the French coast the light
Gleams and is gone; the cliffs of England stand,
Glimmering and vast, out in the tranquil bay.
Come to the window, sweet is the night-air!
Only, from the long line of spray
Where the sea meets the moon-blanch'd land,
Listen! you hear the grating roar
Of pebbles which the waves draw back, and fling,
At their return, up the high strand,
Begin, and cease, and then again begin,
With tremulous cadence slow, and bring
The eternal note of sadness in.

Sophocles long ago
Heard it on the Ægæan, and it brought
Into his mind the turbid ebb and flow
Of human misery; we
Find also in the sound a thought,
Hearing it by this distant northern sea.

The Sea of Faith
Was once, too, at the full, and round earth's shore
Lay like the folds of a bright girdle furl'd.
But now I only hear
Its melancholy, long, withdrawing roar,
Retreating, to the breath
Of the night-wind, down the vast edges drear
And naked shingles of the world.

Ah, love, let us be true
To one another! for the world, which seems
To lie before us like a land of dreams,
So various, so beautiful, so new,
Hath really neither joy, nor love, nor light,
Nor certitude, nor peace, nor help for pain;
And we are here as on a darkling plain
Swept with confused alarms of struggle and flight,
Where ignorant armies clash by night.

THYRSIS

A MONODY IN COMMEMORATION OF ARTHUR HUGH CLOUGH, 1861

How changed is here each spot man makes or fills!
    In the two Hinkseys nothing keeps the same;
        The village street its haunted mansion lacks,
    And from the sign is gone Sibylla's name,
        And from the roofs the twisted chimney-stacks—
            Are ye too changed, ye hills?
    See, 'tis no foot of unfamiliar men
        To-night from Oxford up your pathway strays!
        Here came I often, often, in old days—
    Thyrsis and I; we still had Thyrsis then.

Runs it not here, the track by Childsworth Farm,
    Past the high wood, to where the elm-tree crowns
        The hill behind whose ridge the sunset flames?
    The signal-elm, that looks on Ilsley Downs,
        The Vale, the three lone weirs, the youthful Thames?—
            This winter-eve is warm,
    Humid the air! leafless, yet soft as spring,
        The tender purple spray on copse and briars!
        And that sweet city with her dreaming spires,
    She needs not June for beauty's heightening.

Lovely all times she lies, lovely to-night!—
    Only, methinks, some loss of habit's power
        Befalls me wandering through this upland dim.

Once pass'd I blindfold here, at any hour;
  Now seldom come I, since I came with him.
    That single elm-tree bright
Against the west—I miss it! is it gone?
  We prized it dearly; while it stood, we said,
  Our friend, the Gipsy-Scholar, was not dead;
While the tree lived, he in these fields lived on.

Too rare, too rare, grow now my visits here,
  But once I knew each field, each flower, each stick;
    And with the country-folk acquaintance made
By barn in threshing-time, by new-built rick.
    Here, too, our shepherd-pipes we first assay'd.
    Ah me! this many a year
My pine is lost, my shepherd's holiday!
  Needs must I lose them, needs with heavy heart
  Into the world and wave of men depart;
But Thyrsis of his own will went away.

It irk'd him to be here, he could not rest.
  He loved each simple joy the country yields,
    He loved his mates; but yet he could not keep,
For that a shadow lour'd on the fields,
    Here with the shepherds and the silly sheep.
    Some life of men unblest
He knew, which made him droop, and fill'd his head.
  He went; his piping took a troubled sound
  Of storms that rage outside our happy ground;
He could not wait their passing, he is dead.

So, some tempestuous morn in early June,
  When the year's primal burst of bloom is o'er,
    Before the roses and the longest day—
When garden-walks and all the grassy floor
    With blossoms red and white of fallen May
    And chestnut-flowers are strewn—
So have I heard the cuckoo's parting cry,
  From the wet field, through the vext garden-trees,
  Come with the volleying rain and tossing breeze:
The bloom is gone, and with the bloom go I!

Too quick despairer, wherefore wilt thou go?
  Soon will the high Midsummer pomps come on,
    Soon will the musk carnations break and swell,
  Soon shall we have gold-dusted snap-dragon,
    Sweet-William with his homely cottage-smell,
      And stocks in fragrant blow;
  Roses that down the alleys shine afar,
    And open, jasmine-muffled lattices,
    And groups under the dreaming garden trees,
  And the full moon, and the white evening-star.

He harkens not! light comer, he is flown!
  What matters it? next year he will return,
    And we shall have him in the sweet spring-days,
  With whitening hedges, and uncrumpling fern,
    And blue-bells trembling by the forest-ways,
      And scent of hay new-mown.
  But Thyrsis never more we swains shall see;
    See him come back, and cut a smoother reed,
    And blow a strain the world at last shall heed—
  For Time, not Corydon, hath conquer'd thee!

Alack, for Corydon no rival now!—
  But when Sicilian shepherds lost a mate,
    Some good survivor with his flute would go,
  Piping a ditty sad for Bion's fate;
    And cross the unpermitted ferry's flow,
      And relax Pluto's brow,
  And make leap up with joy the beauteous head
    Of Proserpine, among whose crowned hair
    Are flowers first open'd on Sicilian air,
  And flute his friend, like Orpheus, from the dead.

O easy access to the hearer's grace
  When Dorian shepherds sang to Proserpine!
    For she herself had trod Sicilian fields,
  She knew the Dorian water's gush divine,
    She knew each lily white which Enna yields,
      Each rose with blushing face;

She loved the Dorian pipe, the Dorian strain.
But ah, of our poor Thames she never heard!
Her foot the Cumner cowslips never stirr'd;
And we should tease her with our plaint in vain!

Well! wind-dispersed and vain the words will be,
    Yet, Thyrsis, let me give my grief its hour
    In the old haunt, and find our tree-topp'd hill!
Who, if not I, for questing here hath power?
    I know the wood which hides the daffodil,
        I know the Fyfield tree,
    I know what white, what purple fritillaries
    The grassy harvest of the river-fields,
    Above by Ensham, down by Sandford, yields,
And what sedged brooks are Thames's tributaries;

I know these slopes; who knows them if not I?—
    But many a dingle on the loved hill-side,
        With thorns once studded, old, white-blossom'd trees,
    Where thick the cowslips grew, and far descried
    High tower'd the spikes of purple orchises,
            Hath since our day put by
    The coronals of that forgotten time;
        Down each green bank hath gone the ploughboy's team,
    And only in the hidden brookside gleam
Primroses, orphans of the flowery prime.

Where is the girl, who by the boatman's door,
    Above the locks, above the boating throng,
        Unmoor'd our skiff when through the Wytham flats,
    Red loosestrife and blond meadow-sweet among
    And darting swallows and light water-gnats,
            We track'd the shy Thames shore?
    Where are the mowers, who, as the tiny swell
        Of our boat passing heaved the river-grass,
        Stood with suspended scythe to see us pass?—
They all are gone, and thou art gone as well!

Yes, thou art gone! and round me too the night
    In ever-nearing circle weaves her shade.
        I see her veil draw soft across the day,

I feel her slowly chilling breath invade
   The cheek grown thin, the brown hair sprent with gray;
     I feel her finger light
Laid pausefully upon life's headlong train;—
   The foot less prompt to meet the morning dew,
   The heart less bounding at emotion new,
And hope, once crush'd, less quick to spring again.

And long the way appears, which seem'd so short
   To the less practised eye of sanguine youth;
     And high the mountain-tops, in cloudy air,
   The mountain-tops where is the throne of Truth,
     Tops in life's morning-sun so bright and bare!
       Unbreachable the fort
Of the long-batter'd world uplifts its wall;
   And strange and vain the earthly turmoil grows,
   And near and real the charm of thy repose,
And night as welcome as a friend would fall.

But hush! the upland hath a sudden loss
   Of quiet!—Look, adown the dusk hill-side,
   A troop of Oxford hunters going home,
As in old days, jovial and talking, ride!
   From hunting with the Berkshire hounds they come.
     Quick! let me fly, and cross
Into yon further field!—'Tis done, and see,
   Back'd by the sunset, which doth glorify
   The orange and pale violet evening-sky,
Bare on its lonely ridge, the Tree! the Tree!

I take the omen! Eve lets down her veil,
   The white fog creeps from bush to bush about,
     The west unflushes, the high stars grow bright,
And in the scatter'd farms the lights come out.
   I cannot reach the signal-tree to-night,
     Yet, happy omen, hail!
Hear it from thy broad lucent Arnovale
   (For there thine earth-forgetting eyelids keep
   The morningless and unawakening sleep
Under the flowery oleanders pale),

Hear it, O Thyrsis, still our tree is there!—
   Ah, vain! These English fields, this upland dim,
     These brambles pale with mist engarlanded,
   That lone, sky-pointing tree, are not for him;
      To a boon southern country he is fled,
       And now in happier air,
   Wandering with the great Mother's train divine
     (And purer or more subtle soul than thee,
     I trow, the mighty Mother doth not see)
   Within a folding of the Apennine,

Thou hearest the immortal chants of old!—
   Putting his sickle to the perilous grain
     In the hot cornfield of the Phrygian king,
   For thee the Lityerses-song again
     Young Daphnis with his silver voice doth sing;
      Sings his Sicilian fold,
   His sheep, his hapless love, his blinded eyes—
     And how a call celestial round him rang,
     And heavenward from the fountain-brink he sprang,
   And all the marvel of the golden skies.

There thou art gone, and me thou leavest here
   Sole in these fields! yet will I not despair.
     Despair I will not, while I yet descry
   'Neath the mild canopy of English air
     That lonely tree against the western sky.
      Still, still these slopes, 'tis clear,
   Our Gipsy-Scholar haunts, outliving thee!
     Fields where soft sheep from cages pull the hay,
     Woods with anemones in flower till May,
   Know him a wanderer still; then why not me?

A fugitive and gracious light he seeks,
   Shy to illumine; and I seek it too.
     This does not come with houses or with gold,
   With place, with honour, and a flattering crew;
     'Tis not in the world's market bought and sold—
      But the smooth-slipping weeks

Drop by, and leave its seeker still untired;
  Out of the heed of mortals he is gone,
  He wends unfollow'd, he must house alone;
Yet on he fares, by his own heart inspired.

Thou too, O Thyrsis, on like quest wast bound;
  Thou wanderedst with me for a little hour!
    Men gave thee nothing; but this happy quest,
  If men esteemed thee feeble, gave thee power,
    If men procured thee trouble, gave thee rest.
      And this rude Cumner ground,
  Its fir-topped Hurst, its farms, its quiet fields,
    Here cam'st thou in thy jocund youthful time,
    Here was thine height of strength, thy golden prime!
And still the haunt beloved a virtue yields.

What though the music of thy rustic flute
  Kept not for long its happy, country tone;
    Lost it too soon, and learnt a stormy note
  Of men contention-tost, of men who groan,
    Which task'd thy pipe too sore, and tired thy throat—
      It fail'd, and thou wast mute!
  Yet hadst thou always visions of our light,
    And long with men of care thou couldst not stay.
    And soon thy foot resumed its wandering way,
Left human haunt, and on alone till night.

Too rare, too rare, grow now my visits here!
  'Mid city-noise, not, as with thee of yore,
    Thyrsis! in reach of sheep-bells is my home.
  —Then through the great town's harsh, heart-wearying roar,
    Let in thy voice a whisper often come,
      To chase fatigue and fear:
Why faintest thou! I wander'd till I died.
  Roam on! The light we sought is shining still.
  Dost thou ask proof? Our tree yet crowns the hill,
Our Scholar travels yet the loved hill-side.

WORLDLY PLACE

Even in a palace, life may be led well!
So spake the imperial sage, purest of men,
Marcus Aurelius. But the stifling den
Of common life, where, crowded up pell-mell,
Our freedom for a little bread we sell,
And drudge under some foolish master's ken
Who rates us if we peer outside our pen—
Match'd with a palace, is not this a hell?
Even in a palace! On his truth sincere,
Who spoke these words, no shadow ever came;
And when my ill-school'd spirit is aflame
Some nobler, ampler stage of life to win,
I'll stop, and say: "There were no succour here!
The aids to noble life are all within."

SIDNEY DOBELL [1824–1874]

ENGLAND TO AMERICA

Nor force nor fraud shall sunder us! O ye
Who north or south, on east or western land,
Native to noble sounds, say truth for truth,
Freedom for freedom, love for love, and God
For God; O ye who in eternal youth
Speak with a living and creative flood
This universal English, and do stand
Its breathing book; live worthy of that grand,
Heroic utterance—parted, yet a whole,
Far, yet unsevered,—children brave and free
Of the great Mother-tongue, and ye shall be
Lords of an Empire wide as Shakspere's soul,
Sublime as Milton's immemorial theme,
And rich as Chaucer's speech, and fair as Spenser's dream.

DANTE GABRIEL ROSSETTI [1828–1882]

THE BLESSED DAMOZEL

THE blessed damozel leaned out
   From the golden bar of Heaven;
Her eyes were deeper than the depth
   Of waters stilled at even;
She had three lilies in her hand,
   And the stars in her hair were seven.

Her robe, ungirt from clasp to hem,
   No wrought flowers did adorn,
But a white rose of Mary's gift,
   For service meetly worn;
Her hair that lay along her back
   Was yellow like ripe corn.

Her seemed she scarce had been a day
   One of God's choristers;
The wonder was not yet quite gone
   From that still look of hers;
Albeit, to them she left, her day
   Had counted as ten years.

(To one, it is ten years of years.
   . . . Yet now, and in this place,
Surely she leaned o'er me—her hair
   Fell all about my face. . . .
Nothing: the autumn fall of leaves.
   The whole year sets apace.)

It was the rampart of God's house
   That she was standing on;
By God built over the sheer depth
   The which is Space begun;
So high, that looking downward thence
   She scarce could see the sun.

It lies in Heaven, across the flood
   Of ether, as a bridge.
Beneath, the tides of day and night
   With flame and darkness ridge
The void, as low as where this earth
   Spins like a fretful midge.

Around her, lovers, newly met
   'Mid deathless love's acclaims,
Spoke evermore among themselves
   Their heart-remembered names;
And the souls mounting up to God
   Went by her like thin flames.

And still she bowed herself and stooped
   Out of the circling charm;
Until her bosom must have made
   The bar she leaned on warm,
And the lilies lay as if asleep
   Along her bended arm.

From the fixed place of Heaven she saw
   Time like a pulse shake fierce
Through all the world. Her gaze still strove
   Within the gulf to pierce
Its path; and now she spoke as when
   The stars sang in their spheres.

The sun was gone now; the curled moon
   Was like a little feather
Fluttering far down the gulf; and now
   She spoke through the still weather.
Her voice was like the voice the stars
   Had when they sang together.

(Ah sweet! Even now, in that bird's song,
   Strove not her accents there,
Fain to be hearkened? When those bells
   Possessed the mid-day air,
Strove not her steps to reach my side
   Down all the echoing stair?)

"I wish that he were come to me,
    For he will come," she said.
"Have I not prayed in Heaven?—on earth,
    Lord, Lord, has he not pray'd?
Are not two prayers a perfect strength?
    And shall I feel afraid?

"When round his head the aureole clings,
    And he is clothed in white,
I'll take his hand and go with him
    To the deep wells of light;
As unto a stream we will step down,
    And bathe there in God's sight.

"We two will stand beside that shrine,
    Occult, withheld, untrod,
Whose lamps are stirred continually
    With prayer sent up to God;
And see our old prayers, granted, melt
    Each like a little cloud.

"We two will lie i' the shadow of
    That living mystic tree
Within whose secret growth the Dove
    Is sometimes felt to be,
While every leaf that His plumes touch
    Saith His Name audibly.

"And I myself will teach to him,
    I myself, lying so,
The songs I sing here; which his voice
    Shall pause in, hushed and slow,
And find some knowledge at each pause,
    Or some new thing to know."

(Alas! We two, we two, thou say'st!
    Yea, one wast thou with me
That once of old. But shall God lift
    To endless unity
The soul whose likeness with thy soul
    Was but its love for thee?)

"We two," she said, "will seek the groves
  Where the lady Mary is,
With her five handmaidens, whose names
  Are five sweet symphonies,
Cecily, Gertrude, Magdalen,
  Margaret and Rosalys.

"Circlewise sit they, with bound locks
  And foreheads garlanded;
Into the fine cloth white like flame
  Weaving the golden thread,
To fashion the birth-robes for them
  Who are just born, being dead.

"He shall fear, haply, and be dumb:
  Then will I lay my cheek
To his, and tell about our love,
  Not once abashed or weak:
And the dear Mother will approve
  My pride, and let me speak.

"Herself shall bring us, hand in hand,
  To Him round whom all souls
Kneel, the clear-ranged unnumbered heads
  Bowed with their aureoles:
And angels meeting us shall sing
  To their citherns and citoles.

"There will I ask of Christ the Lord
  Thus much for him and me:—
Only to live as once on earth
  With Love, only to be,
As then awhile, forever now
  Together, I and he."

She gazed and listened and then said,
  Less sad of speech than mild,—
"All this is when he comes." She ceased.
  The light thrilled towards her, fill'd

With angels in strong level flight.
   Her eyes prayed, and she smil'd.

(I saw her smile.) But soon their path
   Was vague in distant spheres:
And then she cast her arms along
   The golden barriers,
And laid her face between her hands,
   And wept. (I heard her tears.)

SONNETS

LOVESIGHT

WHEN do I see thee most, beloved one?
When in the light the spirits of mine eyes
Before thy face, their altar, solemnize
The worship of that Love through thee made known?
Or when in the dusk hours, (we two alone,)
Close-kissed and eloquent of still replies
Thy twilight-hidden glimmering visage lies,
And my soul only sees thy soul its own?
O love, my love! if I no more should see
Thyself, nor on the earth the shadow of thee,
Nor image of thine eyes in any spring,—
How then should sound upon Life's darkening slope
The ground-whirl of the perished leaves of Hope,
The wind of Death's imperishable wing?

INCLUSIVENESS

THE changing guests, each in a different mood,
Sit at the roadside table and arise:
And every life among them in likewise
Is a soul's board set daily with new food.
What man has bent o'er his son's sleep, to brood
How that face shall watch his when cold it lies?—
Or thought, as his own mother kissed his eyes,

Of what her kiss was when his father wooed?
May not this ancient room thou sit'st in dwell
In separate living souls for joy or pain?
Nay, all its corners may be painted plain
Where Heaven shows pictures of some life spent well;
And may be stamped, a memory all in vain,
Upon the sight of lidless eyes in Hell.

TRUE WOMAN

To be a sweetness more desired than Spring;
A bodily beauty more acceptable
Than the wild rose-tree's arch that crowns the fell;
To be an essence more environing
Than wine's drained juice; a music ravishing
More than the passionate pulse of Philomel;—
To be all this 'neath one soft bosom's swell
That is the flower of life:—how strange a thing!
How strange a thing to be what Man can know
But as a sacred secret! Heaven's own screen
Hides her soul's purest depth and loveliest glow;
Closely withheld, as all things most unseen,—
The wave-bowered pearl,—the heart-shaped seal of green
That flecks the snowdrop underneath the snow.

KNOWN IN VAIN

As two whose love, first foolish, widening scope,
Knows suddenly, to music high and soft,
The holy of holies; who because they scoffed
Are now amazed with shame, nor dare to cope
With the whole truth aloud, lest heaven should ope;
Yet, at their meetings, laugh not as they laughed
In speech; nor speak, at length; but sitting oft
Together, within hopeless sight of hope
For hours are silent:—So it happeneth
When Work and Will awake too late, to gaze

After their life sailed by, and hold their breath.
Ah! who shall dare to search through what sad maze
Thenceforth their incommunicable ways
Follow the desultory feet of Death?

BODY'S BEAUTY

Of Adam's first wife, Lilith, it is told
(The witch he loved before the gift of Eve,)
That, ere the snake's, her sweet tongue could deceive,
And her enchanted hair was the first gold.
And still she sits, young while the earth is old,
And, subtly of herself contemplative,
Draws men to watch the bright web she can weave,
Till heart and body and life are in its hold.
The rose and poppy are her flowers; for where
Is he not found, O Lilith, whom shed scent
And soft-shed kisses and soft sleep shall snare?
Lo! as that youth's eyes burned at thine, so went
Thy spell through him, and left his straight neck bent
And round his heart one strangling golden hair.

RETRO ME SATHANA

Get thee behind me. Even as, heavy-curled,
Stooping against the wind, a charioteer
Is snatched from out his chariot by the hair,
So shall Time be; and as the void car, hurled
Abroad by reinless steeds, even so the world:
Yea, even as chariot-dust upon the air,
It shall be sought and not found anywhere.
Get thee behind me, Satan. Oft unfurled,
Thy perilous wings can beat and break like lath
Much mightiness of men to win thee praise.
Leave these weak feet to tread in narrow ways.
Thou still, upon the broad vine-sheltered path,
Mayst wait the turning of the phials of wrath
For certain years, for certain months and days.

A SUPERSCRIPTION

Look in my face; my name is Might-have-been;
I am also called No-more, Too-late, Farewell;
Unto thine ear I hold the dead-sea shell
Cast up thy Life's foam-fretted feet between;
Unto thine eyes the glass where that is seen
Which had Life's form and Love's, but by my spell
Is now a shaken shadow intolerable,
Of ultimate things unuttered the frail screen.
Mark me, how still I am! But should there dart
One moment through thy soul the soft surprise
Of that winged Peace which lulls the breath of sighs,—
Then shalt thou see me smile, and turn apart
Thy visage to mine ambush at thy heart,
Sleepless with cold commemorative eyes.

[From THE HOUSE OF LIFE.]

ALGERNON CHARLES SWINBURNE
[1837–1909]

SHAKSPERE

Not if men's tongues and angels' all in one
Spake, might the word be said that might speak Thee.
Streams, winds, woods, flowers, fields, mountains, yea, the sea,
What power is in them all to praise the sun?
His praise is this,—he can be praised of none.
Man, woman, child, praise God for him; but he
Exults not to be worshipped, but to be.
He is; and, being, beholds his work well done.
All joy, all glory, all sorrow, all strength, all mirth,
Are his: without him, day were night on earth.
Time knows not his from time's own period.
All lutes, all harps, all viols, all flutes, all lyres,
Fall dumb before him ere one string suspires.
All stars are angels; but the sun is God.

WHEN THE HOUNDS OF SPRING

WHEN the hounds of spring are on winter's traces,
   The mother of months in meadow or plain
Fills the shadows and windy places
   With lisp of leaves and ripple of rain;
And the brown bright nightingale amourous
Is half assuaged for Itylus,
For the Thracian ships and the foreign faces,
   The tongueless vigil, and all the pain.

Come with bows bent and with emptying of quivers,
   Maiden most perfect, lady of light,
With a noise of winds and many rivers,
   With a clamour of waters, and with might;
Bind on thy sandals, O thou most fleet,
Over the splendour and speed of thy feet,
For the faint east quickens, the wan west shivers,
   Round the feet of the day and the feet of the night.

Where shall we find her, how shall we sing to her,
   Fold our hands round her knees, and cling?
O that man's heart were as fire and could spring to her,
   Fire, or the strength of the streams that spring!
For the stars and the winds are unto her
As raiment, as songs of the harp-player;
For the risen stars and the fallen cling to her,
   And the southwest-wind and the west-wind sing.

For winter's rains and ruins are over,
   And all the season of snows and sins;
The days dividing lover and lover,
   The light that loses, the night that wins;
And time remembered is grief forgotten,
And frosts are slain and flowers begotten,
And in green underwood and cover
   Blossom by blossom the spring begins.

The full streams feed on flower of rushes,
  Ripe grasses trammel a travelling foot,
The faint fresh flame of the young year flushes
  From leaf to flower and flower to fruit;
And fruit and leaf are as gold and fire,
And the oat is heard above the lyre,
And the hoofed heel of a satyr crushes
  The chestnut-husk at the chestnut root.

And Pan by noon and Bacchus by night,
  Fleeter of foot than the fleet-foot kid,
Follows with dancing and fills with delight
  The Mænad and the Bassarid;
And soft as lips that laugh and hide
The laughing leaves of the trees divide,
And screen from seeing and leave in sight
  The god pursuing, the maiden hid.

The ivy falls with the Bacchanal's hair
  Over her eyebrows hiding her eyes;
The wild vine slipping down leaves bare
  Her bright breast shortening into sighs;
The wild vine slips with the weight of its leaves,
But the berried ivy catches and cleaves
To the limbs that glitter, the feet that scare
  The wolf that follows, the fawn that flies.

[Chorus from ATALANTA IN CALYDON.]

A FORSAKEN GARDEN

IN a coign of the cliff between lowland and highland,
  At the sea-down's edge between windward and lee,
Walled round with rocks as an inland island,
  The ghost of a garden fronts the sea.
A girdle of brushwood and thorn encloses
  The steep square slope of the blossomless bed
Where the weeds that grew green from the graves of its roses
  Now lie dead.

The fields fall southward, abrupt and broken,
  To the low last edge of the long lone land.
If a step should sound or a word be spoken,
  Would a ghost not rise at the strange guest's hand?
So long have the gray bare walks lain guestless,
  Through branches and briars if a man make way,
He shall find no life but the sea-wind's, restless
  Night and day.

The dense hard passage is blind and stifled
  That crawls by a track none turn to climb
To the strait waste place that the years have rifled
  Of all but the thorns that are touched not of time.
The thorns he spares when the rose is taken;
  The rocks are left when he wastes the plain;
The wind that wanders, the weeds wind-shaken,
  These remain.

Not a flower to be pressed of the foot that falls not;
  As the heart of a dead man the seed-plots are dry;
From the thicket of thorns whence the nightingale calls not,
  Could she call, there were never a rose to reply.
Over the meadows that blossom and wither,
  Rings but the note of a sea-bird's song.
Only the sun and the rain come hither
  All year long.

The sun burns sear, and the rain dishevels
  One gaunt bleak blossom of scentless breath.
Only the wind here hovers and revels
  In a round where life seems barren as death.
Here there was laughing of old, there was weeping,
  Haply, of lovers none ever will know,
Whose eyes went seaward a hundred sleeping
  Years ago.

Heart handfast in heart as they stood, "Look thither,"
  Did he whisper? "Look forth from the flowers to the sea;
For the foam-flowers endure when the rose-blossoms wither,
  And men that love lightly may die—But we?"

And the same wind sang, and the same waves whitened,
   And or ever the garden's last petals were shed,
In the lips that had whispered, the eyes that had lightened,
   Love was dead.

Or they loved their life through, and then went whither?
   And were one to the end—but what end who knows?
Love deep as the sea as a rose must wither,
   As the rose-red seaweed that mocks the rose.
Shall the dead take thought for the dead to love them?
   What love was ever as deep as a grave?
They are loveless now as the grass above them
   Or the wave.

All are at one now, roses and lovers,
   Not known of the cliffs and the fields and the sea.
Not a breath of the time that has been hovers
   In the air now soft with a summer to be.
Not a breath shall there sweeten the seasons hereafter
   Of the flowers or the lovers that laugh now or weep,
When, as they that are free now of weeping and laughter,
   We shall sleep.

Here death may deal not again forever;
   Here change may come not till all change end.
From the graves they have made they shall rise up never,
   Who have left naught living to ravage and rend.
Earth, stones, and thorns of the wild ground growing,
   When the sun and the rain live, these shall be;
Till a last wind's breath upon all these blowing
   Roll the sea.

Till the slow sea rise and the sheer cliff crumble,
   Till terrace and meadow the deep gulfs drink,
Till the strength of the waves of the high tides humble
   The fields that lessen, the rocks that shrink,
Here now in his triumph where all things falter,
   Stretched out on the spoils that his own hand spread,
As a god self-slain on his own strange altar,
   Death lies dead.

LOVE AT SEA

WE are in love's land to-day;
    Where shall we go?
Love, shall we start or stay,
    Or sail or row?
There's many a wind and way,
And never a May but May;
We are in love's land to-day;
    Where shall we go?

Our landwind is the breath
Of sorrows kissed to death
    And joys that were:
Our ballast is a rose;
Our way lies where God knows
    And love knows where.
        We are in love's land to-day—

Our seamen are fledged Loves,
Our masts are bills of doves,
    Our decks fine gold;
Our ropes are dead maids' hair,
Our stores are love-shafts fair
    And manifold.
        We are in love's land to-day—

Where shall we land you, sweet?
On fields of strange men's feet,
    Or fields near home?
Or where the fire-flowers blow,
Or where the flowers of snow
    Or flowers of foam?
        We are in love's hand to-day—

Land me, she says, where love
Shows but one shaft, one dove,

One heart, one hand.
—A shore like that, my dear,
Lies where no man will steer,
No maiden land.

[Imitated from THEOPHILE GAUTIER.]

HYMN TO PROSERPINE

AFTER THE PROCLAMATION IN ROME OF THE CHRISTIAN FAITH

Vicisti, Galilæe

I HAVE lived long enough, having seen one thing, that love
    hath an end;
Goddess and maiden and queen, be near me now and befriend.
Thou art more than the day or the morrow, the seasons that
    laugh or that weep;
For these give joy and sorrow; but thou, Proserpina, sleep.
Sweet is the treading of wine, and sweet the feet of the
    dove;
But a goodlier gift is thine than foam of the grapes or love.
Yea, is not even Apollo, with hair and harpstring of gold,
A bitter God to follow, a beautiful God to behold?
I am sick of singing: the bays burn deep and chafe: I am fain
To rest a little from praise and grievous pleasure and pain.
For the Gods we know not of, who give us our daily breath,
We know they are cruel as love or life, and lovely as death.
O Gods dethroned and deceased, cast forth, wiped out in a
    day!
From your wrath is the world released, redeemed from your
    chains, men say.
New Gods are crowned in the city; their flowers have broken
    your rods;
They are merciful, clothed with pity, the young compassion-
    ate Gods.
But for me their new device is barren, the days are bare;
Things long past over suffice, and men forgotten that were.
Time and the Gods are at strife; ye dwell in the midst thereof,
Draining a little life from the barren breasts of love.

I say to you, cease, take rest; yea, I say to you all be at peace,
Till the bitter milk of her breast and the barren bosom shall
  cease.
Wilt thou yet take all, Galilean? but these thou shalt not take,
The laurel, the palms and the pæan, the breast of the nymphs
  in the brake;
Breasts more soft than a dove's, that tremble with tenderer
  breath;
And all the wings of the Loves, and all the joy before death;
All the feet of the hours that sound as a single lyre,
Dropped and deep in the flowers, with strings that flicker like
  fire,
More than these wilt thou give, things fairer than all these
  things?
Nay, for a little we live, and life hath mutable wings.
A little while and we die; shall life not thrive as it may?
For no man under the sky lives twice, outliving his day.
And grief is a grievous thing, and a man hath enough of his
  tears:
Why should he labour, and bring fresh grief to blacken his years?
Thou hast conquered, O pale Galilean; the world has grown
  gray from thy breath;
We have drunken of things Lethean, and fed on the fulness
  of death.
Laurel is green for a season, and love is sweet for a day;
But love grows bitter with treason, and laurel outlives not May.
Sleep, shall we sleep after all? for the world is not sweet in
  the end;
For the old faiths loosen and fall, the new years ruin and
  rend.
Fate is a sea without shore, and the soul is a rock that abides;
But her ears are vexed with the roar and her face with the
  foam of the tides.
O lips that the live blood faints in, the leavings of rack and
  rods!
O ghastly glories of saints, dead limbs of gibbeted Gods!
Though all men abase them before you in spirits, and all knees
  bend,
I kneel not, neither adore you, but standing, look to the end;

All delicate days and pleasant, all spirits and sorrows are cast
Far out with the foam of the present that sweeps to the surf
of the past:
Where beyond the extreme sea-wall, and between the remote
sea gates,
Waste water washes, and tall ships founder, and deep death waits:
Where, mighty with deepening sides, clad about with the seas
as with wings,
And impelled of invisible tides, fulfilled of unspeakable things,
White-eyed and poisonous-finned, shark-toothed and serpen-
tine-curled,
Rolls, under the whitening wind of the future, the wave of
the world.
The depths stand naked in sunder behind it, the storms flee
away;
In the hollow before it the thunder is taken and snared as a
prey;
In its sides is the north-wind bound; and its salt is of all men's
tears;
With light of ruin, and sound of changes, and pulse of years:
With travail of day after day, and with trouble of hour upon
hour;
And bitter as blood is the spray; and the crests are as fangs
that devour:
And its vapour and storm of its steam as the sighing of spirits
to be;
And its noise as the noise in a dream; and its depth as the roots
of the sea:
And the height of its head as the height of the utmost stars
of the air:
And the ends of the earth at the might thereof tremble, and
time is made bare.
Will ye bridle the deep sea with reins, will ye chasten the high
sea with rods?
Will ye take her to chain her with chains, who is older than
all ye Gods?
All ye as a wind shall go by, as a fire shall ye pass and be past;
Ye are Gods, and behold, ye shall die, and the waves be upon
you at last.

In the darkness of time, in the deeps of the years, in the
changes of things,

Ye shall sleep as a slain man sleeps, and the world shall forget you for kings.

Though the feet of thine high priests tread where thy lords
and our forefathers trod,

Though these that were Gods are dead, and thou being dead
art a God,

Though before thee the thronged Cytherean be fallen, and
hidden her head,

Yet thy kingdom shall pass, Galilean, thy dead shall go down
to the dead.

Of the maiden thy mother men sing as a goddess with grace
clad around;

Thou art throned where another was king; where another
was queen she is crowned.

Yea, once we had sight of another: but now she is queen, say
these.

Not as thine, not as thine was our mother, a blossom of flowering seas,

Clothed round with the world's desire as with raiment, and
fair as the foam,

And fleeter than kindled fire, and a goddess, and mother of
Rome.

For thine came pale and a maiden, and sister to sorrow; but
ours,

Her deep hair heavily laden with odour, and colour of flowers,

White rose of the rose-white water, a silver splendour, a
flame,

Bent down into us that besought her, and earth grew sweet
with her name.

For thine came weeping, a slave among slaves, and rejected;
but she

Came flushed from the full-flushed wave, and imperial, her
foot on the sea.

And the wonderful waters knew her, the winds and the viewless ways,

And the roses grew rosier, and bluer the sea-blue stream of
the bays.

Ye are fallen, our lords, by what token? we wist that ye should
    not fall.
Ye were all so fair that are broken; and one more fair than
    ye all.
But I turn to her still, having seen she shall surely abide in
    the end;
Goddess and maiden and queen, be near me now and befriend.
O daughter of earth, of my mother, her crown and blossom
    of birth,
I am also, I also thy brother; I go as I came unto earth.
In the night where thine eyes are as moons are in heaven, the
    night where thou art,
Where the silence is more than all tunes, where sleep over-
    flows from the heart,
Where the poppies are sweet as the rose in our world, and the
    red rose is white,
And the wind falls faint as it blows with the fume of the flowers
    of the night,
And the murmur of spirits that sleep in the shadow of Gods
    from afar
Grows dim in thine ears and deep as the deep dim soul of a
    star,
In the sweet low light of thy face, under heavens untrod by
    the sun,
Let my soul with their souls find place, and forget what is
    done and undone.
Thou art more than the Gods who number the days of our
    temporal breath;
For these give labour and slumber; but thou, Proserpina, death.
Therefore now at thy feet I abide for a season in silence. I
    know
I shall die as my fathers died, and sleep as they sleep; even
    so.
For the glass of the years is brittle wherein we gaze for a span
A little soul for a little bears up this Corpse which is man.[1]
So long I endure, no longer; and laugh not again, neither weep;
For there is no God found stronger than death; and death is
    a sleep.

[1] Ψυχάριον εἶ βαστάζον νεκρόν.—Epictetus.

COVENTRY PATMORE [1823–1896]

THE REVELATION

An idle poet, here and there,
  Looks round him; but, for all the rest,
The world, unfathomably fair,
  Is duller than a witling's jest.
Love wakes men, once a life-time each,
  They lift their heavy lids, and look;
And, lo, what one sweet page can reach,
  They read with joy, then shut the book.
And some give thanks, and some blaspheme,
  And most forget; but, either way,
That and the Child's unheeded dream
  Is all the light of all their day.

THE SPIRIT'S EPOCHS

Not in the crises of events,
  Of compassed hopes, or fears fulfilled,
Or acts of gravest consequence,
  Are life's delight and depth revealed.
The day of days was not the day;
  That went before, or was postponed;
The night Death took our lamp away
  Was not the night on which we groaned.
I drew my bride, beneath the moon,
  Across my theshold; happy hour!
But, ah, the walk that afternoon
  We saw the water-flags in flower!

[Preludes from THE ANGEL IN THE HOUSE.]

GEORGE MEREDITH [1828-1909]

LUCIFER IN STARLIGHT

On a starred night Prince Lucifer uprose.
Tired of his dark dominion, swung the fiend
Above the rolling ball in cloud part screened,
Where sinners hugged their spectre of repose.
Poor prey to his hot fit of pride were those.
And now upon his western wing he leaned,
Now his huge bulk o'er Afric's sands careened,
Now the black planet shadowed Arctic snows.
Soaring through wider zones that pricked his scars
With memory of the old revolt from Awe,
He reached a middle height, and at the stars,
Which are the brain of heaven, he looked, and sank.
Around the ancient track marched, rank on rank,
The army of unalterable law.

LOVE'S DEATH

In our old shipwrecked days there was an hour
When, in the firelight steadily aglow,
Joined slackly, we beheld the red chasm grow
Among the clicking coals. Our library-bower
That eve was left to us; and hushed we sat
As lovers to whom Time is whispering.
From sudden-opened doors we heard them sing;
The nodding elders mixed good wine with chat.
Well knew we that Life's greatest treasure lay
With us, and of it was our talk. "Ah, yes!
Love dies!" I said: I never thought it less.
She yearned to me that sentence to unsay.
Then when the fire domed blackening, I found
Her cheek was salt against my kiss, and swift
Up the sharp scale of sobs her breast did lift:—
Now am I haunted by that taste! that sound.

[From Modern Love.]

LOVE IN THE VALLEY

UNDER yonder beech-tree single on the greensward,
  Couch'd with her arms behind her golden head,
Knees and tresses folded to slip and ripple idly,
  Lies my young love sleeping in the shade.
Had I the heart to slide an arm beneath her,
  Press her parting lips as her waist I gather slow,
Waking in amazement she could not but embrace me:
  Then would she hold me and never let me go?

Shy as the squirrel and wayward as the swallow,
  Swift as the swallow along the river's light
Circleting the surface to meet his mirror'd winglets,
  Fleeter she seems in her stay than in her flight.
Shy as the squirrel that leaps among the pine-tops,
  Wayward as the swallow overhead at set of sun,
She whom I love is hard to catch and conquer,
  Hard, but oh the glory of the winning were she won!

When her mother tends her before the laughing mirror,
  Tying up her laces, looping up her hair,
Often she thinks, were this wild thing wedded,
  More love should I have, and much less care.
When her mother tends her before the lighted mirror,
  Loosening her laces, combing down her curls,
Often she thinks, were this wild thing wedded,
  I should miss but one for many boys and girls.

Heartless she is as the shadow in the meadows
  Flying to the hills on a blue and breezy noon.
No, she is athirst and drinking up her wonder:
  Earth to her is young as the slip of the new moon.
Deals she an unkindness, 'tis but her rapid measure,
  Even as in a dance; and her smile can heal no less:
Like the swinging May-cloud that pelts the flowers with hail-
    stones
  Off a sunny border, she was made to bruise and bless.

Lovely are the curves of the white owl sweeping
  Wavy in the dusk lit by one large star.
Lone on the fir-branch, his rattle-note unvaried,
  Brooding o'er the gloom, spins the brown evejar.
Darker grows the valley, more and more forgetting:
  So were it with me if forgetting could be will'd.
Tell the grassy hollow that holds the bubbling well-spring,
  Tell it to forget the source that keeps it fill'd.

Stepping down the hill with her fair companions,
  Arm in arm, all against the raying West,
Boldly she sings, to the merry tune she marches,
  Brave is her shape, and sweeter unpossess'd.
Sweeter, for she is what my heart first awaking
  Whisper'd the world was; morning light is she.
Love that so desires would fain keep her changeless;
  Fain would fling the net, and fain would have her free.

Happy happy time, when the white star hovers
  Low over dim fields fresh with bloomy dew,
Near the face of dawn, that draws athwart the darkness,
  Threading it with colour, like yewberries the yew.
Thicker crowd the shades as the grave East deepens
  Glowing, and with crimson a long cloud swells.
Maiden still the morn is; and strange she is, and secret;
  Strange her eyes; her cheeks are cold as cold sea-shells.

Sunrays, leaning on our southern hills and lighting
  Wild cloud-mountains that drag the hills along,
Oft ends the day of your shifting brilliant laughter
  Chill as a dull face frowning on a song.
Ay, but shows the South-West a ripple-feather'd bosom
  Blown to silver while the clouds are shaken and ascend
Scaling the mid-heavens as they stream, there comes a sunset
  Rich, deep like love in beauty without end.

When at dawn she sighs, and like an infant to the window
  Turns grave eyes craving light, released from dreams,
Beautiful she looks, like a white water-lily
  Bursting out of bud in havens of the streams.

When from bed she rises clothed from neck to ankle
   In her long nightgown sweet as boughs of May,
Beautiful she looks, like a tall garden-lily
   Pure from the night, and splendid for the day.

Mother of the dews, dark eye-lash'd twilight,
   Low-lidded twilight, o'er the valley's brim,
Rounding on thy breast sings the dew-delighted skylark,
   Clear as though the dew-drops had their voice in him,
Hidden where the rose-flush drinks the rayless planet,
   Fountain-full he pours the spraying fountain-showers.
Let me hear her laughter, I would have her ever
   Cool as dew in twilight, the lark above the flowers.

All the girls are out with their baskets for the primrose;
   Up lanes, woods through, they troop in joyful bands.
My sweet leads: she knows not why, but now she loiters,
   Eyes the bent anemones, and hangs her hands.
Such a look will tell that the violets are peeping,
   Coming the rose; and unaware a cry
Springs in her bosom for odours and for colour,
   Covert and the nightingale; she knows not why.

Kerchief'd head and chin she darts between her tulips,
   Streaming like a willow grey in arrowy rain:
Some bend beaten cheek to gravel, and their angel
   She will be; she lifts them, and on she speeds again.
Black the driving raincloud breasts the iron gateway:
   She is forth to cheer a neighbour lacking mirth.
So when sky and grass met rolling dumb for thunder
   Saw I once a white dove, sole light of earth.

Prim little scholars are the flowers of her garden,
   Train'd to stand in rows, and asking if they please.
I might love them well but for loving more the wild ones:
   O my wild ones! they tell me more than these.
You, my wild one, you tell of honied field-rose,
   Violet, blushing eglantine in life; and even as they,
They by the wayside are earnest of your goodness,
   You are of life's, on the banks that line the way.

Peering at her chamber the white crowns the red rose,
  Jasmine winds the porch with stars two and three.
Parted is the window; she sleeps; the starry jasmine
  Breathes a falling breath that carries thoughts of me.
Sweeter unpossess'd, have I said of her my sweetest?
  Not while she sleeps: while she sleeps the jasmine breathes,
Luring her to love; she sleeps; the starry jasmine
  Bears me to her pillow under white rose-wreaths.

Yellow with birdfoot-trefoil are the grass-glades;
  Yellow with cinquefoil of the dew-grey leaf;
Yellow with stonecrop; the moss-mounds are yellow;
  Blue-neck'd the wheat sways, yellowing to the sheaf.
Green-yellow, bursts from the copse the laughing yaffle;
  Sharp as a sickle is the edge of shade and shine:
Earth in her heart laughs looking at the heavens,
  Thinking of the harvest: I look and think of mine.

This I may know: her dressing and undressing
  Such a change of light shows as when the skies in sport
Shift from cloud to moonlight; or edging over thunder
  Slips a ray of sun; or sweeping into port
White sails furl; or on the ocean borders
  White sails lean along the waves leaping green.
Visions of her shower before me, but from eyesight
  Guarded she would be like the sun were she seen.

Front door and back of the moss'd old farmhouse
  Open with the morn, and in a breezy link
Freshly sparkles garden to stripe-shadow'd orchard,
  Green across a rill where on sand the minnows wink.
Busy in the grass the early sun of summer
  Swarms, and the blackbird's mellow fluting notes
Call my darling up with round and roguish challenge:
  Quaintest, richest carol of all the singing throats!

Cool was the woodside; cool as her white dairy
  Keeping sweet the cream-pan; and there the boys from school,
Cricketing below, rush'd brown and red with sunshine;
  O the dark translucence of the deep-eyed cool!

Spying from the farm, herself she fetch'd a pitcher
　　Full of milk, and tilted for each in turn the beak.
Then a little fellow, mouth up and on tiptoe,
　　Said, "I will kiss you": she laugh'd and lean'd her cheek.

Doves of the fir-wood walling high our red roof
　　Through the long noon coo, crooning through the coo.
Loose droop the leaves, and down the sleepy roadway
　　Sometimes pipes a chaffinch; loose droops the blue.
Cows flap a slow tail knee-deep in the river,
　　Breathless, given up to sun and gnat and fly.
Nowhere is she seen; and if I see her nowhere,
　　Lightning may come, straight rains and tiger sky.

O the golden sheaf, the rustling treasure-armful!
　　O the nutbrown tresses nodding interlaced!
O the treasure-tresses one another over
　　Nodding! O the girdle slack about the waist!
Slain are the poppies that shot their random scarlet
　　Quick amid the wheat-ears: wound about the waist,
Gather'd, see these brides of Earth one blush of ripeness!
　　O the nutbrown tresses nodding interlaced!

Large and smoky red the sun's cold disk drops,
　　Clipp'd by naked hills, on violet shaded snow:
Eastward large and still lights up a bower of moonrise,
　　Whence at her leisure steps the moon aglow.
Nightlong on black print-branches our beech-tree
　　Gazes in this whiteness: nightlong could I.
Here may life on death or death on life be painted.
　　Let me clasp her soul to know she cannot die!

Gossips count her faults; they scour a narrow chamber
　　Where there is no window, read not heaven or her.
"When she was a tiny," one aged woman quavers,
　　Plucks at my heart and leads me by the ear.
Faults she had once as she learn'd to run and tumbled:
　　Faults of feature some see, beauty not complete.
Yet, good gossips, beauty that makes holy
　　Earth and air, may have faults from head to feet.

Hither she comes; she comes to me; she lingers,
  Deepens her brown eyebrows, while in new surprise
High rise the lashes in wonder of a stranger;
  Yet am I the light and living of her eyes.
Something friends have told her fills her heart to brimming,
  Nets her in her blushes, and wounds her, and tames.—
Sure of her haven, O like a dove alighting,
  Arms up, she dropp'd: our souls were in our names.

Soon will she lie like a white frost sunrise.
  Yellow oats and brown wheat, barley pale as rye,
Long since your sheaves have yielded to the thresher,
  Felt the girdle loosen'd, seen the tresses fly.
Soon will she lie like a blood-red sunset.
  Swift with the to-morrow, green-wing'd Spring!
Sing from the South-west, bring her back the truants,
  Nightingale and swallow, song and dipping wing.

Soft new beech-leaves, up to beamy April
  Spreading bough on bough a primrose mountain, you
Lucid in the moon, raise lilies to the skyfields,
  Youngest green transfused in silver shining through:
Fairer than the lily, than the wild white cherry:
  Fair as in image my seraph love appears
Borne to me by dreams when dawn is at my eyelids:
  Fair as in the flesh she swims to me on tears.

Could I find a place to be alone with heaven,
  I would speak my heart out: heaven is my need.
Every woodland tree is flushing like the dogwood,
  Flashing like the whitebeam, swaying like the reed.
Flushing like the dogwood crimson in October;
  Streaming like the flag-reed South-west blown;
Flashing as in gusts the sudden-lighted whitebeam:
  All seem to know what is for heaven alone.

CHRISTINA ROSSETTI [1830–1894]

SONG

WHEN I am dead, my dearest,
  Sing no sad songs for me;
Plant thou no roses at my head,
  Nor shady cypress-tree:
Be the green grass above me
  With showers and dewdrops wet;
And if thou wilt, remember,
  And if thou wilt, forget.

I shall not see the shadows,
  I shall not feel the rain;
I shall not hear the nightingale
  Sing on, as if in pain:
And dreaming through the twilight
  That doth not rise nor set,
Haply I may remember,
  And haply may forget.

UP–HILL

DOES the road wind up-hill all the way?
  Yes, to the very end.
Will the day's journey take the whole long day?
  From morn to night, my friend.

But is there for the night a resting-place?
  A roof for when the slow dark hours begin.
May not the darkness hide it from my face?
  You cannot miss that inn.

Shall I meet other wayfarers at night?
  Those who have gone before.
Then must I knock, or call when just in sight?
  They will not keep you standing at that door.

Shall I find comfort, travel-sore and weak?
  Of labour you shall find the sum.
Will there be beds for me and all who seek?
  Yea, beds for all who come.

WILLIAM MORRIS [1834–1896]

THE GILLIFLOWER OF GOLD

A GOLDEN gilliflower to-day
I wore upon my helm alway,
And won the prize of this tourney.
    Hah! hah! la belle jaune giroflée.

However well Sir Giles might sit,
His sun was weak to wither it,
Lord Miles's blood was dew on it:
    Hah! hah! la belle jaune giroflée.

Although my spear in splinters flew,
From John's steel-coat, my eye was true;
I wheel'd about, and cried for you,
    Hah! hah! la belle jaune giroflée.

Yea, do not doubt my heart was good,
Though my sword flew like rotten wood,
To shout, although I scarcely stood,
    Hah! hah! la belle jaune giroflée.

My hand was steady too, to take
My axe from round my neck, and break
John's steel-coat up for my love's sake.
    Hah! hah! la belle jaune giroflée.

When I stood in my tent again,
Arming afresh, I felt a pain
Take hold of me, I was so fain—
    Hah! hah! la belle jaune giroflée—

To hear: *Honneur aux fils des preux!*
Right in my ears again, and shew
The gilliflower blossom'd new.
    Hah! hah! la belle jaune giroflée.

The Sieur Guillaume against me came,
His tabard bore three points of flame
From a red heart; with little blame,—
    Hah! hah! la belle jaune giroflée,—

Our tough spears crackled up like straw;
He was the first to turn and draw
His sword, that had nor speck nor flaw;
    Hah! hah! la belle jaune giroflée.

But I felt weaker than a maid,
And my brain, dizzied and afraid,
Within my helm a fierce tune play'd,
    Hah! hah! la belle jaune giroflée,

Until I thought of your dear head,
Bow'd to the gilliflower bed,
The yellow flowers stain'd with red;
    Hah! hah! la belle jaune giroflée.

Crash! how the swords met: *giroflée!*
The fierce tune in my helm would play,
La belle! la belle! jaune giroflée!
    Hah! hah! la belle jaune giroflée.

Once more the great swords met again:
"*La belle! la belle!*" but who fell then?
Le Sieur Guillaume, who struck down ten;
    Hah! hah! la belle jaune giroflée.

And as with mazed and unarm'd face,
Toward my own crown and the Queen's place,
They led me at a gentle pace,—
    Hah! hah! la belle jaune giroflée,—

I almost saw your quiet head
Bow'd o'er the gilliflower bed,
The yellow flowers stain'd with red.
     Hah! hah! la belle jaune giroflée.

THE HAYSTACK IN THE FLOODS

HAD she come all the way for this,
To part at last without a kiss?
Yea, had she borne the dirt and rain
That her own eyes might see him slain
Beside the haystack in the floods?

Along the dripping leafless woods,
The stirrup touching either shoe,
She rode astride as troopers do;
With kirtle kilted to her knee,
To which the mud splash'd wretchedly;
And the wet dripp'd from every tree
Upon her head and heavy hair,
And on her eyelids broad and fair;
The tears and rain ran down her face.

By fits and starts they rode apace,
And very often was his place
Far off from her; he had to ride
Ahead, to see what might betide
When the roads cross'd; and sometimes, when
There rose a murmuring from his men,
Had to turn back with promises.
Ah me! she had but little ease;
And often for pure doubt and dread
She sobb'd, made giddy in the head
By the swift riding; while, for cold,
Her slender fingers scarce could hold
The wet reins; yea, and scarcely, too,
She felt the foot within her shoe

Against the stirrup: all for this,
To part at last without a kiss
Beside the haystack in the floods.

For when they near'd that old soak'd hay,
They saw across the only way
That Judas, Godmar, and the three
Red running lions dismally
Grinn'd from his pennon, under which
In one straight line along the ditch,
They counted thirty heads.
                              So then
While Robert turn'd round to his men,
She saw at once the wretched end,
And, stooping down, tried hard to rend
Her coif the wrong way from her head,
And hid her eyes; while Robert said:
"Nay, love, 'tis scarcely two to one;
At Poictiers where we made them run
So fast—why, sweet my love, good cheer,
The Gascon frontier is so near,
Nought after us."
                              But: "O!" she said,
"My God! my God! I have to tread
The long way back without you; then
The court at Paris; those six men;
The gratings of the Chatelet;
The swift Seine on some rainy day
Like this, and people standing by,
And laughing, while my weak hands try
To recollect how strong men swim.
All this, or else a life with him,
For which I should be damned at last,
Would God that this next hour were past!"

Ie answer'd not, but cried his cry,
"St. George for Marny!" cheerily;
And laid his hand upon her rein.
Alas! no man of all his train

Gave back that cheery cry again;
And, while for rage his thumb beat fast
Upon his sword-hilt, some one cast
About his neck a kerchief long,
And bound him.

> Then they went along
To Godmar; who said: "Now, Jehane,
Your lover's life is on the wane
So fast, that, if this very hour
You yield not as my paramour,
He will not see the rain leave off:
Nay, keep your tongue from gibe and scoff
Sir Robert, or I slay you now."

She laid her hand upon her brow,
Then gazed upon the palm, as though
She thought her forehead bled, and: "No!"
She said, and turn'd her head away,
As there was nothing else to say,
And everything was settled: red
Grew Godmar's face from chin to head:
"Jehane, on yonder hill there stands
My castle, guarding well my lands;
What hinders me from taking you,
And doing that I list to do
To your fair wilful body, while
Your knight lies dead?"

> A wicked smile
Wrinkled her face, her lips grew thin,
A long way out she thrust her chin:
"You know that I should strangle you
While you were sleeping; or bite through
Your throat, by God's help: ah!" she said.
"Lord Jesus, pity your poor maid!
For in such wise they hem me in,
I cannot choose but sin and sin,
Whatever happens: yet I think
They could not make me eat or drink,
And so should I just reach my rest."

"Nay, if you do not my behest,
O Jehane! though I love you well,"
Said Godmar, "would I fail to tell
All that I know?"   "Foul lies," she said.
"Eh? lies, my Jehane? by God's head,
At Paris folks would deem them true!
Do you know, Jehane, they cry for you:
'Jehane the brown! Jehane the brown!
Give us Jehane to burn or drown!'
Eh!—gag me Robert!—sweet my friend,
This were indeed a piteous end
For those long fingers, and long feet,
And long neck, and smooth shoulders sweet;
An end that few men would forget
That saw it. So, an hour yet:
Consider, Jehane, which to take
Of life or death!"

                    So, scarce awake,
Dismounting, did she leave that place,
And totter some yards: with her face
Turn'd upward to the sky she lay.
Her head on a wet heap of hay,
And fell asleep: and while she slept,
And did not dream, the minutes crept
Round to the twelve again; but she,
Being waked at last, sigh'd quietly,
And strangely childlike came, and said:
"I will not." Straightway Godmar's head,
As though it hung on strong wires, turn'd
Most sharply round, and his face burn'd.

For Robert, both his eyes were dry,
He could not weep, but gloomily
He seem'd to watch the rain; yea, too,
His lips were firm; he tried once more
To touch her lips; she reach'd out, sore
And vain desire so tortured them,
The poor gray lips, and now the hem
Of his sleeve brush'd them.

With a start
Up Godmar rose, thrust them apart;
From Robert's throat he loosed the bands
Of silk and mail; with empty hands
Held out, she stood and gazed, and saw,
The long bright blade without a flaw
Glide out from Godmar's sheath, his hand
In Robert's hair; she saw him bend
Back Robert's head; she saw him send
The thin steel down; the blow told well,
Right backward the knight Robert fell,
And moaned as dogs do, being half dead,
Unwitting, as I deem: so then
Godmar turn'd grinning to his men,
Who ran, some five or six, and beat
His head to pieces at their feet.

Then Godmar turn'd again and said:
"So, Jehane, the first fitte is read!
Take note, my lady, that your way
Lies backward to the Chatelet!"
She shook her head and gazed awhile
At her cold hands with a rueful smile,
As though this thing had made her mad.

This was the parting that they had
Beside the haystack in the floods.

ROBERT LOUIS STEVENSON [1850–1894]

THE LAND OF COUNTERPANE

WHEN I was sick and lay a-bed,
I had two pillows at my head,
And all my toys beside me lay
To keep me happy all the day.

And sometimes for an hour or so
I watched my leaden soldiers go,
With different uniforms and drills,
Among the bed-clothes, through the hills;

And sometimes sent my ships in fleets
All up and down among the sheets;
Or brought my trees and houses out,
And planted cities all about.

I was the giant great and still
That sits upon the pillow-hill,
And sees before him, dale and plain,
The pleasant land of counterpane.

[From A CHILD'S GARDEN OF VERSES.]

MY WIFE

TRUSTY, dusky, vivid, true,
With eyes of gold and bramble-dew,
  Steel-true and blade-straight,
The great artificer
  Made my mate.

Honour, anger, valour, fire;
A love that life could never tire,
  Death quench or evil stir,
The mighty master
  Gave to her.

Teacher, tender, comrade, wife,
A fellow-farer true through life,
   Heart-whole and soul-free
The august father
   Gave to me.

REQUIEM

UNDER the wide and starry sky,
Dig the grave and let me lie.
Glad did I live and gladly die,
   And I laid me down with a will.

This be the verse you grave for me:
Here he lies where he longed to be;
Home is the sailor, home from sea,
   And the hunter home from the hill.

RUDYARD KIPLING [1865–]

THE LAST CHANTEY

"And there was no more sea."

THUS said the Lord in the Vault above the Cherubim
Calling to the Angels and the Souls in their degree:
   "Lo! Earth has passed away
   On the smoke of Judgment Day,
That Our word may be established shall We gather up the
      sea?"

Loud sang the souls of the jolly, jolly mariners:
"Plague upon the hurricane that made us furl and flee!
   But the war is done between us
   In the deep the Lord hath seen us—
Our bones we'll leave the barracout, and God may sink the
      sea!"

Then said the soul of Judas that betrayèd Him:
"Lord, hast thou forgotten Thy covenant with me?
How once a year I go
To cool me on the floe?
And Ye take my day of mercy if Ye take away the sea!"

Then said the soul of the Angel of the Off-shore Wind:
(He that bits the thunder when the bull-mouthed breakers
flee):
"I have watch and ward to keep
O'er Thy wonders on the deep,
And Ye take mine honour from me if Ye take away the sea."

Loud sang the souls of the jolly, jolly mariners:
"Nay, but we were angry, and a hasty folk are we;
If we worked the ship together
Till she foundered in foul weather,
Are we babes that we should clamour for a vengeance on the
sea?"

Then said the soul of the slaves that men threw overboard:
"Kennelled in the picaroon a weary band were we;
But Thy arm was strong to save,
And it touched us on the wave,
And we drowsed the long tides idle till Thy Trumpets tore
the sea."

Then cried the soul of the stout Apostle Paul to God:
"Once we frapped a ship, and she laboured woundily.
There were fourteen score of these,
And they blessed Thee on their knees,
When they learned Thy Grace and Glory under Malta by the
sea!"

Loud sang the souls of the jolly, jolly mariners,
Plucking at their harps, and they plucked unhandily:
"Our thumbs are rough and tarred,
And the tune is something hard—
May we lift a Deep-sea Chantey such as seamen use at sea?"

Then sang the souls of the gentlemen-adventurers—
Fettered wrist to bar all for red iniquity:
  "Ho, we revel in our chains
  O'er the sorrow that was Spain's;
Heave or sink it, leave or drink it, we were masters of the sea!"

Up spake the soul of a grey Gothavn 'speckshioner—
(He that led the flinching in the fleets of fair Dundee)
  "Oh, the ice-blink white and near,
  And the bowhead breaching clear!
Will Ye whelm them all for wantonness that wallow in the
    sea?"

Loud sang the souls of the jolly, jolly mariners,
Crying, "Under Heaven, here is neither lead nor lee!
  Must we sing forevermore"
  On the windless, glassy floor?
Take back your golden fiddles and we'll beat to open sea!"

Then stooped the Lord, and He called the good sea up to Him,
And 'stablished its borders unto all eternity,
  That such as have no pleasure
  For to praise the Lord by measure,
They may enter into galleons and serve Him on the sea.

Sun, wind, and cloud shall fail not from the face of it,
Stinging, ringing spindrift, nor the fulmar flying free;
  And the ships shall go abroad
  To the Glory of the Lord
Who heard the silly sailor-folks and gave them back their sea!

RECESSIONAL

(1897)

God of our fathers, known of old,
　Lord of our far-flung battle-line,
Beneath whose awful Hand we hold
　Dominion over palm and pine—
Lord God of Hosts, be with us yet,
Lest we forget—lest we forget!

The tumult and the shouting dies;
　The captains and the kings depart:
Still stands Thine ancient sacrifice,
　An humble and a contrite heart.
Lord God of Hosts, be with us yet,
Lest we forget—lest we forget!

Far-called, our navies melt away;
　On dune and headland sinks the fire:
Lo, all our pomp of yesterday
　Is one with Nineveh and Tyre!
Judge of the Nations, spare us yet,
Lest we forget—lest we forget!

If, drunk with sight of power, we loose
　Wild tongues that have not Thee in awe,
Such boastings as the Gentiles use,
　Or lesser breeds without the Law—
Lord God of Hosts, be with us yet,
Lest we forget—lest we forget!

For heathen heart that puts her trust
　In reeking tube and iron shard,
All valiant dust that builds on dust,
　And guarding, calls not Thee to guard,
For frantic boast and foolish word—
Thy Mercy on Thy People, Lord!

　　　　　　　　　　　　　　Amen.

INDEX OF AUTHORS

INDEX OF FIRST LINES

531